PRAISE FOR THE

ALMANAC *of* ARCHITECTURE & DESIGN

"This is the book that informs decision makers like no other."
SOCIETY FOR MARKETING PROFESSIONAL SERVICES

....

"The definitive fact book on architecture and design."
THE AMERICAN INSTITUTE OF ARCHITECTS

....

"No comparable resource exists."
LIBRARY JOURNAL

....

"A comprehensive media guide to architecture and design's defining moments."
THE DESIGN FUTURES COUNCIL

....

"A core reference title for personal, professional, and academic reference collections."
MIDWEST BOOK REVIEW

....

"This Almanac, filled with resources, can help all those involved in the building arts to better fulfill this unusual moment's potential."
ARCHITECTURAL RECORD

DesignIntelligence®

ALMANAC *of*
ARCHITECTURE
& DESIGN 2016
17TH EDITION

DesignIntelligence®

ALMANAC *of* ARCHITECTURE & DESIGN 2016

17TH EDITION

FOUNDING EDITOR AND PUBLISHER
JAMES P. CRAMER

EDITOR
JANE PARADISE WOLFORD, PH.D.

Library of Design Management

Greenway Communications

Almanac of Architecture & Design

Publisher and Founding Editor:	**James P. Cramer, Hon. AIA**
Almanac Editor:	**Jane Paradise Wolford, Ph.D., LEED AP**
Publisher:	**Bob Fisher**
Principal for Research and Administration:	**Mary Pereboom**
Art Director:	**Austin M. Cramer**
Graphic Design and Layout:	**Tredeau Design**
Web Development Advisor:	**Ryan James Cramer**
Research Editors:	**Margot Montouchet; Doug Parker, AIA; Donna Eubanks Pennell; and *DesignIntelligence* Research**

Greenway Communications, LLC

Chairman:	**Arol Wolford, Hon. AIA**
President/CEO:	**James P. Cramer, Hon. AIA**

Greenway Communications, LLC
25 Technology Parkway South, Suite 101
Peachtree Corners, GA 30092
(678) 879-0929
www.di.net

Publisher's Cataloging-in-Publication
Almanac of architecture & design / James P. Cramer
and Jane Paradise Wolford, editors
  2016 ed.
  p. cm.
  Almanac of architecture and design
  Includes bibliographical references and index
  ISBN-13 978-0-9964401-1-0

  1. Architecture—Directories. 2. Architectural design. 3.
Architecture—United States. I. Title: Almanac of architecture
and design

NA9.A27 2011   720

Contents

Note: Please visit us online at www.di.net/almanac/ for enhanced searchability throughout the entire expanded online version of the *Almanac*.

The State of the Art

Architects and designers have an inner drive to re-make the world around them. To improve it. Architects have an imagination that allows them to dwell in worlds beyond current realities.

And too, architects and designers are perpetually dissatisfied. This is actually a useful trait because it drives them to solve problems and invent new things all the time. This creative power not only makes the world a better place but it creates economic value. All around the world, architects and designers are acting as economic multipliers.

Here at *DesignIntelligence* and the *Almanac of Architecture & Design*, we like to track and measure progress. We have grown and expanded our data collection every year. And now, this 17th edition of the Almanac has established a new record for the sharing of data about professional practices and the award-winning work that is created by them.

Indeed, the inner drive to improve the world's built environment benefits us all. Architects understand the blend of the creative and the practical. They understand the taffy-pull between the two, where the really interesting solutions reveal themselves. We see innovation unfolding at satisfying and accelerated levels.

The power of design has never been more urgently needed to address global challenges. And while the design professions are relatively small, they carry great clout. There is potential for even more Impact. The growth of the design profession means that in 2016 we have reached full employment and there is a greater need for more architects and designers than ever before. The top 100 firms in this Almanac will invoice well over $10 Billion dollars. That is just the largest 100 of over 10,000 firms. We rate and list the top 1,000. These are not only going concerns but also places of inspiration. Many are reinventing the industry norms. Our research reveals that there is strength, too, in small and medium size firms. Furthermore, the design professions are expanding beyond traditional boundaries. The data that is organized through our research, combined with the graphs and pictures, show how firms are leading not only in financial terms but also in the advancing quality of the work. Form and function. This translates into community development, planning, and placemaking. All for the common good. We celebrate design excellence.

We welcome you to visit with us about research needs that you have. We like to cover new ground. To solve puzzles. At our fundamental base we track trends every day. Thousands of them. All sizes.

We have discovered that architects and designers are not only adept at design, but also adept at business—clearly articulating value propositions to clients and communities. The trends we watch now include sustainability and all the savvy that goes along with it— integrated, collaborative design. Globalization. Talent shortages. Technology is marching forward at advanced rates never before experienced. Demographic shifts show that the average age of the population is rising. People are living long, healthier and more productive lives. The productivity of design firms is advancing—thanks to better management. Architects and designers now show themselves to be leaders with strategic optimism. Design goes far beyond aesthetics, and so metrics count. Design matters.

As a reader of this *Almanac* we hope you will come to experience the richness of a new profession. Check out our web site at www.di.net/almanac and you will see even more data and information chronicled into meaningful information that you can use to understand and plan forward.

All of our research is underwritten by the Design Futures Council. Without them, this 17th edition would not be published. You can visit the DFC web site at www.designfuturescouncil.com. The DFC generates the flow of ideas to further strengthen our research and the applications that can further advance the quality of life and prosperity, worldwide.

Wishing you good health and prosperity,

Jim Cramer, Hon. AIA, Hon. IIDA, CAE
Jane Paradise Wolford, Ph.D., LEED AP

NORTH AMERICA'S
TOP 1,000 ARCHITECTURE
AND DESIGN FIRMS |

This chapter features an alphabetical listing
of leading North American architecture and
design firms with data about the type of
services they offer; their size, headquarters,
and geography; the market segments they
work in; and metrics from the *DI Index*.

America's Leading Architecture & Design Firms 2016

This section of the *Almanac* features an alphabetical listing of leading North American design and engineering firms selected by the editors. Each year, *DesignIntelligence* polls architects and designers in North America regarding their firms' officers, firm size, primary services offered, market segments and geographical locations served, and the nature of their practices. The firms are invited to participate in additional research underwritten by the Design Futures Council, which includes surveys about trends and market shifts, compensation and fees, technology, mergers and acquisitions, and management strategies.

The key to interpreting the tables is featured below. Firm size, headquarters (HQ), firm type, and markets are determined by *DesignIntelligence* surveys or from record files. Although the concept of headquarters might be less normative than in the past, this convention is still often used for diagnostic purposes in many market-data studies. If your firm has no headquarters and we have listed one, please make sure to complete a survey next year at di.net. The list of services includes market segments and specific professional specializations. The DI Index was determined by survey responses, with further research conducted by *DesignIntelligence* analysts. The criteria include geographic service coverage and reputation (awards as listed in the *Almanac of Architecture & Design* and recognition in professional and business publications). Of the five tiers, only firms in the top three (as represented by 3–5 bars) are included due to space considerations. Abbreviations were used in some firm names due to space constraints: architecture = Arch.; architects = Archts.; associates = Assoc.; construction = Const.; engineers = Engrs.

Principals of firms who want to be included in our next *Almanac* can obtain and/or fill in a survey at di.net; email the editor, Jane Wolford, at jwolford@di.net for a copy; or call *DesignIntelligence* at (678) 879-0929. Firms appearing in this *Almanac* can expect to receive a copy of next year's survey in the mail soon or can request a survey by contacting DI or the editor.

KEY

Rank
Refers to DI Ranking (chapter 2)

Size

	Small	20 employees or less
	Medium	21–100 employees
	Large	101–450 employees
	Extra Large	451+ employees

HQ
Listed by state, Canada (CAN) or Mexico (MEX)

Regions Served

E	East	C	Canada
M	Midwest	G	Global
S	South		
W	West		

Services Offered

A	Architecture	L	Landscape
D	Design/Build		Architecture
E	Engineering (MEP)	O	Other
G	Graphic Design		(inc. industrial design)
I	Interior Design	P	Planning
		U	Urban Design

Market Segments

C	Corporate	M	Museum/Cultural
E	Higher Education	R	Religious
K	K-12	Rs	Residential-Single
G	Government	Rm	Residential-Multi.
Hc	Healthcare	Rc	Retail/Commercial
H	Hospitality	S	Sports
I	Industrial/Tech.	O	Other

DI Brand Recognition Index

Top tier global and categorical leader recognition

Exceptional national and categorical leader recognition

Strong regional and categorical leader recognition

Notable and growing with emerging categorical recognition

Professional practice notable in city and region

© Adrian Smith + Gordon Gill Architecture /photograph by ShuHe Photography

Waldorf Astoria Beijing, Beijing, China | Adrian Smith + Gordon Gill Architecture

Rank	Firm/Web	Size	HQ	Regions		Services		Markets		DI Index
264	**4240 Architecture** www.4240architecture.com	👥👥	CO	E M S W C G		A D E G I L P U O		C E K G Hc H I M R Rs Rm Rc S O		
A	**A. Morton Thomas & Associates** www.amtengineering.com	👥👥👥	MD	E M S W C G		A D E G I L P U O		C E K G Hc H I M R Rs Rm Rc S O		
	A4 Architecture www.a4arch.com	👤	RI	E M S W C G		A D E G I L P U O		C E K G Hc H I M R Rs Rm Rc S O		
	Abell & Associates Architects www.jamesabell.com	👤	AZ	E M S W C G		A D E G I L P U O		C E K G Hc H I M R Rs Rm Rc S O		
128	**AC Martin** www.acmartin.com	👥👥👥	CA	E M S W C G		A D E G I L P U O		C E K G Hc H I M R Rs Rm Rc S O		
	Acai Associates www.acaiworld.com	👥👥	FL	E M S W C G		A D E G I L P U O		C E K G Hc H I M R Rs Rm Rc S O		
	ACI/Boland www.aci-boland.com	👥👥	MO	E M S W C G		A D E G I L P U O		C E K G Hc H I M R Rs Rm Rc S O		
	Adache Group Architects www.adache.com	👥👥	FL	E M S W C G		A D E G I L P U O		C E K G Hc H I M R Rs Rm Rc S O		
	Adamson Associates Architects www.adamson-associates.com	👥👥👥	CAN	E M S W C G		A D E G I L P U O		C E K G Hc H I M R Rs Rm Rc S O		
	ADD Inc www.addinc.com	👥👥👥	MA	E M S W C G		A D E G I L P U O		C E K G Hc H I M R Rs Rm Rc S O		
30	**Adrian Smith + Gordon Gill Architecture** www.smithgill.com	👥👥👥	IL	E M S W C G		A D E G I L P U O		C E K G Hc H I M R Rs Rm Rc S O		
2	**AECOM (Architecture)** www.aecom.com	👥👥👥👥	CA	E M S W C G		A D E G I L P U O		C E K G Hc H I M R Rs Rm Rc S O		
151	**Aedas** www.aedas.com	👥👥👥	NY	E M S W C G		A D E G I L P U O		C E K G Hc H I M R Rs Rm Rc S O		
	AEDIS Architects www.aedisarchitects.com	👥👥	CA	E M S W C G		A D E G I L P U O		C E K G Hc H I M R Rs Rm Rc S O		
333	**Affiniti Architects** www.affinitiarchitects.com	👥👥	FL	E M S W C G		A D E G I L P U O		C E K G Hc H I M R Rs Rm Rc S O		
	Aguirre Roden www.aguirreroden.com	👥👥	TX	E M S W C G		A D E G I L P U O		C E K G Hc H I M R Rs Rm Rc S O		
	Aidlin Darling Design www.aidlin-darling-design.com	👤	CA	E M S W C G		A D E G I L P U O		C E K G Hc H I M R Rs Rm Rc S O		

DI Brand Recognition Index

Top tier global and categorical leader recognition

Exceptional national and categorical leader recognition

Strong regional and categorical leader recognition

Notable and growing with emerging categorical recognition

Professional practice notable in city and region

Rank	Firm/Web	Size	HQ	Regions	Services	Markets	DI Index
	AIP Design www.aipdesign.com		FL	E M S W C G	A D E G I L P U O	C E K G Hc H I M R Rs Rm Rc S O	
146	**Albert Kahn Associates** www.albertkahn.com		MI	E M S W C G	A D E G I L P U O	C E K G Hc H I M R Rs Rm Rc S O	
	Alliance Architects www.alliancearch.com		TX	E M S W C G	A D E G I L P U O	C E K G Hc H I M R Rs Rm Rc S O	
267	**Allied Works Architecture** www.alliedworks.com		OR	E M S W C G	A D E G I L P U O	C E K G Hc H I M R Rs Rm Rc S O	
	Alliiance www.alliiance.us		MN	E M S W C G	A D E G I L P U O	C E K G Hc H I M R Rs Rm Rc S O	
	alt32 Architecture I Design www.alt32.com		KY	E M S W C G	A D E G I L P U O	C E K G Hc H I M R Rs Rm Rc S O	
163	**Altoon Partners** www.altoonpartners.com		CA	E M S W C G	A D E G I L P U O	C E K G Hc H I M R Rs Rm Rc S O	
	AM Partners www.ampartners.com		HI	E M S W C G	A D E G I L P U O	C E K G Hc H I M R Rs Rm Rc S O	
	Ammon Heisler Sachs Architects www.ahsarch.com		MD	E M S W C G	A D E G I L P U O	C E K G Hc H I M R Rs Rm Rc S O	
	Anderson Brulé Architects www.aba-arch.com		CA	E M S W C G	A D E G I L P U O	C E K G Hc H I M R Rs Rm Rc S O	
177	**Anderson Mason Dale Architects** www.amdarchitects.com		CO	E M S W C G	A D E G I L P U O	C E K G Hc H I M R Rs Rm Rc S O	
	Andre Kikoski Architect www.akarch.com		NY	E M S W C G	A D E G I L P U O	C E K G Hc H I M R Rs Rm Rc S O	
	Andrea Cochran Landscape Architecture www.acochran.com		CA	E M S W C G	A D E G I L P U O	C E K G Hc H I M R Rs Rm Rc S O	
	Andreozzi Architects www.andreozzi.com		RI	E M S W C G	A D E G I L P U O	C E K G Hc H I M R Rs Rm Rc S O	
102	**Ankrom Moisan Architects** www.ankrommoisan.com		OR	E M S W C G	A D E G I L P U O	C E K G Hc H I M R Rs Rm Rc S O	
	Anmahian Winton Architects www.aw-arch.com		MA	E M S W C G	A D E G I L P U O	C E K G Hc H I M R Rs Rm Rc S O	
315	**Ann Beha Architects** www.annbeha.com		MA	E M S W C G	A D E G I L P U O	C E K G Hc H I M R Rs Rm Rc S O	

Size

	Small	20 employees or less
	Medium	21–100 employees
	Large	101–450 employees
	Extra Large	451+ employees

Regions East (E), Midwest (M), South (S), West (W), Canada (C), Global (G)

Services Architecture (A), Design/Build (D), Engineering-MEP (E), Graphic Design (G), Interior Design (I), Landscape Architecture (L), Planning (P), Urban Design (U), Other-including Industrial Design (O)

Markets Corporate (C), Higher Ed. (E), K-12 (K), Government (G), Healthcare (Hc), Hospitality (H), Industrial/Tech. (I), Museum/Cultural (M), Religious (R), Residential-Single (Rs), Residential-Multi. (Rm), Retail/Commercial (Rc), Sports (S), Other (O)

Rank	Firm/Web	Size	HQ	Regions	Services	Markets	DI Index
	Anova Nexus www.anovanexus.com	👥	CA	E M S W C G	A D E G I L P U O	C E K G Hc H I M R Rs Rm Rc S O	
	Antinozzi Associates www.antinozzi.com	👥	CT	E M S W C G	A D E G I L P U O	C E K G Hc H I M R Rs Rm Rc S O	
	Apostolou Associates www.apostolouassociates.com	👤	PA	E M S W C G	A D E G I L P U O	C E K G Hc H I M R Rs Rm Rc S O	
	App Architecture www.app-arch.com	👥	OH	E M S W C G	A D E G I L P U O	C E K G Hc H I M R Rs Rm Rc S O	
	ARC/Architectural Resources Cambridge www.arcusa.com	👥	MA	E M S W C G	A D E G I L P U O	C E K G Hc H I M R Rs Rm Rc S O	
	Archicon www.archicon.com	👥	AZ	E M S W C G	A D E G I L P U O	C E K G Hc H I M R Rs Rm Rc S O	
	Archimages www.archimages-stl.com	👥	MO	E M S W C G	A D E G I L P U O	C E K G Hc H I M R Rs Rm Rc S O	
	Archiphy www.archiphy.com	👤	TX	E M S W C G	A D E G I L P U O	C E K G Hc H I M R Rs Rm Rc S O	
	Architects BCRA www.bcradesign.com	👥👥	WA	E M S W C G	A D E G I L P U O	C E K G Hc H I M R Rs Rm Rc S O	
	Architects Design Group www.adgusa.org	👥	FL	E M S W C G	A D E G I L P U O	C E K G Hc H I M R Rs Rm Rc S O	
87	**Architects Hawaii** www.ahldesign.com	👥	HI	E M S W C G	A D E G I L P U O	C E K G Hc H I M R Rs Rm Rc S O	
	Architects Pacific www.architectspacificinc.com	👤	HI	E M S W C G	A D E G I L P U O	C E K G Hc H I M R Rs Rm Rc S O	
	Architects Studio www.architectsstudio.us	👤	HI	E M S W C G	A D E G I L P U O	C E K G Hc H I M R Rs Rm Rc S O	
	Architectura www.architecturapc.com	👥	NY	E M S W C G	A D E G I L P U O	C E K G Hc H I M R Rs Rm Rc S O	
	Architectural Concepts www.arconcepts.com	👥	PA	E M S W C G	A D E G I L P U O	C E K G Hc H I M R Rs Rm Rc S O	
	Arch | Nexus www.archnexus.com	👥	UT	E M S W C G	A D E G I L P U O	C E K G Hc H I M R Rs Rm Rc S O	
	Architectural Resource Team www.art-team.com	👤	AZ	E M S W C G	A D E G I L P U O	C E K G Hc H I M R Rs Rm Rc S O	

DI Brand Recognition Index

Top tier global and categorical leader recognition

Exceptional national and categorical leader recognition

Strong regional and categorical leader recognition

Notable and growing with emerging categorical recognition

Professional practice notable in city and region

Rank	Firm/Web	Size	HQ	Regions	Services	Markets	DI Index
	Architectural Resources www.archres.com		NY	E M S W C G	A D E G I L P U O	C E K G Hc H I M R Rs Rm Rc S O	
	Architectural Resources Group www.argsf.com		CA	E M S W C G	A D E G I L P U O	C E K G Hc H I M R Rs Rm Rc S O	
	Architectural Resources Inc. www.arimn.com		MN	E M S W C G	A D E G I L P U O	C E K G Hc H I M R Rs Rm Rc S O	
	Architectural Studio www.archstudioofl.com		FL	E M S W C G	A D E G I L P U O	C E K G Hc H I M R Rs Rm Rc S O	
	Architecture Incorporated www.architectureinc.com		SD	E M S W C G	A D E G I L P U O	C E K G Hc H I M R Rs Rm Rc S O	
	Architecture Is Fun www.architectureisfun.com		IL	E M S W C G	A D E G I L P U O	C E K G Hc H I M R Rs Rm Rc S O	
	Architecture PML www.archpml.com		CO	E M S W C G	A D E G I L P U O	C E K G Hc H I M R Rs Rm Rc S O	
	Architecture, Inc. www.archinc.com		VA	E M S W C G	A D E G I L P U O	C E K G Hc H I M R Rs Rm Rc S O	
223	**Architekton** www.architekton.com		AZ	E M S W C G	A D E G I L P U O	C E K G Hc H I M R Rs Rm Rc S O	
258	**Arcturis** www.arcturis.com		MO	E M S W C G	A D E G I L P U O	C E K G Hc H I M R Rs Rm Rc S O	
	Aria Group Architects www.ariainc.com		IL	E M S W C G	A D E G I L P U O	C E K G Hc H I M R Rs Rm Rc S O	
	ARIUMae www.ARIUMae.com		MD	E M S W C G	A D E G I L P U O	C E K G Hc H I M R Rs Rm Rc S O	
	Arkinetics www.arkinetics.com		OH	E M S W C G	A D E G I L P U O	C E K G Hc H I M R Rs Rm Rc S O	
91	**Arquitectonica** www.arquitectonica.com		FL	E M S W C G	A D E G I L P U O	C E K G Hc H I M R Rs Rm Rc S O	
109	**Array Architects** www.array-architects.com		PA	E M S W C G	A D E G I L P U O	C E K G Hc H I M R Rs Rm Rc S O	
	Arrington Watkins Architects www.awarch.com		AZ	E M S W C G	A D E G I L P U O	C E K G Hc H I M R Rs Rm Rc S O	
162	**Arrowstreet** www.arrowstreet.com		MA	E M S W C G	A D E G I L P U O	C E K G Hc H I M R Rs Rm Rc S O	

Size

Small	20 employees or less
Medium	21–100 employees
Large	101–450 employees
Extra Large	451+ employees

Regions East (E), Midwest (M), South (S), West (W), Canada (C), Global (G)

Services Architecture (A), Design/Build (D), Engineering-MEP (E), Graphic Design (G), Interior Design (I), Landscape Architecture (L), Planning (P), Urban Design (U), Other-including Industrial Design (O)

Markets Corporate (C), Higher Ed. (E), K-12 (K), Government (G), Healthcare (Hc), Hospitality (H), Industrial/Tech. (I), Museum/Cultural (M), Religious (R), Residential-Single (Rs), Residential-Multi. (Rm), Retail/Commercial (Rc), Sports (S), Other (O)

Rank	Firm/Web	Size	HQ	Regions	Services	Markets	DI Index
	Artekna www.artekna.com	👥👥	IN	E M S W C G	A D E G I L P U O	C E K G Hc H I M R Rs Rm Rc S O	
157	**Ascension Group Architects** www.ascensiongroup.biz	👥👥	TX	E M S W C G	A D E G I L P U O	C E K G Hc H I M R Rs Rm Rc S O	
115	**ASD | SKY** www.asdnet.com	👥👥👥	GA	E M S W C G	A D E G I L P U O	C E K G Hc H I M R Rs Rm Rc S O	
286	**Ashley McGraw Architects** www.ashleymcgraw.com	👥👥	NY	E M S W C G	A D E G I L P U O	C E K G Hc H I M R Rs Rm Rc S O	
	ATI Architects & Engineers www.atiae.com	👥👥	CA	E M S W C G	A D E G I L P U O	C E K G Hc H I M R Rs Rm Rc S O	
	Atkin Olshin Schade Architects www.aosarchitects.com	👥👥	PA	E M S W C G	A D E G I L P U O	C E K G Hc H I M R Rs Rm Rc S O	
	Austin Kuester www.austinkuester.com	👥	VA	E M S W C G	A D E G I L P U O	C E K G Hc H I M R Rs Rm Rc S O	
56	**Ayers Saint Gross** www.asg-architects.com	👥👥👥	MD	E M S W C G	A D E G I L P U O	C E K G Hc H I M R Rs Rm Rc S O	
B	**Baird Sampson Neuert Architects** www.bsnarchitects.com	👥	CAN	E M S W C G	A D E G I L P U O	C E K G Hc H I M R Rs Rm Rc S O	
230	**Baker Barrios Architects** www.bakerbarrios.com	👥👥👥	FL	E M S W C G	A D E G I L P U O	C E K G Hc H I M R Rs Rm Rc S O	
53	**Ballinger** www.ballinger-ae.com	👥👥👥	PA	E M S W C G	A D E G I L P U O	C E K G Hc H I M R Rs Rm Rc S O	
123	**BAR Architects** www.bararch.com	👥👥	CA	E M S W C G	A D E G I L P U O	C E K G Hc H I M R Rs Rm Rc S O	
317	**Bargmann Hendrie & Archetype** www.bhplus.com	👥👥	MA	E M S W C G	A D E G I L P U O	C E K G Hc H I M R Rs Rm Rc S O	
289	**Barker Rinker Seacat Architecture** www.brsarch.com	👥👥	CO	E M S W C G	A D E G I L P U O	C E K G Hc H I M R Rs Rm Rc S O	
	Barry Davis Architects www.barrydavisarchitects.com	👥	AL	E M S W C G	A D E G I L P U O	C E K G Hc H I M R Rs Rm Rc S O	
	BartonPartners www.bartonpartners.com	👥👥	PA	E M S W C G	A D E G I L P U O	C E K G Hc H I M R Rs Rm Rc S O	
218	**Baskervill** www.baskervill.com	👥👥	VA	E M S W C G	A D E G I L P U O	C E K G Hc H I M R Rs Rm Rc S O	

DI Brand Recognition Index

Top tier global and categorical leader recognition

Notable and growing with emerging categorical recognition

Exceptional national and categorical leader recognition

Professional practice notable in city and region

Strong regional and categorical leader recognition

Casey Dunn Photography

Nutrabolt Corporate Headquarters, Bryan, TX | The Beck Group (Architecture)

The Beck Group

Harim Group Headquarters, Seoul, South Korea | The Beck Group (Architecture)

Rank	Firm/Web	Size	HQ	Regions	Services	Markets	DI Index
	Bassetti Architects www.bassettiarch.com	👤	WA	E M S W C G	A D E G I L P U O	C E K G Hc H I M R Rs Rm Rc S O	▁▃▁▁
	BAUER Architects www.bauer-architects.com	👤	CA	E M S W C G	A D E G I L P U O	C E K G Hc H I M R Rs Rm Rc S O	▃▅▃▁
	Bauer Latoza Studio www.bauerlatozastudio.com	👥	IL	E M S W C G	A D E G I L P U O	C E K G Hc H I 'M R Rs Rm Rc S O	▃▅▃▁
	Bay Tree Design www.baytreedesign.com	👤	CA	E M S W C G	A D E G I L P U O	C E K G Hc H I M R Rs Rm Rc S O	▃▅▃▁
180	**BBG-BBGM** www.bbg-bbgm.com	👥👤	NY	E M S W C G	A D E G I L P U O	C E K G Hc H I M R Rs Rm Rc S O	▃▅▆█
	BBH Design www.bbh-design.com	👥	NC	E M S W C G	A D E G I L P U O	C E K G Hc H I M R Rs Rm Rc S O	▃▅▆
	BBL Architects www.bblarchitects.com	👥	OR	E M S W C G	A D E G I L P U O	C E K G Hc H I M R Rs Rm Rc S O	▃▅▃▁
	BC Architects www.bcarchitects.com	👤	FL	E M S W C G	A D E G I L P U O	C E K G Hc H I M R Rs Rm Rc S O	▁▃▅▁
254	**BCA** www.BCAarchitects.com	👥	CA	E M S W C G	A D E G I L P U O	C E K G Hc H I M R Rs Rm Rc S O	▃▅▃▁
236	**BCK - IBI Group** www.bckpc.com	👥	NY	E M S W C G	A D E G I L P U O	C E K G Hc H I M R Rs Rm Rc S O	▃▅▃▁
	BEA Architects www.beai.com	👥	FL	E M S W C G	A D E G I L P U O	C E K G Hc H I M R Rs Rm Rc S O	▃▅▃▁
	Beacon Architectural Associates www.beaconarch.com	👤	MA	E M S W C G	A D E G I L P U O	C E K G Hc H I M R Rs Rm Rc S O	▃▅▃▁
	Beame Architectural Partnership www.bapdesign.com	👤	FL	E M S W C G	A D E G I L P U O	C E K G Hc H I M R Rs Rm Rc S O	▃▅▃▁
	Beatty, Harvey, Coco Architects www.bhc-architects.com	👥	NY	E M S W C G	A D E G I L P U O	C E K G Hc H I M R Rs Rm Rc S O	▁▃▅▁
60	**The Beck Group (Architecture)** www.beckgroup.com	👥👥	TX	E M S W C G	A D E G I L P U O	C E K G Hc H I M R Rs Rm Rc S O	▃▅▆█
	Becker + Becker Associates www.beckerandbecker.com	👤	CT	E M S W C G	A D E G I L P U O	C E K G Hc H I M R Rs Rm Rc S O	▃▅▃▁
	Bell/Knott & Associates www.bellknott.com	👥	KS	E M S W C G	A D E G I L P U O	C E K G Hc H I M R Rs Rm Rc S O	▃▅▃▁

DI Brand Recognition Index

▃▅▆█ Top tier global and categorical leader recognition

▃▅▆ Exceptional national and categorical leader recognition

▃▅▁ Strong regional and categorical leader recognition

▁▃▁▁ Notable and growing with emerging categorical recognition

▁▁▁ Professional practice notable in city and region

Rank	Firm/Web	Size	HQ	Regions	Services	Markets	DI Index
	Benjamin Woo Architects www.benwooarchitects.com	👤	HI	E M S W C G	A D E G I L P U O	C E K G Hc H I M R Rs Rm Rc S O	
	Bennett Sullivan Associates www.bennettsullivan.com	👥	CT	E M S W C G	A D E G I L P U O	C E K G Hc H I M R Rs Rm Rc S O	
255	**Bennett Wagner & Grody Architects** www.bwgarchitects.com	👥	CO	E M S W C G	A D E G I L P U O	C E K G Hc H I M R Rs Rm Rc S O	
	Bentel & Bentel Architects/Planners www.bentelandbentel.com	👤	NY	E M S W C G	A D E G I L P U O	C E K G Hc H I M R Rs Rm Rc S O	
	Berger Partnership www.bergerpartnership.com	👥	WA	E M S W C G	A D E G I L P U O	C E K G Hc H I M R Rs Rm Rc S O	
83	**Bergmann Associates** www.bergmannpc.com	👥👥	NY	E M S W C G	A D E G I L P U O	C E K G Hc H I M R Rs Rm Rc S O	
206	**Bergmeyer Associates** www.bergmeyer.com	👥	MA	E M S W C G	A D E G I L P U O	C E K G Hc H I M R Rs Rm Rc S O	
148	**Bermello Ajamil & Partners** www.bamiami.com	👥	FL	E M S W C G	A D E G I L P U O	C E K G Hc H I M R Rs Rm Rc S O	
272	**Bernardon Haber Holloway** www.bernardon.com	👥	PA	E M S W C G	A D E G I L P U O	C E K G Hc H I M R Rs Rm Rc S O	
78	**Beyer Blinder Belle** www.beyerblinderbelle.com	👥👥	NY	E M S W C G	A D E G I L P U O	C E K G Hc H I M R Rs Rm Rc S O	
90	**BHDP Architecture** www.bhdp.com	👥👥	OH	E M S W C G	A D E G I L P U O	C E K G Hc H I M R Rs Rm Rc S O	
	BHM Architecture www.bhm.us.com	👤	FL	E M S W C G	A D E G I L P U O	C E K G Hc H I M R Rs Rm Rc S O	
	Bialosky & Partners Architects www.bialosky.com	👥	OH	E M S W C G	A D E G I L P U O	C E K G Hc H I M R Rs Rm Rc S O	
291	**Bignell Watkins Hasser Architects** www.bigwaha.com	👥	MD	E M S W C G	A D E G I L P U O	C E K G Hc H I M R Rs Rm Rc S O	
	Bing Thom Architects www.bingthomarchitects.com	👥	CAN	E M S W C G	A D E G I L P U O	C E K G Hc H I M R Rs Rm Rc S O	
	Bingham Hill Architects www.bharch.ca	👤	CAN	E M S W C G	A D E G I L P U O	C E K G Hc H I M R Rs Rm Rc S O	
	Bionic www.bioniclandscape.com	👥	CA	E M S W C G	A D E G I L P U O	C E K G Hc H I M R Rs Rm Rc S O	

Size

👤	Small	20 employees or less
👥	Medium	21–100 employees
👥👥	Large	101–450 employees
👥👥👥	Extra Large	451+ employees

Regions East (E), Midwest (M), South (S), West (W), Canada (C), Global (G)

Services Architecture (A), Design/Build (D), Engineering-MEP (E), Graphic Design (G), Interior Design (I), Landscape Architecture (L), Planning (P), Urban Design (U), Other-including Industrial Design (O)

Markets Corporate (C), Higher Ed. (E), K-12 (K), Government (G), Healthcare (Hc), Hospitality (H), Industrial/Tech. (I), Museum/Cultural (M), Religious (R), Residential-Single (Rs), Residential-Multi. (Rm), Retail/Commercial (Rc), Sports (S), Other (O)

Rank	Firm/Web	Size	HQ	Regions	Services	Markets	DI Index
285	**bKL Architecture** www.bklarch.com	👥	IL	E M S W C G	A D E G I L P U O	C E K G Hc H I M R Rs Rm Rc S O	▪▫▪▪
	BKV Group www.bkvgroup.com	👥	MN	E M S W C G	A D E G I L P U O	C E K G Hc H I M R Rs Rm Rc S O	▪▪▫▫
	Blackburn Architects www.blackburnarch.com	👤	DC	E M S W C G	A D E G I L P U O	C E K G Hc H I M R Rs Rm Rc S O	▪▪▪▫
	Blackney Hayes Architects www.blackneyhayes.com	👥	PA	E M S W C G	A D E G I L P U O	C E K G Hc H I M R Rs Rm Rc S O	▪▪▫▫
	blank studio design + architecture www.blankspaces.net	👤	AZ	E M S W C G	A D E G I L P U O	C E K G Hc H I M R Rs Rm Rc S O	▪▪▪▫
165	**BLT Architects** www.blta.com	👥	PA	E M S W C G	A D E G I L P U O	C E K G Hc H I M R Rs Rm Rc S O	▪▪▪▫
171	**BNIM Architects** www.bnim.com	👥	MO	E M S W C G	A D E G I L P U O	C E K G Hc H I M R Rs Rm Rc S O	▪▪▪▪
321	**Boggs & Partners Architects** www.boggspartners.com	👤	MD	E M S W C G	A D E G I L P U O	C E K G Hc H I M R Rs Rm Rc S O	▪▪▫▫
221	**Bohlin Cywinski Jackson** www.bcj.com	👥👤	N/A	E M S W C G	A D E G I L P U O	C E K G Hc H I M R Rs Rm Rc S O	▪▪▪▪
117	**BOKA Powell** www.bokapowell.com	👥	TX	E M S W C G	A D E G I L P U O	C E K G Hc H I M R Rs Rm Rc S O	▪▪▫▫
	Bond Architects www.bondarchitectsinc.com	👥	MO	E M S W C G	A D E G I L P U O	C E K G Hc H I M R Rs Rm Rc S O	▪▪▪▫
140	**BOORA Architects** www.boora.com	👥	OR	E M S W C G	A D E G I L P U O	C E K G Hc H I M R Rs Rm Rc S O	▪▪▪▫
	Booth Hansen www.boothhansen.com	👤	IL	E M S W C G	A D E G I L P U O	C E K G Hc H I M R Rs Rm Rc S O	▪▪▫▫
	Borrelli + Partners www.borrelliarchitects.com	👤	FL	E M S W C G	A D E G I L P U O	C E K G Hc H I M R Rs Rm Rc S O	▪▪▫▫
302	**Bostwick Design Partnership** www.bostwickdesign.com	👥	OH	E M S W C G	A D E G I L P U O	C E K G Hc H I M R Rs Rm Rc S O	▪▪▫▫
	Boulder Associates www.boulderassociates.com	👥	CO	E M S W C G	A D E G I L P U O	C E K G Hc H I M R Rs Rm Rc S O	▪▪▫▫
	Bouril Design Studio www.bourildesign.com	👥	WI	E M S W C G	A D E G I L P U O	C E K G Hc H I M R Rs Rm Rc S O	▪▪▪▫

DI Brand Recognition Index

▪▪▪▪ Top tier global and categorical leader recognition	▪▪▫▫ Notable and growing with emerging categorical recognition
▪▪▪▫ Exceptional national and categorical leader recognition	▪▫▫▫ Professional practice notable in city and region
▪▪▫▫ Strong regional and categorical leader recognition	

Rank	Firm/Web	Size	HQ	Regions	Services	Markets	DI Index
	Bradley & Bradley Architects and Engineers www.bradleyandbradley.net	👤	IL	E M S W C G	A D E G I L P U O	C E K G Hc H I M R Rs Rm Rc S O	
	Brasher Design www.brasherdesign.com	👤	MD	E M S W C G	A D E G I L P U O	C E K G Hc H I M R Rs Rm Rc S O	
	Braun & Steidl Architects www.bsa-net.com	👤	OH	E M S W C G	A D E G I L P U O	C E K G Hc H I M R Rs Rm Rc S O	
	BRB Architects www.brb.com	👥	NY	E M S W C G	A D E G I L P U O	C E K G Hc H I M R Rs Rm Rc S O	
	Brooks + Scarpa www.brooksscarpa.com	👥	CA	E M S W C G	A D E G I L P U O	C E K G Hc H I M R Rs Rm Rc S O	
	Brown Craig Turner www.brownandcraig.com	👤	MD	E M S W C G	A D E G I L P U O	C E K G Hc H I M R Rs Rm Rc S O	
	Brown Reynolds Watford Architects www.brwarch.com	👥	TX	E M S W C G	A D E G I L P U O	C E K G Hc H I M R Rs Rm Rc S O	
	Browning Day Mullins Dierdorf Architects www.bdmd.com	👥	IN	E M S W C G	A D E G I L P U O	C E K G Hc H I M R Rs Rm Rc S O	
	BRPH www.brph.com	👥	FL	E M S W C G	A D E G I L P U O	C E K G Hc H I M R Rs Rm Rc S O	
	BRR Architecture www.brrarch.com	👥	KS	E M S W C G	A D E G I L P U O	C E K G Hc H I M R Rs Rm Rc S O	
	Bruce Mau Design www.brucemaudesign.com	👤	CAN	E M S W C G	A D E G I L P U O	C E K G Hc H I M R Rs Rm Rc S O	
217	**Bruner/Cott & Associates** www.brunercott.com	👥	MA	E M S W C G	A D E G I L P U O	C E K G Hc H I M R Rs Rm Rc S O	
64	**BSA LifeStructures** www.bsals.com	👥👥	IN	E M S W C G	A D E G I L P U O	C E K G Hc H I M R Rs Rm Rc S O	
	Buckman Architectural Group www.buckmanarchitecturalgroup.com	👤	NJ	E M S W C G	A D E G I L P U O	C E K G Hc H I M R Rs Rm Rc S O	
	Bull Stockwell Allen www.bsaarchitects.com	👥	CA	E M S W C G	A D E G I L P U O	C E K G Hc H I M R Rs Rm Rc S O	
244	**Bullock Tice Associates** www.bullocktice.com	👥	FL	E M S W C G	A D E G I L P U O	C E K G Hc H I M R Rs Rm Rc S O	
	Bumpus & Associates www.bumpusandassociates.com	👤	FL	E M S W C G	A D E G I L P U O	C E K G Hc H I M R Rs Rm Rc S O	

Size

👤	Small	20 employees or less
👥	Medium	21–100 employees
👥👥	Large	101–450 employees
👥👥👥	Extra Large	451+ employees

Regions East (E), Midwest (M), South (S), West (W), Canada (C), Global (G)

Services Architecture (A), Design/Build (D), Engineering-MEP (E), Graphic Design (G), Interior Design (I), Landscape Architecture (L), Planning (P), Urban Design (U), Other-including Industrial Design (O)

Markets Corporate (C), Higher Ed. (E), K-12 (K), Government (G), Healthcare (Hc), Hospitality (H), Industrial/Tech. (I), Museum/Cultural (M), Religious (R), Residential-Single (Rs), Residential-Multi. (Rm), Retail/Commercial (Rc), Sports (S), Other (O)

Rank	Firm/Web	Size	HQ	Regions	Services	Markets	DI Index
	Burgess & Niple www.burgessniple.com	👥👥	OH	E M S W C G	A D E G I L P U O	C E K G Hc H I M R Rs Rm Rc S O	
	Burka Architects www.burka.net	👥👥	CAN	E M S W C G	A D E G I L P U O	C E K G Hc H I M R Rs Rm Rc S O	
	Burkett Design www.burkettdesign.com	👥👥	CO	E M S W C G	A D E G I L P U O	C E K G Hc H I M R Rs Rm Rc S O	
	Burns & McDonnell www.burnsmcd.com	👥👥👥👥👥	MO	E M S W C G	A D E G I L P U O	C E K G Hc H I M R Rs Rm Rc S O	
	Busch Architects www.busch-architects.com	👥👥	MN	E M S W C G	A D E G I L P U O	C E K G Hc H I M R Rs Rm Rc S O	
	Butler Design Group www.butlerdesigngroup.com	👥👥	AZ	E M S W C G	A D E G I L P U O	C E K G Hc H I M R Rs Rm Rc S O	
	BWA Architecture & Planning www.bwa-architects.com	👥	PA	E M S W C G	A D E G I L P U O	C E K G Hc H I M R Rs Rm Rc S O	
67	**BWBR Architects** www.bwbr.com	👥👥👥	MN	E M S W C G	A D E G I L P U O	C E K G Hc H I M R Rs Rm Rc S O	
C	**C.N. Carley Associates** www.cncarley.com	👥	NH	E M S W C G	A D E G I L P U O	C E K G Hc H I M R Rs Rm Rc S O	
	C.T. Hsu + Associates www.cthsu.com	👥	FL	E M S W C G	A D E G I L P U O	C E K G Hc H I M R Rs Rm Rc S O	
	CA Architects www.ca-arch.com	👥👥👥👥👥	TX	E M S W C G	A D E G I L P U O	C E K G Hc H I M R Rs Rm Rc S O	
5	**Callison RTKL** www.rtkl.com	👥	AR	E M S W C G	A D E G I L P U O	C E K G Hc H I M R Rs Rm Rc S O	
	CAMA www.camainc.com	👥	CT	E M S W C G	A D E G I L P U O	C E K G Hc H I M R Rs Rm Rc S O	
119	**Cambridge Seven Associates** www.c7a.com	👥👥	MA	E M S W C G	A D E G I L P U O	C E K G Hc H I M R Rs Rm Rc S O	
	Canin Associates www.canin.com	👥👥	FL	E M S W C G	A D E G I L P U O	C E K G Hc H I M R Rs Rm Rc S O	
14	**CannonDesign** www.cannondesign.com	👥👥👥👥👥	N/A	E M S W C G	A D E G I L P U O	C E K G Hc H I M R Rs Rm Rc S O	
	Carde Ten Architects www.cardeten.com	👥	CA	E M S W C G	A D E G I L P U O	C E K G Hc H I M R Rs Rm Rc S O	

DI Brand Recognition Index

Top tier global and categorical leader recognition

Exceptional national and categorical leader recognition

Strong regional and categorical leader recognition

Notable and growing with emerging categorical recognition

Professional practice notable in city and region

Rank	Firm/Web	Size	HQ	Regions	Services	Markets	DI Index
186	**Carrier Johnson + CULTURE** www.carrierjohnson.com	👥	CA	E M S W C G	A D E G I L P U O	C E K G Hc H I M R Rs Rm Rc S O	▪▪▪
	Cascade Design Collaborative www.cascadedesigncollab.com	👤	WA	E M S W C G	A D E G I L P U O	C E K G Hc H I M R Rs Rm Rc S O	▪▪
224	**CASCO** www.cascocorp.com	👥👥	MO	E M S W C G	A D E G I L P U O	C E K G Hc H I M R Rs Rm Rc S O	▪▪
332	**Cass Sowatsky Consulting Architects** www.csc-a.com	👤	CA	E M S W C G	A D E G I L P U O	C E K G Hc H I M R Rs Rm Rc S O	▪▪▪
	Catalyst Architects www.catalystarch.com	👥	SC	E M S W C G	A D E G I L P U O	C E K G Hc H I M R Rs Rm Rc S O	▪▪
	CBLH Design www.cblhdesign.com	👤	OH	E M S W C G	A D E G I L P U O	C E K G Hc H I M R Rs Rm Rc S O	▪▪
70	**CBT** www.cbtarchitects.com	👥👥	MA	E M S W C G	A D E G I L P U O	C E K G Hc H I M R Rs Rm Rc S O	▪▪
	CCBG Architects www.ccbg-arch.com	👤	AZ	E M S W C G	A D E G I L P U O	C E K G Hc H I M R Rs Rm Rc S O	▪▪
282	**CDH Partners** www.cdhpartners.com	👥	GA	E M S W C G	A D E G I L P U O	C E K G Hc H I M R Rs Rm Rc S O	▪▪
	CDS International www.cdsintl.com	👤	HI	E M S W C G	A D E G I L P U O	C E K G Hc H I M R Rs Rm Rc S O	▪▪
	Cecil Baker + Partners www.cecilbakerpartners.com	👤	PA	E M S W C G	A D E G I L P U O	C E K G Hc H I M R Rs Rm Rc S O	▪▪
	Celli-Flynn Brennan Architects & Planners www.cfbarchitects.com	👤	PA	E M S W C G	A D E G I L P U O	C E K G Hc H I M R Rs Rm Rc S O	▪▪
252	**Centerbrook Architects and Planners** www.centerbrook.com	👥	CT	E M S W C G	A D E G I L P U O	C E K G Hc H I M R Rs Rm Rc S O	▪▪▪
212	**CetraRuddy** www.cetraruddy.com	👥	NY	E M S W C G	A D E G I L P U O	C E K G Hc H I M R Rs Rm Rc S O	▪▪
	Chambers, Murphy & Burge Architects www.cmbarchitects.com	👤	OH	E M S W C G	A D E G I L P U O	C E K G Hc H I M R Rs Rm Rc S O	▪▪
316	**Champalimaud** www.champalimauddesign.com	👥	NY	E M S W C G	A D E G I L P U O	C E K G Hc H I M R Rs Rm Rc S O	▪▪▪
	Champlin Architecture www.charchitects.com	👥	OH	E M S W C G	A D E G I L P U O	C E K G Hc H I M R Rs Rm Rc S O	▪▪

Size

👤	Small	20 employees or less
👥	Medium	21–100 employees
👥👥	Large	101–450 employees
👥👥👥	Extra Large	451+ employees

Regions East (E), Midwest (M), South (S), West (W), Canada (C), Global (G)

Services Architecture (A), Design/Build (D), Engineering-MEP (E), Graphic Design (G), Interior Design (I), Landscape Architecture (L), Planning (P), Urban Design (U), Other-including Industrial Design (O)

Markets Corporate (C), Higher Ed. (E), K-12 (K), Government (G), Healthcare (Hc), Hospitality (H), Industrial/Tech. (I), Museum/Cultural (M), Religious (R), Residential-Single (Rs), Residential-Multi. (Rm), Retail/Commercial (Rc), Sports (S), Other (O)

Rank	Firm/Web	Size	HQ	Regions	Services	Markets	DI Index
	Charlan Brock & Associates www.cbaarchitects.com	👤	FL	E M S W C G	A D E G I L P U O	C E K G Hc H I M R Rs Rm Rc S O	▄▃▁▁
	Chiodini Associates www.chiodini.com	👤	MO	E M S W C G	A D E G I L P U O	C E K G Hc H I M R Rs Rm Rc S O	▄▃▁▁
	Chipman Design Architecture www.chipmandesignarch.com	👥	IL	E M S W C G	A D E G I L P U O	C E K G Hc H I M R Rs Rm Rc S O	▄▃▁▁
331	**Cho Benn Holback + Associates** www.cbhassociates.com	👥	MD	E M S W C G	A D E G I L P U O	C E K G Hc H I M R Rs Rm Rc S O	▄▃▁▁
277	**Christner** www.christnerinc.com	👥	MO	E M S W C G	A D E G I L P U O	C E K G Hc H I M R Rs Rm Rc S O	▄▃▁▁
	Cibinel Architecture www.cibinel.com	👤	CAN	E M S W C G	A D E G I L P U O	C E K G Hc H I M R Rs Rm Rc S O	▄▃▁▁
	City Architecture www.cityarch.com	👥	OH	E M S W C G	A D E G I L P U O	C E K G Hc H I M R Rs Rm Rc S O	▄▃▁▁
	CJMW Architecture www.cjmw.com	👥	NC	E M S W C G	A D E G I L P U O	C E K G Hc H I M R Rs Rm Rc S O	▄▃▁▁
	CJS Group Architects www.cjsgrouparchitects.com	👤	HI	E M S W C G	A D E G I L P U O	C E K G Hc H I M R Rs Rm Rc S O	▄▃▁▁
	Clark Nexsen www.clarknexsen.com	👥👥👥	VA	E M S W C G	A D E G I L P U O	C E K G Hc H I M R Rs Rm Rc S O	▄▄▃▁
	Claude Cormier + Associates www.claudecormier.com	👥	CAN	E M S W C G	A D E G I L P U O	C E K G Hc H I M R Rs Rm Rc S O	▄▅▆▇
	Clohessy Harris & Kaiser www.chkarch.com	👤	CT	E M S W C G	A D E G I L P U O	C E K G Hc H I M R Rs Rm Rc S O	▄▃▁▁
219	**CMA** www.cmarch.com	👥👥	MN	E M S W C G	A D E G I L P U O	C E K G Hc H I M R Rs Rm Rc S O	▄▃▁▁
94	**CO Architects** www.coarchitects.com	👥	CA	E M S W C G	A D E G I L P U O	C E K G Hc H I M R Rs Rm Rc S O	▄▃▁▁
	Colgan Perry Lawler Aurell Architects www.cpla-arch.com	👤	NY	E M S W C G	A D E G I L P U O	C E K G Hc H I M R Rs Rm Rc S O	▄▃▁▁
	Colimore Architects www.colimore.com	👤	MD	E M S W C G	A D E G I L P U O	C E K G Hc H I M R Rs Rm Rc S O	▄▃▁▁
	Collaborative Design Group www.collaborativedesigngroup.com	👥	MN	E M S W C G	A D E G I L P U O	C E K G Hc H I M R Rs Rm Rc S O	▄▃▁▁

DI Brand Recognition Index

▄▅▆▇ Top tier global and categorical leader recognition

▄▄▃▁ Exceptional national and categorical leader recognition

▄▃▁▁ Strong regional and categorical leader recognition

▄▃▁▁ Notable and growing with emerging categorical recognition

▄▁▁▁ Professional practice notable in city and region

Rank	Firm/Web	Size	HQ	Regions	Services	Markets	DI Index
	Collective Invention www.collectiveinvention.com	Small	CA	E M S W C G	A D E G I L P U O	C E K G Hc H I M R Rs Rm Rc S O	
	CollinsWoerman www.collinswoerman.com	Medium	WA	E M S W C G	A D E G I L P U O	C E K G Hc H I M R Rs Rm Rc S O	
266	**Cook + Fox Architects** www.cookplusfox.com	Medium	NY	E M S W C G	A D E G I L P U O	C E K G Hc H I M R Rs Rm Rc S O	
46	**Cooper Carry** www.coopercarry.com	Large	GA	E M S W C G	A D E G I L P U O	C E K G Hc H I M R Rs Rm Rc S O	
214	**Cooper Robertson** www.cooperrobertson.com	Medium	NY	E M S W C G	A D E G I L P U O	C E K G Hc H I M R Rs Rm Rc S O	
	Corbin Design www.corbindesign.com	Small	MI	E M S W C G	A D E G I L P U O	C E K G Hc H I M R Rs Rm Rc S O	
	Cordogan, Clark and Associates www.cordoganclark.com	Medium	IL	E M S W C G	A D E G I L P U O	C E K G Hc H I M R Rs Rm Rc S O	
	CORE www.coredc.com	Small	DC	E M S W C G	A D E G I L P U O	C E K G Hc H I M R Rs Rm Rc S O	
26	**Corgan Associates** www.corgan.com	Extra Large	TX	E M S W C G	A D E G I L P U O	C E K G Hc H I M R Rs Rm Rc S O	
	Cowart Group www.cowartgroup.com	Small	GA	E M S W C G	A D E G I L P U O	C E K G Hc H I M R Rs Rm Rc S O	
	CR Architecture + Design www.cr-architects.com	Medium	OH	E M S W C G	A D E G I L P U O	C E K G Hc H I M R Rs Rm Rc S O	
169	**Crabtree, Rohrbaugh & Associates** www.cra-architects.com	Medium	PA	E M S W C G	A D E G I L P U O	C E K G Hc H I M R Rs Rm Rc S O	
	Crafton Tull www.craftontull.com	Large	AR	E M S W C G	A D E G I L P U O	C E K G Hc H I M R Rs Rm Rc S O	
	Craig Gaulden Davis www.cgdarch.com	Small	SC	E M S W C G	A D E G I L P U O	C E K G Hc H I M R Rs Rm Rc S O	
	Cram and Ferguson Architects www.cramandferguson.com	Small	MA	E M S W C G	A D E G I L P U O	C E K G Hc H I M R Rs Rm Rc S O	
313	**Crawford Architects** www.crawfordarch.com	Small	MO	E M S W C G	A D E G I L P U O	C E K G Hc H I M R Rs Rm Rc S O	
152	**Cromwell Architects Engineers** www.cromwell.com	Large	AR	E M S W C G	A D E G I L P U O	C E K G Hc H I M R Rs Rm Rc S O	

Size

Small	20 employees or less	
Medium	21–100 employees	
Large	101–450 employees	
Extra Large	451+ employees	

Regions East (E), Midwest (M), South (S), West (W), Canada (C), Global (G)

Services Architecture (A), Design/Build (D), Engineering-MEP (E), Graphic Design (G), Interior Design (I), Landscape Architecture (L), Planning (P), Urban Design (U), Other-including Industrial Design (O)

Markets Corporate (C), Higher Ed. (E), K-12 (K), Government (G), Healthcare (Hc), Hospitality (H), Industrial/Tech. (I), Museum/Cultural (M), Religious (R), Residential-Single (Rs), Residential-Multi. (Rm), Retail/Commercial (Rc), Sports (S), Other (O)

Rank	Firm/Web	Size	HQ	Regions	Services	Markets	DI Index
262	**CSArch** www.csarchpc.com	👥👥	NY	E M S W C G	A D E G I L P U O	C E K G Hc H I M R Rs Rm Rc S O	▂▃▁▁
	CSHQA www.cshqa.com	👥	ID	E M S W C G	A D E G I L P U O	C E K G Hc H I M R Rs Rm Rc S O	▂▃▁▁
	CSO Architects www.csoinc.net	👥	IN	E M S W C G	A D E G I L P U O	C E K G Hc H I M R Rs Rm Rc S O	▂▃▄▁
52	**CTA Architects Engineers** www.ctagroup.com	👥👥	MT	E M S W C G	A D E G I L P U O	C E K G Hc H I M R Rs Rm Rc S O	▃▄▅▁
	Cuhaci & Peterson www.c-p.com	👥	FL	E M S W C G	A D E G I L P U O	C E K G Hc H I M R Rs Rm Rc S O	▂▃▄▁
39	**Cuningham Group Architecture** www.cuningham.com	👥👥	MN	E M S W C G	A D E G I L P U O	C E K G Hc H I M R Rs Rm Rc S O	▃▄▅▆
	Cunningham I Quill Architects www.cunninghamquill.com	👥	DC	E M S W C G	A D E G I L P U O	C E K G Hc H I M R Rs Rm Rc S O	▂▃▁▁
	Cutler Associates www.cutlerdb.com	👥👥	MA	E M S W C G	A D E G I L P U O	C E K G Hc H I M R Rs Rm Rc S O	▂▃▁▁
D	**D-2 Architecture** www.d2-architecture.com	👥	TX	E M S W C G	A D E G I L P U O	C E K G Hc H I M R Rs Rm Rc S O	▂▃▁▁
	D.W. Arthur Associates Architecture www.dwarthur.com	👥	MA	E M S W C G	A D E G I L P U O	C E K G Hc H I M R Rs Rm Rc S O	▂▃▁▁
	D2CA Architects www.d2ca.com	👤	PA	E M S W C G	A D E G I L P U O	C E K G Hc H I M R Rs Rm Rc S O	▂▃▁▁
	DAG Architects www.dagarchitects.com	👥	FL	E M S W C G	A D E G I L P U O	C E K G Hc H I M R Rs Rm Rc S O	▂▃▁▁
	Dahlin Group www.dahlingroup.com	👥👥	CA	E M S W C G	A D E G I L P U O	C E K G Hc H I M R Rs Rm Rc S O	▂▃▁▁
	Daniel P. Coffey & Associates www.dpcaltd.com	👥	IL	E M S W C G	A D E G I L P U O	C E K G Hc H I M R Rs Rm Rc S O	▂▃▁▁
	Daniel Smith & Associates www.dsaarch.com	👥	CA	E M S W C G	A D E G I L P U O	C E K G Hc H I M R Rs Rm Rc S O	▂▃▄▁
	Danielian Associates www.danielian.com	👥	CA	E M S W C G	A D E G I L P U O	C E K G Hc H I M R Rs Rm Rc S O	▂▃▁▁
143	**Dattner Architects** www.dattner.com	👥👥	NY	E M S W C G	A D E G I L P U O	C E K G Hc H I M R Rs Rm Rc S O	▂▃▄▁

DI Brand Recognition Index

▂▃▄▅▆ Top tier global and categorical leader recognition

▂▃▄▁ Exceptional national and categorical leader recognition

▂▃▁▁ Strong regional and categorical leader recognition

▂▁▁▁ Notable and growing with emerging categorical recognition

▪▁▁▁ Professional practice notable in city and region

Rank	Firm/Web	Size	HQ	Regions	Services	Markets	DI Index
	David Baker Architects www.dbarchitect.com	Medium	CA	E M S W C G	A D E G I L P U O	C E K G Hc H I M R Rs Rm Rc S O	
	David Jameson Architect Inc www.davidjamesonarchitect.com	Small	CA	E M S W C G	A D E G I L P U O	C E K G Hc H I M R Rs Rm Rc S O	
	David M. Schwarz Architects www.dmsas.com	Medium	DC	E M S W C G	A D E G I L P U O	C E K G Hc H I M R Rs Rm Rc S O	
	David Oakey Designs www.davidoakeydesigns.com	Small	GA	E M S W C G	A D E G I L P U O	C E K G Hc H I M R Rs Rm Rc S O	
246	**Davis** www.thedavisexperience.com	Medium	AZ	E M S W C G	A D E G I L P U O	C E K G Hc H I M R Rs Rm Rc S O	
104	**Davis Brody Bond** www.davisbrody.com	Medium	NY	E M S W C G	A D E G I L P U O	C E K G Hc H I M R Rs Rm Rc S O	
195	**Davis Carter Scott** www.dcsdesign.com	Medium	VA	E M S W C G	A D E G I L P U O	C E K G Hc H I M R Rs Rm Rc S O	
105	**Davis Partnership Architects** www.davispartner.com	Medium	CO	E M S W C G	A D E G I L P U O	C E K G Hc H I M R Rs Rm Rc S O	
294	**DDG** www.ddg-usa.com	Medium	MD	E M S W C G	A D E G I L P U O	C E K G Hc H I M R Rs Rm Rc S O	
	De-Spec www.de-spec.com	Small	NY	E M S W C G	A D E G I L P U O	C E K G Hc H I M R Rs Rm Rc S O	
110	**Dekker/Perich/Sabatini** www.dpsdesign.org	Large	NM	E M S W C G	A D E G I L P U O	C E K G Hc H I M R Rs Rm Rc S O	
	Delawie www.delawie.com	Medium	CA	E M S W C G	A D E G I L P U O	C E K G Hc H I M R Rs Rm Rc S O	
	DES Architects + Engineers www.des-ae.com	Large	CA	E M S W C G	A D E G I L P U O	C E K G Hc H I M R Rs Rm Rc S O	
	The Design Alliance Architects www.tda-architects.com	Medium	PA	E M S W C G	A D E G I L P U O	C E K G Hc H I M R Rs Rm Rc S O	
	Design Collective www.designcollective.com	Large	MD	E M S W C G	A D E G I L P U O	C E K G Hc H I M R Rs Rm Rc S O	
	Design Development Architects www.designdevelopment.com	Small	NC	E M S W C G	A D E G I L P U O	C E K G Hc H I M R Rs Rm Rc S O	
	Design Partners www.designpartnersinc.com	Small	HI	E M S W C G	A D E G I L P U O	C E K G Hc H I M R Rs Rm Rc S O	

Size

Small	20 employees or less	
Medium	21–100 employees	
Large	101–450 employees	
Extra Large	451+ employees	

Regions East (E), Midwest (M), South (S), West (W), Canada (C), Global (G)

Services Architecture (A), Design/Build (D), Engineering-MEP (E), Graphic Design (G), Interior Design (I), Landscape Architecture (L), Planning (P), Urban Design (U), Other-including Industrial Design (O)

Markets Corporate (C), Higher Ed. (E), K-12 (K), Government (G), Healthcare (Hc), Hospitality (H), Industrial/Tech. (I), Museum/Cultural (M), Religious (R), Residential-Single (Rs), Residential-Multi. (Rm), Retail/Commercial (Rc), Sports (S), Other (O)

Rank	Firm/Web	Size	HQ	Regions	Services	Markets	DI Index
	Design Partnership of Cambridge www.design-partnership.com		MA	E M S W C G	A D E G I L P U O	C E K G Hc H I M R Rs Rm Rc S O	
229	Design Workshop www.designworkshop.com		CO	E M S W C G	A D E G I L P U O	C E K G Hc H I M R Rs Rm Rc S O	
	DesignGroup www.designgroup.us.com		OH	E M S W C G	A D E G I L P U O	C E K G Hc H I M R Rs Rm Rc S O	
	DesignLAB architects www.designlabarch.com		MA	E M S W C G	A D E G I L P U O	C E K G Hc H I M R Rs Rm Rc S O	
160	Devenney Group Architects www.devenneygroup.com		AZ	E M S W C G	A D E G I L P U O	C E K G Hc H I M R Rs Rm Rc S O	
18	Dewberry (Architecture) www.dewberry.com		VA	E M S W C G	A D E G I L P U O	C E K G Hc H I M R Rs Rm Rc S O	
	DeWolff Partnership Architects www.dewolff.com		NY	E M S W C G	A D E G I L P U O	C E K G Hc H I M R Rs Rm Rc S O	
	DGA www.dgaonline.com		CA	E M S W C G	A D E G I L P U O	C E K G Hc H I M R Rs Rm Rc S O	
	DHK Architects www.dhkinc.com		MA	E M S W C G	A D E G I L P U O	C E K G Hc H I M R Rs Rm Rc S O	
	Dialog www.dialogdesign.ca		CAN	E M S W C G	A D E G I L P U O	C E K G Hc H I M R Rs Rm Rc S O	
	Diamond Schmitt Architects www.dsai.ca		CAN	E M S W C G	A D E G I L P U O	C E K G Hc H I M R Rs Rm Rc S O	
	Dick & Fritsche Design Group www.dfdg.com		AZ	E M S W C G	A D E G I L P U O	C E K G Hc H I M R Rs Rm Rc S O	
	DiClemente Siegel Design www.dsdonline.com		MI	E M S W C G	A D E G I L P U O	C E K G Hc H I M R Rs Rm Rc S O	
	Diedrich www.diedrichllc.com		GA	E M S W C G	A D E G I L P U O	C E K G Hc H I M R Rs Rm Rc S O	
	Diekema Hamann www.dhae.com		MI	E M S W C G	A D E G I L P U O	C E K G Hc H I M R Rs Rm Rc S O	
	DiGiorgio Associates www.daiarchitects.com		MA	E M S W C G	A D E G I L P U O	C E K G Hc H I M R Rs Rm Rc S O	
311	DiMella Shaffer www.dimellashaffer.com		MA	E M S W C G	A D E G I L P U O	C E K G Hc H I M R Rs Rm Rc S O	

DI Brand Recognition Index

Top tier global and categorical leader recognition

Exceptional national and categorical leader recognition

Strong regional and categorical leader recognition

Notable and growing with emerging categorical recognition

Professional practice notable in city and region

DLR Group

Joplin High School, Joplin, MO | DLR Group

DLR Group

Harbor College Library, Wilmington, CA | DLR Group

Rank	Firm/Web	Size	HQ	Regions	Services	Markets	DI Index
	Dirk Denison Architects www.dirkdenisonarchitects.com	👤	IL	E M S W C G	A D E G I L P U O	C E K G Hc H I M R Rs Rm Rc S O	◧
	DLA Architects www.dla-ltd.com	👥	IL	E M S W C G	A D E G I L P U O	C E K G Hc H I M R Rs Rm Rc S O	◧
20	**DLR Group** www.dlrgroup.com	👥👥👥	N/A	E M S W C G	A D E G I L P U O	C E K G Hc H I M R Rs Rm Rc S O	▅
	DMR www.dmrarchitects.com	👥	NJ	E M S W C G	A D E G I L P U O	C E K G Hc H I M R Rs Rm Rc S O	◧
	DNK www.dnkarchitects.com	👤	OH	E M S W C G	A D E G I L P U O	C E K G Hc H I M R Rs Rm Rc S O	◧
	Domokur Architects www.domokur.com	👤	OH	E M S W C G	A D E G I L P U O	C E K G Hc H I M R Rs Rm Rc S O	◧
	Domus Studio www.domusstudio.com	👤	CA	E M S W C G	A D E G I L P U O	C E K G Hc H I M R Rs Rm Rc S O	◧
	Dore & Whittier www.doreandwhittier.com	👥	VT	E M S W C G	A D E G I L P U O	C E K G Hc H I M R Rs Rm Rc S O	◧
	Dorsky + Yue International www.dorskyyue.com	👥	OH	E M S W C G	A D E G I L P U O	C E K G Hc H I M R Rs Rm Rc S O	▆
270	**Dougherty + Dougherty Architects** www.ddarchitecture.com	👥	CA	E M S W C G	A D E G I L P U O	C E K G Hc H I M R Rs Rm Rc S O	◧
	Douglas Cardinal Architect www.djcarchitect.com	👤	CAN	E M S W C G	A D E G I L P U O	C E K G Hc H I M R Rs Rm Rc S O	▆
	DOWA - IBI Group www.dowa-ibigroup.com	👥	OR	E M S W C G	A D E G I L P U O	C E K G Hc H I M R Rs Rm Rc S O	◧
	DRS Architects www.drsarchitects.com	👥	PA	E M S W C G	A D E G I L P U O	C E K G Hc H I M R Rs Rm Rc S O	◧
	Drummey Rosane Anderson www.draarchitects.com	👥	MA	E M S W C G	A D E G I L P U O	C E K G Hc H I M R Rs Rm Rc S O	◧
	DTJ Design www.dtjdesign.com	👥	CO	E M S W C G	A D E G I L P U O	C E K G Hc H I M R Rs Rm Rc S O	◧
	Duany Plater-Zyberk & Company www.dpz.com	👥	FL	E M S W C G	A D E G I L P U O	C E K G Hc H I M R Rs Rm Rc S O	▆
	Dubbe-Moulder Architects www.dubbe-moulder.com	👤	WY	E M S W C G	A D E G I L P U O	C E K G Hc H I M R Rs Rm Rc S O	◧

DI Brand Recognition Index

▅ Top tier global and categorical leader recognition	◧ Notable and growing with emerging categorical recognition
▆ Exceptional national and categorical leader recognition	▪ Professional practice notable in city and region
◧ Strong regional and categorical leader recognition	

Rank	Firm/Web	Size	HQ	Regions	Services	Markets	DI Index
	Dujardin Design Associates www.dujardindesign.com	Small	CT	E M S W C G	A D E G I L P U O	C E K G Hc H I M R Rs Rm Rc S O	
263	**DWL Architects + Planners** www.dwlarchitects.com	Medium	AZ	E M S W C G	A D E G I L P U O	C E K G Hc H I M R Rs Rm Rc S O	
328	**Dykeman** www.dykeman.net	Medium	WA	E M S W C G	A D E G I L P U O	C E K G Hc H I M R Rs Rm Rc S O	
E	**E+H Architects** www.eandharch.com	Small	TN	E M S W C G	A D E G I L P U O	C E K G Hc H I M R Rs Rm Rc S O	
	EAPC Architects and Engineers www.eapc.net	Medium	ND	E M S W C G	A D E G I L P U O	C E K G Hc H I M R Rs Rm Rc S O	
	Eckert Wordell www.eckert-wordell.com	Medium	MI	E M S W C G	A D E G I L P U O	C E K G Hc H I M R Rs Rm Rc S O	
	EDG www.edgdesign.com	Medium	CA	E M S W C G	A D E G I L P U O	C E K G Hc H I M R Rs Rm Rc S O	
	Edge & Tinney Architects www.edge-tinney.com	Small	OH	E M S W C G	A D E G I L P U O	C E K G Hc H I M R Rs Rm Rc S O	
278	**EDI International** www.EDI-International.com	Medium	TX	E M S W C G	A D E G I L P U O	C E K G Hc H I M R Rs Rm Rc S O	
85	**EDSA** www.edsaplan.com	Large	FL	E M S W C G	A D E G I L P U O	C E K G Hc H I M R Rs Rm Rc S O	
	Edward J. Cuhaci and Associates Architects Inc www.cuhaci.com	Small	CAN	E M S W C G	A D E G I L P U O	C E K G Hc H I M R Rs Rm Rc S O	
	EHDD www.ehdd.com	Medium	CA	E M S W C G	A D E G I L P U O	C E K G Hc H I M R Rs Rm Rc S O	
	Eight, Inc. www.eightinc.com	Medium	CA	E M S W C G	A D E G I L P U O	C E K G Hc H I M R Rs Rm Rc S O	
	Eisenman Architects www.eisenmanarchitects.com	Medium	NY	E M S W C G	A D E G I L P U O	C E K G Hc H I M R Rs Rm Rc S O	
	Elena Kalman Architect www.kalmandesign.com	Small	CT	E M S W C G	A D E G I L P U O	C E K G Hc H I M R Rs Rm Rc S O	
29	**Elkus Manfredi Architects** www.elkus-manfredi.com	Large	MA	E M S W C G	A D E G I L P U O	C E K G Hc H I M R Rs Rm Rc S O	
275	**Ellenzweig** www.ellenzweig.com	Medium	MA	E M S W C G	A D E G I L P U O	C E K G Hc H I M R Rs Rm Rc S O	

Size

Small	20 employees or less	
Medium	21–100 employees	
Large	101–450 employees	
Extra Large	451+ employees	

Regions East (E), Midwest (M), South (S), West (W), Canada (C), Global (G)

Services Architecture (A), Design/Build (D), Engineering-MEP (E), Graphic Design (G), Interior Design (I), Landscape Architecture (L), Planning (P), Urban Design (U), Other-including Industrial Design (O)

Markets Corporate (C), Higher Ed. (E), K-12 (K), Government (G), Healthcare (Hc), Hospitality (H), Industrial/Tech. (I), Museum/Cultural (M), Religious (R), Residential-Single (Rs), Residential-Multi. (Rm), Retail/Commercial (Rc), Sports (S), Other (O)

Rank	Firm/Web	Size	HQ	Regions	Services	Markets	DI Index
168	**Elness Swenson Graham Architects** www.esgarch.com	👥	MN	E M S W C G	A D E G I L P U O	C E K G Hc H I M R Rs Rm Rc S O	▂▃▅▇
	Emc2 Group Architects www.emc2architects.com	👤	AZ	E M S W C G	A D E G I L P U O	C E K G Hc H I M R Rs Rm Rc S O	▅▂▁▁
	Emersion Design www.emersiondesign.com	👥	OH	E M S W C G	A D E G I L P U O	C E K G Hc H I M R Rs Rm Rc S O	▄▅▁▁
234	**Engberg Anderson** www.engberganderson.com	👥	WI	E M S W C G	A D E G I L P U O	C E K G Hc H I M R Rs Rm Rc S O	▄▅▁▁
43	**Ennead Architects** www.ennead.com	👥👥👥	NY	E M S W C G	A D E G I L P U O	C E K G Hc H I M R Rs Rm Rc S O	▃▅▆▇
	ENTOS Design www.entosdesign.com	👤	TX	E M S W C G	A D E G I L P U O	C E K G Hc H I M R Rs Rm Rc S O	▅▄▁▁
	Environetics www.environetics.com	👥	CA	E M S W C G	A D E G I L P U O	C E K G Hc H I M R Rs Rm Rc S O	▅▄▁▁
	Eppstein Uhen Architects www.eua.com	👥👥👥	WI	E M S W C G	A D E G I L P U O	C E K G Hc H I M R Rs Rm Rc S O	▅▄▁▁
89	**Epstein** www.epsteinglobal.com	👥👥👥	IL	E M S W C G	A D E G I L P U O	C E K G Hc H I M R Rs Rm Rc S O	▃▅▆▇
	Escher Architect www.escherdesigninc.com	👥	VT	E M S W C G	A D E G I L P U O	C E K G Hc H I M R Rs Rm Rc S O	▅▄▁▁
	ESI Design www.esidesign.com	👥	NY	E M S W C G	A D E G I L P U O	C E K G Hc H I M R Rs Rm Rc S O	▂▃▅▇
203	**Eskew+Dumez+Ripple** www.eskewdumezripple.com	👥	LA	E M S W C G	A D E G I L P U O	C E K G Hc H I M R Rs Rm Rc S O	▄▅▆▁
	ESP Associates www.espassociates.com	👥👥👥	NC	E M S W C G	A D E G L P U O	C E K G Hc H I M R Rs Rm Rc S O	▅▄▁▁
	The Evans Group www.theevansgroup.com	👥	FL	E M S W C G	A D E G I L P U O	C E K G Hc H I M R Rs Rm Rc S O	▅▄▁▁
36	**EwingCole** www.ewingcole.com	👥👥👥	PA	E M S W C G	A D E G I L P U O	C E K G Hc H I M R Rs Rm Rc S O	▃▅▆▇
17	**EYP** www.eypaedesign.com	👥👥👥👥	NY	E M S W C G	A D E G I L P U O	C E K G Hc H I M R Rs Rm Rc S O	▄▅▆▁
	EYP/BJAC www.eypaedesign.com	👥	NC	E M S W C G	A D E G I L P U O	C E K G Hc H I M R Rs Rm Rc S O	▅▄▁▁

DI Brand Recognition Index

▂▃▅▇ Top tier global and categorical leader recognition

▄▅▆▁ Exceptional national and categorical leader recognition

▅▄▁▁ Strong regional and categorical leader recognition

▅▂▁▁ Notable and growing with emerging categorical recognition

▂▁▁▁ Professional practice notable in city and region

Jason A. Knowles © Fentress Architects

Sanford Consortium for Regenerative Medicine, La Jolla, CA | Fentress Architects

Nick Merrick © Hedrich Blessing

Ralph L. Carr Colorado Judicial Center, Denver, CO | Fentress Architects

Rank	Firm/Web	Size	HQ	Regions	Services	Markets	DI Index
F	**Facility Design Group (FDG)** www.fdgatlanta.com	♛♛♛	GA	E M S W C G	A D E G I L P U O	C E K G Hc H I M R Rs Rm Rc S O	▄▟▁▁
145	**Fanning/Howey Associates** www.fhai.com	♛♛♛	OH	E M S W C G	A D E G I L P U O	C E K G Hc H I M R Rs Rm Rc S O	▄▟▟▁
	Fathom www.gofathom.com	♛	PA	E M S W C G	A D E G I L P U O	C E K G Hc H I M R Rs Rm Rc S O	▄▟▟▁
48	**Fentress Architects** www.fentressarchitects.com	♛♛♛	CO	E M S W C G	A D E G I L P U O	C E K G Hc H I M R Rs Rm Rc S O	▄▟▟▟
	Fergus Garber Group www.fgg-arch.com	♛♛	CA	E M S W C G	A D E G I L P U O	C E K G Hc H I M R Rs Rm Rc S O	▄▟▁▁
	Ferguson & Shamamian Architects www.fergusonshamamian.com	♛♛	NY	E M S W C G	A D E G I L P U O	C E K G Hc H I M R Rs Rm Rc S O	▄▟▁▁
	Ferguson Pape Baldwin Architects www.fpbarch.com	♛♛	CA	E M S W C G	A D E G I L P U O	C E K G Hc H I M R Rs Rm Rc S O	▄▟▁▁
320	**Ferraro Choi** www.ferrarochoi.com	♛♛	HI	E M S W C G	A D E G I L P U O	C E K G Hc H I M R Rs Rm Rc S O	▄▟▁▁
	FFA www.ffadesign.com	♛♛	OR	E M S W C G	A D E G I L P U O	C E K G Hc H I M R Rs Rm Rc S O	▄▟▁▁
98	**FFKR Architects** www.ffkr.com	♛♛♛	UT	E M S W C G	A D E G I L P U O	C E K G Hc H I M R Rs Rm Rc S O	▄▟▁▁
	FGM Architects www.fgmarchitects.com	♛♛	IL	E M S W C G	A D E G I L P U O	C E K G Hc H I M R Rs Rm Rc S O	▄▟▁▁
207	**Field Paoli Architects** www.fieldpaoli.com	♛♛	CA	E M S W C G	A D E G I L P U O	C E K G Hc H I M R Rs Rm Rc S O	▄▟▁▁
310	**Finegold Alexander Architects** www.faainc.com	♛♛	MA	E M S W C G	A D E G I L P U O	C E K G Hc H I M R Rs Rm Rc S O	▄▟▁▁
	Fishbeck Thompson Carr & Huber www.ftch.com	♛♛♛	MI	E M S W C G	A D E G I L P U O	C E K G Hc H I M R Rs Rm Rc S O	▄▟▟▁
	FitzGerald Associates Architects www.fitzgeraldassociates.net	♛♛	IL	E M S W C G	A D E G I L P U O	C E K G Hc H I M R Rs Rm Rc S O	▄▟▁▁
77	**FKP Architects** www.fkp.com	♛♛	TX	E M S W C G	A D E G I L P U O	C E K G Hc H I M R Rs Rm Rc S O	▄▟▟▁
	Flansburgh Architects www.faiarchitects.com	♛	MA	E M S W C G	A D E G I L P U O	C E K G Hc H I M R Rs Rm Rc S O	▄▟▁▁

DI Brand Recognition Index

▄▟▟▟ Top tier global and categorical leader recognition

▄▟▟▁ Exceptional national and categorical leader recognition

▄▟▁▁ Strong regional and categorical leader recognition

▄▟▁▁ Notable and growing with emerging categorical recognition

▄▁▁▁ Professional practice notable in city and region

Rank	Firm/Web	Size	HQ	Regions	Services	Markets	DI Index
	Fletcher Thompson www.fletcherthompson.com	Large	CT	E M S W C G	A D E G I L P U O	C E K G Hc H I M R Rs Rm Rc S O	
	Flewelling & Moody www.flewelling-moody.com	Medium	CA	E M S W C G	A D E G I L P U O	C E K G Hc H I M R Rs Rm Rc S O	
	Foor & Associates Architects www.foorassocs.com	Small	NY	E M S W C G	A D E G I L P U O	C E K G Hc H I M R Rs Rm Rc S O	
	Ford Powell & Carson www.fpcarch.com	Medium	TX	E M S W C G	A D E G I L P U O	C E K G Hc H I M R Rs Rm Rc S O	
	Foreman Architects Engineers www.foremangroup.com	Large	PA	E M S W C G	A D E G I L P U O	C E K G Hc H I M R Rs Rm Rc S O	
312	**Forum Architecture & Interior Design** www.forumarchitecture.com	Medium	FL	E M S W C G	A D E G I L P U O	C E K G Hc H I M R Rs Rm Rc S O	
306	**Forum Studio** www.forumstudio.com	Medium	MO	E M S W C G	A D E G I L P U O	C E K G Hc H I M R Rs Rm Rc S O	
	Foss Architecture & Interiors www.fossarch.com	Small	ND	E M S W C G	A D E G I L P U O	C E K G Hc H I M R Rs Rm Rc S O	
176	**FOX Architects** www.fox-architects.com	Medium	VA	E M S W C G	A D E G I L P U O	C E K G Hc H I M R Rs Rm Rc S O	
113	**Francis Cauffman** www.franciscauffman.com	Large	NY	E M S W C G	A D E G I L P U O	C E K G Hc H I M R Rs Rm Rc S O	
	Franklin Associates Architects www.franklinarch.com	Medium	TN	E M S W C G	A D E G I L P U O	C E K G Hc H I M R Rs Rm Rc S O	
75	**FRCH Design Worldwide** www.frch.com	Large	OH	E M S W C G	A D E G I L P U O	C E K G Hc H I M R Rs Rm Rc S O	
	Frederick + Frederick Architects www.f-farchitects.com	Small	SC	E M S W C G	A D E G I L P U O	C E K G Hc H I M R Rs Rm Rc S O	
138	**FreemanWhite** www.freemanwhite.com	Large	NC	E M S W C G	A D E G I L P U O	C E K G Hc H I M R Rs Rm Rc S O	
308	**Freiheit & Ho Architects** www.fhoarch.com	Medium	WA	E M S W C G	A D E G I L P U O	C E K G Hc H I M R Rs Rm Rc S O	
	French + Ryan www.frenchryan.com	Small	DE	E M S W C G	A D E G I L P U O	C E K G Hc H I M R Rs Rm Rc S O	
	French Associates www.frenchaia.com	Medium	MI	E M S W C G	A D E G I L P U O	C E K G Hc H I M R Rs Rm Rc S O	

Size

Small	20 employees or less	
Medium	21–100 employees	
Large	101–450 employees	
Extra Large	451+ employees	

Regions East (E), Midwest (M), South (S), West (W), Canada (C), Global (G)

Services Architecture (A), Design/Build (D), Engineering-MEP (E), Graphic Design (G), Interior Design (I), Landscape Architecture (L), Planning (P), Urban Design (U), Other-including Industrial Design (O)

Markets Corporate (C), Higher Ed. (E), K-12 (K), Government (G), Healthcare (Hc), Hospitality (H), Industrial/Tech. (I), Museum/Cultural (M), Religious (R), Residential-Single (Rs), Residential-Multi. (Rm), Retail/Commercial (Rc), Sports (S), Other (O)

Rank	Firm/Web	Size	HQ	Regions	Services	Markets	DI Index
	Friedmutter Group www.friedmuttergroup.com	👤👤👤	NV	E M S W C G	A D E G I L P U O	C E K G Hc H I M R Rs Rm Rc S O	▪▮▮__
	Fugleberg Koch www.fuglebergkoch.com	👤	FL	E M S W C G	A D E G I L P U O	C E K G Hc H I M R Rs Rm Rc S O	▪▮▮__
	Fusco, Shaffer & Pappas www.fuscoshafferpappas.com	👤👤	MI	E M S W C G	A D E G I L P U O	C E K G Hc H I M R Rs Rm Rc S O	▪▮▮__
66	**FXFOWLE Architects** www.fxfowle.com	👤👤👤	NY	E M S W C G	A D E G I L P U O	C E K G Hc H I M R Rs Rm Rc S O	▪▮▮▮▮
G	**Gantt Huberman Architects** www.gantthuberman.com	👤👤	NC	E M S W C G	A D E G I L P U O	C E K G Hc H I M R Rs Rm Rc S O	▪▮▮▮_
	Garcia Stromberg www.garciastromberg.com	👤	FL	E M S W C G	A D E G I L P U O	C E K G Hc H I M R Rs Rm Rc S O	▪▮▮__
	Gardner Architects www.gardnerarchitects.com	👤	AL	E M S W C G	A D E G I L P U O	C E K G Hc H I M R Rs Rm Rc S O	▪▮▮__
	Gaudreau www.gaudreauinc.com	👤	MD	E M S W C G	A D E G I L P U O	C E K G Hc H I M R Rs Rm Rc S O	▪▮▮__
	Gauthier, Alvarado & Associates www.gaa-ae.com	👤👤	VA	E M S W C G	A D E G I L P U O	C E K G Hc H I M R Rs Rm Rc S O	▪▮▮__
	Gawron Turgeon Architects www.gawronturgeon.com	👤	ME	E M S W C G	A D E G I L P U O	C E K G Hc H I M R Rs Rm Rc S O	▪▮▮__
92	**GBBN Architects** www.gbbn.com	👤👤👤	OH	E M S W C G	A D E G I L P U O	C E K G Hc H I M R Rs Rm Rc S O	▪▮▮▮▮
	GBD Architects www.gbdarchitects.com	👤👤	OR	E M S W C G	A D E G I L P U O	C E K G Hc H I M R Rs Rm Rc S O	▪▮▮__
	GDA Architects www.gdainet.com	👤👤👤	TX	E M S W C G	A D E G I L P U O	C E K G Hc H I M R Rs Rm Rc S O	▪▮▮__
114	**Gehry Partners** www.foga.com	👤👤👤	CA	E M S W C G	A D E G I L P U O	C E K G Hc H I M R Rs Rm Rc S O	▪▮▮▮▮
1	**Gensler** www.gensler.com	👤👤👤👤	CA	E M S W C G	A D E G I L P U O	C E K G Hc H I M R Rs Rm Rc S O	▪▮▮▮▮
	The Gettys Group www.gettys.com	👤👤👤	IL	E M S W C G	A D E G I L P U O	C E K G Hc H I M R Rs Rm Rc S O	▪▮▮__
124	**GGLO** www.gglo.com	👤👤👤	WA	E M S W C G	A D E G I L P U O	C E K G Hc H I M R Rs Rm Rc S O	▪▮▮▮_

DI Brand Recognition Index

▪▮▮▮▮ Top tier global and categorical leader recognition

▪▮▮▮_ Exceptional national and categorical leader recognition

▪▮▮__ Strong regional and categorical leader recognition

▪▮___ Notable and growing with emerging categorical recognition

▪____ Professional practice notable in city and region

Ryan Center for the Musical Arts, Evanston, IL | Goettsch Partners

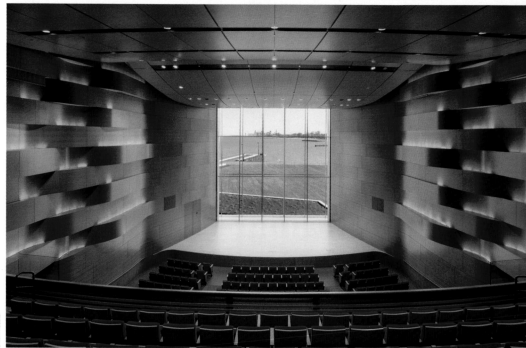

Ryan Center for the Musical Arts, Evanston, IL | Goettsch Partners

Rank	Firm/Web	Size	HQ	Regions	Services	Markets	DI Index
325	**GH2 Architects** www.gh2.com		OK	E M S W C G	A D E G I L P U O	C E K G Hc H I M R Rs Rm Rc S O	
24	**GHAFARI** www.ghafari.com		MI	E M S W C G	A D E G I L P U O	C E K G Hc H I M R Rs Rm Rc S O	
	Gibbs Gage Architects www.gibbsgage.com		CAN	E M S W C G	A D E G I L P U O	C E K G Hc H I M R Rs Rm Rc S O	
	Giffin Bolte Jurgens www.gbjarch.com		OR	E M S W C G	A D E G I L P U O	C E K G Hc H I M R Rs Rm Rc S O	
	Gignac Associates www.gignacarchitects.com		TX	E M S W C G	A D E G I L P U O	C E K G Hc H I M R Rs Rm Rc S O	
	Gilmore Group www.gilmoregroup.com		NY	E M S W C G	A D E G I L P U O	C E K G Hc H I M R Rs Rm Rc S O	
121	**gkkworks** www.gkkworks.com		CA	E M S W C G	A D E G I L P U O	C E K G Hc H I M R Rs Rm Rc S O	
	Glidden Spina & Partners www.gsp-architects.com		FL	E M S W C G	A D E G I L P U O	C E K G Hc H I M R Rs Rm Rc S O	
	Godsey Associates Architects www.godseyassociates.com		KY	E M S W C G	A D E G I L P U O	C E K G Hc H I M R Rs Rm Rc S O	
82	**Goettsch Partners** www.gpchicago.com		IL	E M S W C G	A D E G I L P U O	C E K G Hc H I M R Rs Rm Rc S O	
81	**Good Fulton & Farrell** www.gff.com		TX	E M S W C G	A D E G I L P U O	C E K G Hc H I M R Rs Rm Rc S O	
	Goodwyn, Mills & Cawood www.gmcnetwork.com		AL	E M S W C G	A D E G I L P U O	C E K G Hc H I M R Rs Rm Rc S O	
142	**Goody Clancy** www.goodyclancy.com		MA	E M S W C G	A D E G I L P U O	C E K G Hc H I M R Rs Rm Rc S O	
	Goshow Architects www.gaarchitectsllp.com		NY	E M S W C G	A D E G I L P U O	C E K G Hc H I M R Rs Rm Rc S O	
129	**Gould Evans** www.gouldevans.com		MO	E M S W C G	A D E G I L P U O	C E K G Hc H I M R Rs Rm Rc S O	
	GPD Group www.gpdgroup.com		OH	E M S W C G	A D E G I L P U O	C E K G Hc H I M R Rs Rm Rc S O	
	Graham Landscape Architecture www.grahamlandarch.com		MD	E M S W C G	A D E G I L P U O	C E K G Hc H I M R Rs Rm Rc S O	

DI Brand Recognition Index

Top tier global and categorical leader recognition

Exceptional national and categorical leader recognition

Strong regional and categorical leader recognition

Notable and growing with emerging categorical recognition

Professional practice notable in city and region

Rank	Firm/Web	Size	HQ	Regions	Services	Markets	DI Index
	Gray Organschi Architecture www.grayorganschi.com	👥	CT	E M S W C G	A D E G I L P U O	C E K G Hc H I M R Rs Rm Rc S O	
	GRC Architects www.grcarchitects.com	🧍	CAN	E M S W C G	A D E G I L P U O	C E K G Hc H I M R Rs Rm Rc S O	
	GREC Architects www.grecstudio.com	👥	IL	E M S W C G	A D E G I L P U O	C E K G Hc H I M R Rs Rm Rc S O	
68	**GreenbergFarrow** www.greenbergfarrow.com	👥	GA	E M S W C G	A D E G I L P U O	C E K G Hc H I M R Rs Rm Rc S O	
25	**Gresham, Smith and Partners** www.gspnet.com	👥	TN	E M S W C G	A D E G I L P U O	C E K G Hc H I M R Rs Rm Rc S O	
100	**Grimm + Parker Architects** www.grimmandparker.com	👥	MD	E M S W C G	A D E G I L P U O	C E K G Hc H I M R Rs Rm Rc S O	
	Group 70 International www.group70int.com	🧍	HI	E M S W C G	A D E G I L P U O	C E K G Hc H I M R Rs Rm Rc S O	
197	**Gruen Associates** www.gruenassociates.com	👥	CA	E M S W C G	A D E G I L P U O	C E K G Hc H I M R Rs Rm Rc S O	
	Gruzen Samton www.gruzensamton.com	👥	NY	E M S W C G	A D E G I L P U O	C E K G Hc H I M R Rs Rm Rc S O	
	GSBS Architects www.gsbsarchitects.com	👥	UT	E M S W C G	A D E G I L P U O	C E K G Hc H I M R Rs Rm Rc S O	
261	**GSR Andrade Architects** www.gsr-andrade.com	👥	TX	E M S W C G	A D E G I L P U O	C E K G Hc H I M R Rs Rm Rc S O	
300	**GUND Partnership** www.gundpartnership.com	👥	MA	E M S W C G	A D E G I L P U O	C E K G Hc H I M R Rs Rm Rc S O	
198	**Gwathmey Siegel Kaufman Architects** www.gwathmey-siegel.com	👥	NY	E M S W C G	A D E G I L P U O	C E K G Hc H I M R Rs Rm Rc S O	
205	**GWWO Architects** www.gwwoinc.com	👥	MD	E M S W C G	A D E G I L P U O	C E K G Hc H I M R Rs Rm Rc S O	
H	**H&A Architects & Engineers** www.ha-inc.com	👥	VA	E M S W C G	A D E G I L P U O	C E K G Hc H I M R Rs Rm Rc S O	
199	**H+L Architecture** www.hlarch.com	👥	CO	E M S W C G	A D E G I L P U O	C E K G Hc H I M R Rs Rm Rc S O	
	H2L2 www.h2l2.com	🧍	PA	E M S W C G	A D E G I L P U O	C E K G Hc H I M R Rs Rm Rc S O	

Size
🧍 Small — 20 employees or less
👥 Medium — 21–100 employees
👥 Large — 101–450 employees
👥 Extra Large — 451+ employees

Regions East (E), Midwest (M), South (S), West (W), Canada (C), Global (G)

Services Architecture (A), Design/Build (D), Engineering-MEP (E), Graphic Design (G), Interior Design (I), Landscape Architecture (L), Planning (P), Urban Design (U), Other-including Industrial Design (O)

Markets Corporate (C), Higher Ed. (E), K-12 (K), Government (G), Healthcare (Hc), Hospitality (H), Industrial/Tech. (I), Museum/Cultural (M), Religious (R), Residential-Single (Rs), Residential-Multi. (Rm), Retail/Commercial (Rc), Sports (S), Other (O)

Rank	Firm/Web	Size	HQ	Regions	Services	Markets	DI Index
	H3 Hardy Collaboration Architecture www.h3hc.com	👥	NY	E M S W C G	A D E G I L P U O	C E K G Hc H I M R Rs Rm Rc S O	
	Hacker www.hackerarchitects.com	👥	OR	E M S W C G	A D E G I L P U O	C E K G Hc H I M R Rs Rm Rc S O	
	Hahnfeld Hoffer Stanford www.hahnfeld.com	👤	TX	E M S W C G	A D E G I L P U O	C E K G Hc H I M R Rs Rm Rc S O	
257	**Hamilton Anderson** www.hamilton-anderson.com	👥	MI	E M S W C G	A D E G I L P U O	C E K G Hc H I M R Rs Rm Rc S O	
173	**Hanbury Evans Wright Vlattas + Company** www.hewv.com	👥	VA	E M S W C G	A D E G I L P U O	C E K G Hc H I M R Rs Rm Rc S O	
172	**Handel Architects** www.handelarchitects.com	👥👥	NY	E M S W C G	A D E G I L P U O	C E K G Hc H I M R Rs Rm Rc S O	
	Hardy McCullah/MLM Architects www.hmmlmarchitects.com	👤	TX	E M S W C G	A D E G I L P U O	C E K G Hc H I M R Rs Rm Rc S O	
	Hargreaves Associates www.hargreaves.com	👥	CA	E M S W C G	A D E G I L P U O	C E K G Hc H I M R Rs Rm Rc S O	
38	**Harley Ellis Devereaux** www.harleyellisdevereaux.com	👥👥	MI	E M S W C G	A D E G I L P U O	C E K G Hc H I M R Rs Rm Rc S O	
	Harold Massop Associates Architects www.hmaarchitects.net	👤	CO	E M S W C G	A D E G I L P U O	C E K G Hc H I M R Rs Rm Rc S O	
	Harriman Architects + Engineers www.harriman.com	👥	ME	E M S W C G	A D E G I L P U O	C E K G Hc H I M R Rs Rm Rc S O	
	Harrison Design Associates www.harrisondesign.com	👥	GA	E M S W C G	A D E G I L P U O	C E K G Hc H I M R Rs Rm Rc S O	
116	**Hart	Howerton** www.harthowerton.com	👥👥	NY	E M S W C G	A D E G I L P U O	C E K G Hc H I M R Rs Rm Rc S O	
296	**Hartman Design Group** www.hartmandesigngroup.com	👥	MD	E M S W C G	A D E G I L P U O	C E K G Hc H I M R Rs Rm Rc S O	
209	**Harvard Jolly Architecture** www.harvardjolly.com	👥	FL	E M S W C G	A D E G I L P U O	C E K G Hc H I M R Rs Rm Rc S O	
	Hasenstab Architects www.hasenstabinc.com	👥👥	OH	E M S W C G	A D E G I L P U O	C E K G Hc H I M R Rs Rm Rc S O	
	Hastings & Chivetta Architects www.hastingschivetta.com	👥	MO	E M S W C G	A D E G I L P U O	C E K G Hc H I M R Rs Rm Rc S O	

DI Brand Recognition Index

Top tier global and categorical leader recognition

Exceptional national and categorical leader recognition

Strong regional and categorical leader recognition

Notable and growing with emerging categorical recognition

Professional practice notable in city and region

© 2015 Dave Burk

Cleveland Clinic Abu Dhabi, Abu Dhabi, United Arab Emirates | HDR

Rank	Firm/Web	Size	HQ	Regions	Services	Markets	DI Index
235	**Hawley Peterson Snyder** www.hpsarch.com		CA	E M S W C G	A D E G I L P U O	C E K G Hc H I M R Rs Rm Rc S O	
	Hayes Architecture/Interiors www.hayesstudio.com		AZ	E M S W C G	A D E G I L P U O	C E K G Hc H I M R Rs Rm Rc S O	
23	**HBA/Hirsch Bedner Associates** www.hbadesign.com		GA	E M S W C G	A D E G I L P U O	C E K G Hc H I M R Rs Rm Rc S O	
	HBE www.hbecorp.com		MO	E M S W C G	A D E G I L P U O	C E K G Hc H I M R Rs Rm Rc S O	
	HBRA www.hbra-arch.com		IL	E M S W C G	A D E G I L P U O	C E K G Hc H I M R Rs Rm Rc S O	
	HBT Architects www.hbtarchitects.com		NY	E M S W C G	A D E G I L P U O	C E K G Hc H I M R Rs Rm Rc S O	
	HDA www.hdai.com		MO	E M S W C G	A D E G I L P U O	C E K G Hc H I M R Rs Rm Rc S O	
	HDA Architects www.hd-architects.com		AZ	E M S W C G	A D E G I L P U O	C E K G Hc H I M R Rs Rm Rc S O	
7	**HDR** www.hdrarchitecture.com		NE	E M S W C G	A D E G I L P U O	C E K G Hc H I M R Rs Rm Rc S O	
	Heery International www.heery.com		GA	E M S W C G	A D E G I L P U O	C E K G Hc H I M R Rs Rm Rc S O	
243	**Helix Architecture + Design** www.helixkc.com		MO	E M S W C G	A D E G I L P U O	C E K G Hc H I M R Rs Rm Rc S O	
	Heller Manus Architects www.hellermanus.com		CA	E M S W C G	A D E G I L P U O	C E K G Hc H I M R Rs Rm Rc S O	
249	**Helman Hurley Charvat Peacock/Architects** www.hhcp.com		FL	E M S W C G	A D E G I L P U O	C E K G Hc H I M R Rs Rm Rc S O	
	Helpern Architects www.helpern.com		NY	E M S W C G	A D E G I L P U O	C E K G Hc H I M R Rs Rm Rc S O	
	Hennebery Eddy Architects www.henneberyeddy.com		OR	E M S W C G	A D E G I L P U O	C E K G Hc H I M R Rs Rm Rc S O	
	Herman Gibans Fodor www.hgfarchitects.com		OH	E M S W C G	A D E G I L P U O	C E K G Hc H I M R Rs Rm Rc S O	
	Herschman Architects www.herschmanarchitects.com		OH	E M S W C G	A D E G I L P U O	C E K G Hc H I M R Rs Rm Rc S O	

DI Brand Recognition Index

Top tier global and categorical leader recognition

Exceptional national and categorical leader recognition

Strong regional and categorical leader recognition

Notable and growing with emerging categorical recognition

Professional practice notable in city and region

David Wakely

California State University, Monterey Bay Business and Information Technology Building, Marina, CA | HMC Architects

David Wakely

California State University, Monterey Bay Business and Information Technology Building, Marina, CA | HMC Architects

Rank	Firm/Web	Size	HQ	Regions	Services	Markets	DI Index
	HFR Design www.hfrdesign.com	👥	TN	E M S W C G	A D E G I L P U O ·	C E K G Hc H I M R Rs Rm Rc S O	📊
21	**HGA Architects and Engineers** www.hga.com	👥👥	MN	E M S W C G	A D E G I L P U O	C E K G Hc H I M R Rs Rm Rc S O	📊
	HH Architects www.hharchitects.com	👥	TX	E M S W C G	A D E G I L P U O	C E K G Hc H I M R Rs Rm Rc S O	📊
178	**Hickok Cole Architects** www.hickokcole.com	👥	DC	E M S W C G	A D E G I L P U O	C E K G Hc H I M R Rs Rm Rc S O	📊
96	**Highland Associates** www.highlandassociates.com	👥	PA	E M S W C G	A D E G I L P U O	C E K G Hc H I M R Rs Rm Rc S O	📊
	Historic Buildings Architects www.hba-llc.com	👤	NJ	E M S W C G	A D E G I L P U O	C E K G Hc H I M R Rs Rm Rc S O	📊
	Historical Concepts www.historicalconcepts.com	👥	GA	E M S W C G	A D E G I L P U O	C E K G Hc H I M R Rs Rm Rc S O	📊
133	**Hixson** www.hixson-inc.com	👥	OH	E M S W C G	A D E G I L P U O	C E K G Hc H I M R Rs Rm Rc S O	📊
	HKIT Architects www.hkit.com	👥	CA	E M S W C G	A D E G I L P U O	C E K G Hc H I M R Rs Rm Rc S O	📊
10	**HKS, Inc.** www.hksinc.com	👥👥	TX	E M S W C G	A D E G I L P U O	C E K G Hc H I M R Rs Rm Rc S O	📊
72	**HLW International** www.hlw.com	👥	NY	E M S W C G	A D E G I L P U O	C E K G Hc H I M R Rs Rm Rc S O	📊
	HMA Architects www.hmarch.com	👥	MN	E M S W C G	A D E G I L P U O	C E K G Hc H I M R Rs Rm Rc S O	📊
41	**HMC Architects** www.hmcarchitects.com	👥	CA	E M S W C G	A D E G I L P U O	C E K G Hc H I M R Rs Rm Rc S O	📊
	HMFH Architects www.hmfh.com	👥	MA	E M S W C G	A D E G I L P U O	C E K G Hc H I M R Rs Rm Rc S O	📊
156	**Hnedak Bobo Group** www.hbginc.com	👥	TN	E M S W C G	A D E G I L P U O	C E K G Hc H I M R Rs Rm Rc S O	📊
122	**Hobbs+Black Architects** www.hobbs-black.com	👥	MI	E M S W C G	A D E G I L P U O	C E K G Hc H I M R Rs Rm Rc S O	📊
307	**Hodges & Associates Architects** www.hodgesusa.com	👥	TX	E M S W C G	A D E G I L P U O	C E K G Hc H I M R Rs Rm Rc S O	📊

DI Brand Recognition Index

📊 Top tier global and categorical leader recognition

📊 Exceptional national and categorical leader recognition

📊 Strong regional and categorical leader recognition

📊 Notable and growing with emerging categorical recognition

📊 Professional practice notable in city and region

Rank	Firm/Web	Size	HQ	Regions	Services	Markets	DI Index
	Hoerr Schaudt www.hoerrschaudt.com	👥	IL	E M S W C G	A D E G I L P U O	C E K G Hc H I M R Rs Rm Rc S O	
4	**HOK** www.hok.com	👥👥	MO	E M S W C G	A D E G I L P U O	C E K G Hc H I M R Rs Rm Rc S O	
330	**Holabird & Root** www.holabird.com	👥	IL	E M S W C G	A D E G I L P U O	C E K G Hc H I M R Rs Rm Rc S O	
269	**Hollis + Miller Architects** www.hollisandmiller.com	👥	KS	E M S W C G	A D E G I L P U O	C E K G Hc H I M R Rs Rm Rc S O	
216	**Holzman Moss Bottino Architecture** www.holzmanmoss.com	👥	NY	E M S W C G	A D E G I L P U O	C E K G Hc H I M R Rs Rm Rc S O	
	Hood Design www.wjhooddesign.com	👥	CA	E M S W C G	A D E G I L P U O	C E K G Hc H I M R Rs Rm Rc S O	
55	**Hord Coplan Macht** www.hcm2.com	👥👥	MD	E M S W C G	A D E G I L P U O	C E K G Hc H I M R Rs Rm Rc S O	
319	**Hornberger + Worstell** www.hornbergerworstell.com	👥	CA	E M S W C G	A D E G I L P U O	C E K G Hc H I M R Rs Rm Rc S O	
	Horty Elving www.healthcarearchitects.com	👥	MN	E M S W C G	A D E G I L P U O	C E K G Hc H I M R Rs Rm Rc S O	
	Huckabee www.huckabee-inc.com	👥	TX	E M S W C G	A D E G I L P U O	C E K G Hc H I M R Rs Rm Rc S O	
	Humphreys & Partners Architects www.humphreys.com	👥👥	TX	E M S W C G	A D E G I L P U O	C E K G Hc H I M R Rs Rm Rc S O	
329	**Humphries Poli Architects** www.hparch.com	👥	CO	E M S W C G	A D E G I L P U O	C E K G Hc H I M R Rs Rm Rc S O	
159	**Hunton Brady Architects** www.huntonbrady.com	👥	FL	E M S W C G	A D E G I L P U O	C E K G Hc H I M R Rs Rm Rc S O	
196	**Huntsman Architectural Group** www.huntsmanag.com	👥	NY	E M S W C G	A D E G I L P U O	C E K G Hc H I M R Rs Rm Rc S O	
	Hutker Architects www.hutkerarchitects.com	👥	MA	E M S W C G	A D E G I L P U O	C E K G Hc H I M R Rs Rm Rc S O	
	HWH Architects Engineers Planners www.hwhaep.com	👤	OH	E M S W C G	A D E G I L P U O	C E K G Hc H I M R Rs Rm Rc S O	
I	**IA Interior Architects** www.interiorarchitects.com	👥👥	CA	E M S W C G	A D E G I L P U O	C E K G Hc H I M R Rs Rm Rc S O	

Size

👤	Small	20 employees or less
👥	Medium	21–100 employees
👥👥	Large	101–450 employees
👥👥👥	Extra Large	451+ employees

Regions East (E), Midwest (M), South (S), West (W), Canada (C), Global (G)

Services Architecture (A), Design/Build (D), Engineering-MEP (E), Graphic Design (G), Interior Design (I), Landscape Architecture (L), Planning (P), Urban Design (U), Other-including Industrial Design (O)

Markets Corporate (C), Higher Ed. (E), K-12 (K), Government (G), Healthcare (Hc), Hospitality (H), Industrial/Tech. (I), Museum/Cultural (M), Religious (R), Residential-Single (Rs), Residential-Multi. (Rm), Retail/Commercial (Rc), Sports (S), Other (O)

Rank	Firm/Web	Size	HQ	Regions	Services	Markets	DI Index
265	**ICON Architecture** www.iconarch.com	👥	MA	E M S W / C G	A D E G I / L P U O	C E K G Hc H I / M R Rs **Rm** Rc S O	▂▃▁
	IDC Architects (a division of CH2M Hill) www.idcarchitects.com	👥	OR	E M S W / C G	A D E G I / L P U O	C E K G Hc H I / M R Rs Rm Rc S O	▂▂▁
288	**IKM** www.ikminc.com	👥	PA	E M S W / C G	A D E G I / L P U O	C E K G Hc H I / M R Rs Rm Rc S O	▃▃▁
	Indovina Associates Architects www.indovina.net	👤	PA	E M S W / C G	A D E G I / L P U O	C E K G Hc H I / M R **Rs** Rm Rc S O	▂▃▁
	Innova Group www.theinnovagroup.com	👥	TX	E M S W / C G	A D E G I / L P U O	C E K G Hc H I / M R Rs Rm Rc S O	▃▄▅
240	**Integrated Architecture** www.intarch.com	👥	MI	E M S W / C G	A D E G I / L P U O	C E K G Hc H I / M R Rs **Rm** Rc S O	▃▄▅
	Integrated Design Solutions www.ids-troy.com	👥👤	MI	E M S W / C G	A D E G I / L P U O	C E K G Hc H I / **M R** Rs Rm **Rc** S O	▃▃▁
	Interplan www.interplanllc.com	👥👤	FL	E M S W / C G	A D E G I / L P U O	C E K G Hc H I / M R Rs Rm **Rc** S O	▂▃▁
231	**INVISION** www.invisionarch.com	👥	IA	E M S W / C G	A D E G I / L P U O	C E K G Hc H I / M R Rs **Rm** Rc S O	▃▃▁
	Ittner Architects www.ittnerarchitects.com	👤	MO	E M S W / C G	A D E G I / L P U O	C E K G Hc H I / M R Rs Rm Rc S O	▂▃▁
J	**Jackson & Ryan Architects** www.jacksonryan.com	👤	TX	E M S W / C G	A D E G I / L P U O	C E K G Hc H I / **M R Rs** Rm Rc S O	▃▄▁
3	**Jacobs (Architecture)** www.jacobs.com	👥👥👤	CA	E M S W / C G	A D E G I / L P U O	C E K G Hc H I / M R Rs Rm Rc S O	▄▅▆
	Jahn www.jahn-us.com	👥	IL	E M S W / C G	A D E G I / L P U O	C E K G Hc H I / M R Rs Rm Rc S O	▄▅▆
	James Carpenter Design Associates www.jcdainc.com	👥	NY	E M S W / C G	A D E G I / L P U O	C E K G Hc H I / M R **Rs** Rc S O	▄▅▆
	James G. Rogers Architects www.jgr-architects.com	👤	CT	E M S W / C G	A D E G I / L P U O	C E K G Hc H I / M R Rs Rm **Rc** S O	▂▃▁
	JBA Architects www.jbapc.net	👤	OH	E M S W / C G	A D E G I / L P U O	C E K G Hc H I / M R Rs Rm Rc S O	▃▃▁
324	**JBHM Architects** www.jbhm.com	👥	MS	E M S W / C G	A D E G I / L P U O	C E K G Hc H I / M R Rs Rm Rc S O	▃▃▁

DI Brand Recognition Index

▄▅▆▇   Top tier global and categorical leader recognition

▃▄▅▆   Exceptional national and categorical leader recognition

▂▃▄   Strong regional and categorical leader recognition

▂▃▁   Notable and growing with emerging categorical recognition

▂▁▁   Professional practice notable in city and region

Rank	Firm/Web	Size	HQ	Regions	Services	Markets	DI Index
118	**JCJ Architecture** www.jcj.com	Large	CT	E M S W C G	A D E G I L P U O	C E K G Hc H I M R Rs Rm Rc S O	
	Jeffrey Berman Architects www.jbarch.com	Medium	NY	E M S W C G	A D E G I L P U O	C E K G Hc H I M R Rs Rm Rc S O	
	Jensen & Halstead www.jensenandhalstead.com	Medium	IL	E M S W C G	A D E G I L P U O	C E K G Hc H I M R Rs Rm Rc S O	
	Jensen Architects www.jensen-architects.com	Medium	CA	E M S W C G	A D E G I L P U O	C E K G Hc H I M R Rs Rm Rc S O	
161	**Jerde** www.jerde.com	Large	CA	E M S W C G	A D E G I L P U O	C E K G Hc H I M R Rs Rm Rc S O	
250	**JHP Architecture/Urban Design** www.jhparch.com	Medium	TX	E M S W C G	A D E G I L P U O	C E K G Hc H I M R Rs Rm Rc S O	
323	**JKR Partners** www.jkrpartners.com	Medium	PA	E M S W C G	A D E G I L P U O	C E K G Hc H I M R Rs Rm Rc S O	
84	**JLG Architects** www.jlgarchitects.com	Medium	MN	E M S W C G	A D E G I L P U O	C E K G Hc H I M R Rs Rm Rc S O	
271	**JMZ Architects and Planners** www.jmzarchitects.com	Medium	NY	E M S W C G	A D E G I L P U O	C E K G Hc H I M R Rs Rm Rc S O	
	Jochum Architects www.jochumarchitects.com	Small	CA	E M S W C G	A D E G I L P U O	C E K G Hc H I M R Rs Rm Rc S O	
	John Ciardullo Associates www.jca-ny.com	Medium	NY	E M S W C G	A D E G I L P U O	C E K G Hc H I M R Rs Rm Rc S O	
	John Lape Architect www.jl-architecture.com	Medium	OR	E M S W C G	A D E G I L P U O	C E K G Hc H I M R Rs Rm Rc S O	
	John Poe Architects www.johnpoe.com	Small	OH	E M S W C G	A D E G I L P U O	C E K G Hc H I M R Rs Rm Rc S O	
164	**John Portman & Associates** www.portmanusa.com	Medium	GA	E M S W C G	A D E G I L P U O	C E K G Hc H I M R Rs Rm Rc S O	
	John Ronan Architects www.jrarch.com	Medium	IL	E M S W C G	A D E G I L P U O	C E K G Hc H I M R Rs Rm Rc S O	
	John Schlesinger, A.I.A., Architect www.jschlesinger.com	Medium	CA	E M S W C G	A D E G I L P U O	C E K G Hc H I M R Rs Rm Rc S O	
	John Snyder Architects www.js-architects.com	Small	NY	E M S W C G	A D E G I L P U O	C E K G Hc H I M R Rs Rm Rc S O	

Size

Small	20 employees or less
Medium	21–100 employees
Large	101–450 employees
Extra Large	451+ employees

Regions East (E), Midwest (M), South (S), West (W), Canada (C), Global (G)

Services Architecture (A), Design/Build (D), Engineering-MEP (E), Graphic Design (G), Interior Design (I), Landscape Architecture (L), Planning (P), Urban Design (U), Other-including Industrial Design (O)

Markets Corporate (C), Higher Ed. (E), K-12 (K), Government (G), Healthcare (Hc), Hospitality (H), Industrial/Tech. (I), Museum/Cultural (M), Religious (R), Residential-Single (Rs), Residential-Multi. (Rm), Retail/Commercial (Rc), Sports (S), Other (O)

Rank	Firm/Web	Size	HQ	Regions	Services	Markets	DI Index
	Johnsen Schmaling Architects www.johnsenschmaling.com	👤	WI	E M S W C G	A D E G I L P U O	C E K G Hc H I M R Rs Rm Rc S O	▄█▄_
	Johnson Fain www.johnsonfain.com	👥	CA	E M S W C G	A D E G I L P U O	C E K G Hc H I M R Rs Rm Rc S O	▄▄█
	Johnson Nathan Strohe www.jgjohnson.com	👤	CO	E M S W C G	A D E G I L P U O	C E K G Hc H I M R Rs Rm Rc S O	▄█▄_
	Jonathan Nehmer + Associates www.nehmer.com	👥	DC	E M S W C G	A D E G I L P U O	C E K G Hc H I M R Rs Rm Rc S O	▄█▄_
	Jonathan Segal www.jonathansegalarchitect.com	👤	CA	E M S W C G	A D E G I L P U O	C E K G Hc H I M R Rs Rm Rc S O	▄▄██
	Jones I Haydu www.joneshaydu.com	👤	CA	E M S W C G	A D E G I L P U O	C E K G Hc H I M R Rs Rm Rc S O	▄▄█_
	Joseph Wong Design Associates www.jwdainc.com	👥	CA	E M S W C G	A D E G I L P U O	C E K G Hc H I M R Rs Rm Rc S O	▄█▄_
222	**JPC Architects** www.jpcarchitects.com	👥	WA	E M S W C G	A D E G I L P U O	C E K G Hc H I M R Rs Rm Rc S O	▄█▄_
	JSA www.jsainc.com	👥	NH	E M S W C G	A D E G I L P U O	C E K G Hc H I M R Rs Rm Rc S O	▄▄█
	JZMK Partners www.jzmkpartners.com	👤	CA	E M S W C G	A D E G I L P U O	C E K G Hc H I M R Rs Rm Rc S O	▄█▄_
K 191	**ka** www.kainc.com	👥👥	OH	E M S W C G	A D E G I L P U O	C E K G Hc H I M R Rs Rm Rc S O	▄█▄_
	KAA Design Group www.kaadesigngroup.com	👥	CA	E M S W C G	A D E G I L P U O	C E K G Hc H I M R Rs Rm Rc S O	▄█▄_
	Kaestle Boos Associates www.kba-architects.com	👤	CT	E M S W C G	A D E G I L P U O	C E K G Hc H I M R Rs Rm Rc S O	▄█▄_
136	**Kahler Slater** www.kahlerslater.com	👥👥	WI	E M S W C G	A D E G I L P U O	C E K G Hc H I M R Rs Rm Rc S O	▄▄██
	KAI Design & Build www.kai-db.com	👥	MO	E M S W C G	A D E G I L P U O	C E K G Hc H I M R Rs Rm Rc S O	▄█▄_
	Kann Partners www.kannpartners.com	👥	MD	E M S W C G	A D E G I L P U O	C E K G Hc H I M R Rs Rm Rc S O	▄█▄_
	Karn Charuhas Chapman & Twohey www.kcct.com	👥	DC	E M S W C G	A D E G I L P U O	C E K G Hc H I M R Rs Rm Rc S O	▄█▄_

DI Brand Recognition Index

▄█████ Top tier global and categorical leader recognition	▄█▄_ Notable and growing with emerging categorical recognition
▄▄██ Exceptional national and categorical leader recognition	▄___ Professional practice notable in city and region
▄█▄_ Strong regional and categorical leader recognition	

Erna Peter of Erna Peter Photography

Surrey Civic Centre, Surrey, British Columbia, Canada | Kasian Architecture Interior Design and Planning

Rank	Firm/Web	Size	HQ	Regions	Services	Markets	DI Index
50	**Kasian Architecture Interior Design and Planning** www.kasian.com	¡¡¡	CAN	E M S W C G	A D E G I L P U O	C E K G Hc H I M R Rs Rm Rc S O	
	KBJ Architects www.kbj.com	¡¡	FL	E M S W C G	A D E G I L P U O	C E K G Hc H I M R Rs Rm Rc S O	
260	**KCBA Architects** www.kcba-architects.com	¡¡	PA	E M S W C G	A D E G I L P U O	C E K G Hc H I M R Rs Rm Rc S O	
	KDF Architecture www.kdfarchitecture.com	¡¡	WA	E M S W C G	A D E G I L P U O	C E K G Hc H I M R Rs Rm Rc S O	
	Keffer/Overton Architects www.k-o.com	¡¡	IA	E M S W C G	A D E G I L P U O	C E K G Hc H I M R Rs Rm Rc S O	
	Kendall/Heaton Associates www.kendall-heaton.com	¡¡	TX	E M S W C G	A D E G I L P U O	C E K G Hc H I M R Rs Rm Rc S O	
	Kenneth Boroson Architects www.kbarch.com	¡¡	CT	E M S W C G	A D E G I L P U O	C E K G Hc H I M R Rs Rm Rc S O	
	Kerns Group Architects www.kernsgroup.com	¡	VA	E M S W C G	A D E G I L P U O	C E K G Hc H I M R Rs Rm Rc S O	
	Kevin Daly Architects www.dalygenik.com	¡	CA	E M S W C G	A D E G I L P U O	C E K G Hc H I M R Rs Rm Rc S O	
	Kevin Roche John Dinkeloo & Associates www.krjda.com	¡¡	CT	E M S W C G	A D E G I L P U O	C E K G Hc H I M R Rs Rm Rc S O	
	Kieran Timberlake www.kierantimberlake.com	¡¡	PA	E M S W C G	A D E G I L P U O	C E K G Hc H I M R Rs Rm Rc S O	
	Kiku Obata & Company www.kikuobata.com	¡	MO	E M S W C G	A D E G I L P U O	C E K G Hc H I M R Rs Rm Rc S O	
	Killefer Flammang Architects www.kfarchitects.com	¡¡	CA	E M S W C G	A D E G I L P U O	C E K G Hc H I M R Rs Rm Rc S O	
	King+King Architects www.kingarch.com	¡¡	NY	E M S W C G	A D E G I L P U O	C E K G Hc H I M R Rs Rm Rc S O	
	Kirkegaard Associates www.kirkegaard.com	¡¡	IL	E M S W C G	A D E G I L P U O	C E K G Hc H I M R Rs Rm Rc S O	
47	**Kirksey** www.kirksey.com	¡¡¡	TX	E M S W C G	A D E G I L P U O	C E K G Hc H I M R Rs Rm Rc S O	
	Kitchen & Associates www.kitchenandassociates.com	¡	NJ	E M S W C G	A D E G I L P U O	C E K G Hc H I M R Rs Rm Rc S O	

DI Brand Recognition Index

Top tier global and categorical leader recognition

Exceptional national and categorical leader recognition

Strong regional and categorical leader recognition

Notable and growing with emerging categorical recognition

Professional practice notable in city and region

J.J. Jetel

UNO Soccer Academy High School, Chicago, IL | Wight & Company

Allison Evans Photography

Ping Tom Memorial Park Fieldhouse, Chicago, IL | Wight & Company

Rank	Firm/Web	Size	HQ	Regions	Services	Markets	DI Index
	KlingStubbins, a Jacobs Company www.klingstubbins.com	👤👤👤	PA	E M S W C G	A D E G I L P U O	C E K G Hc H I M R Rs Rm Rc S O	📊
	Kluber Architects + Engineers www.kluberinc.com	👤👤	IL	E M S W C G	A D E G I L P U O	C E K G Hc H I M R Rs Rm Rc S O	📊
	KMA Architecture www.kma-ae.com	👤👤	CA	E M S W C G	A D E G I L P U O	C E K G Hc H I M R Rs Rm Rc S O	📊
135	**KMD Architects** www.kmdarchitects.com	👤👤👤	CA	E M S W C G	A D E G I L P U O	C E K G Hc H I M R Rs Rm Rc S O	📊
	KMW Architecture www.kmwarch.com	👤👤	MA	E M S W C G	A D E G I L P U O	C E K G Hc H I M R Rs Rm Rc S O	📊
	Knowles Blunck Architecture www.kba-studio.com	👤	IA	E M S W C G	A D E G I L P U O	C E K G Hc H I M R Rs Rm Rc S O	📊
	Koch Architects www.kocharchitects.com	👤👤	CA	E M S W C G	A D E G I L P U O	C E K G Hc H I M R Rs Rm Rc S O	📊
	Kodet Architectural Group www.kodet.com	👤	MN	E M S W C G	A D E G I L P U O	C E K G Hc H I M R Rs Rm Rc S O	📊
11	**Kohn Pedersen Fox** www.kpf.com	👤👤👤👤👤	NY	E M S W C G	A D E G I L P U O	C E K G Hc H I M R Rs Rm Rc S O	📊
	Koning Eizenberg Architecture www.kearch.com	👤	CA	E M S W C G	A D E G I L P U O	C E K G Hc H I M R Rs Rm Rc S O	📊
	Kosinski Architecture www.kosinskiarchitecture.com	👤👤	FL	E M S W C G	A D E G I L P U O	C E K G Hc H I M R Rs Rm Rc S O	📊
245	**KPS Group** www.kpsgroup.com	👤👤	AL	E M S W C G	A D E G I L P U O	C E K G Hc H I M R Rs Rm Rc S O	📊
	Kromm Rikimaru and Johansen www.krjarch.com	👤	MO	E M S W C G	A D E G I L P U O	C E K G Hc H I M R Rs Rm Rc S O	📊
	KSQ Architects www.ksqarchitects.com	👤👤	NY	E M S W C G	A D E G I L P U O	C E K G Hc H I M R Rs Rm Rc S O	📊
	KTGY Group www.ktgy.com	👤	CA	E M S W C G	A D E G I L P U O	C E K G Hc H I M R Rs Rm Rc S O	📊
	Kubala Washatko Architects www.tkwa.com	👤	WI	E M S W C G	A D E G I L P U O	C E K G Hc H I M R Rs Rm Rc S O	📊
	Kuhlman Design Group www.kdginc.com	👤👤👤	MO	E M S W C G	A D E G I L P U O	C E K G Hc H I M R Rs Rm Rc S O	📊

DI Brand Recognition Index

📶 Top tier global and categorical leader recognition

📶 Exceptional national and categorical leader recognition

📶 Strong regional and categorical leader recognition

📶 Notable and growing with emerging categorical recognition

📶 Professional practice notable in city and region

Rank	Firm/Web	Size	HQ	Regions	Services	Markets	DI Index
	Kurtz Associates Architects www.kurtzarch.com		IL	E M S W C G	A D E G I L P U O	C E K G Hc H I M R Rs Rm Rc S O	
	Kwan Henmi www.kwanhenmi.com		CA	E M S W C G	A D E G I L P U O	C E K G Hc H I M R Rs Rm Rc S O	
	KYA Design Group www.kyadesigngroup.com		HI	E M S W C G	A D E G I L P U O	C E K G Hc H I M R Rs Rm Rc S O	
	KZF Design www.kzf.com		OH	E M S W C G	A D E G I L P U O	C E K G Hc H I M R Rs Rm Rc S O	
L	**L. R. Kimball (Architecture)** www.lrkimball.com		PA	E M S W C G	A D E G I L P U O	C E K G Hc H I M R Rs Rm Rc S O	
	L2Partridge www.partridgearch.com		PA	E M S W C G	A D E G I L P U O	C E K G Hc H I M R Rs Rm Rc S O	
	Laguarda Low Architects www.laguardalow.com		TX	E M S W C G	A D E G I L P U O	C E K G Hc H I M R Rs Rm Rc S O	
	LAI Design Group www.laidesigngroup.com		CO	E M S W C G	A D E G I L P U O	C E K G Hc H I M R Rs Rm Rc S O	
189	**Lake/Flato Architects** www.lakeflato.com		TX	E M S W C G	A D E G I L P U O	C E K G Hc H I M R Rs Rm Rc S O	
	Landworks Studio www.landworks-studio.com		MA	E M S W C G	A D E G I L P U O	C E K G Hc H I M R Rs Rm Rc S O	
298	**Langdon Wilson International** www.langdonwilson.com		CA	E M S W C G	A D E G I L P U O	C E K G Hc H I M R Rs Rm Rc S O	
225	**Lantz-Boggio Architects** www.lantz-boggio.com		CO	E M S W C G	A D E G I L P U O	C E K G Hc H I M R Rs Rm Rc S O	
	Larson & Darby Group www.larsondarby.com		IL	E M S W C G	A D E G I L P U O	C E K G Hc H I M R Rs Rm Rc S O	
	Lawrence Group www.thelawrencegroup.com		MO	E M S W C G	A D E G I L P U O	C E K G Hc H I M R Rs Rm Rc S O	
	Lawson Group Architects www.lawsongroup.net		FL	E M S W C G	A D E G I L P U O	C E K G Hc H I M R Rs Rm Rc S O	
	LCA Architects www.lca-architects.com		CA	E M S W C G	A D E G I L P U O	C E K G Hc H I M R Rs Rm Rc S O	
	Lee Harris Pomeroy Architects www.lhparch.com		NY	E M S W C G	A D E G I L P U O	C E K G Hc H I M R Rs Rm Rc S O	

Size

	Small	20 employees or less
	Medium	21–100 employees
	Large	101–450 employees
	Extra Large	451+ employees

Regions East (E), Midwest (M), South (S), West (W), Canada (C), Global (G)

Services Architecture (A), Design/Build (D), Engineering-MEP (E), Graphic Design (G), Interior Design (I), Landscape Architecture (L), Planning (P), Urban Design (U), Other-including Industrial Design (O)

Markets Corporate (C), Higher Ed. (E), K-12 (K), Government (G), Healthcare (Hc), Hospitality (H), Industrial/Tech. (I), Museum/Cultural (M), Religious (R), Residential-Single (Rs), Residential-Multi. (Rm), Retail/Commercial (Rc), Sports (S), Other (O)

Rank	Firm/Web	Size	HQ	Regions	Services	Markets	DI Index
184	**Legat Architects** www.legat.com	👤👤	IL	E M S W C G	A D E G I L P U O	C E K G Hc H I M R Rs Rm Rc S O	
	Lehrer Architects www.lehrerarchitects.com	👤	CA	E M S W C G	A D E G I L P U O	C E K G Hc H I M R Rs Rm Rc S O	
16	**LEO A DALY** www.leodaly.com	👤👤👤👤	NE	E M S W C G	A D E G I L P U O	C E K G Hc H I M R Rs Rm Rc S O	
	Leotta Designers www.leottadesigners.com	👤	FL	E M S W C G	A D E G I L P U O	C E K G Hc H I M R Rs Rm Rc S O	
	Levi + Wong Design Associates www.lwda.com	👤	MA	E M S W C G	A D E G I L P U O	C E K G Hc H I M R Rs Rm Rc S O	
	Levin Porter Associates www.levin-porter.com	👤	OH	E M S W C G	A D E G I L P U O	C E K G Hc H I M R Rs Rm Rc S O	
	Levinson Alcoser Associates www.laalp.com	👤👤	TX	E M S W C G	A D E G I L P U O	C E K G Hc H I M R Rs Rm Rc S O	
	LGA www.lgainc.com	👤	NV	E M S W C G	A D E G I L P U O	C E K G Hc H I M R Rs Rm Rc S O	
292	**LGA Partners** www.lga-partners.com	👤👤	PA	E M S W C G	A D E G I L P U O	C E K G Hc H I M R Rs Rm Rc S O	
	LHB Engineers & Architects www.lhbcorp.com	👤👤	MN	E M S W C G	A D E G I L P U O	C E K G Hc H I M R Rs Rm Rc S O	
	Lightowler Johnson Associates www.lja-1.com	👤👤	ND	E M S W C G	A D E G I L P U O	C E K G Hc H I M R Rs Rm Rc S O	
	Lindsay Newman Architecture & Design www.lnarchitecture.com	👤	NY	E M S W C G	A D E G I L P U O	C E K G Hc H I M R Rs Rm Rc S O	
	Lindsay Shives Associates www.lshivesarchitect.com	👤	MA	E M S W C G	A D E G I L P U O	C E K G Hc H I M R Rs Rm Rc S O	
287	**Lindsay, Pope, Brayfield & Associates** www.lpbatlanta.com	👤	GA	E M S W C G	A D E G I L P U O	C E K G Hc H I M R Rs Rm Rc S O	
	LineSync Architecture www.linesync.com	👤	VT	E M S W C G	A D E G I L P U O	C E K G Hc H I M R Rs Rm Rc S O	
71	**Lionakis** www.lionakis.com	👤👤	CA	E M S W C G	A D E G I L P U O	C E K G Hc H I M R Rs Rm Rc S O	
35	**Little** www.littleonline.com	👤👤👤	NC	E M S W C G	A D E G I L P U O	C E K G Hc H I M R Rs Rm Rc S O	

DI Brand Recognition Index

Top tier global and categorical leader recognition

Exceptional national and categorical leader recognition

Strong regional and categorical leader recognition

Notable and growing with emerging categorical recognition

Professional practice notable in city and region

The Spectator Hotel

The Spectator Hotel, Charleston, SC | LS3P Associates Ltd.

Walt Dowdy

IKA, Wilmington, NC | LS3P Associates Ltd.

Rank	Firm/Web	Size	HQ	Regions	Services	Markets	DI Index
127	**LMN Architects** www.lmnarchitects.com	👤👤👤	WA	E M S W C G	A D E G I L P U O	C E K G Hc H I M R Rs Rm Rc S O	▁▃▅▇
	Lockwood Architects www.lockwoodarch.com	👤	CO	E M S W C G	A D E G I L P U O	C E K G Hc H I M R Rs Rm Rc S O	▃▅▁▁
	Loebl Schlossman & Hackl www.lshdesign.com	👤👤	IL	E M S W C G	A D E G I L P U O	C E K G Hc H I M R Rs Rm Rc S O	▁▃▅▁
	Lohan Anderson www.lohananderson.com	👤	IL	E M S W C G	A D E G I L P U O	C E K G Hc H I M R Rs Rm Rc S O	▁▃▅▁
	Looney Ricks Kiss www.lrk.com	👤👤	TN	E M S W C G	A D E G I L P U O	C E K G Hc H I M R Rs Rm Rc S O	▁▃▅▁
106	**Lord, Aeck & Sargent** www.lordaecksargent.com	👤👤👤	GA	E M S W C G	A D E G I L P U O	C E K G Hc H I M R Rs Rm Rc S O	▁▃▅▇
	Lothan Van Hook Destefano Architecture www.lvdarchitecture.com	👤👤	IL	E M S W C G	A D E G I L P U O	C E K G Hc H I M R Rs Rm Rc S O	▁▃▅▇
	Lothrop Associates www.lothropassociates.com	👤👤	NY	E M S W C G	A D E G I L P U O	C E K G Hc H I M R Rs Rm Rc S O	▁▃▅▁
49	**LPA** www.lpainc.com	👤👤👤	CA	E M S W C G	A D E G I L P U O	C E K G Hc H I M R Rs Rm Rc S O	▁▃▅▇
	LPK Architects www.lpkarchitects.com	👤	MS	E M S W C G	A D E G I L P U O	C E K G Hc H I M R Rs Rm Rc S O	▁▃▅▁
	LRS Architects www.lrsarchitects.com	👤👤👤	OR	E M S W C G	A D E G I L P U O	C E K G Hc H I M R Rs Rm Rc S O	▁▃▅▁
42	**LS3P Associates Ltd.** www.LS3P.com	👤👤👤	SC	E M S W C G	A D E G I L P U O	C E K G Hc H I M R Rs Rm Rc S O	▁▃▅▇
220	**LSM** www.lsm.com	👤👤	DC	E M S W C G	A D E G I L P U O	C E K G Hc H I M R Rs Rm Rc S O	▁▃▅▇
	LSW Architects www.lsw-architects.com	👤	WA	E M S W C G	A D E G I L P U O	C E K G Hc H I M R Rs Rm Rc S O	▃▅▁▁
	Luckett & Farley Architects www.luckett-farley.com	👤👤	KY	E M S W C G	A D E G I L P U O	C E K G Hc H I M R Rs Rm Rc S O	▁▃▅▁
	LWC www.lwcinspires.com	👤👤	OH	E M S W C G	A D E G I L P U O	C E K G Hc H I M R Rs Rm Rc S O	▃▅▁▁
	LWPB Architecture www.lwpb.com	👤👤	OK	E M S W C G	A D E G I L P U O	C E K G Hc H I M R Rs Rm Rc S O	▁▃▅▁

DI Brand Recognition Index

▁▃▅▇ Top tier global and categorical leader recognition

▁▃▅▇ Exceptional national and categorical leader recognition

▁▃▅▁ Strong regional and categorical leader recognition

▁▃▁▁ Notable and growing with emerging categorical recognition

▁▁▁▁ Professional practice notable in city and region

Rank	Firm/Web	Size	HQ	Regions	Services	Markets	DI Index
	Lyman Davidson Dooley www.lddi-architects.com	Small	GA	E M S W C G	A D E G I L P U O	C E K G Hc H I M R Rs Rm Rc S O	
M	**M+A Architects** www.ma-architects.com	Medium	OH	E M S W C G	A D E G I L P U O	C E K G Hc H I M R Rs Rm Rc S O	
	Macgregor Associates Architects www.macgregorassoc.com	Small	GA	E M S W C G	A D E G I L P U O	C E K G Hc H I M R Rs Rm Rc S O	
	Machado and Silvetti Associates www.machado-silvetti.com	Medium	MA	E M S W C G	A D E G I L P U O	C E K G Hc H I M R Rs Rm Rc S O	
	Mack Scogin Merrill Elam Architects www.msmearch.com	Medium	GA	E M S W C G	A D E G I L P U O	C E K G Hc H I M R Rs Rm Rc S O	
	MacKay-Lyons Sweetapple Architects www.mlsarchitects.ca	Medium	CAN	E M S W C G	A D E G I L P U O	C E K G Hc H I M R Rs Rm Rc S O	
	Mackenzie www.mcknze.com	Medium	OR	E M S W C G	A D E G I L P U O	C E K G Hc H I M R Rs Rm Rc S O	
314	**Mackey Mitchell Architects** www.mackeymitchell.com	Medium	MO	E M S W C G	A D E G I L P U O	C E K G Hc H I M R Rs Rm Rc S O	
	MacLachlan, Cornelius & Filoni Architects www.mcfarchitects.com	Small	PA	E M S W C G	A D E G I L P U O	C E K G Hc H I M R Rs Rm Rc S O	
179	**Mahlum** www.mahlum.com	Medium	WA	E M S W C G	A D E G I L P U O	C E K G Hc H I M R Rs Rm Rc S O	
	Manasc Isaac Architects www.manascisaac.com	Medium	CAN	E M S W C G	A D E G I L P U O	C E K G Hc H I M R Rs Rm Rc S O	
137	**Mancini - Duffy** www.manciniduffy.com	Medium	NY	E M S W C G	A D E G I L P U O	C E K G Hc H I M R Rs Rm Rc S O	
	Manning Architects www.manningarchitects.com	Medium	LA	E M S W C G	A D E G I L P U O	C E K G Hc H I M R Rs Rm Rc S O	
305	**Margulies Perruzzi Architects** www.mp-architects.com	Medium	MA	E M S W C G	A D E G I L P U O	C E K G Hc H I M R Rs Rm Rc S O	
	Mark Cavagnero Associates www.cavagnero.com	Medium	CA	E M S W C G	A D E G I L P U O	C E K G Hc H I M R Rs Rm Rc S O	
	Marks, Thomas Architects www.marks-thomas.com	Medium	MD	E M S W C G	A D E G I L P U O	C E K G Hc H I M R Rs Rm Rc S O	
	Marlon Blackwell Architect www.marlonblackwell.com	Small	AR	E M S W C G	A D E G I L P U O	C E K G Hc H I M R Rs Rm Rc S O	

Size
- Small — 20 employees or less
- Medium — 21–100 employees
- Large — 101–450 employees
- Extra Large — 451+ employees

Regions East (E), Midwest (M), South (S), West (W), Canada (C), Global (G)

Services Architecture (A), Design/Build (D), Engineering-MEP (E), Graphic Design (G), Interior Design (I), Landscape Architecture (L), Planning (P), Urban Design (U), Other-including Industrial Design (O)

Markets Corporate (C), Higher Ed. (E), K-12 (K), Government (G), Healthcare (Hc), Hospitality (H), Industrial/Tech. (I), Museum/Cultural (M), Religious (R), Residential-Single (Rs), Residential-Multi. (Rm), Retail/Commercial (Rc), Sports (S), Other (O)

Rank	Firm/Web	Size	HQ	Regions	Services	Markets	DI Index
	Marmol Radziner www.marmol-radziner.com	👥	CA	E M S W C G	A D E G I L P U O	C E K G Hc H I M R Rs Rm Rc S O	▂▃▅▇
	Marnell Companies www.marnellcompanies.com	👤	NV	E M S W C G	A D E G I L P U O	C E K G Hc H I M R Rs Rm Rc S O	▂▃▅
	Marsh & Associates www.mai-architects.com	👤	CO	E M S W C G	A D E G I L P U O	C E K G Hc H I M R Rs Rm Rc S O	▂▃▅▇
242	**Marshall Craft Associates** www.marshallcraft.com	👥	MD	E M S W C G	A D E G I L P U O	C E K G Hc H I M R Rs Rm Rc S O	▂▃▅
	Martin Holub Architects & Planners www.mharchitects.com	👤	NY	E M S W C G	A D E G I L P U O	C E K G Hc H I M R Rs Rm Rc S O	▂▃▅
	Martinez + Cutri Architects www.martinezcutri.com	👤	CA	E M S W C G	A D E G I L P U O	C E K G Hc H I M R Rs Rm Rc S O	▂▃▅▇
	Mascari Warner Architects www.mascariwarner.com	👥	CA	E M S W C G	A D E G I L P U O	C E K G Hc H I M R Rs Rm Rc S O	▂▃▅▇
	Mason Architects www.masonarch.com	👥	HI	E M S W C G	A D E G I L P U O	C E K G Hc H I M R Rs Rm Rc S O	▂▃▅▇
	Mathes Brierre Architects www.mathesbrierre.com	👥	LA	E M S W C G	A D E G I L P U O	C E K G Hc H I M R Rs Rm Rc S O	▂▃▅▇
	Matrix Spencer www.matrixdesigncompanies.com	👤	TX	E M S W C G	A D E G I L P U O	C E K G Hc H I M R Rs Rm Rc S O	▂▃▅▇
103	**MBH Architects** www.mbharch.com	👥👥	CA	E M S W C G	A D E G I L P U O	C E K G Hc H I M R Rs Rm Rc S O	▂▃▅▇
	MC Harry & Associates www.mcharry.com	👤	FL	E M S W C G	A D E G I L P U O	C E K G Hc H I M R Rs Rm Rc S O	▂▃▅▇
	MCA Architects www.mca-architects.com	👤	OR	E M S W C G	A D E G I L P U O	C E K G Hc H I M R Rs Rm Rc S O	▂▃▅
	McCall Design Group www.mccalldesign.com	👥	CA	E M S W C G	A D E G I L P U O	C E K G Hc H I M R Rs Rm Rc S O	▂▃▅▇
	McCarty Holsaple McCarty www.mhminc.com	👥	TN	E M S W C G	A D E G I L P U O	C E K G Hc H I M R Rs Rm Rc S O	▂▃▅▇
	McElrath and Oliver Associates www.m-oarchitects.com	👤	AL	E M S W C G	A D E G I L P U O	C E K G Hc H I M R Rs Rm Rc S O	▂▃▅▇
	MCG www.mcgarchitecture.com	👤	CA	E M S W C G	A D E G I L P U O	C E K G Hc H I M R Rs Rm Rc S O	▂▃▅▇

DI Brand Recognition Index

▂▃▅▇ Top tier global and categorical leader recognition

▂▃▅ Exceptional national and categorical leader recognition

▂▃ Strong regional and categorical leader recognition

▂▃ Notable and growing with emerging categorical recognition

▂ Professional practice notable in city and region

Rank	Firm/Web	Size	HQ	Regions	Services	Markets	DI Index
	McGranahan Architects www.mcgranahan.com	●●	WA	E M S W C G	A D E G I L P U O	C E K G Hc H I M R Rs Rm Rc S O	
	McKinley & Associates www.mckinleyassoc.com	●	WV	E M S W C G	A D E G I L P U O	C E K G Hc H I M R Rs Rm Rc S O	
73	**McKissack & McKissack** www.mckissackdc.com	●●●	DC	E M S W C G	A D E G I L P U O	C E K G Hc H I M R Rs Rm Rc S O	
	McMillan Pazdan Smith www.mcmillanpazdansmith.com	●●	SC	E M S W C G	A D E G I L P U O	C E K G Hc H I M R Rs Rm Rc S O	
	McMonigal Architects www.mcmonigal.com	●●	MN	E M S W C G	A D E G I L P U O	C E K G Hc H I M R Rs Rm Rc S O	
147	**Mead & Hunt** www.meadhunt.com	●●●●	WI	E M S W C G	A D E G I L P U O	C E K G Hc H I M R Rs Rm Rc S O	
293	**Meeks + Partners** www.meekspartners.com	●●	TX	E M S W C G	A D E G I L P U O	C E K G Hc H I M R Rs Rm Rc S O	
	Mekus Tanager www.mekustanager.com	●	IL	E M S W C G	A D E G I L P U O	C E K G Hc H I M R Rs Rm Rc S O	
	Melichar Architects www.melichararchitects.com	●	IL	E M S W C G	A D E G I L P U O	C E K G Hc H I M R Rs Rm Rc S O	
268	**Merriman Associates/Architects** www.merrimanassociates.com	●●	TX	E M S W C G	A D E G I L P U O	C E K G Hc H I M R Rs Rm Rc S O	
283	**Meyer, Scherer & Rockcastle** www.msrltd.com	●●	MN	E M S W C G	A D E G I L P U O	C E K G Hc H I M R Rs Rm Rc S O	
	MG Architects www.mgarchitects.com	●●	TX	E M S W C G	A D E G I L P U O	C E K G Hc H I M R Rs Rm Rc S O	
37	**MG2 Corporation** www.MG2.com	●●●	WA	E M S W C G	A D E G I L P U O	C E K G Hc H I M R Rs Rm Rc S O	
	MGA Architecture www.mgahawaii.com	●●	HI	E M S W C G	A D E G I L P U O	C E K G Hc H I M R Rs Rm Rc S O	
327	**MGA Partners Architects** www.mgapartners.com	●●	PA	E M S W C G	A D E G I L P U O	C E K G Hc H I M R Rs Rm Rc S O	
326	**MGE Architects** www.mgearchitects.com	●	FL	E M S W C G	A D E G I L P U O	C E K G Hc H I M R Rs Rm Rc S O	
	MGMA www.morgangick.com	●	VA	E M S W C G	A D E G I L P U O	C E K G Hc H I M R Rs Rm Rc S O	

Size

● Small — 20 employees or less
●● Medium — 21–100 employees
●●● Large — 101–450 employees
●●●● Extra Large — 451+ employees

Regions East (E), Midwest (M), South (S), West (W), Canada (C), Global (G)

Services Architecture (A), Design/Build (D), Engineering-MEP (E), Graphic Design (G), Interior Design (I), Landscape Architecture (L), Planning (P), Urban Design (U), Other-including Industrial Design (O)

Markets Corporate (C), Higher Ed. (E), K-12 (K), Government (G), Healthcare (Hc), Hospitality (H), Industrial/Tech. (I), Museum/Cultural (M), Religious (R), Residential-Single (Rs), Residential-Multi. (Rm), Retail/Commercial (Rc), Sports (S), Other (O)

Rank	Firm/Web	Size	HQ	Regions		Services		Markets			DI Index
	MHAworks www.mhaworks.com		NC	E M S W	C G	A D E G I	L P U O	C E K G Hc H I	M R Rs Rm Rc S O		
	MHTN Architects www.mhtn.com		UT	E M S W	C G	A D E G I	L P U O	C E K G Hc H I	M R Rs Rm Rc S O		
	Michael Graves Architecture & Design www.michaelgraves.com		NJ	E M S W	C G	A D E G I	L P U O	C E K G Hc H I	M R Rs Rm Rc S O		
	Michael Maltzan Architecture www.mmaltzan.com		CA	E M S W	C G	A D E G I	L P U O	C E K G Hc H I	M R Rs Rm Rc S O		
	Michael Van Valkenburgh Associates www.mvvainc.com		NY	E M S W	C G	A D E G I	L P U O	C E K G Hc H I	M R Rs Rm Rc S O		
253	**Miller Dunwiddie Architects** www.millerdunwiddie.com		MN	E M S W	C G	A D E G I	L P U O	C E K G Hc H I	M R Rs Rm Rc S O		
	Miller Dyer Spears www.mds-bos.com		MA	E M S W	C G	A D E G I	L P U O	C E K G Hc H I	M R Rs Rm Rc S O		
141	**Miller Hull Partnership** www.millerhull.com		WA	E M S W	C G	A D E G I	L P U O	C E K G Hc H I	M R Rs Rm Rc S O		
	Milton Glaser www.miltonglaser.com		NY	E M S W	C G	A D E G I	L P U O	C E K G Hc H I	M R Rs Rm Rc S O		
	Mitchell Associates www.mitchellai.com		DE	E M S W	C G	A D E G I	L P U O	C E K G Hc H I	M R Rs Rm Rc S O		
	Mitchell I Giurgola Architects www.mitchellgiurgola.com		NY	E M S W	C G	A D E G I	L P U O	C E K G Hc H I	M R Rs Rm Rc S O		
125	**Mithun** www.mithun.com		WA	E M S W	C G	A D E G I	L P U O	C E K G Hc H I	M R Rs Rm Rc S O		
238	**MKC Associates** www.mkcinc.com		OH	E M S W	C G	A D E G I	L P U O	C E K G Hc H I	M R Rs Rm Rc S O		
	MKTHINK www.mkthink.com		CA	E M S W	C G	A D E G I	L P U O	C E K G Hc H I	M R Rs Rm Rc S O		
280	**MOA Architecture** www.moaarch.com		CO	E M S W	C G	A D E G I	L P U O	C E K G Hc H I	M R Rs Rm Rc S O		
	Moeckel Carbonell Associates www.architectsde.com		DE	E M S W	C G	A D E G I	L P U O	C E K G Hc H I	M R Rs Rm Rc S O		
	Mojo Stumer Associates www.mojostumer.com		NY	E M S W	C G	A D E G I	L P U O	C E K G Hc H I	M R Rs Rm Rc S O		

DI Brand Recognition Index

Top tier global and categorical leader recognition

Notable and growing with emerging categorical recognition

Exceptional national and categorical leader recognition

Professional practice notable in city and region

Strong regional and categorical leader recognition

Rank	Firm/Web	Size	HQ	Regions		Services		Markets		DI Index
	Montalba Architects www.montalbaarchitects.com	Medium	CA	E M S W	C G	A D E G I	L P U O	C E K G Hc H I	M R Rs Rm Rc S O	
80	**Moody - Nolan** www.moodynolan.com	Large	OH	E M S W	C G	A D E G I	L P U O	C E K G Hc H I	M R Rs Rm Rc S O	
	Moon Mayoras Architects www.moonmayoras.com	Small	CA	E M S W	C G	A D E G I	L P U O	C E K G Hc H I	M R Rs Rm Rc S O	
	Moore Ruble Yudell Architects & Planners www.moorerubleyudell.com	Medium	CA	E M S W	C G	A D E G I	L P U O	C E K G Hc H I	M R Rs Rm Rc S O	
	Moriyama & Teshima Architects www.mtarch.com	Small	CAN	E M S W	C G	A D E G I	L P U O	C E K G Hc H I	M R Rs Rm Rc S O	
201	**Morphosis** www.morphosis.com	Medium	CA	E M S W	C G	A D E G I	L P U O	C E K G Hc H I	M R Rs Rm Rc S O	
63	**Morris Architects** www.morrisarchitects.com	Extra Large	TX	E M S W	C G	A D E G I	L P U O	C E K G Hc H I	M R Rs Rm Rc S O	
	Moseley Architects www.moseleyarchitects.com	Large	VA	E M S W	C G	A D E G I	L P U O	C E K G Hc H I	M R Rs Rm Rc S O	
	Mount Vernon Group Architects www.mvgarchitects.com	Medium	MA	E M S W	C G	A D E G I	L P U O	C E K G Hc H I	M R Rs Rm Rc S O	
	MRI Architectural Group www.mriarchitects.com	Small	FL	E M S W	C G	A D E G I	L P U O	C E K G Hc H I	M R Rs Rm Rc S O	
	MS Consultants www.msconsultants.com	Medium	OH	E M S W	C G	A D E G I	L P U O	C E K G Hc H I	M R Rs Rm Rc S O	
303	**MSA Architects** www.msaarch.com	Medium	OH	E M S W	C G	A D E G I	L P U O	C E K G Hc H I	M R Rs Rm Rc S O	
	MSTSD www.mstsd.com	Medium	GA	E M S W	C G	A D E G I	L P U O	C E K G Hc H I	M R Rs Rm Rc S O	
	MTA www.mtalink.com	Medium	CAN	E M S W	C G	A D E G I	L P U O	C E K G Hc H I	M R Rs Rm Rc S O	
	Munger Munger + Associates Architects www.mungermunger.com	Small	OH	E M S W	C G	A D E G I	L P U O	C E K G Hc H I	M R Rs Rm Rc S O	
299	**Munoz & Company** www.munoz-co.com	Medium	TX	E M S W	C G	A D E G I	L P U O	C E K G Hc H I	M R Rs Rm Rc S O	
	Murphy and Dittenhafer www.murphdittarch.com	Medium	MD	E M S W	C G	A D E G I	L P U O	C E K G Hc H I	M R Rs Rm Rc S O	

Size

Small	20 employees or less
Medium	21–100 employees
Large	101–450 employees
Extra Large	451+ employees

Regions East (E), Midwest (M), South (S), West (W), Canada (C), Global (G)

Services Architecture (A), Design/Build (D), Engineering-MEP (E), Graphic Design (G), Interior Design (I), Landscape Architecture (L), Planning (P), Urban Design (U), Other-including Industrial Design (O)

Markets Corporate (C), Higher Ed. (E), K-12 (K), Government (G), Healthcare (Hc), Hospitality (H), Industrial/Tech. (I), Museum/Cultural (M), Religious (R), Residential-Single (Rs), Residential-Multi. (Rm), Retail/Commercial (Rc), Sports (S), Other (O)

Rank	Firm/Web	Size	HQ	Regions	Services	Markets	DI Index
	Murphy Burnham & Buttrick Architects www.mbbarch.com	👥👥	NY	E M S W / C G	A D E G I / L P U O	C E K G Hc H I / M R Rs Rm Rc S O	
	MVE + Partners www.mve-architects.com	👥	CA	E M S W / C G	A D E G I / L P U O	C E K G Hc H I / M R Rs Rm Rc S O	
	MWA Architects www.mwaarchitects.com	👥	CA	E M S W / C G	A D E G I / L P U O	C E K G Hc H I / M R Rs Rm Rc S O	
N 101	**NAC Architecture** www.nacarchitecture.com	👥👥👥	WA	E M S W / C G	A D E G I / L P U O	C E K G Hc H I / M R Rs Rm Rc S O	
	Nacht & Lewis Architects www.nachtlewis.com	👥	CA	E M S W / C G	A D E G I / L P U O	C E K G Hc H I / M R Rs Rm Rc S O	
208	**Nadel** www.nadelarc.com	👥	CA	E M S W / C G	A D E G I / L P U O	C E K G Hc H I / M R Rs Rm Rc S O	
	Nagle Hartray Architecture www.naglehartray.com	👤	IL	E M S W / C G	A D E G I / L P U O	C E K G Hc H I / M R Rs Rm Rc S O	
	nArchitects www.narchitects.com	👤	NY	E M S W / C G	A D E G I / L P U O	C E K G Hc H I / M R Rs Rm Rc S O	
	Nashawtuc Architects www.nasharch.com	👤	MA	E M S W / C G	A D E G I / L P U O	C E K G Hc H I / M R Rs Rm Rc S O	
15	**NBBJ** www.nbbj.com	👥👥👥👥	WA	E M S W / C G	A D E G I / L P U O	C E K G Hc H I / M R Rs Rm Rc S O	
	Neil Hauck Architects www.neilhauckarchitects.com	👤	CT	E M S W / C G	A D E G I / L P U O	C E K G Hc H I / M R Rs Rm Rc S O	
	Nelsen Partners www.nelsenpartners.com	👥	TX	E M S W / C G	A D E G I / L P U O	C E K G Hc H I / M R Rs Rm Rc S O	
61	**NELSON** www.nelsononline.com	👥👥👥	PA	E M S W / C G	A D E G I / L P U O	C E K G Hc H I / M R Rs Rm Rc S O	
	Neumann/Smith Architecture www.neumannsmith.com	👥	MI	E M S W / C G	A D E G I / L P U O	C E K G Hc H I / M R Rs Rm Rc S O	
	Nevue Ngan Associates www.nevuengan.com	👤	OR	E M S W / C G	A D E G I / L P U O	C E K G Hc H I / M R Rs Rm Rc S O	
	Nichols, Melburg & Rossetto Architects www.nmrdesign.com	👥	CA	E M S W / C G	A D E G I / L P U O	C E K G Hc H I / M R Rs Rm Rc S O	
86	**Niles Bolton Associates** www.nilesbolton.com	👥👥👥	GA	E M S W / C G	A D E G I / L P U O	C E K G Hc H I / M R Rs Rm Rc S O	

DI Brand Recognition Index

Top tier global and categorical leader recognition

Exceptional national and categorical leader recognition

Strong regional and categorical leader recognition

Notable and growing with emerging categorical recognition

Professional practice notable in city and region

Rank	Firm/Web	Size	HQ	Regions	Services	Markets	DI Index
	NORR Architects Planners www.norr.com	👥	CAN	E M S W C G	A D E G I L P U O	C E K G Hc H I M R Rs Rm Rc S O	
	Norris Design www.norris-design.com	👥	CO	E M S W C G	A D E G I L P U O	C E K G Hc H I M R Rs Rm Rc S O	
	Northeast Collaborative Architects www.ncarchitects.com	👥	RI	E M S W C G	A D E G I L P U O	C E K G Hc H I M R Rs Rm Rc S O	
	Nudell Architects www.jhn.com	👥	MI	E M S W C G	A D E G I L P U O	C E K G Hc H I M R Rs Rm Rc S O	
O	**O'Brien/Atkins Associates** www.obrienatkins.com	👥	NC	E M S W C G	A D E G I L P U O	C E K G Hc H I M R Rs Rm Rc S O	
	O'Connell Robertson www.oconnellrobertson.com	👥	TX	E M S W C G	A D E G I L P U O	C E K G Hc H I M R Rs Rm Rc S O	
	Oakley Collier Architects www.oakleycollier.com	👥	NC	E M S W C G	A D E G I L P U O	C E K G Hc H I M R Rs Rm Rc S O	
	OBMI www.obmi.com	👥👥	FL	E M S W C G	A D E G I L P U O	C E K G Hc H I M R Rs Rm Rc S O	
	Odell www.odell.com	👥	NC	E M S W C G	A D E G I L P U O	C E K G Hc H I M R Rs Rm Rc S O	
	Office of James Burnett www.ojb.com	👥	TX	E M S W C G	A D E G I L P U O	C E K G Hc H I M R Rs Rm Rc S O	
	Ohlson Lavoie Collaborative www.olcdesigns.com	👥	CO	E M S W C G	A D E G I L P U O	C E K G Hc H I M R Rs Rm Rc S O	
	OKKS Studios www.okksstudios.com	👥	MD	E M S W C G	A D E G I L P U O	C E K G Hc H I M R Rs Rm Rc S O	
	OKW Architects www.okwarchitects.com	👥👥	IL	E M S W C G	A D E G I L P U O	C E K G Hc H I M R Rs Rm Rc S O	
	OLIN www.theolinstudio.com	👥	PA	E M S W C G	A D E G I L P U O	C E K G Hc H I M R Rs Rm Rc S O	
	Olson Kundig Architects www.olsonkundigarchitects.com	👥	WA	E M S W C G	A D E G I L P U O	C E K G Hc H I M R Rs Rm Rc S O	
309	**Omniplan** www.omniplan.com	👥	TX	E M S W C G	A D E G I L P U O	C E K G Hc H I M R Rs Rm Rc S O	
120	**OPN Architects** www.opnarchitects.com	👥👥	IA	E M S W C G	A D E G I L P U O	C E K G Hc H I M R Rs Rm Rc S O	

Size

👤	Small	20 employees or less
👥	Medium	21–100 employees
👥👥	Large	101–450 employees
👥👥👥	Extra Large	451+ employees

Regions East (E), Midwest (M), South (S), West (W), Canada (C), Global (G)

Services Architecture (A), Design/Build (D), Engineering-MEP (E), Graphic Design (G), Interior Design (I), Landscape Architecture (L), Planning (P), Urban Design (U), Other-including Industrial Design (O)

Markets Corporate (C), Higher Ed. (E), K-12 (K), Government (G), Healthcare (Hc), Hospitality (H), Industrial/Tech. (I), Museum/Cultural (M), Religious (R), Residential-Single (Rs), Residential-Multi. (Rm), Retail/Commercial (Rc), Sports (S), Other (O)

Rank	Firm/Web	Size	HQ	Regions	Services	Markets	DI Index
	Opsis Architecture www.opsisarch.com		OR	E M S W C G	A D E G I L P U O	C E K G Hc H I M R Rs Rm Rc S O	
174	**Orcutt I Winslow** www.owp.com		AZ	E M S W C G	A D E G I L P U O	C E K G Hc H I M R Rs Rm Rc S O	
	OSK Design Partners www.oskdesignpartners.com		NJ	E M S W C G	A D E G I L P U O	C E K G Hc H I M R Rs Rm Rc S O	
150	**OTAK** www.otak.com		OR	E M S W C G	A D E G I L P U O	C E K G Hc H I M R Rs Rm Rc S O	
210	**Overland Partners Architects** www.overlandpartners.com		TX	E M S W C G	A D E G I L P U O	C E K G Hc H I M R Rs Rm Rc S O	
126	**OZ Architecture** www.ozarch.com		CO	E M S W C G	A D E G I L P U O	C E K G Hc H I M R Rs Rm Rc S O	
P 112	**P+R Architects** www.prarchitects.com		CA	E M S W C G	A D E G I L P U O	C E K G Hc H I M R Rs Rm Rc S O	
	Pacific Architects www.pacarchitects.com		HI	E M S W C G	A D E G I L P U O	C E K G Hc H I M R Rs Rm Rc S O	
27	**Page** www.pagethink.com		TX	E M S W C G	A D E G I L P U O	C E K G Hc H I M R Rs Rm Rc S O	
	Partners & Sirny Architects www.partnersandsirny.com		MN	E M S W C G	A D E G I L P U O	C E K G Hc H I M R Rs Rm Rc S O	
	Patkau Architects www.patkau.ca		CAN	E M S W C G	A D E G I L P U O	C E K G Hc H I M R Rs Rm Rc S O	
	Patrick Tighe Architecture www.tighearchitecture.com		CA	E M S W C G	A D E G I L P U O	C E K G Hc H I M R Rs Rm Rc S O	
	Paulett Taggart Architects www.ptarc.com		CA	E M S W C G	A D E G I L P U O	C E K G Hc H I M R Rs Rm Rc S O	
58	**Payette** www.payette.com		MA	E M S W C G	A D E G I L P U O	C E K G Hc H I M R Rs Rm Rc S O	
	pb2 Architecture & Engineering www.pb2ae.com		AR	E M S W C G	A D E G I L P U O	C E K G Hc H I M R Rs Rm Rc S O	
69	**PBK** www.pbk.com		TX	E M S W C G	A D E G I L P U O	C E K G Hc H I M R Rs Rm Rc S O	
	PBR Hawaii www.pbrhawaii.com		HI	E M S W C G	A D E G I L P U O	C E K G Hc H I M R Rs Rm Rc S O	

DI Brand Recognition Index

Top tier global and categorical leader recognition

Exceptional national and categorical leader recognition

Strong regional and categorical leader recognition

Notable and growing with emerging categorical recognition

Professional practice notable in city and region

Fernando Guerra

Kristal Kule Finansbank Headquarters, Istanbul, Turkey | Pei Cobb Freed & Partners Architects

Rank	Firm/Web	Size	HQ	Regions		Services		Markets		DI Index
	Peacock Partnership www.peacockarchitects.com	👤	GA	E M S W C G		A D E G I L P U O		C E K G Hc H I M R Rs Rm Rc S O		▁▃▁_
95	**Pei Cobb Freed & Partners Architects** www.pcf-p.com	👤👤👤	NY	E M S W C G		A D E G I L P U O		C E K G Hc H I M R Rs Rm Rc S O		▁▃▅▇
	Pelli Clarke Pelli Architects www.pcparch.com	👤👤	CT	E M S W C G		A D E G I L P U O		C E K G Hc H I M R Rs Rm Rc S O		▁▃▅_
	Pellow + Associates Architects www.pellowarchitects.com	👤👤	CAN	E M S W C G		A D E G I L P U O		C E K G Hc H I M R Rs Rm Rc S O		▁▃▁_
	Perfido Weiskopf Wagstaff + Goettel www.pwwgarch.com	👤	PA	E M S W C G		A D E G I L P U O		C E K G Hc H I M R Rs Rm Rc S O		▁▃▁_
13	**Perkins Eastman** www.perkinseastman.com	👤👤👤👤👤	NY	E M S W C G		A D E G I L P U O		C E K G Hc H I M R Rs Rm Rc S O		▁▃▅▇
6	**Perkins+Will** www.perkinswill.com	👤👤👤👤👤	N/A	E M S W C G		A D E G I L P U O		C E K G Hc H I M R Rs Rm Rc S O		▁▃▅▇
	Perry Dean Rogers | Partners Architects www.perrydean.com	👤👤	MA	E M S W C G		A D E G I L P U O		C E K G Hc H I M R Rs Rm Rc S O		▁▃▅_
	Peter Chermayeff www.peterchermayeff.com	👤	MA	E M S W C G		A D E G I L P U O		C E K G Hc H I M R Rs Rm Rc S O		▁▃▅_
	Peter Henry Architects www.chebucto.ns.ca/Business/PHARCH	👤👤	CAN	E M S W C G		A D E G I L P U O		C E K G Hc H I M R Rs Rm Rc S O		▁▃▁_
204	**Peter Marino Architect** www.petermarinoarchitect.com	👤👤👤	NY	E M S W C G		A D E G I L P U O		C E K G Hc H I M R Rs Rm Rc S O		▁▃▅▇
	Peter Vincent Architects www.pva.com	👤	HI	E M S W C G		A D E G I L P U O		C E K G Hc H I M R Rs Rm Rc S O		▁▃▁_
273	**Pfeiffer Partners Architects** www.pfeifferpartners.com	👤👤	CA	E M S W C G		A D E G I L P U O		C E K G Hc H I M R Rs Rm Rc S O		▁▃▅▇
	PFS Studio www.pfsstudio.com	👤👤	CAN	E M S W C G		A D E G I L P U O		C E K G Hc H I M R Rs Rm Rc S O		▁▃▁_
	PFVS www.pfvs.com	👤👤	GA	E M S W C G		A D E G I L P U O		C E K G Hc H I M R Rs Rm Rc S O		▁▃▁_
	PGAL www.pgal.com	👤👤👤	TX	E M S W C G		A D E G I L P U O		C E K G Hc H I M R Rs Rm Rc S O		▁▃▁_
	PGAV Architects www.pgav.com	👤👤👤	MO	E M S W C G		A D E G I L P U O		C E K G Hc H I M R Rs Rm Rc S O		▁▃▁_

DI Brand Recognition Index

▁▃▅▇ Top tier global and categorical leader recognition

▁▃▅ Exceptional national and categorical leader recognition

▁▃ Strong regional and categorical leader recognition

▁▃▁_ Notable and growing with emerging categorical recognition

▁___ Professional practice notable in city and region

© David Sundberg-Esto

Eaton House, Dublin, Ireland | Pickard Chilton

Rank	Firm/Web	Size	HQ	Regions	Services	Markets	DI Index
	Phillips Partnership www.phillipspart.com	👥👥	GA	E M S W C G	A D E G I L P U O	C E K G Hc H I M R Rs Rm Rc S O	
	Philo Wilke Partnership www.pwarch.com	👥👥	TX	E M S W C G	A D E G I L P U O	C E K G Hc H I M R Rs Rm Rc S O	
	Pica + Sullivan Architects www.picasullivan.com	👤	CA	E M S W C G	A D E G I L P U O	C E K G Hc H I M R Rs Rm Rc S O	
	Pickard Chilton www.pickardchilton.com	👥👥	CT	E M S W C G	A D E G I L P U O	C E K G Hc H I M R Rs Rm Rc S O	
213	**Pieper O'Brien Herr Architects** www.poharchitects.com	👥👥	GA	E M S W C G	A D E G I L P U O	C E K G Hc H I M R Rs Rm Rc S O	
	Pinnacle Architects www.pinnaclearchitects.com	👤	OH	E M S W C G	A D E G I L P U O	C E K G Hc H I M R Rs Rm Rc S O	
	PLANT Architect www.branchplant.com	👤	CAN	E M S W C G	A D E G I L P U O	C E K G Hc H I M R Rs Rm Rc S O	
	Platt Byard Dovell White Architects www.pbdw.com	👥👥	NY	E M S W C G	A D E G I L P U O	C E K G Hc H I M R Rs Rm Rc S O	
	Poggemeyer Design Group www.poggemeyer.com	👥👥👥	OH	E M S W C G	A D E G I L P U O	C E K G Hc H I M R Rs Rm Rc S O	
251	**Polk Stanley Wilcox** www.polkstanleywilcox.com	👥👥	AR	E M S W C G	A D E G I L P U O	C E K G Hc H I M R Rs Rm Rc S O	
	Pope Associates www.popearch.com	👥👥	MN	E M S W C G	A D E G I L P U O	C E K G Hc H I M R Rs Rm Rc S O	
22	**Populous** www.populous.com	👥👥👥	MO	E M S W C G	A D E G I L P U O	C E K G Hc H I M R Rs Rm Rc S O	
	Port City Architecture www.portcityarch.com	👤	ME	E M S W C G	A D E G I L P U O	C E K G Hc H I M R Rs Rm Rc S O	
211	**The Portico Group** www.porticogroup.com	👥👥	WA	E M S W C G	A D E G I L P U O	C E K G Hc H I M R Rs Rm Rc S O	
	PositivEnergy Practice www.pepractice.com	👥👥	IL	E M S W C G	A D E G I L P U O	C E K G Hc H I M R Rs Rm Rc S O	
	Potter Lawson www.potterlawson.com	👥👥	WI	E M S W C G	A D E G I L P U O	C E K G Hc H I M R Rs Rm Rc S O	
	Powers Brown Architecture www.powersbrown.com	👥👥	TX	E M S W C G	A D E G I L P U O	C E K G Hc H I M R Rs Rm Rc S O	

DI Brand Recognition Index

- Top tier global and categorical leader recognition
- Exceptional national and categorical leader recognition
- Strong regional and categorical leader recognition
- Notable and growing with emerging categorical recognition
- Professional practice notable in city and region

Joe Fletcher

888 Brannan, San Francisco, CA | Gensler

Rank	Firm/Web	Size	HQ	Regions	Services	Markets	DI Index
154	**The Preston Partnership** www.theprestonpartnership.com	👥	GA	E M S W C G	A D E G I L P U O	C E K G Hc H I M R Rs Rm Rc S O	▪▫▫
	PS & S Architecture & Engineering www.psands.com	👥	NJ	E M S W C G	A D E G I L P U O	C E K G Hc H I M R Rs Rm Rc S O	▪▫▫
	PW Architects www.pwarchitects.com	👤	MO	E M S W C G	A D E G I L P U O	C E K G Hc H I M R Rs Rm Rc S O	▪▫▫
	PWP Landscape Architecture www.pwpla.com	👤	CA	E M S W C G	A D E G I L P U O	C E K G Hc H I M R Rs Rm Rc S O	▪▪▪
	Pyatok Architects www.pyatok.com	👤	CA	E M S W C G	A D E G I L P U O	C E K G Hc H I M R Rs Rm Rc S O	▪▪▫
Q	**Quinn Evans Architects** www.quinnevans.com	👤	DC	E M S W C G	A D E G I L P U O	C E K G Hc H I M R Rs Rm Rc S O	▪▪▫
	Quorum Architects www.quorumarchitects.com	👤	WI	E M S W C G	A D E G I L P U O	C E K G Hc H I M R Rs Rm Rc S O	▪▫▫
R	**R.L. Engebretson** www.rleco.com	👥	ND	E M S W C G	A D E G I L P U O	C E K G Hc H I M R Rs Rm Rc S O	▪▪▫
33	**Rafael Viñoly Architects** www.rvapc.com	👥👥👥	NY	E M S W C G	A D E G I L P U O	C E K G Hc H I M R Rs Rm Rc S O	▪▪▪▪
	Randall Stout Architects www.stoutarc.com	👤	CA	E M S W C G	A D E G I L P U O	C E K G Hc H I M R Rs Rm Rc S O	▪▫▫
	Randy Brown Architects www.randybrownarchitects.com	👤	NE	E M S W C G	A D E G I L P U O	C E K G Hc H I M R Rs Rm Rc S O	▪▪▪
182	**RAPT Studio** www.raptstudio.com	👥	CA	E M S W C G	A D E G I L P U O	C E K G Hc H I M R Rs Rm Rc S O	▪▪▪
228	**Ratcliff** www.ratcliffarch.com	👥	CA	E M S W C G	A D E G I L P U O	C E K G Hc H I M R Rs Rm Rc S O	▪▪▫
166	**RATIO Architects** www.ratioarchitects.com	👥	IN	E M S W C G	A D E G I L P U O	C E K G Hc H I M R Rs Rm Rc S O	▪▪▫
139	**RBB Architects** www.rbbinc.com	👥	CA	E M S W C G	A D E G I L P U O	C E K G Hc H I M R Rs Rm Rc S O	▪▪▫
	RCM Architects www.rcmarchitects.com	👥	OH	E M S W C G	A D E G I L P U O	C E K G Hc H I M R Rs Rm Rc S O	▪▪▫
88	**RDG Planning & Design** www.rdgusa.com	👥👥👥	IA	E M S W C G	A D E G I L P U O	C E K G Hc H I M R Rs Rm Rc S O	▪▪▫

DI Brand Recognition Index

▪▪▪▪ Top tier global and categorical leader recognition

▪▪▫▫ Notable and growing with emerging categorical recognition

▪▪▪ Exceptional national and categorical leader recognition

▪▫▫▫ Professional practice notable in city and region

▪▪▫ Strong regional and categorical leader recognition

Rank	Firm/Web	Size	HQ	Regions	Services	Markets	DI Index
155	**Rebel Design+Group** www.rebeldesign.com	👥	CA	E M S W C G	A D E G I L P U O	C E K G Hc H I M R Rs Rm Rc S O	▃▄▅▆
	Reed Hilderbrand www.reedhilderbrand.com	👥	MA	E M S W C G	A D E G I L P U O	C E K G Hc H I M R Rs Rm Rc S O	▃▂▃▆
248	**Rees Associates** www.rees.com	👥	OK	E M S W C G	A D E G I L P U O	C E K G Hc H I M R Rs Rm Rc S O	▃▄▃▅
	Renaissance 3 Architects www.r3a.com	👤	PA	E M S W C G	A D E G I L P U O	C E K G Hc H I M R Rs Rm Rc S O	▃▄▅▂
322	**Research Facilities Design** www.rfd.com	👥	CA	E M S W C G	A D E G I L P U O	C E K G Hc H I M R Rs Rm Rc S O	▃▄▅▂
	RicciGreene Associates www.riccigreene.com	👥	NY	E M S W C G	A D E G I L P U O	C E K G Hc H I M R Rs Rm Rc S O	▃▄▅▆
	Richard Brown Architects www.richardbrownarchitects.com	👤	MA	E M S W C G	A D E G I L P U O	C E K G Hc H I M R Rs Rm Rc S O	▃▄▅▂
	Richard Fleischman + Partners Architects www.studiorfa.com	👥	OH	E M S W C G	A D E G I L P U O	C E K G Hc H I M R Rs Rm Rc S O	▃▄▂▂
	Richard Matsunaga & Associates Architects www.rmaia-architects.com	👥	HI	E M S W C G	A D E G I L P U O	C E K G Hc H I M R Rs Rm Rc S O	▃▂▂▂
107	**Richard Meier & Partners Architects** www.richardmeier.com	👥👥	NY	E M S W C G	A D E G I L P U O	C E K G Hc H I M R Rs Rm Rc S O	▃▄▅▆
	richärd+bauer www.richard-bauer.com	👤	AZ	E M S W C G	A D E G I L P U O	C E K G Hc H I M R Rs Rm Rc S O	▃▄▅▂
	Rick Ryniak Architects www.ryniak.com	👤	HI	E M S W C G	A D E G I L P U O	C E K G Hc H I M R Rs Rm Rc S O	▃▄▅▆
	Riecke Sunnland Kono Architects www.rskarchitects.com	👤	HI	E M S W C G	A D E G I L P U O	C E K G Hc H I M R Rs Rm Rc S O	▃▄▅▂
	Risinger + Associates www.risingerassociates.com	👤	IL	E M S W C G	A D E G I L P U O	C E K G Hc H I M R Rs Rm Rc S O	▃▄▂▂
	RJC Architects www.rjcarch.com	👤	CA	E M S W C G	A D E G I L P U O	C E K G Hc H I M R Rs Rm Rc S O	▃▄▅▂
	RKAA Architects www.rkaa.com	👥	AZ	E M S W C G	A D E G I L P U O	C E K G Hc H I M R Rs Rm Rc S O	▃▄▅▆
	RKTB Architects www.rktb.com	👥	NY	E M S W C G	A D E G I L P U O	C E K G Hc H I M R Rs Rm Rc S O	▃▄▅▂

Size

👤	Small	20 employees or less
👥	Medium	21–100 employees
👥👥	Large	101–450 employees
👥👥👥	Extra Large	451+ employees

Regions   East (E), Midwest (M), South (S), West (W), Canada (C), Global (G)

Services   Architecture (A), Design/Build (D), Engineering-MEP (E), Graphic Design (G), Interior Design (I), Landscape Architecture (L), Planning (P), Urban Design (U), Other-including Industrial Design (O)

Markets   Corporate (C), Higher Ed. (E), K-12 (K), Government (G), Healthcare (Hc), Hospitality (H), Industrial/Tech. (I), Museum/Cultural (M), Religious (R), Residential-Single (Rs), Residential-Multi. (Rm), Retail/Commercial (Rc), Sports (S), Other (O)

Rank	Firm/Web	Size	HQ	Regions	Services	Markets	DI Index
	RLF Architecture, Engineering, Interior Design www.rlfarchitects.com	👤👤👤	FL	E M S W C G	A D E G I L P U O	C E K G Hc H I M R Rs Rm Rc S O	▪▍▁▁
	RLPS Architects www.rlps.com	👤	PA	E M S W C G	A D E G I L P U O	C E K G Hc H I M R Rs Rm Rc S O	▪▍▁▁
200	**RMW architecture & interiors** www.rmw.com	👤👤	CA	E M S W C G	A D E G I L P U O	C E K G Hc H I M R Rs Rm Rc S O	▪▍▍▁
132	**RNL** www.rnldesign.com	👤👤👤	CO	E M S W C G	A D E G I L P U O	C E K G Hc H I M R Rs Rm Rc S O	▪▍▍▍
	Rob Wellington Quigley www.robquigley.com	👤	CA	E M S W C G	A D E G I L P U O	C E K G Hc H I M R Rs Rm Rc S O	▪▍▍▁
28	**Robert A.M. Stern Architects** www.ramsa.com	👤👤👤	NY	E M S W C G	A D E G I L P U O	C E K G Hc H I M R Rs Rm Rc S O	▪▍▍▍
	Robert M. Swedroe Architects & Planners www.swedroe.com	👤	FL	E M S W C G	A D E G I L P U O	C E K G Hc H I M R Rs Rm Rc S O	▪▍▍▁
	Robert P. Madison, International www.rpmadison.com	👤👤	OH	E M S W C G	A D E G I L P U O	C E K G Hc H I M R Rs Rm Rc S O	▪▍▍▁
	Robertson Loia Roof www.rlrpc.com	👤👤	GA	E M S W C G	A D E G I L P U O	C E K G Hc H I M R Rs Rm Rc S O	▪▍▍▁
	Rockwell Group www.rockwellgroup.com	👤👤	NY	E M S W C G	A D E G I L P U O	C E K G Hc H I M R Rs Rm Rc S O	▪▍▍▍
	Rodriguez and Quiroga www.rodriguezquiroga.com	👤	FL	E M S W C G	A D E G I L P U O	C E K G Hc H I M R Rs Rm Rc S O	▪▍▍▁
	Roesling Nakamura Terada Architects www.rntarchitects.com	👤👤	CA	E M S W C G	A D E G I L P U O	C E K G Hc H I M R Rs Rm Rc S O	▪▍▁▁
295	**Rogers Partners Architects+Urban Designers** www.rogersarchitects.com	👤👤	NY	E M S W C G	A D E G I L P U O	C E K G Hc H I M R Rs Rm Rc S O	▪▍▍▍
	Ron Yeo Architect www.ronyeo.com	👤👤	CA	E M S W C G	A D E G I L P U O	C E K G Hc H I M R Rs Rm Rc S O	▪▍▍▁
256	**Rosser International** www.rosser.com	👤👤	GA	E M S W C G	A D E G I L P U O	C E K G Hc H I M R Rs Rm Rc S O	▪▍▍▁
276	**Rossetti** www.rossetti.com	👤👤👤	MI	E M S W C G	A D E G I L P U O	C E K G Hc H I M R Rs Rm Rc S O	▪▍▍▁
34	**RSP Architects** www.rsparch.com	👤👤👤	MN	E M S W C G	A D E G I L P U O	C E K G Hc H I M R Rs Rm Rc S O	▪▍▍▁

DI Brand Recognition Index

▪▍▍▍ Top tier global and categorical leader recognition

▪▍▍▍ Exceptional national and categorical leader recognition

▪▍▍▁ Strong regional and categorical leader recognition

▪▍▁▁ Notable and growing with emerging categorical recognition

▪▁▁▁ Professional practice notable in city and region

Anton Grassi

Dudley Square Bruce Bolling Municipal Office Building, Boston, MA | Sasaki Associates, Inc.

Rank	Firm/Web	Size	HQ	Regions	Services	Markets	DI Index
	RSSC Architecture www.rsscarch.com	♦	PA	E M S W C G	A D E G I L P U O	C E K G Hc H I M R Rs Rm Rc S O	
	Rubeling & Associates www.rubeling.com	♦♦	MD	E M S W C G	A D E G I L P U O	C E K G Hc H I M R Rs Rm Rc S O	
	Rule Joy Trammell + Rubio www.rjtplusr.com	♦♦	GA	E M S W C G	A D E G I L P U O	C E K G Hc H I M R Rs Rm Rc S O	
	RWA Architects www.rwaarchitects.com	♦	OH	E M S W C G	A D E G I L P U O	C E K G Hc H I M R Rs Rm Rc S O	
S	**SAA** www.saaia.com	♦♦	CA	E M S W C G	A D E G I L P U O	C E K G Hc H I M R Rs Rm Rc S O	
	Safdie Architects www.msafdie.com	♦	CA	E M S W C G	A D E G I L P U O	C E K G Hc H I M R Rs Rm Rc S O	
	Salerno/Livingston Architects www.slarchitects.com	♦	CA	E M S W C G	A D E G I L P U O	C E K G Hc H I M R Rs Rm Rc S O	
	Salmela Architects www.salmelaarchitect.com	♦	MN	E M S W C G	A D E G I L P U O	C E K G Hc H I M R Rs Rm Rc S O	
	Sandvick Architects www.sandvickarchitects.com	♦♦	OH	E M S W C G	A D E G I L P U O	C E K G Hc H I M R Rs Rm Rc S O	
	Sarah Nettleton Architects www.sarahnettleton.com	♦	MN	E M S W C G	A D E G I L P U O	C E K G Hc H I M R Rs Rm Rc S O	
45	**Sasaki Associates, Inc.** www.sasaki.com	♦♦♦	MA	E M S W C G	A D E G I L P U O	C E K G Hc H I M R Rs Rm Rc S O	
167	**SB Architects** www.sb-architects.com	♦♦	CA	E M S W C G	A D E G I L P U O	C E K G Hc H I M R Rs Rm Rc S O	
149	**SchenkelShultz** www.schenkelshultz.com	♦♦	IN	E M S W C G	A D E G I L P U O	C E K G Hc H I M R Rs Rm Rc S O	
183	**Schmidt Associates** www.schmidt-arch.com	♦♦	OH	E M S W C G	A D E G I L P U O	C E K G Hc H I M R Rs Rm Rc S O	
	Schooley Caldwell Associates www.sca-ae.com	♦	OH	E M S W C G	A D E G I L P U O	C E K G Hc H I M R Rs Rm Rc S O	
	Schwartz/Silver Architects www.schwartzsilver.com	♦	MA	E M S W C G	A D E G I L P U O	C E K G Hc H I M R Rs Rm Rc S O	
	Scott + Cormia www.scottcormia.com	♦	FL	E M S W C G	A D E G I L P U O	C E K G Hc H I M R Rs Rm Rc S O	

DI Brand Recognition Index

Top tier global and categorical leader recognition

Exceptional national and categorical leader recognition

Strong regional and categorical leader recognition

Notable and growing with emerging categorical recognition

Professional practice notable in city and region

Rank	Firm/Web	Size	HQ	Regions	Services	Markets	DI Index
	Seaver Franks Architects www.seaverfranks.com	👤	AZ	E M S W C G	A D E G I L P U O	C E K G Hc H I M R Rs Rm Rc S O	
	SEI Design Group www.seidesigngroup.com	👥	NY	E M S W C G	A D E G I L P U O	C E K G Hc H I M R Rs Rm Rc S O	
	SEM Architects www.semarchitects.com	👤	CO	E M S W C G	A D E G I L P U O	C E K G Hc H I M R Rs Rm Rc S O	
	Semple Brown Design www.sbdesign-pc.com	👤	CO	E M S W C G	A D E G I L P U O	C E K G Hc H I M R Rs Rm Rc S O	
	Setzer Architects www.setzerarchitects.com	👤	MN	E M S W C G	A D E G I L P U O	C E K G Hc H I M R Rs Rm Rc S O	
	SGA Design www.sgadesigngroup.com	👥👥	OK	E M S W C G	A D E G I L P U O	C E K G Hc H I M R Rs Rm Rc S O	
	SGGM Architects + Interior Designers www.sggm.net	👤	IA	E M S W C G	A D E G I L P U O	C E K G Hc H I M R Rs Rm Rc S O	
	SGPA Architecture and Planning www.sgpa.com	👥	CA	E M S W C G	A D E G I L P U O	C E K G Hc H I M R Rs Rm Rc S O	
	SH Architecture www.sh-architecture.com	👤	NV	E M S W C G	A D E G I L P U O	C E K G Hc H I M R Rs Rm Rc S O	
97	**Shalom Baranes Associates** www.sbaranes.com	👥	DC	E M S W C G	A D E G I L P U O	C E K G Hc H I M R Rs Rm Rc S O	
	Shea Architects www.shealink.com	👥	MN	E M S W C G	A D E G I L P U O	C E K G Hc H I M R Rs Rm Rc S O	
	Shepherd Resources www.sriarchitect.com	👤	CO	E M S W C G	A D E G I L P U O	C E K G Hc H I M R Rs Rm Rc S O	
74	**Shepley Bulfinch** www.shepleyfbulfinch.com	👥👥	MA	E M S W C G	A D E G I L P U O	C E K G Hc H I M R Rs Rm Rc S O	
279	**Sherlock Smith & Adams** www.ssainc.com	👥	AL	E M S W C G	A D E G I L P U O	C E K G Hc H I M R Rs Rm Rc S O	
	The Sheward Partnership www.theshewardpartnership.com	👤	PA	E M S W C G	A D E G I L P U O	C E K G Hc H I M R Rs Rm Rc S O	
	Shiffler Associates Architects www.shiffler.com	👤	IA	E M S W C G	A D E G I L P U O	C E K G Hc H I M R Rs Rm Rc S O	
	Shim-Sutcliffe Architects www.shim-sutcliffe.com	👤	CAN	E M S W C G	A D E G I L P U O	C E K G Hc H I M R Rs Rm Rc S O	

Size

👤	Small	20 employees or less
👥	Medium	21–100 employees
👥👥	Large	101–450 employees
👥👥👥	Extra Large	451+ employees

Regions East (E), Midwest (M), South (S), West (W), Canada (C), Global (G)

Services Architecture (A), Design/Build (D), Engineering-MEP (E), Graphic Design (G), Interior Design (I), Landscape Architecture (L), Planning (P), Urban Design (U), Other-including Industrial Design (O)

Markets Corporate (C), Higher Ed. (E), K-12 (K), Government (G), Healthcare (Hc), Hospitality (H), Industrial/Tech. (I), Museum/Cultural (M), Religious (R), Residential-Single (Rs), Residential-Multi. (Rm), Retail/Commercial (Rc), Sports (S), Other (O)

Rank	Firm/Web	Size	HQ	Regions		Services		Markets		DI Index
	Shive Hattery www.shive-hattery.com	🧍🧍🧍	IA	E M S W C G		A D E G I L P U O		C E K G Hc H I M R Rs Rm Rc S O		▂▃▁
153	**SHoP Architects** www.shoparc.com	🧍🧍	NY	E M S W C G		A D E G I L P U O		C E K G Hc H I M R Rs Rm Rc S O		▂▃▅▆
	Shore Point Architecture www.shorepointarch.com	🧍	NJ	E M S W C G		A D E G I L P U O		C E K G Hc H I M R Rs Rm Rc S O		▂▃▁
188	**SHP Leading Design** www.shp.com	🧍🧍	OH	E M S W C G		A D E G I L P U O		C E K G Hc H I M R Rs Rm Rc S O		▂▃▅▁
190	**Shremshock Architects** www.shremshock.com	🧍🧍🧍	OH	E M S W C G		A D E G I L P U O		C E K G Hc H I M R Rs Rm Rc S O		▂▃▁
	Shultz & Associates www.thearchitectfirm.com	🧍	ND	E M S W C G		A D E G I L P U O		C E K G Hc H I M R Rs Rm Rc S O		▂▃▁
	Silver/Petrucelli + Associates www.silverpetrucelli.com	🧍🧍	CT	E M S W C G		A D E G I L P U O		C E K G Hc H I M R Rs Rm Rc S O		▂▃▁
215	**Sink Combs Dethlefs** www.sinkcombs.com	🧍	CO	E M S W C G		A D E G I L P U O		C E K G Hc H I M R Rs Rm Rc S O		▂▃▁
	Sizemore Group www.sizemoregroup.com	🧍🧍	GA	E M S W C G		A D E G I L P U O		C E K G Hc H I M R Rs Rm Rc S O		▂▃▁
	SK+I Architecture www.skiarch.com	🧍🧍	MD	E M S W C G		A D E G I L P U O		C E K G Hc H I M R Rs Rm Rc S O		▂▃▁
8	**Skidmore, Owings & Merrill** www.som.com	🧍🧍🧍🧍	IL	E M S W C G		A D E G I L P U O		C E K G Hc H I M R Rs Rm Rc S O		▂▃▅▆
51	**The SLAM Collaborative** www.slamcoll.com	🧍🧍🧍	CT	E M S W C G		A D E G I L P U O		C E K G Hc H I M R Rs Rm Rc S O		▂▃▅
76	**SLCE Architects** www.slcearch.com	🧍🧍	NY	E M S W C G		A D E G I L P U O		C E K G Hc H I M R Rs Rm Rc S O		▂▃▁
274	**Slifer Designs** www.sliferdesigns.com	🧍🧍	CO	E M S W C G		A D E G I L P U O		C E K G Hc H I M R Rs Rm Rc S O		▂▃▁
	Slocum Platts Architects Design Studio www.slocumplatts.com	🧍	FL	E M S W C G		A D E G I L P U O		C E K G Hc H I M R Rs Rm Rc S O		▂▃▁
131	**Smallwood, Reynolds, Stewart, Stewart & Associates** www.srssa.com	🧍🧍🧍	GA	E M S W C G		A D E G I L P U O		C E K G Hc H I M R Rs Rm Rc S O		▂▃▅
	Smith Consulting Architects www.sca-sd.com	🧍🧍🧍	CA	E M S W C G		A D E G I L P U O		C E K G Hc H I M R Rs Rm Rc S O		▂▃▁

DI Brand Recognition Index

▂▃▅▆ Top tier global and categorical leader recognition

▂▃▅ Exceptional national and categorical leader recognition

▂▃▁ Strong regional and categorical leader recognition

▂▁▁ Notable and growing with emerging categorical recognition

▂▁▁ Professional practice notable in city and region

Rank	Firm/Web	Size	HQ	Regions	Services	Markets	DI Index
12	**SmithGroupJJR** www.smithgroupjjr.com	Extra Large	N/A	E M S W C G	A D E G I L P U O	C E K G Hc H I M R Rs Rm Rc S O	
	SMP Architects www.smparchitects.com	Medium	PA	E M S W C G	A D E G I L P U O	C E K G Hc H I M R Rs Rm Rc S O	
	SMRT www.smrtinc.com	Large	ME	E M S W C G	A D E G I L P U O	C E K G Hc H I M R Rs Rm Rc S O	
	Snow Kreilich Architects www.snowkreilich.com	Small	MN	E M S W C G	A D E G I L P U O	C E K G Hc H I M R Rs Rm Rc S O	
	Soderstrom Architects www.sdra.com	Small	OR	E M S W C G	A D E G I L P U O	C E K G Hc H I M R Rs Rm Rc S O	
40	**Solomon Cordwell Buenz** www.scb.com	Large	IL	E M S W C G	A D E G I L P U O	C E K G Hc H I M R Rs Rm Rc S O	
	Song + Associates www.songandassociates.net/xe	Medium	FL	E M S W C G	A D E G I L P U O	C E K G Hc H I M R Rs Rm Rc S O	
	Southern A&E www.southernae.com	Small	GA	E M S W C G	A D E G I L P U O	C E K G Hc H I M R Rs Rm Rc S O	
	Sowinski Sullivan Architects www.sowinskisullivan.com	Small	NJ	E M S W C G	A D E G I L P U O	C E K G Hc H I M R Rs Rm Rc S O	
	Spector Group Architects www.spectorgroup.com	Small	NY	E M S W C G	A D E G I L P U O	C E K G Hc H I M R Rs Rm Rc S O	
	spg3 www.spg3.com	Medium	PA	E M S W C G	A D E G I L P U O	C E K G Hc H I M R Rs Rm Rc S O	
	SRG www.srgpartnership.com	Small	WA	E M S W C G	A D E G I L P U O	C E K G Hc H I M R Rs Rm Rc S O	
	SRK Architects www.srkarchitects.com	Medium	PA	E M S W C G	A D E G I L P U O	C E K G Hc H I M R Rs Rm Rc S O	
	SSOE Group www.ssoe.com	Extra Large	OH	E M S W C G	A D E G I L P U O	C E K G Hc H I M R Rs Rm Rc S O	
	SSP Architectural Group www.ssparchitects.com	Medium	NJ	E M S W C G	A D E G I L P U O	C E K G Hc H I M R Rs Rm Rc S O	
239	**Staffelbach** www.staffelbach.com	Medium	TX	E M S W C G	A D E G I L P U O	C E K G Hc H I M R Rs Rm Rc S O	
301	**Stanley Beaman & Sears** www.stanleybeamansears.com	Medium	GA	E M S W C G	A D E G I L P U O	C E K G Hc H I M R Rs Rm Rc S O	

Size

♦	Small	20 employees or less
♦♦	Medium	21–100 employees
♦♦♦	Large	101–450 employees
♦♦♦♦	Extra Large	451+ employees

Regions East (E), Midwest (M), South (S), West (W), Canada (C), Global (G)

Services Architecture (A), Design/Build (D), Engineering-MEP (E), Graphic Design (G), Interior Design (I), Landscape Architecture (L), Planning (P), Urban Design (U), Other-including Industrial Design (O)

Markets Corporate (C), Higher Ed. (E), K-12 (K), Government (G), Healthcare (Hc), Hospitality (H), Industrial/Tech. (I), Museum/Cultural (M), Religious (R), Residential-Single (Rs), Residential-Multi. (Rm), Retail/Commercial (Rc), Sports (S), Other (O)

Rank	Firm/Web	Size	HQ	Regions		Services		Markets		DI Index
	Stanley Love-Stanley www.stanleylove-stanleypc.com		GA	E M S W C G		A D E G I L P U O		C E K G Hc H I M R Rs Rm Rc S O		
9	**Stantec Architecture (US)** www.stantec.com		CAN	E M S W C G		A D E G I L P U O		C E K G Hc H I M R Rs Rm Rc S O		
54	**Steelman Partners** www.steelmanpartners.com		NV	E M S W C G		A D E G I L P U O		C E K G Hc H I M R Rs Rm Rc S O		
144	**Steffian Bradley Architects** www.steffian.com		MA	E M S W C G		A D E G I L P U O		C E K G Hc H I M R Rs Rm Rc S O		
	Steinberg Architects www.steinbergarchitects.com		CA	E M S W C G		A D E G I L P U O		C E K G Hc H I M R Rs Rm Rc S O		
	Stengel Hill Architecture www.stengelhill.com		KY	E M S W C G		A D E G I L P U O		C E K G Hc H I M R Rs Rm Rc S O		
237	**Stephen B. Jacobs Group/** **Andi Pepper Designs** www.sbjgroup.com		NY	E M S W C G		A D E G I L P U O		C E K G Hc H I M R Rs Rm Rc S O		
	Stephen Stimson Associates **Landscape Architects** www.stephenstimson.com		MA	E M S W C G		A D E G I L P U O		C E K G Hc H I M R Rs Rm Rc S O		
	Steve Martino Landscape Architect www.stevemartino.net		AZ	E M S W C G		A D E G I L P U O		C E K G Hc H I M R Rs Rm Rc S O		
	Steven Holl Architects www.stevenholl.com		NY	E M S W C G		A D E G I L P U O		C E K G Hc H I M R Rs Rm Rc S O		
175	**Stevens & Wilkinson** www.stevenswilkinson.com		GA	E M S W C G		A D E G I L P U O		C E K G Hc H I M R Rs Rm Rc S O		
	STG Design www.stgdesign.com		TX	E M S W C G		A D E G I L P U O		C E K G Hc H I M R Rs Rm Rc S O		
	Strada www.stradallc.com		PA	E M S W C G		A D E G I L P U O		C E K G Hc H I M R Rs Rm Rc S O		
	Strekalovsky Architecture www.strekalovskyarchitecture.com		MA	E M S W C G		A D E G I L P U O		C E K G Hc H I M R Rs Rm Rc S O		
	Strobel & Hunter www.strobelhunter.com		FL	E M S W C G		A D E G I L P U O		C E K G Hc H I M R Rs Rm Rc S O		
	Studio 2030 www.studio2030.com		MN	E M S W C G		A D E G I L P U O		C E K G Hc H I M R Rs Rm Rc S O		
	Studio Gang www.studiogang.net		IL	E M S W C G		A D E G I L P U O		C E K G Hc H I M R Rs Rm Rc S O		

DI Brand Recognition Index

Top tier global and categorical leader recognition

Exceptional national and categorical leader recognition

Strong regional and categorical leader recognition

Notable and growing with emerging categorical recognition

Professional practice notable in city and region

Rank	Firm/Web	Size	HQ	Regions	Services	Markets	DI Index
	Studio Meng Strazzara www.studioms.com	Small	WA	E M S W C G	A D E G I L P U O	C E K G Hc H I M R Rs Rm Rc S O	
44	**STUDIOS Architecture** www.studiosarchitecture.com	Large	DC	E M S W C G	A D E G I L P U O	C E K G Hc H I M R Rs Rm Rc S O	
	STV Group www.stvinc.com	Medium	NY	E M S W C G	A D E G I L P U O	C E K G Hc H I M R Rs Rm Rc S O	
	Susanka Studios www.susanka.com	Small	MN	E M S W C G	A D E G I L P U O	C E K G Hc H I M R Rs Rm Rc S O	
	SWA Group www.swagroup.com	Large	TX	E M S W C G	A D E G I L P U O	C E K G Hc H I M R Rs Rm Rc S O	
	Swaback Partners www.swabackpartners.com	Medium	AZ	E M S W C G	A D E G I L P U O	C E K G Hc H I M R Rs Rm Rc S O	
93	**Symmes Maini & McKee Associates (SMMA)** www.smma.com	Large	MA	E M S W C G	A D E G I L P U O	C E K G Hc H I M R Rs Rm Rc S O	
T	**TAYLOR** www.wearetaylor.com	Small	CA	E M S W C G	A D E G I L P U O	C E K G Hc H I M R Rs Rm Rc S O	
	tBP/Architecture www.tbparchitecture.com	Medium	CA	E M S W C G	A D E G I L P U O	C E K G Hc H I M R Rs Rm Rc S O	
	TCA Architects www.tcaarchitects.com	Small	CA	E M S W C G	A D E G I L P U O	C E K G Hc H I M R Rs Rm Rc S O	
	TCF Architecture www.tcfarchitecture.com	Medium	WA	E M S W C G	A D E G I L P U O	C E K G Hc H I M R Rs Rm Rc S O	
	TDA Architecture www.thendesign.com	Large	OH	E M S W C G	A D E G I L P U O	C E K G Hc H I M R Rs Rm Rc S O	
	Tecton Architects www.tectonarchitects.com	Small	CT	E M S W C G	A D E G I L P U O	C E K G Hc H I M R Rs Rm Rc S O	
	TEN Arquitectos www.ten-arquitectos.com	Medium	MEX	E M S W C G	A D E G I L P U O	C E K G Hc H I M R Rs Rm Rc S O	
	Terence Williams Architect www.twarchitect.ca	Small	CAN	E M S W C G	A D E G I L P U O	C E K G Hc H I M R Rs Rm Rc S O	
	Terrance J. Cisco Architect www.konaarchitects.com	Medium	HI	E M S W C G	A D E G I L P U O	C E K G Hc H I M R Rs Rm Rc S O	
	Tessier Associates www.tessierarchitects.com	Medium	MA	E M S W C G	A D E G I L P U O	C E K G Hc H I M R Rs Rm Rc S O	

Size

Small	20 employees or less	
Medium	21–100 employees	
Large	101–450 employees	
Extra Large	451+ employees	

Regions East (E), Midwest (M), South (S), West (W), Canada (C), Global (G)

Services Architecture (A), Design/Build (D), Engineering-MEP (E), Graphic Design (G), Interior Design (I), Landscape Architecture (L), Planning (P), Urban Design (U), Other-including Industrial Design (O)

Markets Corporate (C), Higher Ed. (E), K-12 (K), Government (G), Healthcare (Hc), Hospitality (H), Industrial/Tech. (I), Museum/Cultural (M), Religious (R), Residential-Single (Rs), Residential-Multi. (Rm), Retail/Commercial (Rc), Sports (S), Other (O)

Rank	Firm/Web	Size	HQ	Regions	Services	Markets	DI Index
241	**Thalden-Boyd-Emery Architects** www.thaldenboyd.com	👤	MO	E M S W C G	A D E G I L P U O	C E K G Hc H I M R Rs Rm Rc S O	▃▁▁
	Theodore + Theodore Architects www.2tarch.com	👤	ME	E M S W C G	A D E G I L P U O	C E K G Hc H I M R Rs Rm Rc S O	▃▁▁
	Thomas Biro Landscape Architects www.thomasbiro.com	👤	NJ	E M S W C G	A D E G I L P U O	C E K G Hc H I M R Rs Rm Rc S O	▃▃▁
	Thompson & Litton www.t-l.com	👤👤👤	VA	E M S W C G	A D E G I L P U O	C E K G Hc H I M R Rs Rm Rc S O	▃▁▁
	Threshold Acoustics www.thresholdacoustics.com	👤	IL	E M S W C G	A D E G I L P U O	C E K G Hc H I M R Rs Rm Rc S O	▃▃▁
192	**THW Design** www.thw.com	👤👤	GA	E M S W C G	A D E G I L P U O	C E K G Hc H I M R Rs Rm Rc S O	▃▁▁
	Tigerman McCurry Architects www.tigerman-mccurry.com	👤	IL	E M S W C G	A D E G I L P U O	C E K G Hc H I M R Rs Rm Rc S O	▄▅▆▇
232	**TMP Associates** www.tmp-architecture.com	👤👤👤	MI	E M S W C G	A D E G I L P U O	C E K G Hc H I M R Rs Rm Rc S O	▃▁▁
	Tod Williams Billie Tsien Architects www.twbta.com	👤👤	NY	E M S W C G	A D E G I L P U O	C E K G Hc H I M R Rs Rm Rc S O	▄▅▆▇
	Todd & Associates www.toddassoc.com	👤	AZ	E M S W C G	A D E G I L P U O	C E K G Hc H I M R Rs Rm Rc S O	▃▃▁
185	**Torti Gallas and Partners** www.tortigallas.com	👤👤	MD	E M S W C G	A D E G I L P U O	C E K G Hc H I M R Rs Rm Rc S O	▄▅▆
247	**TowerPinkster** www.towerpinkster.com	👤👤	MI	E M S W C G	A D E G I L P U O	C E K G Hc H I M R Rs Rm Rc S O	▃▃▁
	TPG Architecture www.tpgarchitecture.com	👤👤👤	NY	E M S W C G	A D E G I L P U O	C E K G Hc H I M R Rs Rm Rc S O	▃▂▁
318	**TR,i Architects** www.triarchitects.com	👤	MO	E M S W C G	A D E G I L P U O	C E K G Hc H I M R Rs Rm Rc S O	▃▃▁
	TRA Architects www.traarchitects.com	👤	FL	E M S W C G	A D E G I L P U O	C E K G Hc H I M R Rs Rm Rc S O	▃▃▁
	Trivers www.trivers.com	👤👤	MO	E M S W C G	A D E G I L P U O	C E K G Hc H I M R Rs Rm Rc S O	▃▃▁
	TRK Architecture & Facilities Management www.trkinc.com	👤👤	AZ	E M S W C G	A D E G I L P U O	C E K G Hc H I M R Rs Rm Rc S O	▃▃▁

DI Brand Recognition Index

▆▇▇▇ Top tier global and categorical leader recognition

▄▅▆▇ Exceptional national and categorical leader recognition

▃▃▆ Strong regional and categorical leader recognition

▃▁▁ Notable and growing with emerging categorical recognition

▂▁▁ Professional practice notable in city and region

Rank	Firm/Web	Size	HQ	Regions	Services	Markets	DI Index
111	**TRO JB** www.trojb.com	🏅🏅🏅	MA	E M S W C G	A D E G I L P U O	C E K G Hc H I M R Rs Rm Rc S O	
	TruexCullins www.truexcullins.com	🏅	VT	E M S W C G	A D E G I L P U O	C E K G Hc H I M R Rs Rm Rc S O	
	Tryba Architects www.trybaarchitects.com	🏅	CO	E M S W C G	A D E G I L P U O	C E K G Hc H I M R Rs Rm Rc S O	
	Tsao & McKown Architects www.tsao-mckown.com	🏅	NY	E M S W C G	A D E G I L P U O	C E K G Hc H I M R Rs Rm Rc S O	
187	**Tsoi/Kobus & Associates** www.tka-architects.com	🏅🏅	MA	E M S W C G	A D E G I L P U O	C E K G Hc H I M R Rs Rm Rc S O	
202	**TSP** www.teamtsp.com	🏅🏅🏅	SD	E M S W C G	A D E G I L P U O	C E K G Hc H I M R Rs Rm Rc S O	
	Tushie Montgomery Architects www.tmiarchitects.com	🏅	MN	E M S W C G	A D E G I L P U O	C E K G Hc H I M R Rs Rm Rc S O	
	TVA Architects www.tvaarchitects.com	🏅🏅	OR	E M S W C G	A D E G I L P U O	C E K G Hc H I M R Rs Rm Rc S O	
65	**tvsdesign** www.tvs-design.com	🏅🏅🏅	GA	E M S W C G	A D E G I L P U O	C E K G Hc H I M R Rs Rm Rc S O	
U	**Urbahn Architects** www.urbahn.com	🏅	NY	E M S W C G	A D E G I L P U O	C E K G Hc H I M R Rs Rm Rc S O	
297	**Urban Design Associates** www.urbandesignassociates.com	🏅🏅	PA	E M S W C G	A D E G I L P U O	C E K G Hc H I M R Rs Rm Rc S O	
V	**Van H. Gilbert Architect** www.vhgarchitect.com	🏅🏅	NM	E M S W C G	A D E G I L P U O	C E K G Hc H I M R Rs Rm Rc S O	
233	**Van Tilburg, Banvard & Soderbergh** www.vtbs.com	🏅🏅🏅	CA	E M S W C G	A D E G I L P U O	C E K G Hc H I M R Rs Rm Rc S O	
	Vasquez + Marshall & Associates www.vmarch.net	🏅	CA	E M S W C G	A D E G I L P U O	C E K G Hc H I M R Rs Rm Rc S O	
130	**VCBO Architecture** www.vcbo.com	🏅🏅	UT	E M S W C G	A D E G I L P U O	C E K G Hc H I M R Rs Rm Rc S O	
	VEBH Architects www.vebh.com	🏅	PA	E M S W C G	A D E G I L P U O	C E K G Hc H I M R Rs Rm Rc S O	
	Venturi, Scott, Brown and Associates www.vsba.com	🏅	PA	E M S W C G	A D E G I L P U O	C E K G Hc H I M R Rs Rm Rc S O	

Size
- Small — 20 employees or less
- Medium — 21–100 employees
- Large — 101–450 employees
- Extra Large — 451+ employees

Regions East (E), Midwest (M), South (S), West (W), Canada (C), Global (G)

Services Architecture (A), Design/Build (D), Engineering-MEP (E), Graphic Design (G), Interior Design (I), Landscape Architecture (L), Planning (P), Urban Design (U), Other-including Industrial Design (O)

Markets Corporate (C), Higher Ed. (E), K-12 (K), Government (G), Healthcare (Hc), Hospitality (H), Industrial/Tech. (I), Museum/Cultural (M), Religious (R), Residential-Single (Rs), Residential-Multi. (Rm), Retail/Commercial (Rc), Sports (S), Other (O)

Rank	Firm/Web	Size	HQ	Regions	Services	Markets	DI Index
	Vetter Design Group www.vetterdesigngroup.com	👤	OH	E M S W C G	A D E G I L P U O	C E K G Hc H I M R Rs Rm Rc S O	▪▫▫▫
	Vision 3 Architects www.vision3architects.com	👥	RI	E M S W C G	A D E G I L P U O	C E K G Hc H I M R Rs Rm Rc S O	▪▫▫▫
	Visions in Architecture www.viarchitecture.com	👤	NE	E M S W C G	A D E G I L P U O	C E K G Hc H I M R Rs Rm Rc S O	▪▫▫▫
290	**VITETTA** www.vitetta.com	👥👥	PA	E M S W C G	A D E G I L P U O	C E K G Hc H I M R Rs Rm Rc S O	▪▪▫▫
	VJAA www.vjaa.com	👤	MN	E M S W C G	A D E G I L P U O	C E K G Hc H I M R Rs Rm Rc S O	▪▪▪▫
	VLK Architects www.vlkarchitects.com	👤	TX	E M S W C G	A D E G I L P U O	C E K G Hc H I M R Rs Rm Rc S O	▪▪▫▫
304	**VMDO Architects** www.vmdo.com	👥	VA	E M S W C G	A D E G I L P U O	C E K G Hc H I M R Rs Rm Rc S O	▪▪▪▫
31	**VOA Associates** www.voa.com	👥👥	IL	E M S W C G	A D E G I L P U O	C E K G Hc H I M R Rs Rm Rc S O	▪▪▪▪
108	**Vocon** www.vocon.com	👥👥	OH	E M S W C G	A D E G I L P U O	C E K G Hc H I M R Rs Rm Rc S O	▪▪▪▪
	Voith & Mactavish Architects www.voithandmactavish.com	👥	PA	E M S W C G	A D E G I L P U O	C E K G Hc H I M R Rs Rm Rc S O	▪▪▫▫
	VPS Architecture www.vpsarch.com	👤	IN	E M S W C G	A D E G I L P U O	C E K G Hc H I M R Rs Rm Rc S O	▪▪▫▫
	VSBA www.vsba.com	👤	PA	E M S W C G	A D E G I L P U O	C E K G Hc H I M R Rs Rm Rc S O	▪▪▪▫
W	**W Architecture & Landscape Architecture** www.w-architecture.com	👤	NY	E M S W C G	A D E G I L P U O	C E K G Hc H I M R Rs Rm Rc S O	▪▪▫▫
	Wagner Hodgson Landscape Architecture www.wagnerhodgson.com	👥	VT	E M S W C G	A D E G I L P U O	C E K G Hc H I M R Rs Rm Rc S O	▪▪▫▫
193	**Wakefield Beasley & Associates** www.wakefieldbeasley.com	👥	GA	E M S W C G	A D E G I L P U O	C E K G Hc H I M R Rs Rm Rc S O	▪▪▫▫
281	**Wald, Ruhnke & Dost Architects** www.wrdarch.com	👥	CA	E M S W C G	A D E G I L P U O	C E K G Hc H I M R Rs Rm Rc S O	▪▪▫▫
170	**Wallace Roberts & Todd** www.wrtdesign.com	👥👥	PA	E M S W C G	A D E G I L P U O	C E K G Hc H I M R Rs Rm Rc S O	▪▪▫▫

DI Brand Recognition Index

▪▪▪▪ Top tier global and categorical leader recognition

▪▪▪▫ Exceptional national and categorical leader recognition

▪▪▫▫ Strong regional and categorical leader recognition

▪▫▫▫ Notable and growing with emerging categorical recognition

▪▫▫▫ Professional practice notable in city and region

J.J. Jetel

Land O'Frost Corporate Office Headquarters, Munster, IN | Wight & Company

Paul Schlismann Photography

Knoch Knolls Nature Center, Naperville Park District, Naperville, IL | Wight & Company

Rank	Firm/Web	Size	HQ	Regions	Services	Markets	DI Index
	Ware Malcomb www.waremalcomb.com		CA	E M S W C G	A D E G I L P U O	C E K G Hc H I M R Rs Rm Rc S O	
259	**WASA Studio** www.wasallp.com		NY	E M S W C G	A D E G I L P U O	C E K G Hc H I M R Rs Rm Rc S O	
	Waterleaf Architecture & Interiors www.waterleaf.com		OR	E M S W C G	A D E G I L P U O	C E K G Hc H I M R Rs Rm Rc S O	
32	**WATG** www.watg.com		CA	E M S W C G	A D E G I L P U O	C E K G Hc H I M R Rs Rm Rc S O	
	WBCM www.wbcm.com		MD	E M S W C G	A D E G I L P U O	C E K G Hc H I M R Rs Rm Rc S O	
62	**WD Partners** www.wdpartners.com		OH	E M S W C G	A D E G I L P U O	C E K G Hc H I M R Rs Rm Rc S O	
134	**WDG Architecture** www.wdgarch.com		DC	E M S W C G	A D E G I L P U O	C E K G Hc H I M R Rs Rm Rc S O	
	Weiss/Manfredi Architects www.weissmanfredi.com		NY	E M S W C G	A D E G I L P U O	C E K G Hc H I M R Rs Rm Rc S O	
	Wendel www.wendelcompanies.com		NY	E M S W C G	A D E G I L P U O	C E K G Hc H I M R Rs Rm Rc S O	
	West 8 Urban Design & Landscape Architecture www.west8.com/ny		NY	E M S W C G	A D E G I L P U O	C E K G Hc H I M R Rs Rm Rc S O	
99	**Westlake Reed Leskosky** www.wrldesign.com		OH	E M S W C G	A D E G I L P U O	C E K G Hc H I M R Rs Rm Rc S O	
	WGM Design www.wgmdesign.com		NC	E M S W C G	A D E G I L P U O	C E K G Hc H I M R Rs Rm Rc S O	
59	**WHR Architects** www.whrarchitects.com		TX	E M S W C G	A D E G I L P U O	C E K G Hc H I M R Rs Rm Rc S O	
	Widseth Smith Nolting www.widsethsmithnolting.com		MN	E M S W C G	A D E G I L P U O	C E K G Hc H I M R Rs Rm Rc S O	
181	**Wight & Company** www.wightco.com		IL	E M S W C G	A D E G I L P U O	C E K G Hc H I M R Rs Rm Rc S O	
	William McDonough + Partners www.mcdonoughpartners.com		VA	E M S W C G	A D E G I L P U O	C E K G Hc H I M R Rs Rm Rc S O	
	William Nicholas Bodouva + Associates www.bodouva.com		NY	E M S W C G	A D E G I L P U O	C E K G Hc H I M R Rs Rm Rc S O	

DI Brand Recognition Index

Top tier global and categorical leader recognition

Exceptional national and categorical leader recognition

Strong regional and categorical leader recognition

Notable and growing with emerging categorical recognition

Professional practice notable in city and region

Rank	Firm/Web	Size	HQ	Regions	Services	Markets	DI Index
194	**William Rawn Associates, Architects, Inc.** www.rawnarch.com	👥	MA	E M S W C G	A D E G I L P U O	C E K G Hc H I M R Rs Rm Rc S O	
227	**Williams Blackstock Architects** www.wba-architects.com	👥	AL	E M S W C G	A D E G I L P U O	C E K G Hc H I M R Rs Rm Rc S O	
	Wilson Architects www.wilsonarch.com	👥	MA	E M S W C G	A D E G I L P U O	C E K G Hc H I M R Rs Rm Rc S O	
284	**Wilson Architectural Group** www.wilsonargroup.com	👥	TX	E M S W C G	A D E G I L P U O	C E K G Hc H I M R Rs Rm Rc S O	
57	**Wilson Associates** www.wilsonassociates.com	👥👥	TX	E M S W C G	A D E G I L P U O	C E K G Hc H I M R Rs Rm Rc S O	
	Wnuk Spurlock www.wnukspurlock.com	👤	DC	E M S W C G	A D E G I L P U O	C E K G Hc H I M R Rs Rm Rc S O	
	Wold Architects & Engineers www.woldae.com	👥👥	MN	E M S W C G	A D E G I L P U O	C E K G Hc H I M R Rs Rm Rc S O	
	Wolfberg Alvarez & Partners www.wolfbergalvarez.com	👤	FL	E M S W C G	A D E G I L P U O	C E K G Hc H I M R Rs Rm Rc S O	
	Woolpert www.woolpert.com	👥👥👥	OH	E M S W C G	A D E G I L P U O	C E K G Hc H I M R Rs Rm Rc S O	
158	**Workshop Architects** www.workshoparchitects.com	👤	WI	E M S W C G	A D E G I L P U O	C E K G Hc H I M R Rs Rm Rc S O	
	Worn Jerabek Wiltse Architects www.wjaworks.com	👤	IL	E M S W C G	A D E G I L P U O	C E K G Hc H I M R Rs Rm Rc S O	
	WorthGroup Architects www.worthgroup.com	👥	CO	E M S W C G	A D E G I L P U O	C E K G Hc H I M R Rs Rm Rc S O	
	WRT www.wrtdesign.com	👥👥	PA	E M S W C G	A D E G I L P U O	C E K G Hc H I M R Rs Rm Rc S O	
	WTW Architects www.wtwarchitects.com	👥	PA	E M S W C G	A D E G I L P U O	C E K G Hc H I M R Rs Rm Rc S O	
X	**XTEN Architecture** www.xtenarchitecture.com	👤	CA	E M S W C G	A D E G I L P U O	C E K G Hc H I M R Rs Rm Rc S O	
Y	**YFH Architects** www.yfharchitects.com	👤	HI	E M S W C G	A D E G I L P U O	C E K G Hc H I M R Rs Rm Rc S O	
226	**Yost Grube Hall Architecture** www.ygh.com	👥	OR	E M S W C G	A D E G I L P U O	C E K G Hc H I M R Rs Rm Rc S O	

Size
- 👤 Small — 20 employees or less
- 👥 Medium — 21–100 employees
- 👥👥👥 Large — 101–450 employees
- 👥👥👥👥 Extra Large — 451+ employees

Regions East (E), Midwest (M), South (S), West (W), Canada (C), Global (G)

Services Architecture (A), Design/Build (D), Engineering-MEP (E), Graphic Design (G), Interior Design (I), Landscape Architecture (L), Planning (P), Urban Design (U), Other-including Industrial Design (O)

Markets Corporate (C), Higher Ed. (E), K-12 (K), Government (G), Healthcare (Hc), Hospitality (H), Industrial/Tech. (I), Museum/Cultural (M), Religious (R), Residential-Single (Rs), Residential-Multi. (Rm), Retail/Commercial (Rc), Sports (S), Other (O)

Rank	Firm/Web	Size	HQ	Regions	Services	Markets	DI Index
Z	**Zeidler** www.zeidlerpartnership.com	👤👤👤	CAN	E M S W C G	A D E G I L P U O	C E K G Hc H I M R Rs Rm Rc S O	▪▪▪▪▪
19	**ZGF Architects** www.zgf.com	👤👤👤👤	OR	E M S W C G	A D E G I L P U O	C E K G Hc H I M R Rs Rm Rc S O	▪▪▪▪▪
	Ziegler Cooper Architects www.zieglercooper.com	👤👤	TX	E M S W C G	A D E G I L P U O	C E K G Hc H I M R Rs Rm Rc S O	▪▪▪▪
	Ziger/Snead Architects www.zigersnead.com	👤	MD	E M S W C G	A D E G I L P U O	C E K G Hc H I M R Rs Rm Rc S O	▪▪▪▪
	Zimmerman Architectural Studios www.zastudios.com	👤👤👤	WI	E M S W C G	A D E G I L P U O	C E K G Hc H I M R Rs Rm Rc S O	▪▪▪▪
	Zyscovich www.zyscovich.com	👤👤👤	FL	E M S W C G	A D E G I L P U O	C E K G Hc H I M R Rs Rm Rc S O	▪▪▪▪

DI Brand Recognition Index

▪▪▪▪▪ Top tier global and categorical leader recognition

▪▪▪▪ Exceptional national and categorical leader recognition

▪▪▪ Strong regional and categorical leader recognition

▪▪ Notable and growing with emerging categorical recognition

▪ Professional practice notable in city and region

DesignIntelligence 333 |

This chapter features a ranking of America's
top 333 architecture firms, along with useful
contact information and pertinent data.

DesignIntelligence 333

The *DesignIntelligence* 333 ranks the top 333 architecture and design firms in North America. To compile the most accurate and up-to-date information, firms throughout the United States and Canada were surveyed during the spring and summer of 2014. Under the direction of the editors, extensive research was conducted by the *Almanac* staff and the research staff of *DesignIntelligence* to compile a comprehensive geographically and demographically diverse group of firms that would qualify for inclusion. Professional associations, media lists, client organizations, and conference registrations of the Design Futures Council were also studied to determine the most active leading firms. *DesignIntelligence* also researched additional media sources, such as leading professional and business publications read by clients in each of the areas of specialty.

The firms were mailed a letter inviting them to participate in the survey, along with a copy of the survey. The survey asked for information regarding their areas of specialty, employment counts, number of offices, fields of professional practice, 2014 gross professional fee revenues, leading officers of the firms, and other relevant information. The data collected was also used for the *Almanac*'s Directory of North America's Top 1,000 Architecture & Design Firms.

Telephone calls and emails followed mailed surveys if additional information was needed. Each firm included in this *Almanac* was contacted a minimum of three times by mail, email, or telephone. When firms did not respond, estimates were made based on previous surveys completed by the firms for *DesignIntelligence*, listings in business media, and private research databases, reliable information on the Internet regarding employee counts, and other credible sources. At least three independent sources were used to estimate gross revenues when the firms did not supply these figures. Blank fields in the ranking section or missing profile information were due to the firm not returning its survey. The number of reported firm locations and actual locations may differ. Totals may not equal 100 percent due to rounding.

To fill out a survey for next year's Almanac, visit www.di.net/almanac/, call Design-Intelligence at (678) 879-0929, or contact the editor at jwolford@di.net.

Note: n/p = not provided

Shanghai Tower, Shanghai, China | Gensler

1 | Gensler

2 Harrison Street
San Francisco, CA 94105
(415) 433-3700
www.gensler.com
Andy Cohen, Co-CEO
Diane Hoskins, Co-CEO

WORLDWIDE REVENUE	$1,100,000,000
US REVENUE	$803,000,000
WORLDWIDE STAFF	3,700
HEADQUARTERS	San Francisco, CA
YEAR ESTABLISHED	1966
RECENT REPRESENTATIVE PROJECT	

L.A. Live, Los Angeles, CA

GEOGRAPHIC ANALYSIS OF WORK IN THE US

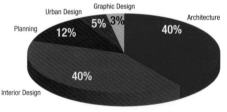

GEOGRAPHIC ANALYSIS OF WORK OUTSIDE THE US

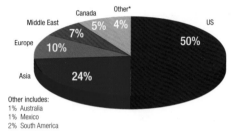

Other includes:
1% Australia
1% Mexico
2% South America

PRIMARY SERVICES OFFERED

MARKET SEGMENTS

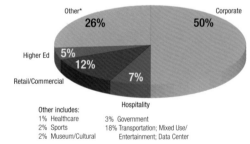

Other includes:
1% Healthcare
2% Sports
2% Museum/Cultural
3% Government
18% Transportation; Mixed Use/
    Entertainment; Data Center

LOCATIONS INCLUDE

Atlanta, GA	Los Angeles, CA	San Francisco, CA	Hong Kong, China
Austin, TX	Miami, CA	San Jose, CA	Mexico City, Mexico
Baltimore, MD	Minneapolis, MN	Seattle, WA	San José, Costa Rica
Boston, MA	Morristown, NJ	Tampa, FL	São Paulo, Brazil
Charlotte, NC	New York, NY	Washington, DC	Seoul, South Korea
Chicago, IL	Newport Beach, RI	Abu Dhabi, UAE	Shanghai, China
Dallas, TX	Oakland, CA	Doha, Qatar	Singapore
Denver, CO	Philadelphia, PA	Dubai, UAE	Sydney, Australia
Detroit, MI	Phoenix, AZ	London, UK	Tokyo, Japan
Houston, TX	Pittsburgh, PA	Bangalore, India	Toronto, ON, Canada
La Crosse, WI	Raleigh-Durham, NC	Bangkok, Thailand	
Las Vegas, NV	San Diego, CA	Beijing, China	**Gensler**

2 | AECOM (Architecture)

1999 Avenue of the Stars, Suite 2600
Los Angeles, CA 90067
(213) 593-8100
www.aecom.com
Michael Burke, Chairman/CEO
Stephen Kadenacy, President/CFO

WORLDWIDE REVENUE	$801,000,000
US REVENUE	$360,700,000
WORLDWIDE STAFF	87,225
HEADQUARTERS	Los Angeles, CA
YEAR ESTABLISHED	1990
RECENT REPRESENTATIVE PROJECT	

Bejing Yanyi Lake Capital Guesthouse,
Beijing, China

GEOGRAPHIC ANALYSIS OF WORK IN THE US

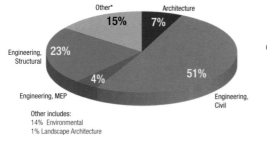

GEOGRAPHIC ANALYSIS OF WORK OUTSIDE THE US

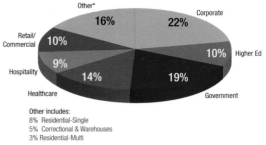

Other includes:
7% Austrailia
1% South America
1% Other

PRIMARY SERVICES OFFERED

Other includes:
14% Environmental
1% Landscape Architecture

MARKET SEGMENTS

Other includes:
8% Residential-Single
5% Correctional & Warehouses
3% Residential-Multi

LOCATIONS INCLUDE

Main Offices include ---
Los Angeles, CA
New York, NY
Abu Dhabi, UAE
Brisbane, Australia
Hong Kong, China
London, UK
Moscow, Russia

3 | Jacobs (Architecture)

155 North Lake Avenue
Pasadena, CA 91101
(626) 578-3500
www.jacobs.com
H. Thomas McDuffie Jr., Group Vice President
Michael Lorenz, VP
Brad Simmons, National Design Operations
Thanyapat Cholvibul, Sr. Design Operations

WORLDWIDE REVENUE	$435,000,000
US REVENUE	$295,970,000
WORLDWIDE STAFF	2,549
HEADQUARTERS	Pasadena, CA
YEAR ESTABLISHED	1947

RECENT REPRESENTATIVE PROJECT
FDA Biodefense Laboratory Complex,
White Oak, MD

GEOGRAPHIC ANALYSIS OF WORK IN THE US

GEOGRAPHIC ANALYSIS OF WORK OUTSIDE THE US

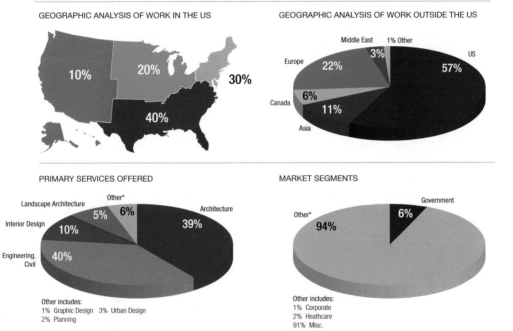

PRIMARY SERVICES OFFERED

Other includes:
1% Graphic Design   3% Urban Design
2% Planning

MARKET SEGMENTS

Other includes:
1% Corporate
2% Heathcare
91% Misc.

LOCATIONS INCLUDE

Arlington, VA
Atlanta, GA
Austin, TX
Baltimore, MD
Boston, MA
Charleston, SC
Chicago, IL
Cincinnati, OH
Dallas, TX
Denver, CO
Honolulu, HI
Houston, TX
Indianapolis, IN
Irvine, CA
Las Vegas, NV

Los Angeles, CA
Louisville, KY
Madison, WI
Miami, FL
Minneapolis, MN
Nashville, TN
New York, NY
Oklahoma City, OK
Orlando, FL
Philadelphia, PA
Phoenix, AZ
Pittsburgh, PA
Portland, OR
Providence, RI

Raleigh, NC
Sacramento, CA
Salt Lake City, UT
San Antonio, TX
San Diego, CA
San Francisco, CA
Seattle, WA
St. Louis, MO
Tampa, FL
Tucson, AZ
Tulsa, OK
Washington, DC
Abu Dhabi, UAE
Al-Khobar, Saudi Arabia

Antwerp, Belgium
Athens, Greece
Aylesbury, UK
Beijing, China
Birmingham, UK
Calgary, Canada
Hong Kong, China
Leeds, UK
London, UK
Madrid, Spain
Melbourne, Australia

Milan, Italy
Moscow, Russia
Mumbai, India
New Delhi, India
Paris, France
Shanghai, China
Singapore
Toronto, ON, Canada
Vancouver, BC, Canada

Anaheim Regional Transportation Intermodal Center, Anaheim, CA | HOK

4 | HOK

10 South Broadway, Suite 200
St. Louis, MO 63102
(314) 421-2000
www.hok.com
Patrick MacLeamy, Chairman/CEO
Bill Hellmuth, President

WORLDWIDE REVENUE	$416,549,000
US REVENUE	$278,380,000
WORLDWIDE STAFF	1,600
HEADQUARTERS	St. Louis, MO
YEAR ESTABLISHED	1955
RECENT REPRESENTATIVE PROJECT	

Hamad International Airport Passenger
Terminal Complex, Doha, Qatar

GEOGRAPHIC ANALYSIS OF WORK IN THE US

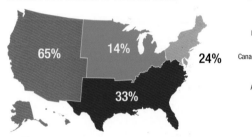

GEOGRAPHIC ANALYSIS OF WORK OUTSIDE THE US

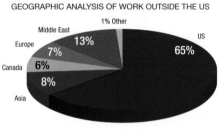

1% Other
Middle East 13%
Europe 7%
Canada 6%
8% Asia
US 65%

PRIMARY SERVICES OFFERED

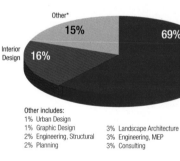

Other* 15%
Architecture 69%
Interior Design 16%

Other includes:
1% Urban Design
1% Graphic Design
2% Engineering, Structural
2% Planning
3% Landscape Architecture
3% Engineering, MEP
3% Consulting

MARKET SEGMENTS

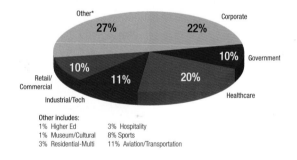

Other* 27%
Corporate 22%
Government 10%
Healthcare 20%
Industrial/Tech 11%
Retail/Commercial 10%

Other includes:
1% Higher Ed
1% Museum/Cultural
3% Residential-Multi
3% Hospitality
8% Sports
11% Aviation/Transportation

LOCATIONS INCLUDE

Atlanta, GA	New York, NY	Calgary, AB, Canada	Toronto, ON, Canada
Chicago, IL	Philadelphia, PA	Dubai, UAE	Vancouver, BC, Canada
Columbus, OH	San Francisco, CA	Hong Kong, China	
Dallas, TX	Seattle, WA	London, UK	
Houston, TX	St. Louis, MO	Mumbai, India	
Kansas City, MO	Tampa, FL	Ottawa, ON, Canada	
Los Angeles, CA	Washington, DC	Shanghai, China	
Miami, FL	Beijing, China		

© Adrian Smith + Gordon Gill Architecture /photograph by Nampoong Sun

FKI Tower, Seoul, South Korea | Adrian Smith + Gordon Gill

5 | Callison RTKL

1717 Pacific Avenue
Dallas,TX 75201
(214) 468-7600
www.rtkl.com
Lance Josal, CEO
Randall Pace, CFO
Bryceon Sumner, COO

WORLDWIDE REVENUE	$390,285,403
US REVENUE	$180,106,235
WORLDWIDE STAFF	2,183
HEADQUARTERS	Seattle, WA
YEAR ESTABLISHED	1946
RECENT REPRESENTATIVE PROJECT	

San Antonio Military Medical Center
(SAMMC), San Antonio, TX

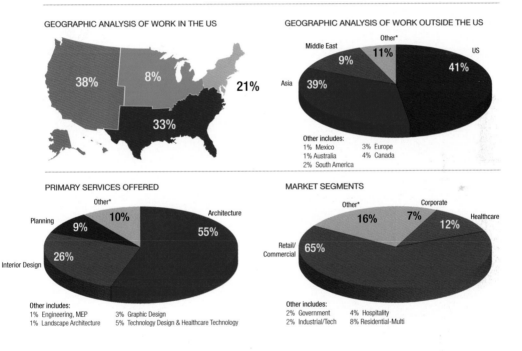

GEOGRAPHIC ANALYSIS OF WORK IN THE US

38% | 8% | 21% | 33%

GEOGRAPHIC ANALYSIS OF WORK OUTSIDE THE US

Other* 11%
Middle East 9%
US 41%
Asia 39%

Other includes:
1% Mexico   3% Europe
1% Australia   4% Canada
2% South America

PRIMARY SERVICES OFFERED

Other* 10%
Planning 9%
Architecture 55%
Interior Design 26%

Other includes:
1% Engineering, MEP   3% Graphic Design
1% Landscape Architecture   5% Technology Design & Healthcare Technology

MARKET SEGMENTS

Other* 16%
Corporate 7%
Healthcare 12%
Retail/ Commercial 65%

Other includes:
2% Government   4% Hospitality
2% Industrial/Tech   8% Residential-Multi

LOCATIONS INCLUDE

Baltimore, MD
Chicago, IL
Dallas, TX
Los Angeles, CA
Miami, FL
New York, NY
Seattle, WA

Scottsdale, AZ
Washington, DC
Abu Dhabi, UAE
Beijing, China
Dubai, UAE
Guangzhou, China
Hong Kong, China

Jeddah, Saudi
   Arabia
London, UK
Mexico City, Mexico
São Paulo, Brazil
Shanghai, China
Toronto, Canada

CALLISONRTKL
A DESIGN CONSULTANCY OF ARCADIS

Nic Lehoux

VanDusen Botanical Garden Visitor Centre, Vancouver, British Columbia, Canada | Perkins + Will

6 | Perkins+Will

330 North Wabash Avenue, Suite 3600
Chicago, IL 60611
(312) 755-0770
www.perkinswill.com
Phil Harrison, President/CEO
Tyson Curcio, COO
Joseph Dailey, CFO

WORLDWIDE REVENUE	$350,000,000
US REVENUE	$194,000,000
WORLDWIDE STAFF	1,515
HEADQUARTERS	23 Global Offices
YEAR ESTABLISHED	1935

RECENT REPRESENTATIVE PROJECT

Texas Children's Hospital Jan & Dan Duncan
Neurological Institute, Houston, TX

GEOGRAPHIC ANALYSIS OF WORK IN THE US

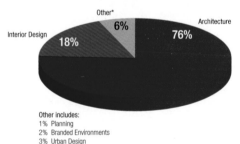

15%   22%   16%
47%

GEOGRAPHIC ANALYSIS OF WORK OUTSIDE THE US

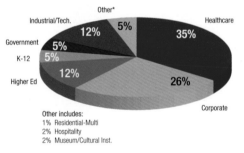

Other*
Canada   8%   US
7%   75%
Middle   10%
East

Other includes:
1% South America   3% Europe
1% Mexico   3% Asia

PRIMARY SERVICES OFFERED

Other*
6%   Architecture
Interior Design   76%
18%

Other includes:
1% Planning
2% Branded Environments
3% Urban Design

MARKET SEGMENTS

Other*
Industrial/Tech.   5%   Healthcare
12%   35%
Government 5%
K-12 5%
12%   26%
Higher Ed
Corporate

Other includes:
1% Residential-Multi
2% Hospitality
2% Museum/Cultural Inst.

LOCATIONS INCLUDE

Atlanta, GA
Austin, TX
Boston, MA
Charlotte, NC
Chicago, IL
Dallas, TX
Houston, TX
Los Angeles, CA

Miami, FL
Minneapolis, MN
New York, NY
Research Triangle
    Park, NC
San Francisco, CA
Seattle, WA
Washington, DC

Dubai, UAE
Dundas, ON,
    Canada
London, UK
Ottawa, ON,
    Canada
São Paulo, Brazil
Shanghai, China

Toronto, ON,
    Canada
Vancouver, BC,
    Canada

PERKINS
+WILL

© 2014 Mark Herboth Photography, LLC

Sheikh Zayed Bin Sultan Al Nahyan Building for Personalized Cancer Care, MD Anderson Cancer Center, University of Texas, Houston, TX | HDR

7 | HDR

8404 Indian Hills Drive
Omaha, NE 68114
(402) 399-1000
www.hdrarchitecture.com
Doug S. Wignall, President
Michael Moran, Director of Operations, Domestic
Scott Butler, Director of Operations, International
Tom Vandeveer, Director of Professional Services

WORLDWIDE REVENUE	$331,450,000
US REVENUE	$251,100,000
WORLDWIDE STAFF	1,412
HEADQUARTERS	Omaha, NE
YEAR ESTABLISHED	1917

RECENT REPRESENTATIVE PROJECT

Parkland Hospital,
Dallas, TX

GEOGRAPHIC ANALYSIS OF WORK IN THE US

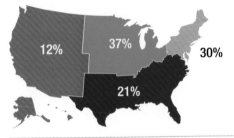

GEOGRAPHIC ANALYSIS OF WORK OUTSIDE THE US

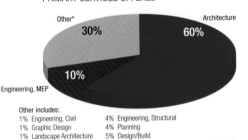

Other* 12%
US 73%
Canada 15%

Other includes:
2% Asia   4% Middle East
2% Australia   4% Europe

PRIMARY SERVICES OFFERED

Other* 30%
Architecture 60%
Engineering, MEP 10%

Other includes:
1% Engineering, Civil   4% Engineering, Structural
1% Graphic Design   4% Planning
1% Landscape Architecture   5% Design/Build
2% Urban Design   9% Product Design, Sustainable Design, Consulting
3% Interior Design

MARKET SEGMENTS

Other* 21%
Higher Ed 6%
Government 14%
Healthcare 59%

Other includes:
1% Sports   2% Retail/Commercial
2% Corporate   16% Science & Technology

LOCATIONS INCLUDE

Alexandria, VA	Lexington, KY	Sacramento, CA	Dubai, UAE
Atlanta, GA	Lincoln, NE	San Antonio, TX	Kingston, ON, Canada
Bethesda, MD	Los Angeles, CA	San Diego, CA	London, ON, Canada
Boise, ID	New York, NY	San Francisco, CA	London, UK
Boston, MA	Oklahoma City, OK	Seattle, WA	Ottawa, ON, Canada
Charleston, SC	Omaha, NE	St. Paul, MN	Shanghai, China
Charlotte, NC	Orlando, FL	Tacoma, WA	Sydney, Australia
Chicago, IL	Phoenix, AZ	Tampa, FL	Toronto, ON, Canada
Dallas, TX	Portland, OR	Tucson, AZ	
Denver, CO	Princeton, NJ	Abu Dhabi, UAE	
Houston, TX	Rochester, MN	Beijing, China	

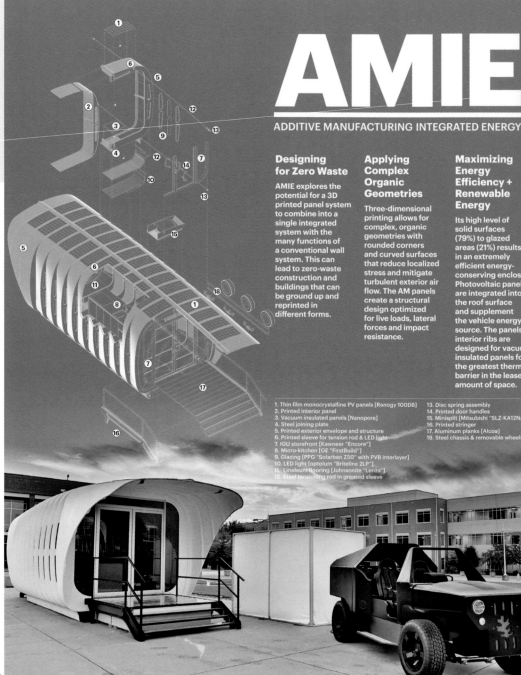

AMIE

ADDITIVE MANUFACTURING INTEGRATED ENERGY

Designing for Zero Waste

AMIE explores the potential for a 3D printed panel system to combine into a single integrated system with the many functions of a conventional wall system. This can lead to zero-waste construction and buildings that can be ground up and reprinted in different forms.

Applying Complex Organic Geometries

Three-dimensional printing allows for complex, organic geometries with rounded corners and curved surfaces that reduce localized stress and mitigate turbulent exterior air flow. The AM panels create a structural design optimized for live loads, lateral forces and impact resistance.

Maximizing Energy Efficiency + Renewable Energy

Its high level of solid surfaces (79%) to glazed areas (21%) results in an extremely efficient energy-conserving enclosure. Photovoltaic panels are integrated into the roof surface and supplement the vehicle energy source. The panels' interior ribs are designed for vacuum insulated panels for the greatest thermal barrier in the least amount of space.

1. Thin film monocrystalline PV panels [Renogy 100DB]
2. Printed interior panel
3. Vacuum insulated panels [Nanopore]
4. Steel joining plate
5. Printed exterior envelope and structure
6. Printed sleeve for tension rod & LED light
7. IGU storefront [Kawneer "Encore"]
8. Micro-kitchen [GE "FirstBuild"]
9. Glazing [PPG "Solarban Z50" with PVB interlayer]
10. LED light [optolum "Briteline 2LP"]
11. Linoleum flooring [Johnsonite "Lenza"]
12. Steel tensioning rod in greased sleeve
13. Disc spring assembly
14. Printed door handles
15. Minisplit [Mitsubishi "SLZ-KA12NA"]
16. Printed stringer
17. Aluminum planks [Alcoa]
18. Steel chassis & removable wheels

AMIE (Additive Manufacturing Integrated Energy), Oak Ridge National Laboratory, TN | SOM

8 | Skidmore, Owings & Merrill

224 South Michigan Avenue
Chicago, IL 60604
(312) 554-9090
www.som.com
Gary Haney, Partner
Jeffrey J. McCarthy, Partner
Gene Schnair, Partner

WORLDWIDE REVENUE	$330,000,000
US REVENUE	$168,000,000
WORLDWIDE STAFF	786
HEADQUARTERS	Chicago, IL
YEAR ESTABLISHED	1936

RECENT REPRESENTATIVE PROJECT

UCSF Neurosciences Lab & Clinical
Research Bldg 19A, San Francisco, CA

GEOGRAPHIC ANALYSIS OF WORK IN THE US

17%
12%
69%
2%

GEOGRAPHIC ANALYSIS OF WORK OUTSIDE THE US

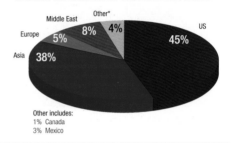

Other* 4%
Middle East 8%
Europe 5%
Asia 38%
US 45%

Other includes:
1% Canada
3% Mexico

PRIMARY SERVICES OFFERED

1% Graphic Design
Planning 7%
Interior Design 6%
Architecture 75%
Engineering, Civil 11%

MARKET SEGMENTS

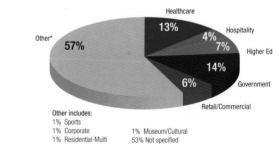

Healthcare 13%
Hospitality 4%
Higher Ed 7%
Government 14%
Retail/Commercial 6%
Other* 57%

Other includes:
1% Sports
1% Corporate
1% Residential-Multi
1% Museum/Cultural
53% Not specified

LOCATIONS INCLUDE

Chicago, IL
Los Angeles, CA
New York, NY
San Francisco, CA

Hong Kong, China
London, UK
Shanghai, China

SOM

Nutrabolt Corporate Headquarters, Bryan, TX | The Beck Group (Architecture)

SaRang Community Church, Seoul, South Korea | The Beck Group (Architecture)

9 | Stantec Architecture (US)

10160 112 Street
Edmonton, Alberta Canada
(780) 917-7000
www.stantec.com
Richard K Allen, President/CEO
Stantis Smith, Executive VP
Anton Germishuizen, Senior VP
Bruce Knepper, VP/Secretary

WORLDWIDE REVENUE	$319,990,974
US REVENUE	$127,513,422
WORLDWIDE STAFF	745
HEADQUARTERS	Edmonton, Alberta, Canada
YEAR ESTABLISHED	1954
RECENT REPRESENTATIVE PROJECT	

UCSF Mission Bay Hospital,
San Francisco, CA

GEOGRAPHIC ANALYSIS OF WORK IN THE US

GEOGRAPHIC ANALYSIS OF WORK OUTSIDE THE US

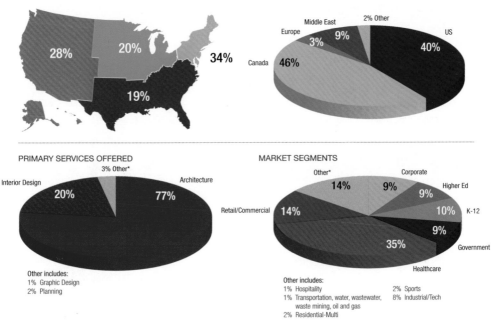

GEOGRAPHIC ANALYSIS OF WORK IN THE US
28% 20% 34% 19%

GEOGRAPHIC ANALYSIS OF WORK OUTSIDE THE US
Middle East 9% — 2% Other
Europe 3%
Canada 46%
US 40%

PRIMARY SERVICES OFFERED
3% Other*
Interior Design 20%
Architecture 77%

Other includes:
1% Graphic Design
2% Planning

MARKET SEGMENTS
Other* 14%
Corporate 9%
Higher Ed 9%
K-12 10%
Government 9%
Healthcare 35%
Retail/Commercial 14%

Other includes:
1% Hospitality
1% Transportation, water, wastewater,
   waste mining, oil and gas
2% Residential-Multi
2% Sports
8% Industrial/Tech

LOCATIONS INCLUDE

Boston, MA
Boulder, CO
Butler, PA
Cleveland, OH
Columbus, OH
Philadelphia, PA -
   Spring Garden
Pittsburgh, PA
Redlands, CA

State College, PA
Washington, DC
Abu Dhabi, UAE
Ahmedabad, India
Calgary, AB, Canada
Doha, Qatar
Dubai, UAE
Edmonton, AB, Canada
Hamilton, ON, Canada

Kamloops, BC, Canada
London, UK
Ottawa, ON, Canada
Regina, SK, Canada
Saskatoon, SK,
   Canada
Toronto, ON, Canada
Vancouver, BC, Canada
Victoria, BC, Canada

Winnipeg, MB, Canada
Yellowknife, NT,
   Canada

Stantec

JW Marriott, Austin, TX | HKS, Inc.

10 | HKS, Inc.

350 North Saint Paul Street, Suite 100
Dallas, TX 75201
(214) 969-5599
www.hksinc.com
Ralph Hawkins, Chairman/CEO
Dan Noble, President/CEO
Craig Beale, Executive VP
Nunzio DeSantis, Executive VP

WORLDWIDE REVENUE	$285,000,000
US REVENUE	$225,000,000
WORLDWIDE STAFF	1,200
HEADQUARTERS	Dallas, TX
YEAR ESTABLISHED	1939
RECENT REPRESENTATIVE PROJECT	

Minnesota Vikings Stadium,
Minneapolis, MN

GEOGRAPHIC ANALYSIS OF WORK IN THE US

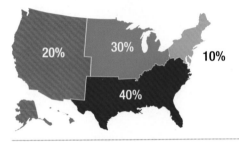

20% 30% 10%
40%

GEOGRAPHIC ANALYSIS OF WORK OUTSIDE THE US

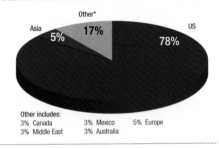

Other* 17%
Asia 5%
US 78%

Other includes:
3% Canada   3% Mexico   5% Europe
3% Middle East   3% Australia

PRIMARY SERVICES OFFERED

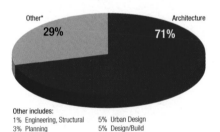

Other* 29%
Architecture 71%

Other includes:
1% Engineering, Structural   5% Urban Design
3% Planning   5% Design/Build
5% Engineering, MEP   10% Graphic Design

MARKET SEGMENTS

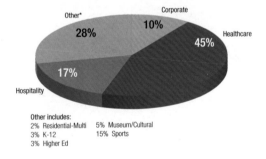

Other* 28%
Corporate 10%
Healthcare 45%
Hospitality 17%

Other includes:
2% Residential-Multi   5% Museum/Cultural
3% K-12   15% Sports
3% Higher Ed

LOCATIONS INCLUDE

Atlanta, GA	Los Angeles, CA	San Diego, CA	São Paulo, Brazil
Chicago, IL	Miami, FL	San Francisco, CA	Shanghai, China
Dallas, TX	New York, NY	Tampa, FL	Singapore
Denver, CO	Orange County, CA	Washington, DC	
Detroit, MI	Orlando, FL	Abu Dhabi, UAE	
Fort Worth, TX	Phoenix, AZ	London, UK	
Houston, TX	Richmond, VA	Mexico City, Mexico	
Indianapolis, IN	Salt Lake City, UT	New Delhi, India	

HKS

Grischa Ruschendorf

Hysan Place, Hong Kong | Kohn Pedersen Fox

11 | Kohn Pedersen Fox

11 West 42nd Street
New York, NY 10036
(212) 977-6500
www.kpf.com
A. Eugene Kohn, Chairman
Paul Katz, Managing Principal
James von Klemperer, Design Principal

WORLDWIDE REVENUE	$220,000,000
US REVENUE	$55,000,000
WORLDWIDE STAFF	500
HEADQUARTERS	New York, NY
YEAR ESTABLISHED	1976
RECENT REPRESENTATIVE PROJECT	University of Michigan Ross School of Business, Ann Arbor, MI

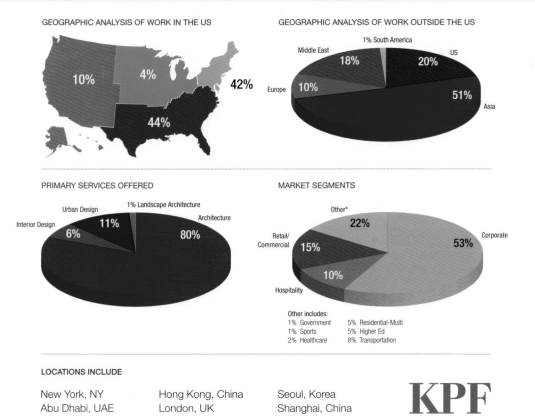

GEOGRAPHIC ANALYSIS OF WORK IN THE US

10% 4% 42% 44%

GEOGRAPHIC ANALYSIS OF WORK OUTSIDE THE US

1% South America
Middle East 18% US 20%
Europe 10% Asia 51%

PRIMARY SERVICES OFFERED

1% Landscape Architecture
Urban Design
Interior Design
Architecture
6% 11% 80%

MARKET SEGMENTS

Other* 22%
Retail/Commercial 15%
Hospitality 10%
Corporate 53%

Other includes:
1% Government   5% Residential-Multi
1% Sports   5% Higher Ed
2% Healthcare   8% Transportation

LOCATIONS INCLUDE

New York, NY
Abu Dhabi, UAE

Hong Kong, China
London, UK

Seoul, Korea
Shanghai, China

KPF

12 | SmithGroupJJR

500 Griswold Street, Suite 1700
Detroit, MI 48226
(313) 983-3600
www.smithgroupjjr.com
David R.H. King, Chairman/Design Director
Carl Roehling, President/CEO
Randal Swiech, COO

WORLDWIDE REVENUE	$190,000,000
US REVENUE	$184,000,000
WORLDWIDE STAFF	750
HEADQUARTERS	11 Global Offices
YEAR ESTABLISHED	1853
RECENT REPRESENTATIVE PROJECT	
Chandler City Hall, Chandler, AZ	

GEOGRAPHIC ANALYSIS OF WORK IN THE US

GEOGRAPHIC ANALYSIS OF WORK OUTSIDE THE US

PRIMARY SERVICES OFFERED

MARKET SEGMENTS

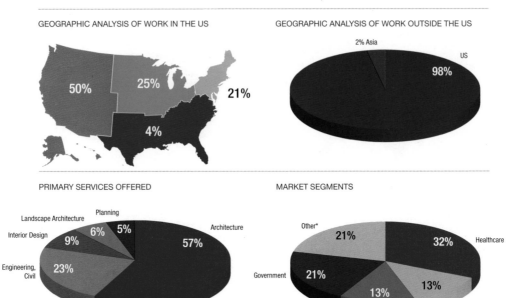

GEOGRAPHIC ANALYSIS OF WORK IN THE US: 50%, 25%, 21%, 4%

GEOGRAPHIC ANALYSIS OF WORK OUTSIDE THE US: 2% Asia, US 98%

PRIMARY SERVICES OFFERED: Landscape Architecture, Planning, Interior Design, Engineering, Civil, Architecture 57%, Engineering, Civil 23%, Interior Design 9%, Landscape Architecture 6%, Planning 5%

MARKET SEGMENTS: Other* 21%, Healthcare 32%, Government 21%, Corporate 13%, Higher Ed 13%, Other includes: 4% Museum/Cultural, 17% Science & Technology

LOCATIONS INCLUDE

Ann Arbor, MI
Chicago, IL
Dallas, TX
Detroit, MI

Los Angeles, CA
Madison, WI
Phoenix, AZ
San Francisco, CA

Washington, DC
Shanghai, China

SMITHGROUP JJR

13 | Perkins Eastman

115 Fifth Avenue
New York, NY 10003
(212) 353-7200
www.perkinseastman.com
Bradford Perkins, Chairman
Mary-Jean Eastman, Managing Principal

WORLDWIDE REVENUE	$185,000,000
US REVENUE	$139,000,000
WORLDWIDE STAFF	950
HEADQUARTERS	New York, NY
YEAR ESTABLISHED	1981

RECENT REPRESENTATIVE PROJECT

Dunbar High School,
Washington, D.C.

GEOGRAPHIC ANALYSIS OF WORK IN THE US

15%   4%   70%

11%

GEOGRAPHIC ANALYSIS OF WORK OUTSIDE THE US

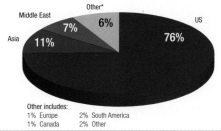

Other*
Middle East   6%   US
7%   76%
Asia   11%

Other includes:
1% Europe   2% South America
1% Canada   2% Other

PRIMARY SERVICES OFFERED

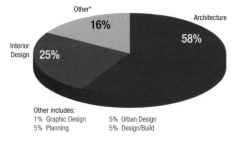

Other*
16%   Architecture
58%
Interior Design
25%

Other includes:
1% Graphic Design   5% Urban Design
5% Planning   5% Design/Build

MARKET SEGMENTS

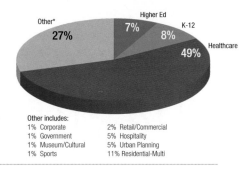

Other*   Higher Ed
27%   7%   K-12
8%
Healthcare
49%

Other includes:
1% Corporate   2% Retail/Commercial
1% Government   5% Hospitality
1% Museum/Cultural   5% Urban Planning
1% Sports   11% Residential-Multi

LOCATIONS INCLUDE

Boston, MA	Pittsburgh, PA	Guayaquil, Ecuador
Charlotte, NC	San Francisco, CA	Mumbai, India
Chicago, IL	Stamford, CT	Shanghai, China
Los Angeles, CA	Washington, DC	Toronto, ON,
New York, NY	Dubai, UAE	Canada

Perkins Eastman

Scott Frances

Dickinson College, Kline Athletic Center, Carlisle, PA | CannonDesign

CannonDesign

University of Utah, Lassonde Studios, Salt Lake City, UT | CannonDesign

14 | CannonDesign

225 North Michigan Avenue, Suite 1100
Chicago IL, 60601
(312) 332-9600
www.cannondesign.com
Gary Miller, Chairman/CEO
Kevin Sticht, COO
David Carlino, CFO

WORLDWIDE REVENUE	$183,800,000
US REVENUE	$153,000,000
WORLDWIDE STAFF	950
HEADQUARTERS	17 Global Offices
YEAR ESTABLISHED	1945
RECENT REPRESENTATIVE PROJECT	

St. Louis Public Library, Central Library,
St. Louis, MO

GEOGRAPHIC ANALYSIS OF WORK IN THE US

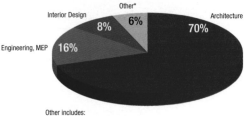

GEOGRAPHIC ANALYSIS OF WORK OUTSIDE THE US

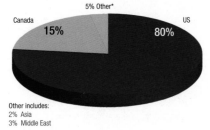

Other includes:
2% Asia
3% Middle East

PRIMARY SERVICES OFFERED

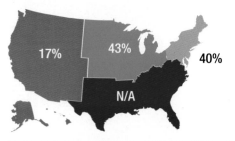

Other includes:
3% Engineering, Structural
3% Design/Build

MARKET SEGMENTS

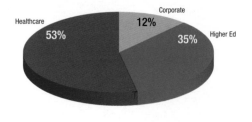

LOCATIONS INCLUDE

Baltimore, MD
Boston, MA
Buffalo, NY
Chicago, IL
Los Angeles, CA
New York, NY
Phoenix, AZ

Pittsburgh, PA
San Francisco, CA
St. Louis, MO
Washington, DC
Abu Dhabi, UAE
Montreal, QC,
    Canada

Mumbai, India
Toronto, ON,
    Canada
Vancouver, BC,
    Canada

CANNONDESIGN

University Medical Center, New Orleans, LA | NBBJ

15 | NBBJ

223 Yale Avenue North
Seattle, WA 98109
(206) 223-5555
www.nbbj.com
Steven McConnell, Managing Partner
Jonathan Ward, Design Partner
Juli Cook, COO
Tim Leberecht, CMO

WORLDWIDE REVENUE	$175,900,000
US REVENUE	$121,500,000
WORLDWIDE STAFF	700
HEADQUARTERS	Seattle, WA
YEAR ESTABLISHED	1943

RECENT REPRESENTATIVE PROJECT

China Trust Commercial Bank Headqtrs.,
Taipei, Taiwan

GEOGRAPHIC ANALYSIS OF WORK IN THE US

63%
11%
15%
11%

GEOGRAPHIC ANALYSIS OF WORK OUTSIDE THE US

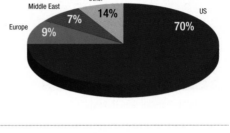

Other
Middle East
14%
US
Europe 7%
9%
70%

PRIMARY SERVICES OFFERED

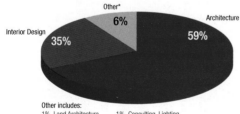

Other*
6%
Architecture
Interior Design
35%
59%

Other includes:
1% Land Architecture   1% Consulting, Lighting
1% Graphic Design   2% Planning
1% Urban Design

MARKET SEGMENTS

Other*
Retail/Commercial 5%   Corporate
12%   18%
Industrial/Tech 6%   7% Higher Ed
8%
44%   Government

Healthcare

Other includes:
1% Sports
4% Urban Design, Planning, EGD

LOCATIONS INCLUDE

Boston, MA	San Francisco, CA	London, UK
Columbus, OH	Seattle, WA	Pune, India
Los Angeles, CA	Beijing, China	Shanghai, China
New York, NY	Hong Kong	

LEO A DALY

Embry-Riddle Aeronautical University, College of Arts & Sciences, Daytona, FL | Leo A Daly

LEO A DALY

Toro Company Corporate Headquarters, Bloomington, MN | Leo A Daly

16 | LEO A DALY

8600 Indian Hills Drive
Omaha, NE 68114
(402) 391-8111
www.leodaly.com
Leo A. Daly III, Chairman/CEO
Dennis Petersen, President
John Kraskiewicz, Senior VP/COO
Jay Brader, Senior VP/CFO

WORLDWIDE REVENUE	$142,000,000
US REVENUE	$134,000,000
WORLDWIDE STAFF	701
HEADQUARTERS	Omaha, NE
YEAR ESTABLISHED	1915

RECENT REPRESENTATIVE PROJECT

Toro Headquarters,
Bloomington, MN

GEOGRAPHIC ANALYSIS OF WORK IN THE US

10%
20%
10%
60%
10%

GEOGRAPHIC ANALYSIS OF WORK OUTSIDE THE US

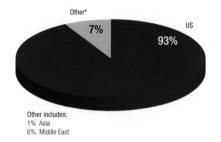

Other*
7%
US
93%

Other includes:
1% Asia
6% Middle East

PRIMARY SERVICES OFFERED

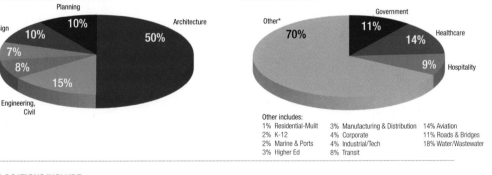

Planning
10%
Interior Design
10%
Architecture
50%
Engineering,
Structural
7%
Engineering,
MEP
8%
15%
Engineering,
Civil

MARKET SEGMENTS

Government
Other*
70%
11%
Healthcare
14%
9%
Hospitality

Other includes:
1% Residential-Mulit	3% Manufacturing & Distribution	14% Aviation
2% K-12	4% Corporate	11% Roads & Bridges
2% Marine & Ports	4% Industrial/Tech	18% Water/Wastewater
3% Higher Ed	8% Transit	

LOCATIONS INCLUDE

Atlanta, GA	Los Angeles, CA	Abu Dhabi, UAE
Dallas, TX	Miami, FL	Doha, Qatar
Denver, CO	Minneapolis, MN	Riyadh, Saudi Arabia
Honolulu, HI	Omaha, NE	
Houston, TX	Washington, DC	
Las Vegas, NV	West Palm Beach, FL	

17 | EYP

257 Fuller Road, NanoFab East
Albany, NY12203
(518) 795-3800
www.eypaedesign.com
Tom Birdsey, President/CEO
David Watkins, WHR Founding Principal
Tom McDougall, Weldt Energy Leader

WORLDWIDE REVENUE	$138,184,652
US REVENUE	$136,053,988
WORLDWIDE STAFF	600
HEADQUARTERS	Albany, NY
YEAR ESTABLISHED	1972
RECENT REPRESENTATIVE PROJECT	

Birch Bayh Federal Building & US Courthouse, Indianapolis, IN

GEOGRAPHIC ANALYSIS OF WORK IN THE US

GEOGRAPHIC ANALYSIS OF WORK OUTSIDE THE US

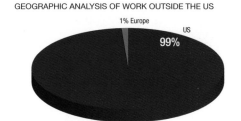

PRIMARY SERVICES OFFERED

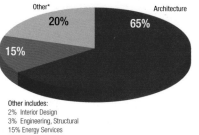

Other includes:
2% Interior Design
3% Engineering, Structural
15% Energy Services

MARKET SEGMENTS

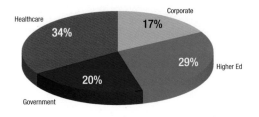

LOCATIONS INCLUDE

Albany, NY
Boston, MA
Charlotte, NC
Dallas, TX

Greenville, SC
Houston, TX
New York, NY
Orlando, FL

Raleigh, NC
Washington, DC

EYP/®
Architecture & Engineering

18 | Dewberry (Architecture)

8401 Arlington Boulevard
Fairfax, VA 22031
(703) 849-0100
www.dewberry.com
Barry Dewberry, Chairman
Donald E. Stone Jr., CEO
James Draheim, President

WORLDWIDE REVENUE	$133,600,000
US REVENUE	$133,600,000
WORLDWIDE STAFF	320
HEADQUARTERS	Fairfax, VA
YEAR ESTABLISHED	1956
RECENT REPRESENTATIVE PROJECT	

RLI Corporate Headquarters,
Peoria, IL

GEOGRAPHIC ANALYSIS OF WORK IN THE US

GEOGRAPHIC ANALYSIS OF WORK OUTSIDE THE US

PRIMARY SERVICES OFFERED

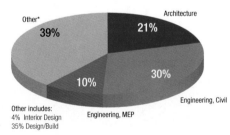

Other includes:
4% Interior Design
35% Design/Build

MARKET SEGMENTS

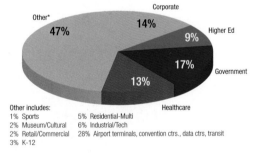

Other includes:
1% Sports   5% Residential-Multi
2% Museum/Cultural 6% Industrial/Tech
2% Retail/Commercial 28% Airport terminals, convention ctrs., data ctrs, transit
3% K-12

LOCATIONS INCLUDE

Atlanta, GA
Baltimore, MD
Baton Rouge, LA
Bloomfield, NJ
Boston, MA
Brooklyn, NY
Carlisle, PA
Chapel Hill, NC
Charleston, WV
Charlotte, NC
Costa Mesa, CA
Dallas, TX
Danville, VA

Deland, FL
Denton, TX
Denver, CO
Elgin, IL
Fairfax, VA
Frederick, MD
Gainesville, VA
Glen Allen, VA
Gulfport, MS
Jacksonville, FL
Lanham, MD
Leesburg, VA
Mobile, AL

Mount Laurel, NJ
New Haven, CT
New Orleans, LA
New York, NY
Orlando, FL
Parsippany, NJ
Pasadena, CA
Pensacola, FL
Peoria, IL

Pittsburgh, PA
Raleigh, NC
Rockville, MD
Roseville, CA
Sacramento, CA
Sarasota, FL
Tulsa, OK
Virginia Beach, VA

Dewberry®

J. Craig Venter Institute, La Jolla, CA | ZGF Architects

Nick Merrick / Hedrich Blessing Photographers

19 | ZGF Architects

1223 S.W. Washington Street, Suite 100
Portland, OR 97205
(503) 224-3860
www.zgf.com
Robert Packard, Managing Partner
Robert Frasca, Partner in Charge of Design

WORLDWIDE REVENUE	$131,689,176
US REVENUE	$131,689,176
WORLDWIDE STAFF	611
HEADQUARTERS	Portland, OR
YEAR ESTABLISHED	1959
RECENT REPRESENTATIVE PROJECT	

Randall Children's Hospital at Legacy Emanuel, Portland, OR

GEOGRAPHIC ANALYSIS OF WORK IN THE US

53% 4% 30% 13%

GEOGRAPHIC ANALYSIS OF WORK OUTSIDE THE US

Other*
10% US 90%

Other includes:
1% Europe   3% Canada
1% Middle East 5% Asia

PRIMARY SERVICES OFFERED

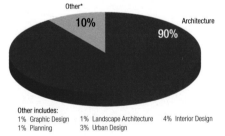

Other*
10% Architecture 90%

Other includes:
1% Graphic Design   1% Landscape Architecture   4% Interior Design
1% Planning   3% Urban Design

MARKET SEGMENTS

Other*
17% Corporate 10% 25% Higher Ed
Healthcare 38% 10% Government

Other includes:
1% Sports   5% Urban Design/Transit
5% Retail/Commercial 6% Residential-Multi

LOCATIONS INCLUDE

Los Angeles, CA
New York, NY
Portland, OR
Seattle, WA

Washington, DC
Vancouver, BC,
  Canada

ZGF
ZIMMER GUNSUL FRASCA ARCHITECTS LLP

Baoshon Long Beach Winder Tower, Shanghai, China | DLR Group

Four Winds, Jeddah, Saudi Arabia | DLR Group

20 | DLR Group

520 Nicollet Mall, Suite 200
Minneapolis, MN 55402
(952) 941-8950
www.dlrgroup.com
Griff Davenport, Managing Principal
Steven McKay, Design Leader

WORLDWIDE REVENUE	$130,000,000
US REVENUE	$127,000,000
WORLDWIDE STAFF	500
HEADQUARTERS	20 Global Offices
YEAR ESTABLISHED	1966

RECENT REPRESENTATIVE PROJECT

Joplin Interim High School,
Joplin, MO

GEOGRAPHIC ANALYSIS OF WORK IN THE US

GEOGRAPHIC ANALYSIS OF WORK OUTSIDE THE US

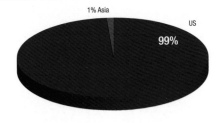

PRIMARY SERVICES OFFERED

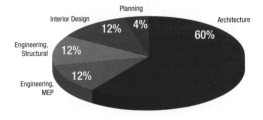

MARKET SEGMENTS

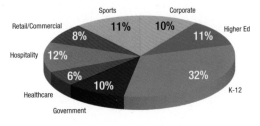

LOCATIONS INCLUDE

Chicago, IL
Colorado Springs, CO
Denver, CO
Des Moines, IA
Honolulu, HI

Kansas City, KS
Las Vegas, NV
Lincoln, NE
Los Angeles, CA
Minneapolis, MN
Omaha, NE

Orlando, FL
Pasadena, CA
Phoenix, AZ
Portland, OR
Riverside, CA
Sacramento, CA

Seattle, WA
Tucson, AZ
Washington, DC
Shanghai, China

Paul Crosby Photography

Macalester College, Janet Wallace Studio Arts Center, St. Paul, MN | HGA Architects and Engineers

21 | HGA Architects and Engineers

420 Fifth Street North, Suite 100
Minneapolis, MN 55401
(612) 758-4000
www.hga.com
Tim Carl, CEO
Daniel Rectenwald, COO

WORLDWIDE REVENUE	$123,900,000
US REVENUE	$120,800,000
WORLDWIDE STAFF	666
HEADQUARTERS	Minneapolis, MN
YEAR ESTABLISHED	1953
RECENT REPRESENTATIVE PROJECT	

Northrop Performing Arts Ctr., Univ. of Minnesota, Minneapolis, MN

GEOGRAPHIC ANALYSIS OF WORK IN THE US

30% 40% 20% 10%

GEOGRAPHIC ANALYSIS OF WORK OUTSIDE THE US

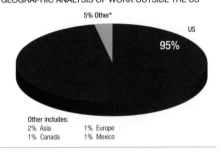

5% Other*
US
95%

Other includes:
2% Asia   1% Europe
1% Canada   1% Mexico

PRIMARY SERVICES OFFERED

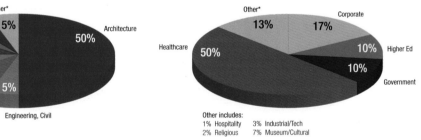

Planning   Other*
Landscape   5%   5%   5%
Architecture
Interior Design   10%   Architecture
                                      50%
Engineering,   10%
Structural   10%   5%
Engineering, MEP

Other includes: Engineering, Civil
2% Urban Design
3% Graphic Design

MARKET SEGMENTS

Other*   Corporate
13%   17%
Healthcare   10%   Higher Ed
50%   10%
                            Government

Other includes:
1% Hospitality   3% Industrial/Tech
2% Religious   7% Museum/Cultural

LOCATIONS INCLUDE

Los Angeles, CA   Sacramento, CA
Milwaukee, WI   San Francisco, CA
Minneapolis, MN   Washington, DC
Rochester, NY

hGA.

22 | Populous

300 Wyandotte Street, Suite 200
Kansas City, MO 64105
(816) 221-1500
www.populous.com
Earl Santee, Sr. Principal
Chris Lee, Sr. Principal
Paul Henry, Sr. Principal

WORLDWIDE REVENUE	$122,444,000
US REVENUE	$74,000,000
WORLDWIDE STAFF	402
HEADQUARTERS	Kansas City, MO
YEAR ESTABLISHED	1983
RECENT REPRESENTATIVE PROJECT	

Marlins Park,
Miami, FL

GEOGRAPHIC ANALYSIS OF WORK IN THE US

GEOGRAPHIC ANALYSIS OF WORK OUTSIDE THE US

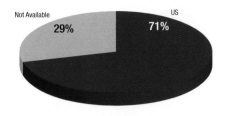

PRIMARY SERVICES OFFERED

Other*
13%
Architecture
70%
Urban Design
5%
Planning
5%

Other includes:
1% Graphic Design
3% Interior Design
9% Design/Build

MARKET SEGMENTS

Other*
24%
Sports
76%

Other includes:
7% Event
17% Museum/Cultural

LOCATIONS INCLUDE

Boston, MA
Denver, CO
Kansas City, MO
Knoxville, TN
Norman, OK

San Francisco, CA
Brisbane, Australia
London, UK
Melbourne, Australia
New Delhi, India

Singapore
Sydney, Australia
Taipei, Taiwan

POPULOUS

23 | HBA/Hirsch Bedner Associates

Two Peachree Pointe, Suite 700
Atlanta, GA 30309
(404) 873-4379
www.hbadesign.com
Michael Bedner, Chairman
Ian Carr, CEO
René Gross Kærskov, CEO

WORLDWIDE REVENUE	$122,000,000
US REVENUE	$117,000,000
WORLDWIDE STAFF	1,200
HEADQUARTERS	Atlanta, GA
YEAR ESTABLISHED	1964
RECENT REPRESENTATIVE PROJECT	

St. Regis,
Atlanta, GA

GEOGRAPHIC ANALYSIS OF WORK IN THE US

0%   100%   0%
0%

GEOGRAPHIC ANALYSIS OF WORK OUTSIDE THE US

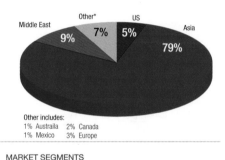

Other* 7%   US 5%   Asia 79%
Middle East 9%

Other includes:
1% Austraila   2% Canada
1% Mexico   3% Europe

PRIMARY SERVICES OFFERED

Interior Design

100%

MARKET SEGMENTS

2% Other*

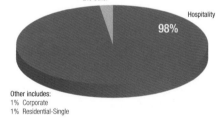

Hospitality 98%

Other includes:
1% Corporate
1% Residential-Single

LOCATIONS INCLUDE

Atlanta, GA
Los Angeles, CA
Miami, FL
San Francisco, CA
Bali, Indonesia
Bangkok, Thailand
Beijing, China
Clark, Philippines

Dubai, UAE
Hong Kong, China
Istanbul, Turkey
Jeddah, Saudi
    Arabia
Kuala Lumpur,
    Malaysia
London, UK

Manila, Philippines
Melbourne, Australia
Moscow, Russia
New Delhi, India
Shanghai, China
Singapore
Tokyo, Japan

HBA

24 | GHAFARI

17101 Michigan Avenue
Dearborn, MI 48126
(313) 441-3000
www.ghafari.com
Yousif Ghafari, Chairman
Kouhalia G. Hammer, President/CEO
Ali Solaksubasi, President/Internatl Operations
Michael Neville, Executive VP

WORLDWIDE REVENUE	$114,900,000
US REVENUE	$86,000,000
WORLDWIDE STAFF	450
HEADQUARTERS	Dearborn, MI
YEAR ESTABLISHED	1982
RECENT REPRESENTATIVE PROJECT	

Jesse White Community Center,
Chicago, IL

GEOGRAPHIC ANALYSIS OF WORK IN THE US

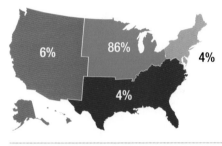

6% 86% 4%
4%

GEOGRAPHIC ANALYSIS OF WORK OUTSIDE THE US

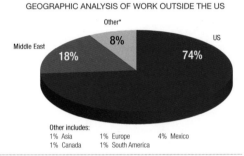

Other*
8%
Middle East
18%
US
74%

Other includes:
1% Asia   1% Europe   4% Mexico
1% Canada   1% South America

PRIMARY SERVICES OFFERED

Other*
58%
Architecture
9%
Engineering, MEP
23%
10%
Engineering, Structural

Other includes:
2% Engineering, Civil   54% Management
2% Interior Design

MARKET SEGMENTS

Other*
67%
Industrial/Tech.
33%

Other includes:
1% Corporate   4% Higher Ed
1% Government   22% Aviation
1% Healthcare   37% Residential-Multi
1% Retail/Commercial

LOCATIONS INCLUDE

Birmingham, AL
Chicago, IL
Dearborn, MI
Indianapolis, IN
Abu Dhabi, UAE
Baroda, India

Doha, Qatar
Jeddah, Saudi
  Arabia
Muscat, Oman
São Paulo, Brazil

GHAFARI ▪▪

ARCHITECTURE | ENGINEERING | CONSULTING

25 | Gresham, Smith and Partners

511 Union Street, Suite 1400
Nashville, TN 37219
(615) 770-8100
www.gspnet.com
Brackney J. Reed, Chairman/COO
James W. Bearden, CEO

WORLDWIDE REVENUE	$110,300,000
US REVENUE	$108,000,000
WORLDWIDE STAFF	625
HEADQUARTERS	Nashville, TN
YEAR ESTABLISHED	1967
RECENT REPRESENTATIVE PROJECT	

Nissan Americas Corporate Facility,
Franklin, TN

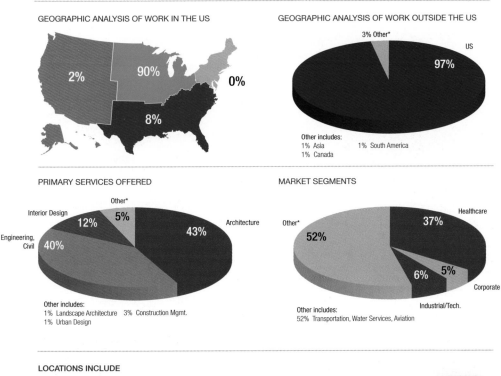

GEOGRAPHIC ANALYSIS OF WORK IN THE US

2%   90%   0%   8%

GEOGRAPHIC ANALYSIS OF WORK OUTSIDE THE US

3% Other*   US   97%

Other includes:
1% Asia   1% South America
1% Canada

PRIMARY SERVICES OFFERED

Other*
Interior Design   5%
12%
Engineering, Civil 40%   43%   Architecture

Other includes:
1% Landscape Architecture   3% Construction Mgmt.
1% Urban Design

MARKET SEGMENTS

Healthcare
Other*   37%
52%
6%   5%   Corporate
Industrial/Tech.

Other includes:
52% Transportation, Water Services, Aviation

LOCATIONS INCLUDE

Atlanta, GA	Dallas, TX	Memphis, TN
Baton Rouge, LA	Fort Lauderdale, FL	Miami, FL
Birmingham, AL	Houston, TX	Nashville, TN
Charlotte, NC	Jackson, MS	Richmond, VA
Chipley, FL	Jacksonville, FL	Tallahassee, FL
Cincinnati, OH	Knoxville, TN	Tampa, FL
Columbus, OH	Louisville, KY	Shanghai, China

GS&P

GRESHAM
SMITH AND
PARTNERS

Nick Merrick © Hedrich Blessing

Undisclosed Services Firm, Dallas, TX | Staffelbach

26 | Corgan Associates

401 North Houston Street
Dallas, TX 75202
(214) 748-2000
www.corgan.com
David Lind, Chairman
Bob Morris, CEO/President
Jon Holzheimer, COO

WORLDWIDE REVENUE	$108,100,000
WORLDWIDE STAFF	497
HEADQUARTERS	Dallas, TX
YEAR ESTABLISHED	1938

RECENT REPRESENTATIVE PROJECT
Blue Cross Blue Shield of Texas,
Richardson, TX

27 | Page

400 West Cesar Chavez, Suite 500
Austin, TX 78701
(512) 472-6721
www.pagethink.com

WORLDWIDE REVENUE	$91,000,000
WORLDWIDE STAFF	415
HEADQUARTERS	Dallas, TX
YEAR ESTABLISHED	1898

RECENT REPRESENTATIVE PROJECT
Architecture of Discovery Green,
Houston, TX

28 | Robert A.M. Stern Architects

460 West 34th Street
New York, NY 10001
(212) 967-5100
www.ramsa.com
Robert Stern, Senior & Founding Partner
Paul Whalen, Partner
Graham Wyatt, Partner
Roger Seifter, Partner

WORLDWIDE REVENUE	$82,304,661
WORLDWIDE STAFF	330
HEADQUARTERS	New York, NY
YEAR ESTABLISHED	1969

RECENT REPRESENTATIVE PROJECT
George W. Bush Presidential Ctr.,
Dallas, TX

29 | Elkus Manfredi Architects

25 Drydock Avenue
Boston, MA 02210
(617) 426-1300
www.elkus-manfredi.com
Howard Elkus, Principal
David Manfredi, Principal
Samuel Norod, Principal
John Martin, Principal

WORLDWIDE REVENUE	$81,593,000
WORLDWIDE STAFF	305
HEADQUARTERS	Boston, MA
YEAR ESTABLISHED	1988

RECENT REPRESENTATIVE PROJECT
Vertex Pharmaceuticals Global Headqtrs.,
Boston, MA

© Adrian Smith + Gordon Gill Architecture /photograph by ShuHe Photography

Waldorf Astoria Beijing, Beijing, China | Adrian Smith + Gordon Gill

30 | Adrian Smith + Gordon Gill Architecture

ADRIAN SMITH + GORDON GILL
ARCHITECTURE

111 West Monroe, Suite 2300
Chicago, IL 60603
(312) 920-1888
www.smithgill.com
Adrian Smith, Partner
Gordon Gill, Partner
Robert Forest, Partner

WORLDWIDE REVENUE	$81,199,000
WORLDWIDE STAFF	125
HEADQUARTERS	Chicago, IL
YEAR ESTABLISHED	2006
RECENT REPRESENTATIVE PROJECT	

FKI Tower,
Seoul, Korea

31 | VOA Associates

224 South Michigan Avenue, Suite 1400
Chicago, IL 60604
(312) 554-1400
www.voa.com
Michael A. Toolis, Chairman/CEO
Percy "Rebel" Roberts III, President/COO
Theodore Fery, Secretary

WORLDWIDE REVENUE	$70,000,000
WORLDWIDE STAFF	375
HEADQUARTERS	Chicago, IL
YEAR ESTABLISHED	1969
RECENT REPRESENTATIVE PROJECT	

Roosevelt University Vertical Campus,
Chicago, IL

32 | WATG

8001 Irvine Center Drive, Suite 500
Irvine, CA 92618
(949) 574-8500
www.watg.com
Michael R. Seyle, President/CEO
Peter Priebe, VP/CFO
Rajesh Chandnani, VP/Strategy Director

WORLDWIDE REVENUE	$68,679,000
WORLDWIDE STAFF	327
HEADQUARTERS	Irvine, CA
YEAR ESTABLISHED	1945
RECENT REPRESENTATIVE PROJECT	

Viceroy Anguilla,
Anguilla

33 | Rafael Viñoly Architects

50 Vandam Street
New York, NY 10013
(212) 924-5060
www.rvapc.com
Rafael Vinoly, President

WORLDWIDE REVENUE	$66,000,000
WORLDWIDE STAFF	500
HEADQUARTERS	New York, NY
YEAR ESTABLISHED	1983

34 | RSP Architects

1220 Marshall Street Northeast
Minneapolis, MN 55413
(612) 677-7100
www.rsparch.com
David Norback, President
Bob Lucius, Principal
Jon Buggy, Principal
Joe Tyndall, Principal

WORLDWIDE REVENUE	$63,486,000
WORLDWIDE STAFF	286
HEADQUARTERS	Minneapolis, MN
YEAR ESTABLISHED	1978

RECENT REPRESENTATIVE PROJECT

Mayo Clinic Square,
Minneapolis, MN

35 | Little

5815 Westpark Drive
Charlotte, NC 28217
(704) 525-6350
www.littleonline.com
Philip Kuttner, CEO
John Komisin, President/COO
Terry Bradshaw, CFO
Jim Williams, National Design Director

WORLDWIDE REVENUE	$60,697,000
WORLDWIDE STAFF	341
HEADQUARTERS	Charlotte, NC
YEAR ESTABLISHED	1964

RECENT REPRESENTATIVE PROJECT

Campbell University School
of Osteopathic Medicine, Buies Creek, NC

36 | EwingCole

100 North 6th Street
Philadelphia, PA 19106
(215) 923-2020
www.ewingcole.com
John Gerbner, CEO
Mark Hebden, President
Joseph Kelly, CFO
Jared Loos, Executive VP

WORLDWIDE REVENUE	$58,000,000
WORLDWIDE STAFF	300
HEADQUARTERS	Philadelphia, PA
YEAR ESTABLISHED	1961

RECENT REPRESENTATIVE PROJECT

Penn Pennsylvania Pavilion Univ.
of PA Health System, Philadelphia, PA

37 | MG2 Corporation

1101 Second Avenue, Suite 100
Seattle, WA 98101
(206) 962-6500
www.MG2.com
Mitch Smith, Chairman/CEO
Russ Hazzard, President

WORLDWIDE REVENUE	$57,171,144
WORLDWIDE STAFF	300
HEADQUARTERS	Seattle, WA
YEAR ESTABLISHED	1971

RECENT REPRESENTATIVE PROJECT

UNIQLO Flagship Store,
Boston, MA

38 | Harley Ellis Devereaux

26913 Northwestern Highway, Suite 200
Southfield, MI 48033
(248) 262-1500
www.harleyellisdevereaux.com
Gary L. Skog, Chairman
J. Peter Devereaux, CEO
Michael Cooper, President

WORLDWIDE REVENUE	$56,914,000
WORLDWIDE STAFF	295
HEADQUARTERS	Detroit, MI
YEAR ESTABLISHED	1908
RECENT REPRESENTATIVE PROJECT	

West Berkeley Library,
Berkeley, CA

39 | Cuningham Group Architecture

201 Main Street Southeast, Suite 325
Minneapolis, MN 55414
(612) 379-3400
www.cuningham.com
James Scheidel, Chairman
Timothy Dufault, President/CEO

WORLDWIDE REVENUE	$56,884,509
WORLDWIDE STAFF	276
HEADQUARTERS	Minneapolis, MN
YEAR ESTABLISHED	1968
RECENT REPRESENTATIVE PROJECT	

Alexandria Area High School,
Alexandria, MN

40 | Solomon Cordwell Buenz

625 North Michigan Avenue, Suite 800
Chicago, IL 60611
(312) 896-1100
www.scb.com
John Lahey, Chairman/Design Principal
Gary Kohn, Managing Principal
Chris Pemberton, Principal

WORLDWIDE REVENUE	$56,600,000
WORLDWIDE STAFF	185
HEADQUARTERS	Chicago, IL
YEAR ESTABLISHED	1931

41 | HMC Architects

633 West 5th Street, 3rd Floor
Los Angeles, CA 90071
(800) 350-9979
www.hmcarchitects.com
Randy Peterson, President/CEO
Brian Staton, Regional Managing Principal
Ric Mangum, Regional Managing Principal

WORLDWIDE REVENUE	$55,000,000
WORLDWIDE STAFF	400
HEADQUARTERS	Ontario, CA
YEAR ESTABLISHED	1940

Tim Griffith

UCLA Landfair Student Apartments, Los Angeles, CA | STUDIOS Architecture

42 | LS3P Associates Ltd.

205 1/2 King Street
Charleston, SC 29401
(843) 577-4444
www.LS3P.com
Thompson Penney, President/CEO/ Chairman
Katherine Peele, Executive VP of Practice
George Temple, Executive VP of Business

WORLDWIDE REVENUE	$53,342,585
WORLDWIDE STAFF	257
HEADQUARTERS	Charleston, SC
YEAR ESTABLISHED	1963

43 | Ennead Architects

320 West 13th Street
New York, NY 10014
(212) 807-7171
www.ennead.com

WORLDWIDE REVENUE	$52,275,000
WORLDWIDE STAFF	174
HEADQUARTERS	New York, NY
YEAR ESTABLISHED	1963

44 | STUDIOS Architecture

STUDIOS architecture

1625 M Street Northwest
Washington, DC   20036
(202)736-5900
www.studiosarchitecture.com
Thomas Yee, Chairman
Todd DeGarmo, President/CEO
Erik Sueberkrop, Chairman Emeritus

WORLDWIDE REVENUE	$52,031,636
WORLDWIDE STAFF	247
HEADQUARTERS	Washington, DC
YEAR ESTABLISHED	1985

45 | Sasaki Associates, Inc.

64 Pleasant Street
Watertown, MA 02472
(617) 926-3300
www.sasaki.com
James Miner, Managing Partner
Mark O. Dawson, Managing Partner
Pablo Savid-Buteler, Managing Principal

WORLDWIDE REVENUE	$51,000,000
WORLDWIDE STAFF	212
HEADQUARTERS	Watertown, MA
YEAR ESTABLISHED	1953

Nick Merrick © Hedrich Blessing

Arraya Center Office Tower, Kuwait City, Kuwait | Fentress Architects

46 | Cooper Carry

191 Peachtree Street Northeast, Suite 2400
Atlanta, GA 30303
(404) 237-2000
www.coopercarry.com
Kevin Cantley, President/CEO
Jerry Cooper, Founding Principal
Roger Miller, Principal
Gar Muse, Principal

WORLDWIDE REVENUE	$48,658,690
WORLDWIDE STAFF	215
HEADQUARTERS	Atlanta, GA
YEAR ESTABLISHED	1960

47 | Kirksey

6909 Portwest Drive
Houston, TX 77024
(713) 850-9600
www.kirksey.com
John Kirksey, President
Wes Good, Managing Principal
Randall Walker, Executive VP

WORLDWIDE REVENUE	$48,200,000
WORLDWIDE STAFF	110
HEADQUARTERS	Houston, TX
YEAR ESTABLISHED	1971

48 | Fentress Architects

FENTRESS

421 Broadway
Denver, CO 80203
(303) 722-5000
www.fentressarchitects.com
Curtis W. Fentress, Founder/Principal-in-Charge
Agatha Kessler, Chairman
Patrick McCue, COO

WORLDWIDE REVENUE	$47,782,004
WORLDWIDE STAFF	150
HEADQUARTERS	Denver, CO
YEAR ESTABLISHED	1980

49 | LPA

5161 California Avenue
Irvine, CA 92617
(949) 261-1001
www.lpainc.com
Robert O. Kupper, CEO
Dan Heinfeld, President
Charles Pruitt, COO/CFO

WORLDWIDE REVENUE	$47,509,890
WORLDWIDE STAFF	300
HEADQUARTERS	Irvine, CA
YEAR ESTABLISHED	1965

Rendering by Interface Multimedia

Half Street Ballpark Mixed-Use Development, Washington, DC | Hord Coplan Macht

50 | Kasian Architecture Interior Design and Planning

1500 West Georgia Street, Suite 1685	WORLDWIDE REVENUE	$47,000,000
Vancouver, BC v6G2z6	WORLDWIDE STAFF	280
(604) 683-4145	HEADQUARTERS	Vancouver, Canada
www.kasian.com	YEAR ESTABLISHED	1985

51 | The SLAM Collaborative

80 Glastonbury Boulevard	WORLDWIDE REVENUE	$46,200,000
Glastonbury, CT 06033	WORLDWIDE STAFF	151
(860) 657-8077	HEADQUARTERS	Glastonbury, CT
www.slamcoll.com	YEAR ESTABLISHED	1976

52 | CTA Architects Engineers

13 North 23rd Street	WORLDWIDE REVENUE	$46,150,000
Billings, MT 59101	WORLDWIDE STAFF	345
(406) 248-7455	HEADQUARTERS	Billings, MT
www.ctagroup.com	YEAR ESTABLISHED	1938

53 | Ballinger

833 Chestnut Street, Suite 1400	WORLDWIDE REVENUE	$46,100,000
Philadelphia, PA 19107	WORLDWIDE STAFF	125
(215) 446-0900	HEADQUARTERS	Philadelphia, PA
www.ballinger-ae.com	YEAR ESTABLISHED	1878

54 | Steelman Partners

3330 West Desert Inn Road	WORLDWIDE REVENUE	$44,000,000
Las Vegas, NV 89012	WORLDWIDE STAFF	200
(702) 873-0221	HEADQUARTERS	Las Vegas, NV
www.steelmanpartners.com	YEAR ESTABLISHED	1987

55 | Hord Coplan Macht   hord | coplan | macht

750 East Pratt Street, Suite 1100	WORLDWIDE REVENUE	$42,833,042
Baltimore, MD 21202	WORLDWIDE STAFF	200
(410) 837-7311	HEADQUARTERS	Baltimore, MD
www.hcm2.com	YEAR ESTABLISHED	1977

Paul Burk Photography

Emory University Freshman Housing Village, Atlanta, GA | Ayers Saint Gross

Brad Feinknopf

University of Delaware Interdisciplinary Science and Engineering Laboratory (ISE-Lab), Newark, DE | Ayers Saint Gross

56 | Ayers Saint Gross

1040 Hull Street, Suite 100	WORLDWIDE REVENUE	$42,242,000
Baltimore, MD 21230	WORLDWIDE STAFF	156
(410) 347-8500	HEADQUARTERS	Baltimore, MD
www.asg-architects.com	YEAR ESTABLISHED	1912

57 | Wilson Associates

3811 Turtle Creek Boulevard, Suite 1600	WORLDWIDE REVENUE	$42,000,000
Dallas, TX 75219	WORLDWIDE STAFF	400
(214) 521-6753	HEADQUARTERS	Dallas, TX
www.wilsonassociates.com	YEAR ESTABLISHED	1971

58 | Payette

290 Congress Street, Fifth Floor	WORLDWIDE REVENUE	$41,668,598
Boston, MA 02210	WORLDWIDE STAFF	169
(617) 895-1000	HEADQUARTERS	Boston, MA
www.payette.com	YEAR ESTABLISHED	1932

59 | WHR Architects

1111 Louisiana Street, 26th Floor	WORLDWIDE REVENUE	$41,000,000
Houston, TX 77002	WORLDWIDE STAFF	114
(713) 665-5665	HEADQUARTERS	Houston, TX
www.whrarchitects.com	YEAR ESTABLISHED	1979

60 | The Beck Group (Architecture)

1807 Ross Avenue, Suite 500	WORLDWIDE REVENUE	$40,880,866
Dallas, TX 75201	WORLDWIDE STAFF	150
(214) 303-6482	HEADQUARTERS	Dallas, TX
www.beckgroup.com	YEAR ESTABLISHED	1912

61 | NELSON

222-230 Walnut Street	WORLDWIDE REVENUE	$40,000,000
Philadelphia, PA 19106	WORLDWIDE STAFF	240
(215) 925-6562	HEADQUARTERS	Philadelphia, PA
www.nelsononline.com	YEAR ESTABLISHED	1977

62 | WD Partners

7007 Discovery Boulevard
Dublin, OH 43017
(614) 634-7000
www.wdpartners.com

WORLDWIDE REVENUE	$39,000,000
WORLDWIDE STAFF	350+
HEADQUARTERS	Dublin, OH
YEAR ESTABLISHED	1968

63 | Morris Architects

1001 Fannin Street, Suite 300
Houston, TX 77002
(713) 622-1180
www.morrisarchitects.com

WORLDWIDE REVENUE	$38,370,000
WORLDWIDE STAFF	462
HEADQUARTERS	Houston, TX
YEAR ESTABLISHED	1938

64 | BSA LifeStructures

9365 Counselors Row
Indianapolis, IN 46240
(317) 819-7878
www.bsals.com

WORLDWIDE REVENUE	$38,200,000
WORLDWIDE STAFF	247
HEADQUARTERS	Indianapolis, IN
YEAR ESTABLISHED	1975

65 | tvsdesign

1230 Peachtree Street NE, Suite 2700
Atlanta, GA 30309
(404) 888-6600
www.tvs-design.com

WORLDWIDE REVENUE	$38,100,000
WORLDWIDE STAFF	167
HEADQUARTERS	Atlanta, GA
YEAR ESTABLISHED	1968

66 | FXFOWLE Architects

22 West 19th Street
New York, NY 10011
(212) 627-1700
www.fxfowle.com

WORLDWIDE REVENUE	$37,293,202
WORLDWIDE STAFF	145
HEADQUARTERS	New York, NY
YEAR ESTABLISHED	1978

67 | BWBR Architects

380 Saint Peter Street, Suite 600
St. Paul, MN 55102
(651) 222-3701
www.bwbr.com

WORLDWIDE REVENUE	$37,020,000
WORLDWIDE STAFF	140
HEADQUARTERS	St. Paul, MN
YEAR ESTABLISHED	1922

68 | GreenbergFarrow

1430 West Peachtree Street, Suite 200	WORLDWIDE REVENUE	$37,000,000
Atlanta, GA 30309	WORLDWIDE STAFF	140
(404) 601-4000	HEADQUARTERS	Atlanta, GA
www.greenbergfarrow.com	YEAR ESTABLISHED	1974

69 | PBK

11 Greenway Plaza	WORLDWIDE REVENUE	$36,500,000
Houston, TX 77046	WORLDWIDE STAFF	220
(713) 965-0608	HEADQUARTERS	Houston, TX
www.pbk.com	YEAR ESTABLISHED	1981

70 | CBT

110 Canal Street	WORLDWIDE REVENUE	$36,000,000
Boston, MA 02114	WORLDWIDE STAFF	220
(617) 262-4354	HEADQUARTERS	Boston, MA
www.cbtarchitects.com	YEAR ESTABLISHED	1967

71 | Lionakis

1919 Nineteenth Street	WORLDWIDE REVENUE	$35,500,000
Sacramento, CA 95811	WORLDWIDE STAFF	21–100
(916) 558-1900	HEADQUARTERS	Sacramento, CA
www.lionakis.com	YEAR ESTABLISHED	1909

72 | HLW International

115 Fifth Avenue, Suite 500	WORLDWIDE REVENUE	$35,200,000
New York, NY 10003	WORLDWIDE STAFF	149
(212) 353-4600	HEADQUARTERS	New York, NY
www.hlw.com	YEAR ESTABLISHED	1885

73 | McKissack & McKissack

901 K Street NW, 6th Floor	WORLDWIDE REVENUE	$35,000,000
Washington, DC 20001	WORLDWIDE STAFF	150
(202) 347-1446	HEADQUARTERS	Washington, DC
www.mckissackdc.com	YEAR ESTABLISHED	1990

Jonathan Hillyer

Salem State University, Frederick E Berry Library & Learning Commons, Salem, MA | Shepley Bulfinch

74 | Shepley Bulfinch

2 Seaport Lane
Boston, MA 02210
(617) 423-1700
www.shepleyfbulfinch.com

WORLDWIDE REVENUE	$33,980,000
WORLDWIDE STAFF	155
HEADQUARTERS	Boston, MA
YEAR ESTABLISHED	1874

75 | FRCH Design Worldwide

311 Elm Street, Suite 600
Cincinnati, OH 45202
(513) 241-3000
www.frch.com

WORLDWIDE REVENUE	$33,500,000
WORLDWIDE STAFF	225
HEADQUARTERS	Cincinnati, OH
YEAR ESTABLISHED	1968

76 | SLCE Architects

1359 Broadway
New York, NY 10018
(212) 979-8400
www.slcearch.com

WORLDWIDE REVENUE	$33,000,000
WORLDWIDE STAFF	5–20
HEADQUARTERS	New York, NY
YEAR ESTABLISHED	1941

77 | FKP Architects

8 Greenway Plaza, Suite 300
Houston, TX 77046
(713) 621-2100
www.fkp.com

WORLDWIDE REVENUE	$32,000,000
WORLDWIDE STAFF	95
HEADQUARTERS	Houston, TX
YEAR ESTABLISHED	1937

78 | Beyer Blinder Belle

41 East 11th Street
New York, NY 10003
(212) 777-7800
www.beyerblinderbelle.com

WORLDWIDE REVENUE	$31,000,000
WORLDWIDE STAFF	175
HEADQUARTERS	New York, NY
YEAR ESTABLISHED	1968

79 | MVE + Partners

1900 Main Street
Irvine, CA 92614
(949) 809-3388
www.mve-architects.com

WORLDWIDE REVENUE	$30,580,715
WORLDWIDE STAFF	90
HEADQUARTERS	Irvine, CA
YEAR ESTABLISHED	1974

80 | Moody - Nolan

300 Spruce Street, Suite 300
Columbus, OH 43215
(614) 461-4664
www.moodynolan.com

WORLDWIDE REVENUE	$30,022,000
WORLDWIDE STAFF	166
HEADQUARTERS	Columbus, OH
YEAR ESTABLISHED	1982

81 | Good Fulton & Farrell

2808 Fairmount Street, Suite 300
Dallas, TX 75201
(214) 303-1500
www.gff.com

WORLDWIDE REVENUE	$30,000,000
WORLDWIDE STAFF	128
HEADQUARTERS	Dallas, TX
YEAR ESTABLISHED	1982

82 | Goettsch Partners

224 South Michigan Avenue, Suite 1700
Chicago, IL 60604
(312) 356-0600
www.gpchicago.com

WORLDWIDE REVENUE	$29,671,000
WORLDWIDE STAFF	110
HEADQUARTERS	Chicago, IL
YEAR ESTABLISHED	1938

83 | Bergmann Associates

28 East Main Street
Rochester, NY 14614
(585) 232-5135
www.bergmannpc.com

WORLDWIDE REVENUE	$29,500,000
WORLDWIDE STAFF	161
HEADQUARTERS	Rochester, NY
YEAR ESTABLISHED	1980

84 | JLG Architects

124 North 3rd Street
Grand Forks, ND 58203
(701) 746-1727
www.jlgarchitects.com

WORLDWIDE REVENUE	$29,200,000
WORLDWIDE STAFF	80
HEADQUARTERS	Grand Forks, ND
YEAR ESTABLISHED	1989

85 | EDSA

1512 East Broward Boulevard, Suite 110
Fort Lauderdale, FL 33301
(954) 524-3330
www.edsaplan.com

WORLDWIDE REVENUE	$29,000,000
WORLDWIDE STAFF	175
HEADQUARTERS	Fort Lauderdale, FL
YEAR ESTABLISHED	1960

86 | Niles Bolton Associates

3060 Peachtree Road Northwest, Suite 600	WORLDWIDE REVENUE	$28,723,000
Atlanta, GA 30305	WORLDWIDE STAFF	130
(404) 365-7600	HEADQUARTERS	Atlanta, GA
www.nilesbolton.com	YEAR ESTABLISHED	1975

87 | Architects Hawaii

733 Bishop Street, Suite 3100	WORLDWIDE REVENUE	$28,299,000
Honolulu, HI 96813	WORLDWIDE STAFF	95
(808) 523-9636	HEADQUARTERS	Honolulu, HI
www.ahldesign.com	YEAR ESTABLISHED	1946

88 | RDG Planning & Design

301 Grand Avenue	WORLDWIDE REVENUE	$28,184,944
Des Moines, IA 50309	WORLDWIDE STAFF	156
(515) 288-3141	HEADQUARTERS	Des Moines, IA
www.rdgusa.com	YEAR ESTABLISHED	1965

89 | Epstein

600 West Fulton	WORLDWIDE REVENUE	$28,100,000
Chicago, IL 60661	WORLDWIDE STAFF	260
(312) 454-9100	HEADQUARTERS	Chicago, IL
www.epsteinglobal.com	YEAR ESTABLISHED	1921

90 | BHDP Architecture

302 West 3rd Street, Suite 500	WORLDWIDE REVENUE	$28,080,000
Cincinnati, OH 45202	WORLDWIDE STAFF	107
(513) 271-1634	HEADQUARTERS	Cincinnati, OH
www.bhdp.com	YEAR ESTABLISHED	1937

91 | Arquitectonica

2900 Oak Avenue	WORLDWIDE REVENUE	$28,050,000
Miami, FL 33133	WORLDWIDE STAFF	355
(305) 372-1812	HEADQUARTERS	Miami, FL
www.arquitectonica.com	YEAR ESTABLISHED	1977

Joe Hanson, JH Photography Inc.

Cincinnati Children's Hospital Medical Center, Clinical Sciences Pavilion, Cincinnati, OH | GBBN Architects

92 | GBBN Architects

332 East Eighth Street	WORLDWIDE REVENUE	$28,000,000
Cincinnati, OH 45202	WORLDWIDE STAFF	120
(513) 241-8700	HEADQUARTERS	Cincinnati, OH
www.gbbn.com	YEAR ESTABLISHED	1958

93 | Symmes Maini & McKee Associates (SMMA)

1000 Massachusetts Avenue	WORLDWIDE REVENUE	$27,800,000
Cambridge, MA 02138	WORLDWIDE STAFF	140
(617) 547-5400	HEADQUARTERS	Cambridge, MA
www.smma.com	YEAR ESTABLISHED	1955

94 | CO Architects

5055 Wilshire Boulevard, 9th Floor	WORLDWIDE REVENUE	$27,754,100
Los Angeles, CA 90036	WORLDWIDE STAFF	87
(323) 525-0500	HEADQUARTERS	Los Angeles, CA
www.coarchitects.com	YEAR ESTABLISHED	1986

95 | Pei Cobb Freed & Partners Architects

88 Pine Street	WORLDWIDE REVENUE	$27,102,000
New York, NY 10005	WORLDWIDE STAFF	103
(212) 751-3122	HEADQUARTERS	New York, NY
www.pcf-p.com	YEAR ESTABLISHED	1955

96 | Highland Associates

102 Highland Avenue	WORLDWIDE REVENUE	$27,000,000
Clarks Summit, PA 18411	WORLDWIDE STAFF	21–100
(570) 586-4334	HEADQUARTERS	Clarks Summit, PA
www.highlandassociates.com	YEAR ESTABLISHED	1988

97 | Shalom Baranes Associates

1010 Wisconsin Avenue Northwest, Suite 900	WORLDWIDE REVENUE	$26,900,000
Washington, DC 20007	WORLDWIDE STAFF	21–100
(202) 342-2200	HEADQUARTERS	Washington, DC
www.sbaranes.com	YEAR ESTABLISHED	1981

98 | FFKR Architects

730 Pacific Avenue
Salt Lake City, UT 84104
(801) 521-6186
www.ffkr.com

WORLDWIDE REVENUE	$26,700,000
WORLDWIDE STAFF	121
HEADQUARTERS	Salt Lake City, UT
YEAR ESTABLISHED	1976

99 | Westlake Reed Leskosky

1422 Euclid Avenue, Suite 300
Cleveland, OH 44115
(216) 522-1350
www.wrldesign.com

WORLDWIDE REVENUE	$26,500,000
WORLDWIDE STAFF	120
HEADQUARTERS	Cleveland, OH
YEAR ESTABLISHED	1905

100 | Grimm + Parker Architects

11720 Beltsville Drive, Suite 600
Calverton, MD 20705
(301) 595-1000
www.grimmandparker.com

WORLDWIDE REVENUE	$26,400,000
WORLDWIDE STAFF	101–450
HEADQUARTERS	Calverton, MD
YEAR ESTABLISHED	1972

101 | NAC Architecture

1203 West Riverside Avenue
Spokane, WA 99201
(509) 954-2888
www.nacarchitecture.com

WORLDWIDE REVENUE	$26,339,196
WORLDWIDE STAFF	150
HEADQUARTERS	Every office
YEAR ESTABLISHED	1960

102 | Ankrom Moisan Architects

6720 Southwest Macadam Avenue, Suite 100
Portland, OR 97219
(503) 245-7100
www.ankrommoisan.com

WORLDWIDE REVENUE	$26,210,825
WORLDWIDE STAFF	265
HEADQUARTERS	Portland, OR
YEAR ESTABLISHED	1983

103 | MBH Architects

2470 Mariner Square Loop
Alameda, CA 94501
(510) 865-8663
www.mbharch.com

WORLDWIDE REVENUE	$26,188,094
WORLDWIDE STAFF	160
HEADQUARTERS	Alameda, CA
YEAR ESTABLISHED	1989

104 | Davis Brody Bond

One New York Plaza, Suite 4200
New York, NY 10004
(212) 633-4700
www.davisbrody.com

WORLDWIDE REVENUE	$26,100,000
WORLDWIDE STAFF	100
HEADQUARTERS	New York, NY
YEAR ESTABLISHED	1952

105 | Davis Partnership Architects

2301 Blake Street, Suite 100
Denver, CO 80205
(303) 861-8555
www.davispartner.com

WORLDWIDE REVENUE	$26,000,000
WORLDWIDE STAFF	21-100
HEADQUARTERS	Denver, CO
YEAR ESTABLISHED	1967

106 | Lord, Aeck & Sargent

1175 Peachtree Street, NE, Suite 2400
Atlanta, GA 30361
(877) 929-1400
www.lordaecksargent.com

WORLDWIDE REVENUE	$25,950,000
WORLDWIDE STAFF	125
HEADQUARTERS	Atlanta, GA
YEAR ESTABLISHED	1989

107 | Richard Meier & Partners Architects

475 Tenth Avenue, 6th Floor
New York, NY 10018
(212) 967-6060
www.richardmeier.com

WORLDWIDE REVENUE	$25,900,000
WORLDWIDE STAFF	100
HEADQUARTERS	New York, NY
YEAR ESTABLISHED	1963

108 | Vocon

3142 Prospect Avenue
Cleveland, OH 44115
(216) 588-0800
www.vocon.com

WORLDWIDE REVENUE	$25,866,150
WORLDWIDE STAFF	132
HEADQUARTERS	Cleveland, OH
YEAR ESTABLISHED	1987

109 | Array Architects

One West Elm Street, Suite 400
Conshohocken, PA 19428
(610) 270-0599
www.array-architects.com

WORLDWIDE REVENUE	$25,500,000
WORLDWIDE STAFF	111
HEADQUARTERS	Conshohocken, PA
YEAR ESTABLISHED	1983

Benjamin Benschneider

Federal Center South Building 1202, U.S. General Services Administration, Seattle, WA | ZGF Architects

110 | Dekker/Perich/Sabatini

7601 Jefferson Northeast, Suite 100	WORLDWIDE REVENUE	$25,211,183
Albuquerque, NM 87109	WORLDWIDE STAFF	150
(505) 761-9700	HEADQUARTERS	Albuquerque, NM
www.dpsdesign.org	YEAR ESTABLISHED	1998

111 | TRO JB

22 Boston Wharf Road	WORLDWIDE REVENUE	$25,150,000
Boston, MA 02210	WORLDWIDE STAFF	170
(617) 502-3400	HEADQUARTERS	Boston, MA
www.trojb.com	YEAR ESTABLISHED	1909

112 | P+R Architects

111 West Ocean Boulevard, 21st Floor	WORLDWIDE REVENUE	$25,100,000
Long Beach, CA 90802	WORLDWIDE STAFF	201
(562) 628-8000	HEADQUARTERS	Long Beach, CA
www.prarchitects.com	YEAR ESTABLISHED	1979

113 | Francis Cauffman

40 Worth Street, Suite 300	WORLDWIDE REVENUE	$25,090,000
New York, NY 10013	WORLDWIDE STAFF	105
(646) 315-7000	HEADQUARTERS	New York, NY
www.franciscauffman.com	YEAR ESTABLISHED	1954

114 | Gehry Partners

12541 Beatrice Street	WORLDWIDE REVENUE	$25,050,000
Los Angeles, CA 90066	WORLDWIDE STAFF	125
(310) 482-3000	HEADQUARTERS	Los Angeles, CA
www.foga.com	YEAR ESTABLISHED	1962

115 | ASD I SKY

55 Ivan Allen Junior Boulevard, Suite 100	WORLDWIDE REVENUE	$25,005,000
Atlanta, GA 30308	WORLDWIDE STAFF	108
(404) 688-3318	HEADQUARTERS	Atlanta, GA
www.asdnet.com	YEAR ESTABLISHED	1963

116 | Hart | Howerton

One Union Street	WORLDWIDE REVENUE	$25,001,000
San Francisco, CA 94111	WORLDWIDE STAFF	125
(415) 439-2200	HEADQUARTERS	San Francisco, CA
www.harthowerton.com	YEAR ESTABLISHED	1967

117 | BOKA Powell

8070 Park Lane, Suite 300	WORLDWIDE REVENUE	$25,000,000
Dallas, TX 75231	WORLDWIDE STAFF	110
(972) 701-9000	HEADQUARTERS	Dallas, TX
www.bokapowell.com	YEAR ESTABLISHED	1975

118 | JCJ Architecture

38 Prospect Street	WORLDWIDE REVENUE	$24,500,000
Hartford, CT 06103	WORLDWIDE STAFF	112
(860) 240-9329	HEADQUARTERS	Hartford, CT
www.jcj.com	YEAR ESTABLISHED	1936

119 | Cambridge Seven Associates

1050 Massachusetts Avenue	WORLDWIDE REVENUE	$24,300,000
Cambridge, MA 02138	WORLDWIDE STAFF	55
(617) 492-7000	HEADQUARTERS	Cambridge, MA
www.c7a.com	YEAR ESTABLISHED	1962

120 | OPN Architects

1200 Fifth Avenue SE, Suite 201	WORLDWIDE REVENUE	$24,040,000
Cedar Rapids, IA 52401	WORLDWIDE STAFF	110
(319) 363-6018	HEADQUARTERS	Cedar Rapids, IA
www.opnarchitects.com	YEAR ESTABLISHED	1979

121 | gkkworks

2355 Main Street, Suite 220	WORLDWIDE REVENUE	$24,030,000
Irvine, CA 92614	WORLDWIDE STAFF	102
(949) 250-1500	HEADQUARTERS	Irvine, CA
www.gkkworks.com	YEAR ESTABLISHED	1991

122 | Hobbs+Black Architects

100 North State Street	WORLDWIDE REVENUE	$24,015,000
Ann Arbor, MI 48104	WORLDWIDE STAFF	98
(734) 663-4189	HEADQUARTERS	Ann Arbor, MI
www.hobbs-black.com	YEAR ESTABLISHED	1969

123 | BAR Architects

901 Battery Street	WORLDWIDE REVENUE	$24,010,000
San Francisco, CA 94111	WORLDWIDE STAFF	89
(415) 293-5700	HEADQUARTERS	San Francisco, CA
www.bararch.com	YEAR ESTABLISHED	1966

124 | GGLO

1301 First Avenue, Suite 301	WORLDWIDE REVENUE	$24,005,000
Seattle, WA 98101	WORLDWIDE STAFF	105
(206) 467-5828	HEADQUARTERS	Seattle, WA
www.gglo.com	YEAR ESTABLISHED	1986

125 | Mithun

Pier 56, 1201 Alaskan Way , Suite 200	WORLDWIDE REVENUE	$24,000,000
Seattle, WA 98101	WORLDWIDE STAFF	130
(206) 623-3344	HEADQUARTERS	Seattle, WA
www.mithun.com	YEAR ESTABLISHED	1949

126 | OZ Architecture

3003 Larimer Street	WORLDWIDE REVENUE	$23,665,000
Denver, CO 80205	WORLDWIDE STAFF	120
(303) 861-5704	HEADQUARTERS	Denver, CO
www.ozarch.com	YEAR ESTABLISHED	1964

127 | LMN Architects

801 2nd Avenue, Suite 501	WORLDWIDE REVENUE	$23,050,000
Seattle, WA 98104	WORLDWIDE STAFF	150
(206) 682-3460	HEADQUARTERS	Seattle, WA
www.lmnarchitects.com	YEAR ESTABLISHED	1979

Rendering courtesy of RNL.

Heart of Jeddah Development, Jeddah, Kingdom of Saudi Arabia | RNL

Frank Ooms

Metropolitan State University Student Success Building, Denver, CO | RNL

128 | AC Martin

444 South Flower Street, Suite 1470
Los Angeles, CA 90071
(213) 683-1900
www.acmartin.com

WORLDWIDE REVENUE	$23,025,000
WORLDWIDE STAFF	101–150
HEADQUARTERS	Los Angeles, CA
YEAR ESTABLISHED	1906

129 | Gould Evans

4041 Mill Street
Kansas City, MO 64111
(800) 297-6655
www.gouldevans.com

WORLDWIDE REVENUE	$23,010,000
WORLDWIDE STAFF	119
HEADQUARTERS	Kansas City, MO
YEAR ESTABLISHED	1974

130 | VCBO Architecture

524 South 600 East
Salt Lake City, UT 84102
(801) 575-8800
www.vcbo.com

WORLDWIDE REVENUE	$23,000,000
WORLDWIDE STAFF	83
HEADQUARTERS	Salt Lake City, UT
YEAR ESTABLISHED	1973

131 | Smallwood, Reynolds, Stewart, Stewart & Associates

3565 Piedmont Road NE, One Piedmont Center, Suite 303
Atlanta, GA 30305
(404) 233-5453
www.srssa.com

WORLDWIDE REVENUE	$22,742,443
WORLDWIDE STAFF	121
HEADQUARTERS	Atlanta, GA
YEAR ESTABLISHED	1979

132 | RNL

RNL

1050 17th Street, Suite A200
Denver, CO 80265
(303) 295-1717
www.rnldesign.com

WORLDWIDE REVENUE	$22,343,000
WORLDWIDE STAFF	121
HEADQUARTERS	Denver, CO
YEAR ESTABLISHED	1956

133 | Hixson

659 Van Meter Avenue
Cincinnati, OH 45202
(513) 241-1230
www.hixson-inc.com

WORLDWIDE REVENUE	$22,300,000
WORLDWIDE STAFF	136
HEADQUARTERS	Cincinnati, OH
YEAR ESTABLISHED	1948

134 | WDG Architecture

1025 Connecticut Avenue NW, Suite 300
Washington, DC 20036
(202) 857-8300
www.wdgarch.com

WORLDWIDE REVENUE	$22,197,000
WORLDWIDE STAFF	151
HEADQUARTERS	Washington, DC
YEAR ESTABLISHED	1938

135 | KMD Architects

222 Vallejo Street
San Francisco, CA 94111
(415) 398-5191
www.kmdarchitects.com

WORLDWIDE REVENUE	$22,000,000
WORLDWIDE STAFF	163
HEADQUARTERS	San Francisco, CA
YEAR ESTABLISHED	1963

136 | Kahler Slater

111 West Wisconsin Avenue
Milwaukee, WI 53203
(414) 272-2000
www.kahlerslater.com

WORLDWIDE REVENUE	$21,500,000
WORLDWIDE STAFF	142
HEADQUARTERS	Milwaukee, WI
YEAR ESTABLISHED	1908

137 | Mancini - Duffy

275 Seventh Avenue, 19th Floor
New York, NY 10001
(212) 938-1260
www.manciniduffy.com

WORLDWIDE REVENUE	$21,400,000
WORLDWIDE STAFF	60
HEADQUARTERS	New York, NY
YEAR ESTABLISHED	1920

138 | FreemanWhite

8845 Red Oak Boulevard
Charlotte, NC 28217
(704) 523-2230
www.freemanwhite.com

WORLDWIDE REVENUE	$21,300,000
WORLDWIDE STAFF	106
HEADQUARTERS	Charlotte, NC
YEAR ESTABLISHED	1892

139 | RBB Architects

10980 Wilshire Boulevard
Los Angeles, CA 90024
(310) 473-3555
www.rbbinc.com

WORLDWIDE REVENUE	$21,100,000
WORLDWIDE STAFF	75
HEADQUARTERS	Los Angeles, CA
YEAR ESTABLISHED	1952

140 | BOORA Architects

720 Southwest Washington, Suite 800
Portland, OR 97205
(503) 226-1575
www.boora.com

WORLDWIDE REVENUE	$21,005,000
WORLDWIDE STAFF	65
HEADQUARTERS	Portland, OR
YEAR ESTABLISHED	1958

141 | Miller Hull Partnership

71 Columbia Street, Suite 600
Seattle, WA 98104
(206) 682-6837
www.millerhull.com

WORLDWIDE REVENUE	$20,981,140
WORLDWIDE STAFF	80
HEADQUARTERS	Seattle, WA
YEAR ESTABLISHED	1977

142 | Goody Clancy

420 Boylston Street
Boston, MA 02116
(617) 262-2760
www.goodyclancy.com

WORLDWIDE REVENUE	$20,600,000
WORLDWIDE STAFF	67
HEADQUARTERS	Boston, MA
YEAR ESTABLISHED	1955

143 | Dattner Architects

1385 Broadway, 15th Floor
New York, NY 10018
(212) 247-2660
www.dattner.com

WORLDWIDE REVENUE	$20,500,000
WORLDWIDE STAFF	110
HEADQUARTERS	New York, NY
YEAR ESTABLISHED	1964

144 | Steffian Bradley Architects

88 Black Falcon Avenue, Suite 353
Boston, MA 02110
(617) 305-7100
www.steffian.com

WORLDWIDE REVENUE	$20,130,000
WORLDWIDE STAFF	140
HEADQUARTERS	Boston, MA
YEAR ESTABLISHED	1932

145 | Fanning/Howey Associates

540 East Market Street
Celina, OH 45822
(419) 586-7771
www.fhai.com

WORLDWIDE REVENUE	$20,100,000
WORLDWIDE STAFF	173
HEADQUARTERS	Celina,OH
YEAR ESTABLISHED	1961

146 | Albert Kahn Associates

7430 2nd Avenue, Suite 700
Detroit, MI 48202
(313) 202-7000
www.albertkahn.com

WORLDWIDE REVENUE	$20,000,000
WORLDWIDE STAFF	200
HEADQUARTERS	Detroit, MI
YEAR ESTABLISHED	1895

147 | Mead & Hunt

2440 Deming Way
Middleton, WI 53562
(608) 273-6380
www.meadhunt.com

WORLDWIDE REVENUE	$19,600,000
WORLDWIDE STAFF	500
HEADQUARTERS	Madison, WI
YEAR ESTABLISHED	1900

148 | Bermello Ajamil & Partners

2601 South Bayshore Drive, Suite 1000
Miami, FL 33133
(305) 859-2050
www.bamiami.com

WORLDWIDE REVENUE	$19,260,000
WORLDWIDE STAFF	90
HEADQUARTERS	Miami, FL
YEAR ESTABLISHED	1939

149 | SchenkelShultz

200 East Robinson Street, Suite 300
Orlando, FL 32801
(407) 872-3322
www.schenkelshultz.com

WORLDWIDE REVENUE	$19,100,000
WORLDWIDE STAFF	45
HEADQUARTERS	Fort Wayne, IN
YEAR ESTABLISHED	1958

150 | OTAK

808 Southwest Third Avenue, Suite 300
Portland, OR 97207
(503) 287-6825
www.otak.com

WORLDWIDE REVENUE	$19,090,000
WORLDWIDE STAFF	176
HEADQUARTERS	Portland, OR
YEAR ESTABLISHED	1980

151 | Aedas

3819 Lyceum Avenue
Los Angeles, CA 90066
(310) 821- 4859
www.aedas.com

WORLDWIDE REVENUE	$19,050,000
WORLDWIDE STAFF	151
HEADQUARTERS	Los Angeles, CA
YEAR ESTABLISHED	1952

152 | Cromwell Architects Engineers

101 South Spring Street
Little Rock, AR 72201
(501) 372-2900
www.cromwell.com

WORLDWIDE REVENUE	$19,030,000
WORLDWIDE STAFF	114
HEADQUARTERS	Little Rock, AR
YEAR ESTABLISHED	1885

153 | SHoP Architects

233 Broadway, 11th Floor
New York, NY 10279
(212) 889-9005
www.shoparc.com

WORLDWIDE REVENUE	$19,000,000
WORLDWIDE STAFF	60
HEADQUARTERS	New York, NY
YEAR ESTABLISHED	1996

154 | The Preston Partnership

115 Perimeter Center Place, Suite 650, South Terraces
Atlanta, GA 30346
(770) 396-7248
www.theprestonpartnership.com

WORLDWIDE REVENUE	$18,900,000
WORLDWIDE STAFF	60
HEADQUARTERS	Atlanta, GA
YEAR ESTABLISHED	1995

155 | Rebel Design+Group

2554 Lincoln Boulevard
Marina Del Rey, CA 90292
(800) 92-REBEL
www.rebeldesign.com

WORLDWIDE REVENUE	$18,792,889
WORLDWIDE STAFF	80
HEADQUARTERS	Marina Del Rey, CA
YEAR ESTABLISHED	1985

156 | Hnedak Bobo Group

104 South Front Street
Memphis, TN 38103
(901) 525-2557
www.hbginc.com

WORLDWIDE REVENUE	$18,500,000
WORLDWIDE STAFF	80
HEADQUARTERS	Memphis, TN
YEAR ESTABLISHED	1979

157 | Ascension Group Architects

1250 East Copeland Road, Suite 500
Arlington, TX 76011
(817) 226-1917
www.ascensiongroup.biz

WORLDWIDE REVENUE	$18,420,000
WORLDWIDE STAFF	50
HEADQUARTERS	Arlington, TX
YEAR ESTABLISHED	2001

158 | Workshop Architects

201 East Pittsburgh Avenue, Suite 301
Milwaukee, WI 53204
(414) 272-8822
www.workshoparchitects.com

WORLDWIDE REVENUE	$18,400,000
WORLDWIDE STAFF	17
HEADQUARTERS	Milwaukee, WI
YEAR ESTABLISHED	1996

159 | Hunton Brady Architects

800 North Magnolia Avenue, Suite 600
Orlando, FL 32803
(407) 839-0886
www.huntonbrady.com

WORLDWIDE REVENUE	$18,373,000
WORLDWIDE STAFF	85
HEADQUARTERS	Orlando, FL
YEAR ESTABLISHED	1947

160 | Devenney Group Architects

201 West Indian School Road
Phoenix, AZ 85013
(602) 943-8950
www.devenneygroup.com

WORLDWIDE REVENUE	$18,200,000
WORLDWIDE STAFF	63
HEADQUARTERS	Phoenix, AZ
YEAR ESTABLISHED	1962

161 | Jerde

913 Ocean Front Walk
Venice, CA 90291
(310) 399-1987
www.jerde.com

WORLDWIDE REVENUE	$18,097,890
WORLDWIDE STAFF	92
HEADQUARTERS	Los Angeles, CA
YEAR ESTABLISHED	1977

162 | Arrowstreet

10 Post Office Square, Suite 700N
Boston, MA 02109
(617) 623-5555
www.arrowstreet.com

WORLDWIDE REVENUE	$18,070,000
WORLDWIDE STAFF	45
HEADQUARTERS	Somerville, MA
YEAR ESTABLISHED	1961

163 | Altoon Partners

617 West 7th Street, Suite 400
Los Angeles, CA 90071
(213) 225-1900
www.altoonpartners.com

WORLDWIDE REVENUE	$18,025,000
WORLDWIDE STAFF	176
HEADQUARTERS	Los Angeles, CA
YEAR ESTABLISHED	1984

164 | John Portman & Associates

303 Peachtree Center Avenue, Suite 575
Atlanta, GA 30303
(404) 614-5555
www.portmanusa.com

WORLDWIDE REVENUE	$18,000,000
WORLDWIDE STAFF	78
HEADQUARTERS	Atlanta, GA
YEAR ESTABLISHED	1953

165 | BLT Architects

1216 Arch Street, Suite 800
Philadelphia, PA 19107
(215) 563-3900
www.blta.com

WORLDWIDE REVENUE	$17,900,000
WORLDWIDE STAFF	63
HEADQUARTERS	Philadelphia, PA
YEAR ESTABLISHED	1961

166 | RATIO Architects

101 South Pennsylvania Street
Indianapolis, IN 46204
(317) 633-4040
www.ratioarchitects.com

WORLDWIDE REVENUE	$17,814,000
WORLDWIDE STAFF	90
HEADQUARTERS	Indianapolis, IN
YEAR ESTABLISHED	1982

167 | SB Architects

One Beach Street, Suite 101
San Francisco, CA 94133
(415) 673-8990
www.sb-architects.com

WORLDWIDE REVENUE	$17,735,517
WORLDWIDE STAFF	82
HEADQUARTERS	San Francisco, CA
YEAR ESTABLISHED	1960

168 | Elness Swenson Graham Architects

500 Washington Avenue, Suite 1080
Minneapolis, MN 55415
(612) 339-5508
www.esgarch.com

WORLDWIDE REVENUE	$17,500,000
WORLDWIDE STAFF	52
HEADQUARTERS	Minneapolis,MN
YEAR ESTABLISHED	1995

169 | Crabtree, Rohrbaugh & Associates

401 East Winding Hill Road
Mechanicsburg, PA 17055
(717) 458-0272
www.cra-architects.com

WORLDWIDE REVENUE	$17,300,000
WORLDWIDE STAFF	70
HEADQUARTERS	Mechanicsburg, PA
YEAR ESTABLISHED	1984

Hanbury Evans Wright Vlattas + Company

Arizona State University Dining Hall, Phoenix, AZ | Hanbury Evans Wright Vlattas + Company

Hanbury Evans Wright Vlattas + Company

University of Michigan East Quad Renovation and Addition, Ann Arbor, MI | Hanbury Evans Wright Vlattas + Company

170 | Wallace Roberts & Todd

1700 Market Street, Suite 2800
Philadelphia, PA 19103
(215) 732-5215
www.wrtdesign.com

WORLDWIDE REVENUE	$17,200,000
WORLDWIDE STAFF	130
HEADQUARTERS	Philadelphia, PA
YEAR ESTABLISHED	1963

171 | BNIM Architects

106 West 14th Street, Suite 200
Kansas City, MO 64105
(816) 783-1500
www.bnim.com

WORLDWIDE REVENUE	$17,100,000
WORLDWIDE STAFF	68
HEADQUARTERS	Kansas City, MO
YEAR ESTABLISHED	1970

172 | Handel Architects

120 Broadway, 6th Floor
New York, NY 10271
(212) 595-4112
www.handelarchitects.com

WORLDWIDE REVENUE	$17,050,000
WORLDWIDE STAFF	105
HEADQUARTERS	New York, NY
YEAR ESTABLISHED	1994

173 | Hanbury Evans Wright Vlattas + Company

HANBURY EVANS
WRIGHT VLATTAS
+ C O M P A N Y
ARCHITECTURE PLANNING

120 Atlantic Street
Norfolk, VA 23510
(757) 321-9600
www.hewv.com

WORLDWIDE REVENUE	$17,000,000
WORLDWIDE STAFF	72
HEADQUARTERS	Norfolk, VA
YEAR ESTABLISHED	1979

174 | Orcutt I Winslow

3003 North Central Avenue, 16th Floor
Phoenix, AZ 85012
(602) 257-1764
www.owp.com

WORLDWIDE REVENUE	$16,900,000
WORLDWIDE STAFF	70
HEADQUARTERS	Phoenix, AZ
YEAR ESTABLISHED	1971

175 | Stevens & Wilkinson

100 Peachtree Street Northwest, Suite 2500
Atlanta, GA 30303
(404) 522-8888
www.stevenswilkinson.com

WORLDWIDE REVENUE	$16,800,000
WORLDWIDE STAFF	99
HEADQUARTERS	Atlanta, GA
YEAR ESTABLISHED	1919

New Trier High School Winnetka Campus Facilities Project, New Trier THSD 203, Winnetka, IL | Wight & Company

176 | FOX Architects

8484 Westpark Drive, Suite 620
McLean, VA 22102
(703) 821-7990
www.fox-architects.com

WORLDWIDE REVENUE	$16,700,000
WORLDWIDE STAFF	66
HEADQUARTERS	McLean, VA
YEAR ESTABLISHED	1993

177 | Anderson Mason Dale Architects

3198 Speer Boulevard
Denver, CO 80211
(303) 294-9448
www.amdarchitects.com

WORLDWIDE REVENUE	$16,520,000
WORLDWIDE STAFF	40
HEADQUARTERS	Denver, CO
YEAR ESTABLISHED	1960

178 | Hickok Cole Architects

1023 31st Street Northwest
Washington, DC 20007
(202) 667-9776
www.hickokcole.com

WORLDWIDE REVENUE	$16,500,000
WORLDWIDE STAFF	85
HEADQUARTERS	Washington, DC
YEAR ESTABLISHED	1987

179 | Mahlum

71 Columbia, 4th Floor
Seattle, WA 98104
(206) 441-4151
www.mahlum.com

WORLDWIDE REVENUE	$16,400,000
WORLDWIDE STAFF	90
HEADQUARTERS	Seattle, WA
YEAR ESTABLISHED	1938

180 | BBG-BBGM

1825 K Street NW, Suite 300
Washington, DC 20006
(202) 452-1644
www.bbg-bbgm.com

WORLDWIDE REVENUE	$16,100,000
WORLDWIDE STAFF	120
HEADQUARTERS	New York, NY
YEAR ESTABLISHED	1984

181 | Wight & Company   Wight

2500 North Frontage Road
Darien, IL 60561
(630) 969-7000
www.wightco.com

WORLDWIDE REVENUE	$16,000,000
WORLDWIDE STAFF	133
HEADQUARTERS	Darien, IL
YEAR ESTABLISHED	1939

Pinnacle Bank Arena, Lincoln, NE | DLR Group

Calaveras County - New San Andreas Courthouse, San Andreas, CA | DLR Group

182 | RAPT Studio

111 Maiden Lane, Suite 350
San Francisco, CA 94108
(415) 788-4400
www.raptstudio.com

WORLDWIDE REVENUE	$16,000,000
WORLDWIDE STAFF	41
HEADQUARTERS	San Francisco, CA
YEAR ESTABLISHED	1985

183 | Schmidt Associates

415 Massachusetts Avenue
Indianapolis, IN 46204
(317) 263-6226
www.schmidt-arch.com

WORLDWIDE REVENUE	$15,990,000
WORLDWIDE STAFF	92
HEADQUARTERS	Indianapolis, IN
YEAR ESTABLISHED	1976

184 | Legat Architects

651 West Washington Boulevard, Suite 1
Chicago, IL 60661
(312) 258-9595
www.legat.com

WORLDWIDE REVENUE	$15,950,000
WORLDWIDE STAFF	21–100
HEADQUARTERS	Chicago, IL
YEAR ESTABLISHED	1964

185 | Torti Gallas and Partners

1300 Spring Street, Suite 400
Silver Spring, MD 20910
(301) 588-4800
www.tortigallas.com

WORLDWIDE REVENUE	$15,900,000
WORLDWIDE STAFF	85
HEADQUARTERS	Silver Spring, MD
YEAR ESTABLISHED	1953

186 | Carrier Johnson + CULTURE

1301 3rd Avenue
San Diego, CA 92101
(619) 239-2353
www.carrierjohnson.com

WORLDWIDE REVENUE	$15,891,398
WORLDWIDE STAFF	64
HEADQUARTERS	San Diego, CA
YEAR ESTABLISHED	1977

187 | Tsoi/Kobus & Associates

One Brattle Square
Cambridge, MA 02238
(617) 475-4000
www.tka-architects.com

WORLDWIDE REVENUE	$15,658,004
WORLDWIDE STAFF	66
HEADQUARTERS	Cambridge, MA
YEAR ESTABLISHED	1983

Joe Harrison, JH Photography, Inc.

Beavercreek Coy/Trebein Campus, Beavercreek, OH | SHP Leading Design

Joe Harrison, JH Photography, Inc.

Lebanon Library Technology Center, Lebanon, OH | SHP Leading Design

188 | SHP Leading Design

SHP LEADING DESIGN

4805 Montgomery Road, Suite 400	WORLDWIDE REVENUE	$15,450,000
Cincinnati, OH 45212	WORLDWIDE STAFF	85
(513) 381-2112	HEADQUARTERS	Cincinnati, OH
www.shp.com	YEAR ESTABLISHED	1901

189 | Lake/Flato Architects

311 3rd Street, Suite 200	WORLDWIDE REVENUE	$15,400,000
San Antonio, TX 78205	WORLDWIDE STAFF	21–100
(210) 227-3335	HEADQUARTERS	San Antonio, TX
www.lakeflato.com	YEAR ESTABLISHED	1984

190 | Shremshock Architects

7400 West Campus Road, Suite 150	WORLDWIDE REVENUE	$15,350,000
New Albany, OH 43054	WORLDWIDE STAFF	101
(614) 545-4550	HEADQUARTERS	Westerville, OH
www.shremshock.com	YEAR ESTABLISHED	1976

191 | ka

1468 West 9th Street, Suite 600	WORLDWIDE REVENUE	$15,300,000
Cleveland, OH 44113	WORLDWIDE STAFF	105
(216) 781-9144	HEADQUARTERS	Cleveland, OH
www.kainc.com	YEAR ESTABLISHED	1960

192 | THW Design

2100 RiverEdge Parkway, Suite 900	WORLDWIDE REVENUE	$15,250,000
Atlanta, GA 30328	WORLDWIDE STAFF	40
(404) 252-8040	HEADQUARTERS	Atlanta, GA
www.thw.com	YEAR ESTABLISHED	1975

193 | Wakefield Beasley & Associates

5200 Avalon Road	WORLDWIDE REVENUE	$15,200,000
Alpharetta, GA 30009	WORLDWIDE STAFF	80
(770) 209-9393	HEADQUARTERS	Norcross, GA
www.wakefieldbeasley.com	YEAR ESTABLISHED	1980

194 | William Rawn Associates, Architects, Inc.

10 Post Office Square, Suite 1010	WORLDWIDE REVENUE	$15,183,654
Boston, MA 02109	WORLDWIDE STAFF	50
(617) 423-3470	HEADQUARTERS	Boston, MA
www.rawnarch.com	YEAR ESTABLISHED	1983

195 | Davis Carter Scott

1676 International Drive, Suite 500	WORLDWIDE REVENUE	$15,100,000
McLean, VA 22102	WORLDWIDE STAFF	21–100
(703) 556-9275	HEADQUARTERS	McLean, VA
www.dcsdesign.com	YEAR ESTABLISHED	1968

196 | Huntsman Architectural Group

50 California Street, 7th Floor	WORLDWIDE REVENUE	$15,000,000
San Francisco, CA 94111	WORLDWIDE STAFF	87
(415) 394-1212	HEADQUARTERS	San Francisco, CA
www.huntsmanag.com	YEAR ESTABLISHED	1981

197 | Gruen Associates

6330 San Vicente Boulevard, Suite 200	WORLDWIDE REVENUE	$14,950,000
Los Angeles, CA 90048	WORLDWIDE STAFF	21–100
(323) 937-4270	HEADQUARTERS	Los Angeles, CA
www.gruenassociates.com	YEAR ESTABLISHED	1946

198 | Gwathmey Siegel Kaufman Architects

525 Broadway, 7th Floor	WORLDWIDE REVENUE	$14,900,000
New York, NY 10012	WORLDWIDE STAFF	45
(212) 947-1240	HEADQUARTERS	New York, NY
www.gwathmey-siegel.com	YEAR ESTABLISHED	1968

199 | H+L Architecture

1755 Blake Street, Suite 400	WORLDWIDE REVENUE	$14,812,710
Denver, CO 80202	WORLDWIDE STAFF	63
(303) 298-4734	HEADQUARTERS	Denver, CO
www.hlarch.com	YEAR ESTABLISHED	1963

200 | RMW architecture & interiors

160 Pine Street, 4th Floor
San Francisco, CA 94111
(415) 781-9800
www.rmw.com

WORLDWIDE REVENUE	$14,800,000
WORLDWIDE STAFF	60
HEADQUARTERS	San Francisco, CA
YEAR ESTABLISHED	1970

201 | Morphosis

3440 Wesley Street
Culver City, CA 90232
(424) 258-6200
www.morphosis.com

WORLDWIDE REVENUE	$14,700,000
WORLDWIDE STAFF	21–100
HEADQUARTERS	Culver City, CA
YEAR ESTABLISHED	1972

202 | TSP

1112 North West Avenue
Sioux Falls, SD 57104
(605) 336-1160
www.teamtsp.com

WORLDWIDE REVENUE	$14,600,000
WORLDWIDE STAFF	101–450
HEADQUARTERS	Sioux Falls, SD
YEAR ESTABLISHED	1930

203 | Eskew+Dumez+Ripple

365 Canal Street, Suite 3150
New Orleans, LA 70130
(504) 561-8686
www.eskewdumezripple.com

WORLDWIDE REVENUE	$14,550,000
WORLDWIDE STAFF	40
HEADQUARTERS	New Orleans, LA
YEAR ESTABLISHED	1989

204 | Peter Marino Architect

150 East 58th Street
New York, NY 10022
(212) 752-5444
www.petermarinoarchitect.com

WORLDWIDE REVENUE	$14,500,000
WORLDWIDE STAFF	167
HEADQUARTERS	New York, NY
YEAR ESTABLISHED	1978

205 | GWWO Architects

800 Wyman Park Drive, Suite 300
Baltimore, MD 21211
(410) 332-1009
www.gwwoinc.com

WORLDWIDE REVENUE	$14,438,710
WORLDWIDE STAFF	55
HEADQUARTERS	Baltimore, MD
YEAR ESTABLISHED	1990

©D. A. Horchner/Design Workshop

Eaton World Headquarters, Beachwood, OH | Design Workshop

©D. A. Horchner/Design Workshop

Bagby Park, Houston, TX | Design Workshop

206 | Bergmeyer Associates

51 Sleeper Street, 6th Floor
Boston, MA 02210
(617) 542-1025
www.bergmeyer.com

WORLDWIDE REVENUE	$14,200,000
WORLDWIDE STAFF	50
HEADQUARTERS	Boston, MA
YEAR ESTABLISHED	1973

207 | Field Paoli Architects

150 California Street, 7th Floor
San Francisco, CA 94111
(415) 788-6606
www.fieldpaoli.com

WORLDWIDE REVENUE	$14,100,000
WORLDWIDE STAFF	25
HEADQUARTERS	San Francisco, CA
YEAR ESTABLISHED	1986

208 | Nadel

1990 South Bundy Drive, 4th Floor
Los Angeles, CA 90025
(310) 826-2100
www.nadelarc.com

WORLDWIDE REVENUE	$14,000,000
WORLDWIDE STAFF	70
HEADQUARTERS	Los Angeles, CA
YEAR ESTABLISHED	1973

209 | Harvard Jolly Architecture

5201 West Kennedy Boulevard, Suite 515
Tampa, FL 33609
(813) 286-8206
www.harvardjolly.com

WORLDWIDE REVENUE	$14,000,000
WORLDWIDE STAFF	65
HEADQUARTERS	Tampa, FL
YEAR ESTABLISHED	1938

210 | Overland Partners Architects

203 East Jones Avenue
San Antonio, TX 78215
(210) 829-7003
www.overlandpartners.com

WORLDWIDE REVENUE	$13,940,000
WORLDWIDE STAFF	58
HEADQUARTERS	San Antonio, TX
YEAR ESTABLISHED	1987

211 | The Portico Group

1500 4th Avenue, 3rd Floor
Seattle, WA 98101
(206) 621-2196
www.porticogroup.com

WORLDWIDE REVENUE	$13,900,000
WORLDWIDE STAFF	52
HEADQUARTERS	Seattle, WA
YEAR ESTABLISHED	1984

212 | CetraRuddy

584 Broadway, Suite 401
New York, NY 10012
(212) 941-9801
www.cetraruddy.com

WORLDWIDE REVENUE	$13,800,000
WORLDWIDE STAFF	86
HEADQUARTERS	New York, NY
YEAR ESTABLISHED	1987

213 | Pieper O'Brien Herr Architects

3000 Royal Boulevard South
Alpharetta, GA 30022
(770) 569-1706
www.poharchitects.com

WORLDWIDE REVENUE	$13,704,000
WORLDWIDE STAFF	55
HEADQUARTERS	Alpharetta, GA
YEAR ESTABLISHED	1971

214 | Cooper Robertson

123 William Street
New York, NY 10038
(212) 247-1717
www.cooperrobertson.com

WORLDWIDE REVENUE	$13,400,000
WORLDWIDE STAFF	52
HEADQUARTERS	New York, NY
YEAR ESTABLISHED	1979

215 | Sink Combs Dethlefs

475 Lincoln Street, Suite 100
Denver, CO 80203
(303) 308-0200
www.sinkcombs.com

WORLDWIDE REVENUE	$13,266,022
WORLDWIDE STAFF	50
HEADQUARTERS	Denver, CO
YEAR ESTABLISHED	1962

216 | Holzman Moss Bottino Architecture

90 Broad Street, Suite 1803
New York, NY 10004
(212) 465-0808
www.holzmanmoss.com

WORLDWIDE REVENUE	$13,200,000
WORLDWIDE STAFF	32
HEADQUARTERS	New York, NY
YEAR ESTABLISHED	2004

217 | Bruner/Cott & Associates

130 Prospect Street
Cambridge, MA 02139
(617) 492-8400
www.brunercott.com

WORLDWIDE REVENUE	$13,150,000
WORLDWIDE STAFF	65
HEADQUARTERS	Cambridge, MA
YEAR ESTABLISHED	1972

218 | Baskervill

101 South 15th Street, Suite 200
Richmond, VA 23219
(804) 343-1010
www.baskervill.com

WORLDWIDE REVENUE	$13,086,957
WORLDWIDE STAFF	95
HEADQUARTERS	Richmond, VA
YEAR ESTABLISHED	1897

219 | CMA

800 Washington Avenue North, Suite 208
Minneapolis, MN 55401
(612) 547-1300
www.cmarch.com

WORLDWIDE REVENUE	$13,000,000
WORLDWIDE STAFF	106
HEADQUARTERS	Minneapolis, MN
YEAR ESTABLISHED	1977

220 | LSM

1212 Banks
Washington, DC 20007
(202) 295-4800
www.lsm.com

WORLDWIDE REVENUE	$12,950,000
WORLDWIDE STAFF	50
HEADQUARTERS	Washington, DC
YEAR ESTABLISHED	1991

221 | Bohlin Cywinski Jackson

8 West Market Street, Suite 1200
Wilkes-Barre, PA 18701
(570) 825-8756
www.bcj.com

WORLDWIDE REVENUE	$12,910,000
WORLDWIDE STAFF	185
HEADQUARTERS	Wilkes Barre, PA
YEAR ESTABLISHED	1965

222 | JPC Architects

909 112th Avenue Northeast, Suite 206
Bellevue, WA 98004
(425) 641-9200
www.jpcarchitects.com

WORLDWIDE REVENUE	$12,900,000
WORLDWIDE STAFF	41
HEADQUARTERS	Bellevue, WA
YEAR ESTABLISHED	1986

223 | Architekton

464 South Farmer Avenue, Suite 101
Tempe, AZ 85281
(480) 894-4637
www.architekton.com

WORLDWIDE REVENUE	$12,850,000
WORLDWIDE STAFF	40
HEADQUARTERS	Tempe, AZ
YEAR ESTABLISHED	1989

224 | CASCO

10877 Watson Road
St. Louis, MO 63127
(314) 821-1100
www.cascocorp.com

WORLDWIDE REVENUE	$12,800,000
WORLDWIDE STAFF	135
HEADQUARTERS	St. Louis, MO
YEAR ESTABLISHED	1959

225 | Lantz-Boggio Architects

5650 DTC Parkway, Suite 200
Englewood, CO 80111
(303) 773-0436
www.lantz-boggio.com

WORLDWIDE REVENUE	$12,402,529
WORLDWIDE STAFF	46
HEADQUARTERS	Englewood, CO
YEAR ESTABLISHED	1984

226 | Yost Grube Hall Architecture

707 Southwest Washington Street, Suite 1200
Portland, OR 97205
(503) 221-0150
www.ygh.com

WORLDWIDE REVENUE	$12,300,000
WORLDWIDE STAFF	58
HEADQUARTERS	Portland, OR
YEAR ESTABLISHED	1964

227 | Williams Blackstock Architects

2204 1st Avenue South, Suite 200
Birmingham, AL 35233
(205) 252-9811
www.wba-architects.com

WORLDWIDE REVENUE	$12,210,000
WORLDWIDE STAFF	32
HEADQUARTERS	Birmingham, AL
YEAR ESTABLISHED	1992

228 | Ratcliff

5856 Doyle Street
Emeryville, CA 94608
(510) 899-6400
www.ratcliffarch.com

WORLDWIDE REVENUE	$12,200,000
WORLDWIDE STAFF	55
HEADQUARTERS	Emeryville, CA
YEAR ESTABLISHED	1906

229 | Design Workshop

1390 Lawrence Street, Suite 200
Denver, CO 80204
(303) 623-5186
www.designworkshop.com

WORLDWIDE REVENUE	$12,100,000
WORLDWIDE STAFF	74
HEADQUARTERS	Denver, CO
YEAR ESTABLISHED	1969

230 | Baker Barrios Architects

189 South Orange Avenue, Suite 1700
Orlando, FL 32801
(407) 926-3000
www.bakerbarrios.com

WORLDWIDE REVENUE	$12,000,000
WORLDWIDE STAFF	101–450
HEADQUARTERS	Orlando, FL
YEAR ESTABLISHED	1993

231 | INVISION

501 Sycamore Street, Suite 101
Waterloo, IA 50704
(319) 233-8419
www.invisionarch.com

WORLDWIDE REVENUE	$11,754,000
WORLDWIDE STAFF	50
HEADQUARTERS	Waterloo, IA
YEAR ESTABLISHED	1914

232 | TMP Associates

1191 West Square Lake Road, Box 289
Bloomfield Hills, MI 48302
(248) 338-4561
www.tmp-architecture.com

WORLDWIDE REVENUE	$11,643,000
WORLDWIDE STAFF	68
HEADQUARTERS	Bloomfield Hills, MI
YEAR ESTABLISHED	1959

233 | Van Tilburg, Banvard & Soderbergh

1738 Berkeley Street
Santa Monica, CA 90404
(310) 394-0273
www.vtbs.com

WORLDWIDE REVENUE	$11,400,000
WORLDWIDE STAFF	105
HEADQUARTERS	Santa Monica, CA
YEAR ESTABLISHED	1994

234 | Engberg Anderson

320 East Buffalo Street, Suite 500
Milwaukee, WI 53202
(414) 944-9000
www.engberganderson.com

WORLDWIDE REVENUE	$11,200,000
WORLDWIDE STAFF	45
HEADQUARTERS	Milwaukee, WI
YEAR ESTABLISHED	1988

235 | Hawley Peterson & Snyder Architects

444 Castro Street, Suite 1000
Mountain View, CA 94041
(650) 968-2944
www.hpsarch.com

WORLDWIDE REVENUE	$11,050,000
WORLDWIDE STAFF	38
HEADQUARTERS	Mountain View, CA
YEAR ESTABLISHED	1957

Nick Merrick © Hedrich Blessing

Epsilon, Irving, TX | Staffelbach

236 | BCK-IBI Group

41 Chenango Street
Binghamton, NY 13901
(607) 772-0007
www.bckpc.com

WORLDWIDE REVENUE	$11,000,000
WORLDWIDE STAFF	56
HEADQUARTERS	Binghamton, NY
YEAR ESTABLISHED	1976

237 | Stephen B. Jacobs Group/Andi Pepper Designs

381 Park Avenue South
New York, NY 10016
(212) 421-3712
www.sbjgroup.com

WORLDWIDE REVENUE	$10,900,000
WORLDWIDE STAFF	40
HEADQUARTERS	New York, NY
YEAR ESTABLISHED	1967

238 | MKC Associates

90 Hidden Ravines Drive
Powell, OH 43065
(866) 675-7584
www.mkcinc.com

WORLDWIDE REVENUE	$10,800,000
WORLDWIDE STAFF	43
HEADQUARTERS	Mansfield, OH
YEAR ESTABLISHED	1924

239 | Staffelbach

STAFFELBACH

2525 McKinnon Street, Suite 800
Dallas, TX 75201
(214) 747-2511
www.staffelbach.com

WORLDWIDE REVENUE	$10,750,000
WORLDWIDE STAFF	78
HEADQUARTERS	Dallas, TX
YEAR ESTABLISHED	1966

240 | Integrated Architecture

4090 Lake Drive Southeast
Grand Rapids, MI 49546
(616) 574-0220
www.intarch.com

WORLDWIDE REVENUE	$10,700,000
WORLDWIDE STAFF	60
HEADQUARTERS	Grand Rapids, MI
YEAR ESTABLISHED	1988

241 | Thalden-Boyd-Emery Architects

1133 Olivette Executive Parkway
Olivette, MO 63132
(314) 727-7000
www.thaldenboyd.com

WORLDWIDE REVENUE	$10,600,000
WORLDWIDE STAFF	5–20
HEADQUARTERS	Olivette, MO
YEAR ESTABLISHED	1962

242 | Marshall Craft Associates

6112 York Road
Baltimore, MD 21212
(410) 532-3131
www.marshallcraft.com

WORLDWIDE REVENUE	$10,500,000
WORLDWIDE STAFF	28
HEADQUARTERS	Baltimore, MD
YEAR ESTABLISHED	1986

243 | Helix Architecture + Design

1629 Walnut Street
Kansas City, MO 64108
(816) 300-0300
www.helixkc.com

WORLDWIDE REVENUE	$10,450,000
WORLDWIDE STAFF	29
HEADQUARTERS	Kansas City, MO
YEAR ESTABLISHED	1992

244 | Bullock Tice Associates

909 East Cervantes Street
Pensacola, FL 32501
(850) 434-5444
www.bullocktice.com

WORLDWIDE REVENUE	$10,400,000
WORLDWIDE STAFF	26
HEADQUARTERS	Pensacola, FL
YEAR ESTABLISHED	1958

245 | KPS Group

2101 First Avenue
Birmingham, AL 35203
(205) 251-0125
www.kpsgroup.com

WORLDWIDE REVENUE	$10,300,000
WORLDWIDE STAFF	42
HEADQUARTERS	Birmingham, AL
YEAR ESTABLISHED	1965

246 | Davis

74 East Rio Salado Parkway, Suite 200
Tempe, AZ 85281
(480) 638-1100
www.thedavisexperience.com

WORLDWIDE REVENUE	$10,250,000
WORLDWIDE STAFF	30
HEADQUARTERS	Tempe, AZ
YEAR ESTABLISHED	1975

247 | TowerPinkster

242 East Kalamazoo Avenue, Suite 200
Kalamazoo, MI 49007
(269) 343-6133
www.towerpinkster.com

WORLDWIDE REVENUE	$10,200,000
WORLDWIDE STAFF	70
HEADQUARTERS	Kalamazoo, MI
YEAR ESTABLISHED	1953

248 | Rees Associates

92111 Lake Hefner Parkway, Suite 300
Oklahoma City, OK 73120
(888) 942-7337
www.rees.com

WORLDWIDE REVENUE	$10,100,000
WORLDWIDE STAFF	64
HEADQUARTERS	Oklahoma City, OK
YEAR ESTABLISHED	1975

249 | Helman Hurley Charvat Peacock/Architects

120 North Orange Avenue
Orlando, FL 32801
(407) 644-2656
www.hhcp.com

WORLDWIDE REVENUE	$10,000,000
WORLDWIDE STAFF	44
HEADQUARTERS	Orlando, FL
YEAR ESTABLISHED	1975

250 | JHP Architecture/Urban Design

8340 Meadow Road, Suite 150
Dallas, TX 75231
(214) 363-5687
www.jhparch.com

WORLDWIDE REVENUE	$9,800,000
WORLDWIDE STAFF	30
HEADQUARTERS	Dallas, TX
YEAR ESTABLISHED	1979

251 | Polk Stanley Wilcox

2222 Cottondale Lane, Suite 100
Little Rock, AR 72202
(501) 378-0878
www.polkstanleywilcox.com

WORLDWIDE REVENUE	$9,780,738
WORLDWIDE STAFF	42
HEADQUARTERS	Little Rock, AR
YEAR ESTABLISHED	1977

252 | Centerbrook Architects and Planners

67 Main Street, P.O. Box 955
Centerbrook, CT 06409
(860) 767-0175
www.centerbrook.com

WORLDWIDE REVENUE	$9,700,000
WORLDWIDE STAFF	21–100
HEADQUARTERS	Centerbrook, CT
YEAR ESTABLISHED	1975

253 | Miller Dunwiddie Architects

123 North 3rd Street, Suite 104
Minneapolis, MN 55401
(612) 337-0000
www.millerdunwiddie.com

WORLDWIDE REVENUE	$9,500,000
WORLDWIDE STAFF	21–100
HEADQUARTERS	Minneapolis, MN
YEAR ESTABLISHED	1963

Joe Harrison, JH Photography, Inc.

Miami University Geothermal Energy Plant, Oxford, OH | SHP Leading Design

Joe Harrison, JH Photography, Inc.

Zane State College Advanced Science and Technology Center, Zanesville, OH | SHP Leading Design

254 | BCA

505 South Market Street	WORLDWIDE REVENUE	$9,400,000
San Jose, CA 95113	WORLDWIDE STAFF	42
(408) 588-3800	HEADQUARTERS	San Jose, CA
www.BCAarchitects.com	YEAR ESTABLISHED	1989

255 | Bennett Wagner & Grody Architects

1301 Wazee Street, Suite 100	WORLDWIDE REVENUE	$9,200,000
Denver, CO 80204	WORLDWIDE STAFF	35
(303) 623-7323	HEADQUARTERS	Denver, CO
www.bwgarchitects.com	YEAR ESTABLISHED	1989

256 | Rosser International

1555 Peachtree Street Northeast, Suite 800	WORLDWIDE REVENUE	$9,121,916
Atlanta, GA 30309	WORLDWIDE STAFF	85
(404) 876-3800	HEADQUARTERS	Atlanta, GA
www.rosser.com	YEAR ESTABLISHED	1947

257 | Hamilton Anderson

1435 Randolph Street, Suite 200	WORLDWIDE REVENUE	$9,120,000
Detroit, MI 48226	WORLDWIDE STAFF	55
(313) 964-0270	HEADQUARTERS	Detroit, MI
www.hamilton-anderson.com	YEAR ESTABLISHED	1994

258 | Arcturis

720 Olive Street, Suite 200	WORLDWIDE REVENUE	$9,110,000
St. Louis, MO 63101	WORLDWIDE STAFF	101
(314) 206-7100	HEADQUARTERS	St. Louis, MO
www.arcturis.com	YEAR ESTABLISHED	1977

259 | WASA Studio

740 Broadway	WORLDWIDE REVENUE	$9,105,000
New York, NY 10003	WORLDWIDE STAFF	70
(212) 420-1160	HEADQUARTERS	New York, NY
www.wasallp.com	YEAR ESTABLISHED	1889

260 | KCBA Architects

8 East Broad Street
Hatfield, PA 19440
(215) 368-5806
www.kcba-architects.com

WORLDWIDE REVENUE	$9,100,000
WORLDWIDE STAFF	60
HEADQUARTERS	Philadelphia, PA
YEAR ESTABLISHED	1972

261 | GSR Andrade Architects

4121 Commerce Street, Suite One
Dallas, TX 75226
(214) 824-7040
www.gsr-andrade.com

WORLDWIDE REVENUE	$9,075,200
WORLDWIDE STAFF	42
HEADQUARTERS	Dallas, TX
YEAR ESTABLISHED	1991

262 | CSArch

40 Beaver Street
Albany, NY 12207
(518) 463-8068
www.csarchpc.com

WORLDWIDE REVENUE	$9,050,000
WORLDWIDE STAFF	64
HEADQUARTERS	Albany, NY
YEAR ESTABLISHED	1991

263 | DWL Architects + Planners

2333 North Central Avenue
Phoenix, AZ 85004
(602) 264-9731
www.dwlarchitects.com

WORLDWIDE REVENUE	$9,000,000
WORLDWIDE STAFF	42
HEADQUARTERS	Phoenix, AZ
YEAR ESTABLISHED	1949

264 | 4240 Architecture

3507 Ringsby Court, Suite 117
Denver, CO 80216
(303) 292-3388
www.4240architecture.com

WORLDWIDE REVENUE	$8,964,166
WORLDWIDE STAFF	23
HEADQUARTERS	Denver, CO
YEAR ESTABLISHED	2003

265 | ICON Architecture

101 Summer Street
Boston, MA 02111
(617) 451-3333
www.iconarch.com

WORLDWIDE REVENUE	$8,930,602
WORLDWIDE STAFF	40
HEADQUARTERS	Boston, MA
YEAR ESTABLISHED	1996

266 | Cook + Fox Architects

641 Avenue of the Americas	WORLDWIDE REVENUE	$8,900,000
New York, NY 10011	WORLDWIDE STAFF	21–100
(212) 477-0287	HEADQUARTERS	New York, NY
www.cookplusfox.com	YEAR ESTABLISHED	2003

267 | Allied Works Architecture

1532 Southwest Morrison Street	WORLDWIDE REVENUE	$8,870,000
Portland, OR 97205	WORLDWIDE STAFF	40
(503) 227-1737	HEADQUARTERS	Portland, OR
www.alliedworks.com	YEAR ESTABLISHED	1994

268 | Merriman Associates/Architects

300 North Field Street	WORLDWIDE REVENUE	$8,800,000
Dallas, TX 75202	WORLDWIDE STAFF	40
(214) 987-1299	HEADQUARTERS	Dallas, TX
www.merrimanassociates.com	YEAR ESTABLISHED	1987

269 | Hollis + Miller Architects

8205 West 108th Terrace	WORLDWIDE REVENUE	$8,800,000
Overland Park, KS 66210	WORLDWIDE STAFF	37
(913) 451-8886	HEADQUARTERS	Overland Park, KS
www.hollisandmiller.com	YEAR ESTABLISHED	1950

270 | Dougherty + Dougherty Architects

3194D Airport Loop Drive	WORLDWIDE REVENUE	$8,800,000
Costa Mesa, CA 92626	WORLDWIDE STAFF	35
(714) 427-0277	HEADQUARTERS	Costa Mesa, CA
www.ddarchitecture.com	YEAR ESTABLISHED	1979

271 | JMZ Architects and Planners

190 Glen Street, P.O. Box 725	WORLDWIDE REVENUE	$8,740,000
Glens Falls, NY 12801	WORLDWIDE STAFF	27
(518) 793-0786	HEADQUARTERS	Glen Falls, NY
www.jmzarchitects.com	YEAR ESTABLISHED	1977

272 | Bernardon Haber Holloway

425 McFarlan Road, Suite 200
Kennett Square, PA 19348
(610) 444-2900
www.bernardon.com

WORLDWIDE REVENUE	$8,700,000
WORLDWIDE STAFF	44
HEADQUARTERS	Kenette Square, PA
YEAR ESTABLISHED	1973

273 | Pfeiffer Partners Architects

811 West 7th Street, 7th Floor
Los Angeles, CA 90017
(213) 624-2775
www.pfeifferpartners.com

WORLDWIDE REVENUE	$8,600,000
WORLDWIDE STAFF	21–100
HEADQUARTERS	Los Angeles, CA
YEAR ESTABLISHED	2004

274 | Slifer Designs

216 Main Street, Suite C-100
Edwards, CO 81632
(970) 926-8200
www.sliferdesigns.com

WORLDWIDE REVENUE	$8,530,000
WORLDWIDE STAFF	41
HEADQUARTERS	Vail, CO
YEAR ESTABLISHED	1984

275 | Ellenzweig

1280 Massachusetts Avenue
Cambridge, MA 02138
(617) 491-5575
www.ellenzweig.com

WORLDWIDE REVENUE	$8,520,000
WORLDWIDE STAFF	55
HEADQUARTERS	Cambridge, MA
YEAR ESTABLISHED	1965

276 | Rossetti

160 West Fort Street, Suite 400
Detroit, MI 48226
(313) 463-5151
www.rossetti.com

WORLDWIDE REVENUE	$8,510,000
WORLDWIDE STAFF	101–450
HEADQUARTERS	Southfield, MI
YEAR ESTABLISHED	1969

277 | Christner

168 North Meramec, Suite 400
St. Louis, MO 63105
(314) 725-2927
www.christnerinc.com

WORLDWIDE REVENUE	$8,505,000
WORLDWIDE STAFF	65
HEADQUARTERS	St. Louis, MO
YEAR ESTABLISHED	1963

278 | EDI International

10550 Richmond Avenue, Suite 160	WORLDWIDE REVENUE	$8,500,000
Houston, TX 77042	WORLDWIDE STAFF	52
(713) 375-1400	HEADQUARTERS	Houston, TX
www.EDI-International.com	YEAR ESTABLISHED	1976

279 | Sherlock Smith & Adams

3047 Carter Hill Road	WORLDWIDE REVENUE	$8,460,000
Montgomery, AL 36111	WORLDWIDE STAFF	63
(334) 263-6481	HEADQUARTERS	Montgomery, AL
www.ssainc.com	YEAR ESTABLISHED	1946

280 | MOA Architecture

821 17th Street, Suite 400	WORLDWIDE REVENUE	$8,440,000
Denver, CO 80202	WORLDWIDE STAFF	26
(303) 308-1190	HEADQUARTERS	Denver, CO
www.moaarch.com	YEAR ESTABLISHED	1981

281 | Wald, Ruhnke & Dost Architects

2340 Garden Road, Suite 100	WORLDWIDE REVENUE	$8,400,000
Monterey, CA 93940	WORLDWIDE STAFF	38
(831) 649-4642	HEADQUARTERS	Monterey, CA
www.wrdarch.com	YEAR ESTABLISHED	1990

282 | CDH Partners

675 Tower Road	WORLDWIDE REVENUE	$8,390,796
Marietta, GA 30060	WORLDWIDE STAFF	65
(770) 423-0016	HEADQUARTERS	Marietta, GA
www.cdhpartners.com	YEAR ESTABLISHED	1977

283 | Meyer, Scherer & Rockcastle

710 South 2nd Street, 8th Floor	WORLDWIDE REVENUE	$8,350,263
Minneapolis, MN 55401	WORLDWIDE STAFF	40
(612) 375-0336	HEADQUARTERS	Minneapolis,MN
www.msrltd.com	YEAR ESTABLISHED	1981

bKL Architecture

Fusion92, Chicago, IL | bKL Architecture

bKL Architecture

Fusion92, Chicago, IL | bKL Architecture

284 | Wilson Architectural Group

5051 Westheimer, Suite 200
Houston, TX 77056
(713) 621-8714
www.wilsonargroup.com

WORLDWIDE REVENUE	$8,345,000
WORLDWIDE STAFF	38
HEADQUARTERS	Houston, TX
YEAR ESTABLISHED	1986

285 | bKL Architecture

bKL
ARCHITECTURE

225 North Columbus Drive, Suite 100
Chicago, IL 60601
(312) 881-5999
www.bklarch.com

WORLDWIDE REVENUE	$8,300,000
WORLDWIDE STAFF	60
HEADQUARTERS	Chicago, IL
YEAR ESTABLISHED	2010

286 | Ashley McGraw Architects

125 East Jefferson Street, 15th Floor
Syracuse, NY 13202
(315) 425-1814
www.ashleymcgraw.com

WORLDWIDE REVENUE	$8,200,000
WORLDWIDE STAFF	40
HEADQUARTERS	Syracuse, NY
YEAR ESTABLISHED	1981

287 | Lindsay, Pope, Brayfield & Associates

344 West Pike Street
Lawrenceville, GA 30046
(770) 963-8989
www.lpbatlanta.com

WORLDWIDE REVENUE	$8,150,000
WORLDWIDE STAFF	5–20
HEADQUARTERS	Lawrenceville, GA
YEAR ESTABLISHED	1975

288 | IKM

One PPG Place
Pittsburgh, PA 15222
(412) 281-1337
www.ikminc.com

WORLDWIDE REVENUE	$8,100,000
WORLDWIDE STAFF	45
HEADQUARTERS	Pittsburgh, PA
YEAR ESTABLISHED	1911

289 | Barker Rinker Seacat Architecture

3457 Ringsby Court, Unit 200
Denver, CO 80216
(303) 455-1366
www.brsarch.com

WORLDWIDE REVENUE	$8,025,000
WORLDWIDE STAFF	28
HEADQUARTERS	Denver, CO
YEAR ESTABLISHED	1975

290 | VITETTA

1510 Chester Pike, Suite 104	WORLDWIDE REVENUE $8,010,000
Eddystone, PA 19022	WORLDWIDE STAFF 130
(215) 218-4747	HEADQUARTERS Philadelphia, PA
www.vitetta.com	YEAR ESTABLISHED 1967

291 | Bignell Watkins Hasser Architects

One Park Place, Suite 250	WORLDWIDE REVENUE $8,000,000
Annapolis, MD 21401	WORLDWIDE STAFF 38
(410) 224-2727	HEADQUARTERS Annapolis,MD
www.bigwaha.com	YEAR ESTABLISHED 1977

292 | LGA Partners

1425 Forbes Avenue, Suite 400	WORLDWIDE REVENUE $7,990,472
Pittsburgh, PA 15219	WORLDWIDE STAFF 45
(412) 243-3430	HEADQUARTERS Pittsburgh, PA
www.lga-partners.com	YEAR ESTABLISHED 1993

293 | Meeks + Partners

16000 Memorial Dr., Suite 100	WORLDWIDE REVENUE $7,920,000
Houston, TX 77079	WORLDWIDE STAFF 35
(281) 558-8787	HEADQUARTERS Houston, TX
www.meekspartners.com	YEAR ESTABLISHED 1974

294 | DDG

3700 O'Donnell Street	WORLDWIDE REVENUE $7,844,397
Baltimore, MD 21224	WORLDWIDE STAFF 68
(410) 962-0505	HEADQUARTERS Baltimore, MD
www.ddg-usa.com	YEAR ESTABLISHED 1972

295 | Rogers Partners Architects+Urban Designers

100 Reade Street	WORLDWIDE REVENUE $7,800,000
New York, NY 10013	WORLDWIDE STAFF 30
(212) 309-7570	HEADQUARTERS New York, NY
www.rogersarchitects.com	YEAR ESTABLISHED 2013

296 | Hartman Design Group

111 Rockville Pike, Suite 425	WORLDWIDE REVENUE $7,800,000
Rockville, MD 20850	WORLDWIDE STAFF 26
(301) 838-9306	HEADQUARTERS Washington, DC
www.hartmandesigngroup.com	YEAR ESTABLISHED 1987

297 | Urban Design Associates

3 PPG Place, 3rd Floor	WORLDWIDE REVENUE $7,700,000
Pittsburgh, PA 15222	WORLDWIDE STAFF 25
(412) 263-5200	HEADQUARTERS Pittsburgh, PA
www.urbandesignassociates.com	YEAR ESTABLISHED 1964

298 | Langdon Wilson International

1055 Wilshire Boulevard, Suite 1500	WORLDWIDE REVENUE $7,500,000
Los Angeles, CA 90017	WORLDWIDE STAFF 90
(213) 250-1186	HEADQUARTERS Los Angeles, CA
www.langdonwilson.com	YEAR ESTABLISHED 1951

299 | Muñoz & Company

1017 North Main Street, Suite 300	WORLDWIDE REVENUE $7,450,000
San Antonio, TX 78212	WORLDWIDE STAFF 50
(210) 349-1163	HEADQUARTERS San Antonio, TX
www.kellmunoz.com	YEAR ESTABLISHED 1927

300 | GUND Partnership

47 Thorndike Street	WORLDWIDE REVENUE $7,440,000
Cambridge, MA 02141	WORLDWIDE STAFF 21-100
(617) 250-6800	HEADQUARTERS Cambridge, MA
www.gundpartnership.com	YEAR ESTABLISHED 1971

301 | Stanley Beaman & Sears

180 Peachtree Street, Northwest, Suite 600	WORLDWIDE REVENUE $7,410,000
Atlanta, GA 30303	WORLDWIDE STAFF 57
(404) 524-2200	HEADQUARTERS Atlanta, GA
www.stanleybeamansears.com	YEAR ESTABLISHED 1991

302 | Bostwick Design Partnership

2729 Prospect Avenue
Cleveland, OH 44115
(216) 621-7900
www.bostwickdesign.com

WORLDWIDE REVENUE	$7,405,000
WORLDWIDE STAFF	40
HEADQUARTERS	Cleveland, OH
YEAR ESTABLISHED	1962

303 | MSA Architects

316 West 4th Street, 6th Floor
Cincinnati, OH 45202
(513) 241-5666
www.msaarch.com

WORLDWIDE REVENUE	$7,400,000
WORLDWIDE STAFF	44
HEADQUARTERS	Cincinnati, OH
YEAR ESTABLISHED	1985

304 | VMDO Architects

200 East Market Street
Charlottesville, VA 22902
(434) 296-5684
www.vmdo.com

WORLDWIDE REVENUE	$7,330,000
WORLDWIDE STAFF	50
HEADQUARTERS	Charlottesville, VA
YEAR ESTABLISHED	1976

305 | Margulies Perruzzi Architects

308 Congress Street
Boston, MA 02210
(617) 482-3232
www.mp-architects.com

WORLDWIDE REVENUE	$7,300,000
WORLDWIDE STAFF	31
HEADQUARTERS	Boston, MA
YEAR ESTABLISHED	1988

306 | Forum Studio

2199 Innerbelt Business Center Drive
St. Louis, MO 63114
(314) 429-1010
www.forumstudio.com

WORLDWIDE REVENUE	$7,200,000
WORLDWIDE STAFF	37
HEADQUARTERS	St. Louis, MO
YEAR ESTABLISHED	1999

307 | Hodges & Associates Architects

13642 Omega
Dallas, TX 75244
(972) 387-1000
www.hodgesusa.com

WORLDWIDE REVENUE	$7,120,000
WORLDWIDE STAFF	30
HEADQUARTERS	Dallas, TX
YEAR ESTABLISHED	1977

308 | Freiheit & Ho Architects

5209 Lake Washington Boulevard NE, Suite 200	WORLDWIDE REVENUE	$7,100,000
Kirkland, WA 98033	WORLDWIDE STAFF	40
(425) 827-2100	HEADQUARTERS	Kirkland, WA
www.fhoarch.com	YEAR ESTABLISHED	1985

309 | Omniplan

1845 Woodall Rodgers Freeway, Suite 1500	WORLDWIDE REVENUE	$7,050,000
Dallas, TX 75201	WORLDWIDE STAFF	30
(214) 826-7080	HEADQUARTERS	Dallas, TX
www.omniplan.com	YEAR ESTABLISHED	1956

310 | Finegold Alexander Architects

77 North Washington Street	WORLDWIDE REVENUE	$7,000,000
Boston, MA 02114	WORLDWIDE STAFF	30
(617) 227-9272	HEADQUARTERS	Boston, MA
www.faainc.com	YEAR ESTABLISHED	1961

311 | DiMella Shaffer

281 Summer Street	WORLDWIDE REVENUE	$6,900,000
Boston, MA 02210	WORLDWIDE STAFF	65
(617) 426-5004	HEADQUARTERS	Boston, MA
www.dimellashaffer.com	YEAR ESTABLISHED	1967

312 | Forum Architecture & Interior Design

745 Orienta Avenue, Suite 1121	WORLDWIDE REVENUE	$6,900,000
Altamonte Springs, FL 32701	WORLDWIDE STAFF	46
(407) 830-1400	HEADQUARTERS	Altamonte Springs, FL
www.forumarchitecture.com	YEAR ESTABLISHED	1986

313 | Crawford Architects

1801 McGee, Suite 200	WORLDWIDE REVENUE	$6,800,000
Kansas City, MO 64108	WORLDWIDE STAFF	5–20
(816) 421-2640	HEADQUARTERS	Kansas City, MO
www.crawfordarch.com	YEAR ESTABLISHED	2001

314 | Mackey Mitchell Architects

900 Spruce Street, Suite 500
St. Louis, MO 63103
(314) 421-1815
www.mackeymitchell.com

WORLDWIDE REVENUE	$6,770,000
WORLDWIDE STAFF	40
HEADQUARTERS	St. Louis, MO
YEAR ESTABLISHED	1968

315 | Ann Beha Architects

33 Kingston Street
Boston, MA 02111
(617) 338-3000
www.annbeha.com

WORLDWIDE REVENUE	$6,700,000
WORLDWIDE STAFF	21–100
HEADQUARTERS	Boston, MA
YEAR ESTABLISHED	1977

316 | Champalimaud

475 Tenth Avenue, 10th Floor
New York, NY 10018
(212) 807-8869
www.champalimauddesign.com

WORLDWIDE REVENUE	$6,600,000
WORLDWIDE STAFF	21–100
HEADQUARTERS	New York, NY
YEAR ESTABLISHED	1981

317 | Bargmann Hendrie & Archetype

300 A Street
Boston, MA 02210
(617) 350-0450
www.bhplus.com

WORLDWIDE REVENUE	$6,410,000
WORLDWIDE STAFF	30
HEADQUARTERS	Boston, MA
YEAR ESTABLISHED	1980

318 | TR,i Architects

9812 Manchester Road
St. Louis, MO 63119
(314) 395-9750
www.triarchitects.com

WORLDWIDE REVENUE	$6,400,000
WORLDWIDE STAFF	16
HEADQUARTERS	St. Louis, MO
YEAR ESTABLISHED	1989

319 | Hornberger + Worstell

170 Maiden Lane
San Francisco, CA 94108
(415) 391-1080
www.hornbergerworstell.com

WORLDWIDE REVENUE	$6,300,000
WORLDWIDE STAFF	38
HEADQUARTERS	San Francisco, CA
YEAR ESTABLISHED	1980

320 | Ferraro Choi

1240 Ala Moana Boulevard, Suite 510
Honolulu, HI 96814
(808) 533-8880
www.ferrarochoi.com

WORLDWIDE REVENUE	$6,250,000
WORLDWIDE STAFF	75
HEADQUARTERS	Honolulu, HI
YEAR ESTABLISHED	1988

321 | Boggs & Partners Architects

410 Severn Avenue, Suite 406
Annapolis, MD 21403
(410) 268-3797
www.boggspartners.com

WORLDWIDE REVENUE	$6,200,000
WORLDWIDE STAFF	10
HEADQUARTERS	Annapolis,MD
YEAR ESTABLISHED	1996

322 | Research Facilities Design

3965 Fifth Avenue, Suite 400
San Diego, CA 92103
(619) 297-0159
www.rfd.com

WORLDWIDE REVENUE	$6,000,000
WORLDWIDE STAFF	25
HEADQUARTERS	San Diego, CA
YEAR ESTABLISHED	1984

323 | JKR Partners

100 Penn Square East, Suite 1080
Philadelphia, PA 19107
(215) 928-9331
www.jkrpartners.com

WORLDWIDE REVENUE	$5,750,000
WORLDWIDE STAFF	40
HEADQUARTERS	Philadelphia, PA
YEAR ESTABLISHED	1984

324 | JBHM Architects

308 East Pearl Street, Suite 300
Jackson, MS 39201
(601) 352-2699
www.jbhm.com

WORLDWIDE REVENUE	$5,721,000
WORLDWIDE STAFF	29
HEADQUARTERS	Jackson, MS
YEAR ESTABLISHED	1970

325 | GH2 Architects

320 South Boston, Suite 1600
Tulsa, OK 74103
(918) 587-6158
www.gh2.com

WORLDWIDE REVENUE	$5,602,956
WORLDWIDE STAFF	33
HEADQUARTERS	Tulsa, OK
YEAR ESTABLISHED	1973

326 | MGE Architects

3081 Salzedo Street, Third Floor
Coral Gables, FL 33134
(305) 444-0413
www.mgearchitects.com

WORLDWIDE REVENUE	$5,600,000
WORLDWIDE STAFF	17
HEADQUARTERS	Coral Gables, FL
YEAR ESTABLISHED	1982

327 | MGA Partners Architects

234 Market Street
Philadelphia, PA 19106
(215) 925-0100
www.mgapartners.com

WORLDWIDE REVENUE	$5,568,000
WORLDWIDE STAFF	25
HEADQUARTERS	Philadelphia, PA
YEAR ESTABLISHED	1958

328 | Dykeman

1716 West Marine View Drive, Suite 200
Everett, WA 98201
(425) 259-3161
www.dykeman.net

WORLDWIDE REVENUE	$5,500,000
WORLDWIDE STAFF	20
HEADQUARTERS	Everett, WA
YEAR ESTABLISHED	1967

329 | Humphries Poli Architects

2100 Downing Street
Denver, CO 80205
(303) 607-0040
www.hparch.com

WORLDWIDE REVENUE	$5,425,000
WORLDWIDE STAFF	22
HEADQUARTERS	Denver, CO
YEAR ESTABLISHED	1994

330 | Holabird & Root

140 South Dearborn Street
Chicago, IL 60603
(312) 357-1771
www.holabird.com

WORLDWIDE REVENUE	$5,420,000
WORLDWIDE STAFF	24
HEADQUARTERS	Chicago, IL
YEAR ESTABLISHED	1880

331 | Cho Benn Holback + Associates

100 North Charles Street
Baltimore, MD 21201
(410) 576-0440
www.cbhassociates.com

WORLDWIDE REVENUE	$5,400,000
WORLDWIDE STAFF	32
HEADQUARTERS	Baltimore, MD
YEAR ESTABLISHED	1979

332 | Cass Sowatsky Consulting Architects

3569 Fifth Avenue
San Diego, CA 92103
(619) 298-3480
www.csc-a.com

WORLDWIDE REVENUE	$5,300,000
WORLDWIDE STAFF	19
HEADQUARTERS	San Diego, CA
YEAR ESTABLISHED	1983

333 | Affiniti Architects

6100 Broken South Parkway NW, Suite 8
Boca Raton, FL 33487
(561) 750-0445
www.affinitiarchitects.com

WORLDWIDE REVENUE	$5,263,950
WORLDWIDE STAFF	21
HEADQUARTERS	Boca Raton, FL
YEAR ESTABLISHED	1993

3

BUILDING TYPES |

Listings of architecturally significant
airports, aquariums, art museums,
convention centers, and sports stadiums,
with their requisite architectural statistics,
are available in this chapter.

Airports: 1990–2015

Airports have evolved over the past century from small, utilitarian structures to sprawling multi-purpose complexes. Engineering challenges, the popularity of regional airlines, the need to accommodate larger jets, and expansion in Asia have resulted in the construction of countless new airport terminals since 1990. Many of those noteworthy for their architecture or engineering are listed in the following chart.

Airport	Location	Architect	Opened
Astana International Airport (KZT), Passenger Terminal	Astana, Kazakhstan	Kisho Kurokawa Architect & Associates (Japan)	2005
Barcelona International Airport (BCN), T1	Barcelona, Spain	Taller de Arquitectura (Spain)	2009
Barcelona International Airport (BCN), South Terminal	Barcelona, Spain	Taller de Arquitectura (Spain)	2005
Beihai Fucheng Airport (BHY), Domestic Terminal	Beihai, Guangxi, China	Llewelyn-Davies Ltd. (UK)	2000
Beijing Capital International Airport (PEK), Terminal 3	Beijing, China	Foster + Partners (UK) with Beijing Institute of Architectural Design (China)	2008
Ben Gurion Airport (TLV), Airside Complex, Terminal 3	Tel Aviv, Israel	Moshe Safdie and Associates and TRA Architects—a joint venture	2004
Ben Gurion Airport (TLV), Landside Complex, Terminal 3	Tel Aviv, Israel	Skidmore, Owings & Merrill; Moshe Safdie and Associates; Karmi Associates (Israel); Lissar Eldar Architects (Israel) joint venture	2002
Bilbao Airport (BIO), Terminal Building	Bilbao, Spain	Santiago Calatrava (Spain)	2000
Buffalo Niagara International Airport (BUF), Passenger Terminal	Cheektowaga, NY	Cannon Design; William Nicholas Bodouva + Associates; Kohn Pedersen Fox— a joint venture	1997
Carrasco International Airport (MVD), New Terminal	Montevideo, Uruguay	Rafael Viñoly Architects with Carla Bechelli Arquitectos (Argentina)	2009
Central Japan International Airport (NGO)	Tokoname City, Aichi Prefecture, Japan	Nikken Sekkei (Japan); Azusa Sekkei (Japan); Hellmuth, Obata & Kassabaum/ Arup (UK)—a joint venture	2005
Changi Airport (SIN), Terminal 3	Singapore	CPG Corporation (Singapore); Skidmore, Owings & Merrill	2008
Charles de Gaulle Airport (CDG), Terminal 2E	Paris, France	Aéroports de Paris (France)	2003
Charles de Gaulle Airport (CDG), Terminal 2F	Paris, France	Aéroports de Paris (France)	1998

Airports: 1990–2015

Airport	Location	Architect	Opened
Chicago-O'Hare International Airport (ORD), Terminal 5	Chicago, IL	Perkins+Will with Heard & Associates	1994
Chongqing Jiangbei International Airport (CKG)	Chongqing, China	Llewelyn-Davies Ltd. (UK) with Arup (UK)	2004
Cologne/Bonn Airport (CGN), Terminal 2	Cologne, Germany	Murphy/Jahn	2000
Copenhagen International Airport (CPH), Terminal 3	Copenhagen, Denmark	Vilhelm Lauritzen AS (Denmark)	1998
Dallas-Fort Worth International Airport (DFW), Terminal D	Dallas/Fort Worth, TX	HNTB Architecture; HKS, Inc.; Corgan	2005
Denver International Airport (DEN)	Denver, CO	Fentress Bradburn Architects	1995
Detroit Metropolitan Wayne County Airport (DTW), North Terminal	Romulus, MI	Gensler; GHAFARI; Hamilton Anderson Associates	2008
Detroit Metropolitan Wayne County Airport (DTW), McNamara Terminal	Romulus, MI	SmithGroup	2002
Dubai International Airport (DXB), Terminal 3	Dubai, UAE	Paul Andreu Architecte (France)	2007
Dusseldorf International Airport (DUS)	Dusseldorf, Germany	JSK Architekten (Germany); Perkins+Will	2001–2003
Enfidha – Zine el Abidine Ben Ali Airport (NBE)	Enfidha, Tunisia	ADPi Designers & Planners (France)	2009
EuroAirport Basel-Mulhouse-Freiburg (BSL), South Terminal	Saint Louis Cédex, France	Aegerter and Bosshardt (Switzerland)	2005
Frankfurt Airport (FRA), Terminal 2	Frankfurt, Germany	Perkins+Will; JSK Architekten (Germany)	1994
Fukuoka International Airport (FUK), International Terminal	Hakata-ku, Fukuoka City, Japan	Hellmuth, Obata & Kassabaum; Azusa Sekkei (Japan); Mishima Architects (Japan); MHS Planners, Architects & Engineers Co. (Japan)	1999
Gardermoen Airport (GEN)	Oslo, Norway	AVIAPLAN (Norway); Niels Torp Architects (Norway)	1998
Graz International Airport (GRZ), Passenger Terminal	Graz, Austria	Pittino & Ortner Architekturbüro (Austria)	2005
Graz International Airport (GRZ), Passenger Terminal expansion	Graz, Austria	Riegler Riewe Architekten (Austria)	1994
Guangzhou Baiyun International Airport (CAN)	Guangdong, China	Parsons Brinckerhoff with URS Corporation	2004
Hamad International Airport (DOH)	Doha, Qatar	HOK	2014

Airport	Location	Architect	Opened
Hamburg Airport (HAM), New Terminal 1	Hamburg, Germany	gmp Architekten (Germany) with von Gerkan, Marg & Partner Architekten (Germany)	2005
Hamburg Airport (HAM), Terminal 4 (now Terminal 2)	Hamburg, Germany	von Gerkan, Marg & Partner Architekten (Germany)	1991
Haneda Airport (HND), New International Terminal	Tokyo, Japan	Unknown	2010
Haneda Airport (HND), Terminal 2	Tokyo, Japan	Cesar Pelli & Associates; Jun Mitsui & Associates Inc. Architects (Japan)	2004
Heathrow Airport (LHR), Terminal 2	London, UK	Luis Vidal + Architects (Spain); Foster + Partners	2014
Heathrow Airport (LHR), Terminal 5	London, UK	Richard Rogers Partnership (UK)	2008
Heathrow Airport (LHR), Pier 4A	London, UK	Nicholas Grimshaw & Partners (UK)	1993
Heathrow Airport (LHR), Europier	London, UK	Richard Rogers Partnership (UK)	1992
Hong Kong International Airport (HKG)	Hong Kong, China	Foster + Partners (UK)	1998
Incheon International Airport (ICN), Integrated Transportation Center	Seoul, South Korea	Terry Farrell and Partners (UK)	2002
Incheon International Airport (ICN)	Seoul, South Korea	Fentress Bradburn Architects with BHJW and Korean Architects Collaborative International (South Korea)	2001
Indianapolis Airport (IND), Passenger Terminal	Indianapolis, IN	Hellmuth, Obata & Kassabaum	2008
Indira Ghandi International Airport (DEL), Terminal 3	New Delhi, India	Hellmuth, Obata & Kassabaum with Mott MacDonald Group (UK)	2010
Jinan International Airport (TNA)	Jinan, China	Integrated Design Associates	2005
John F. Kennedy International Airport (JFK), Terminal 5	Jamaica, NY	Gensler	2008
John F. Kennedy International Airport (JFK), American Airlines Terminal, Phase 1	Jamaica, NY	DMJM Harris	AECOM	2005–2007
John F. Kennedy International Airport (JFK), Terminal 4	Jamaica, NY	Skidmore, Owings & Merrill	2001
John F. Kennedy International Airport (JFK), Terminal 1	Jamaica, NY	William Nicholas Bodouva + Associates	1998
Jorge Chávez International Airport (LIM), New Terminal	Lima, Peru	Arquitectonica	2005
Kansai International Airport (KIA)	Osaka Bay, Japan	Renzo Piano Building Workshop (Italy) with Nikken Sekkei (Japan), Aéroports de Paris (France), Japan Airport Consultants Inc. (Japan)	1994

Airports: 1990–2015

Airport	Location	Architect	Opened
King Fahd International Airport (DMM)	Dammam, Saudi Arabia	Minoru Yamasaki Associates (Japan)	1999
King Shaka International Airport (DUR)	Durban, South Africa	Osmond Lange Architects and Planners (South Africa)	2010
Kuala Lumpur International Airport (KUL)	Kuala Lumpur, Malaysia	Kisho Kurokawa Architect & Associates (Japan) with Akitek Jururancang (Malaysia)	1998
Learmonth International Airport (LEA)	Exeter, Australia	JCY Architects and Urban Designers (Australia)	1999
Lester B. Pearson International Airport (YYZ), Pier F at Terminal 1	Toronto, ON, Canada	Architects Canada; Moshe Safdie and Associates; Skidmore, Owings & Merrill; Adamson Associates Architects (Canada)	2007
Lester B. Pearson International Airport (YYZ), New Terminal 1	Toronto, ON, Canada	Skidmore, Owings & Merrill; Moshe Safdie and Associates; Adamson Associates Architects (Canada)	2004
Logan International Airport (BOS), Terminal A	Boston, MA	Hellmuth, Obata & Kassabaum with C&R/Rizvi, Inc.	2005
Madrid Barajas International Airport (MAD), Terminal 3	Madrid, Spain	Richard Rogers Partnership (UK) with Estudio Lamela (Spain)	2005
Málaga Airport (AGP), Terminal 3	Malaga, Spain	Bruce S. Fairbanks (Spain)	2010
Malaga Airport (AGP), Pablo Ruiz Picasso Terminal	Malaga, Spain	Taller de Arquitectura (Spain)	1991
McCarran International Airport (LAS), Satellite D	Las Vegas, NV	LEO A DALY; Tate & Snyder	1998
Mineta San José International Airport (SJC), Terminals A and B	San Jose, CA	Fentress Architects	2010
Mineta San José International Airport (SJC), Terminals A and B Concourses	San Jose, CA	Gensler	2010
Ministro Pistarini International Airport (EZE), Terminal A	Buenos Aires, Argentina	Estudio M/SG/S/S/S (Spain) with Urgell/Fazio/Penedo/Urgell (Spain)	2000
Munich International Airport (MUC), Terminal 2	Munich, Germany	K+P Architekten und Stadtplaner (Germany)	2003
Munich International Airport (MUC), Airport Center	Munich, Germany	Murphy/Jahn	1999
Munich International Airport (MUC)	Munich, Germany	Von Busse & Partners (Germany)	1992
Orlando International Airport (MCO), Airside 2	Orlando, FL	Hellmuth, Obata & Kassabaum	2000
Ottawa International Airport (YOW), Passenger Terminal	Ottawa, ON, Canada	Brisbin Brook Beynon Architects (Canada); Stantec	2003

Airport	Location	Architect	Opened
Philadelphia International Airport (PHL), International Terminal A-West	Philadelphia, PA	Kohn Pedersen Fox	2003
Pointe à Pitre Le Raizet International Airport (PTP)	Pointe à Pitre, Guadeloupe	Aéroports de Paris (France)	1996
Pulkovo International Airport (LED)	St. Petersburg, Russia	Grimshaw with Pascall + Watson (UK)	2015
Raleigh-Durham International Airport (RDU), Terminal 2 Phase 1	Raleigh-Durham, NC	Fentress Architects	2008
Raleigh-Durham International Airport (RDU), Terminal 2 Phase 2	Raleigh-Durham, NC	Fentress Architects	2011
Ronald Reagan Washington National Airport (DCA), North Terminal	Washington, DC	Cesar Pelli & Associates; LEO A DALY	1997
Sacramento International Airport (SMF), Central Terminal B and Airside Concourse	Sacramento, CA	Corgan Associates with Fentress Architects	2011
San Francisco International Airport (SFO), International Terminal	San Francisco, CA	Skidmore, Owings & Merrill with Del Campo & Maru and Michael Willis Architects	2000
San Francisco International Airport (SFO), Terminal 2	San Francisco, CA	Gensler	2011
San Pablo Airport (SVQ)	Seville, Spain	Rafael Moneo (Spain)	1992
Seattle-Tacoma International Airport (SEA), Central Terminal	Seattle, WA	Fentress Bradburn Architects	2005
Seattle-Tacoma International Airport (SEA), Concourse A	Seattle, WA	NBBJ	2004
Sendai International Airport (SDJ)	Natori, Japan	Hellmuth, Obata & Kassabaum; Nikken Sekkei (Japan)	1998
Shanghai Pudong International Airport (PVG), Terminal 2	Shanghai, China	Shanghai Xian Dai Architectural Design Group (China)	2007
Shanghai Pudong International Airport (PVG)	Shanghai, China	Aéroports de Paris (France)	1999
Shenzhen Baoan International Airport (SZX), Domestic Terminal	Shenzhen, China	Llewelyn-Davies Ltd. (UK)	2001
Shenzhen Baoan International Airport (SZX), Terminal 3	Shenzhen, China	Studio Fuksas (Italy)	2013
Sheremetyevo International Airport (SVO), Terminal 3	Moscow, Russia	ADPi Designers & Planners (France)	2009

Airports: 1990–2015

Airport	Location	Architect	Opened
Southampton Airport (SOU)	Southampton, UK	Manser Associates (UK)	1994
Stansted Airport (STN)	London, UK	Foster + Partners (UK)	1991
Suvarnabhumi Airport (BK)	Samut Prakarn (Bangkok), Thailand	MJTA (Murphy/Jahn; TAMS Consultants Inc.; ACT Engineering)	2006
Tianjin Binhai International Airport (TSN), Terminal	Dongli, China	Kohn Pedersen Fox with Netherlands Airport Consultants (Netherlands)	2008
Toulouse-Blagnac International Airport (TLS), Hall D	Toulouse, France	Cardete Huet Architectes (France)	2010
Winnipeg James Armstrong Richardson International Airport (YWG)	Winnipeg, MB, Canada	Pelli Clarke Pelli Architects and Stantec	2011
Zurich Airport (ZRH), Airside Centre	Zurich, Switzerland	Nicholas Grimshaw & Partners (UK) with Itten+Brechbühl (Switzerland)	2004

Source: DesignIntelligence

Aquariums

The opening of Boston's New England Aquarium in 1969 ushered in a new age for aquariums, combining the traditional ideas found in the classic aquariums of the early 20th century with new technology and revised educational and research commitments. Aquariums have since proliferated. The following pages highlight the major free-standing aquariums in the United States.

Aquarium	Location	Opened	Cost
Alaska SeaLife Center	Seward, AK	1998	$56 M
Aquarium of the Bay	San Francisco, CA	1996	$38 M
Aquarium of the Pacific	Long Beach, CA	1998	$117 M
Audubon Aquarium of Americas	New Orleans, LA	1990	$42 M
Belle Isle Aquarium	Royal Oak, MI	1904	$175,000
Birch Aquarium at Scripps Institution of Oceanography, UCSD	La Jolla, CA	1992	$14 M
Colorado's Ocean Journey Architects	Denver, CO	1999	$94 M
Flint RiverQuarium	Albany, GA	2004	$30 M
Florida Aquarium	Tampa, FL	1994	$84 M
Georgia Aquarium	Atlanta, GA	2005	$280 M ($110 M addition)
Great Lakes Aquarium	Duluth, MN	2000	$34 M
Greater Cleveland Aquarium	Cleveland, OH	2012	$33 M
John G. Shedd Aquarium	Chicago, IL	1930	$ 3.25 M ($45 M addition)
Maritime Aquarium at Norwalk	Norwalk, CT	1988	$11.5 M ($9 M addition)
Monterey Bay Aquarium	Monterey, CA	1984	$55 M ($57 M addition)
Mystic Aquarium	Mystic, CT	1973	$1.74 M ($52 M expansion)
National Aquarium	Washington, DC	1931	n/a
National Aquarium in Baltimore	Baltimore, MD	1981	$21.3 M ($35 M 1990 addition; $66 M 2005 addition)

Total Square Ft. (original/current)	Tank Capacity (orig./current, in gal.)	Architect
115,000	400,000	Cambridge Seven Associates with Livingston Slone
48,000	707,000	Esherick Homsey Dodge and Davis
156,735	900,000	A joint venture of Hellmuth, Obata & Kassabaum and Esherick Homsey Dodge and Davis
110,000	1.19 M	The Bienville Group: a joint venture of The Mathes Group, Eskew + Architects, Billes/Manning Architects, Hewitt Washington & Associates, Concordia
10,000	32,000	Albert Kahn Associates, Inc.
34,000	150,000	Wheeler Wimer Blackman & Associates
107,000	1 M	Odyssea: a joint venture of RNL and Anderson Mason Dale
30,000	175,000	Antoine Predock Architect with Robbins Bell Kreher Inc.
152,000	1 M	Hellmuth, Obata & Kassabaum and Esherick Homsey Dodge and Davis
500,000/584,000	8 M/9.3 M	Thompson, Ventulett, Stainback & Associates (PGAV Destinations, 2010 expansion)
62,382	170,000	Hammel, Green and Abrahamson
70,000	1 M	Marinescape (New Zealand); (John N. Richardson, original 1892 Powerhouse building)
225,000/395,000	1.5 M/3 M	Graham, Anderson, Probst, & White (Lohan Associates, 1991 addition)
102,000/135,000	150,000	Graham Gund Architects Inc. (original building and 2001 addition)
216,000/307,000	900,000/1.9 M	Esherick Homsey Dodge and Davis (original building and 1996 addition)
76,000/137,000	1.6 M/2.3 M	Flynn, Dalton and van Dijk (Cesar Pelli & Associates, 1999 expansion)
13,500	32,000	York & Sawyer Architects
209,000/324,000/ 389,400	1 M/1.5 M/ 1.578 M	Cambridge Seven Associates (Grieves & Associates, 1990 addition; Chermayeff, Sollogub and Poole, 2005 addition)

Aquariums

Aquarium	Location	Opened	Cost
New England Aquarium	Boston, MA	1969	$8 M ($20.9 M 1998 addition; $19.3 M 2001 expansion)
New Jersey State Aquarium	Camden, NJ	1992	$52 M
New York Aquarium at Coney Island	Brooklyn, NY	1957	n/a
Newport Aquarium	Newport, KY	1999	$40 M ($4.5 M expansion)
North Carolina Aquarium at Fort Fisher	Kure Beach, NC	1976	$1.5 M ($17.5 M expansion)
North Carolina Aquarium at Pine Knoll Shores	Pine Knoll Shores, NC	1976	$4 M ($25 M expansion)
North Carolina Aquarium on Roanoke Island	Manteo, NC	1976	$1.6 M ($16 M expansion)
Oklahoma Aquarium	Tulsa, OK	2003	$15 M
Oregon Coast Aquarium	Newport, OR	1992	$25.5 M
Ripley's Aquarium	Myrtle Beach, SC	1997	$40 M
Ripley's Aquarium of the Smokies	Gatlinburg, TN	2000	$49 M
Seattle Aquarium	Seattle, WA	1977	n/a ($20 M expansion)
South Carolina Aquarium	Charleston, SC	2000	$69 M
Steinhart Aquarium at the California Academy of Science	San Francisco, CA	2008	$438 M*
Tennessee Aquarium	Chattanooga, TN	1992	$45 M ($30 M addition)
Texas State Aquarium	Corpus Christi, TX	1990	$31 M ($14 M addition)
Virginia Aquarium & Science Center	Virginia Beach, VA	1986	$7.5 M ($35 M expansion)
Waikiki Aquarium	Honolulu, HI	1955	$400,000
Wonders of Wildlife at the American National Fish and Wildlife Museum	Springfield, MO	2001	$34 M

* Combines figures for the Steinhart Aquarium, Morrison Planetarium, and Kimball Natural History Museum.

Source: DesignIntelligence

Total Square Ft. (original/current)	Tank Capacity (orig./current, in gal.)	Architect
75,000/1 M	1 M	Cambridge Seven Associates (Schwartz/Silver Architects, 1998 addition; E. Verner Johnson and Associates, 2001 expansion)
120,000	1 M	The Hillier Group
150,000	1.8 M	n/a
100,000/121,200	1 M/1.01 M	GBBN Architects (original and 2005 expansion)
30,000/84,000	77,000/455,000	Cambridge Seven Associates (BMS Architects, 2002 expansion)
29,000/93,000	25,000/433,000	Hayes, Howell & Associates (BMS Architects, 2006 expansion)
34,000/68,000	5,000/400,000	Lyles, Bissett, Carlisle and Wolff Associates of North Carolina Inc. with Cambridge Seven Associates (BMS Architects, 2000 expansion)
71,600	500,000	SPARKS
51,000	1.4 M	SRG Partnership
87,000	1.3 M	Enartec
115,000	1.3 M	Helman Hurley Charvat Peacock/Architects
68,000/86,000	753,000/873,000	Fred Bassetti & Co. (Miller Hull Partnership and Mithun, 2007 expansion)
93,000	1 M	Eskew + Architects with Clark and Menefee Architects
410,000*	500,000	Renzo Piano Building Workshop (Italy) with Stantec Architecture
130,000/190,000	400,000/1.1 M	Cambridge Seven Associates (Chermayeff, Sollogub & Poole, 2005 addition)
43,000/73,800	325,000/725,000	Phelps, Bomberger, and Garza (Corpus Christi Design Associates, 2003 addition)
41,500/120,000	100,000/800,000	E. Verner Johnson and Associates (original building and 1996 expansion)
19,000	152,000	Hart Wood and Edwin A. Weed with Ossipoff, Snyder, and Rowland
92,000	500,000	Cambridge Seven Associates

Art Museums

By some calculations there are more than 16,000 museums in the United States. While the collections they hold are often priceless, the facilities that contain them are frequently significant, especially amidst the recent museum-building boom led by world-class architects. The following chart, while not comprehensive, lists architecturally significant US art museums.

Museum	Location	Architect (original)
Akron Art Museum	Akron, OH	Dalton, van Dijk, Johnson & Partners (conversion of the original 1899 post office)
Albright-Knox Art Gallery	Buffalo, NY	Edward B. Green
Allen Memorial Art Museum	Oberlin, OH	Cass Gilbert
Amon Carter Museum	Fort Worth, TX	Philip Johnson
Anchorage Museum of History and Art	Anchorage, AK	Kirk, Wallace, and McKinley with Schultz/Maynard
Art Institute of Chicago	Chicago, IL	Shepley, Rutan, and Coolidge
Art Museum of South Texas	Corpus Christi, TX	Philip Johnson
Asian Art Museum	San Francisco, CA	Gae Aulenti (Italy) with Hellmuth, Obata & Kassabaum, LDa Architects, and Robert Wong Architects (adapted the 1917 main library by George Kelham)
Aspen Art Museum	Aspen, CO	Shigeru Ban (Japan)
Baltimore Museum of Art	Baltimore, MD	John Russell Pope
Barnes Foundation	Merion, PA	Paul Philippe Cret
Barnes Foundation	Philadelphia, PA	Tod Williams Billie Tsien Architects
Bass Museum of Art	Miami, FL	B. Robert Swartburg (adapted the 1930 Miami Beach Library by Russell Pancoast)
Bechtler Museum of Modern Art	Charlotte, NC	Mario Botta (Switzerland)
Bellevue Art Museum	Bellevue, WA	Steven Holl Architects
Berkeley Art Museum + Pacific Film Archive	Berkeley, CA	Mario J. Ciampi & Associates
Birmingham Museum of Art	Birmingham, AL	Warren, Knight and Davis
Bowdoin College Museum of Art	Brunswick, ME	McKim, Mead and White
The Broad	Los Angeles, CA	Diller Scofidio + Renfro with Gensler

Opened	Architect (expansion)
1981	Coop Himmelb(l)au (Austria) with Westlake Reed Leskosky, 2007 John S. and James L. Knight Building
1905	Skidmore, Owings & Merrill, 1961 addition
1917	Venturi, Scott Brown and Associates, 1977 addition
1961	Johnson/Burgee Architects, 1977 expansion; Philip Johnson/Alan Ritchie Architects, 2001 expansion
1968	Kenneth Maynard Associates, 1974 addition; Mitchell | Giurgola Architects with Maynard and Partch, 1986 addition; David Chipperfield Architects with Kumin Associates Inc., 2009 expansion
1893	Skidmore, Owings & Merrill, 1977 Arthur Rubloff Building; Hammond, Beebe and Babka, 1988 Daniel F. and Ada L. Rice Building; Renzo Piano Building Workshop (Italy) , with Interactive Design Inc., 2009 Modern Wing
1972	Legorreta + Legorreta (Mexico) with Dykema Architects, 2006 William B. and Maureen Miller Building
2003	—
2014	—
1929	John Russell Pope, 1937 Jacobs Wing; Wrenn, Lewis & Jancks, 1950 May Wing, 1956 Woodward Wing and 1957 Cone Wing; Bower Lewis & Thrower Architects, 1994 West Wing for Contemporary Art
1925	—
2012	—
1964	Arata Isozaki & Associates (Japan) with Spillis Candela DMJM | AECOM, 2002 expansion
2010	—
2001	—
1970	—
1959	Warren, Knight and Davis, 1965 west wing, 1967 east wing, 1974 expansion, 1979 addition, and 1980 expansion; Edward Larrabee Barnes Associates, 1993 expansion
1894	Machado and Silvetti Associates, 2007 entry pavilion
2015	—

Art Museums

Museum	Location	Architect (original)
Brooklyn Museum	Brooklyn, NY	McKim, Mead, and White
Butler Institute of American Art	Youngstown, OH	McKim, Mead and White
Cantor Center	Palo Alto, CA	Ennead Architects
Chazen Museum of Art (formerly Elvehjem Museum of Art)	Madison, WI	Harry Weese
Cincinnati Art Museum	Cincinnati, OH	James McLaughlin
Cleveland Museum of Art	Cleveland, OH	Benjamin Hubbell and W. Dominick Benes
Clyfford Still Museum	Denver, CO	Allied Works Architecture
Colorado Springs Fine Arts Center	Colorado Springs, CO	John Gaw Meem
Columbus Museum of Art	Columbus, OH	Richards, McCarty and Bulford
Contemporary Art Museum St. Louis	St. Louis, MO	Allied Works Architecture
Contemporary Arts Museum, Houston	Houston, TX	Gunnar Birkerts and Associates
Corcoran Gallery of Art	Washington, DC	Ernest Flagg
Cranbrook Art Museum	Cranbrook, MI	Eliel Saarinen
Crocker Art Museum	Sacramento, CA	Seth Babson (architect of the original 1872 Crocker family mansion and art gallery)
Crystal Bridges Museum of American Art	Bentonville, AR	Moshe Safdie
Dallas Museum of Art	Dallas, TX	Edward Larrabee Barnes Associates
Dayton Art Institute	Dayton, OH	Edward B. Green
de Young Museum	San Francisco, CA	Herzog & de Meuron (Switzerland) with Fong & Chan Archite
Denver Art Museum	Denver, CO	Gio Ponti (Italy) with James Sudler Associates
Denver Museum of Contemporary Art	Denver, CO	Adjaye Associates (UK)
Des Moines Art Center	Des Moines, IA	Eliel Saarinen
Detroit Institute of Arts	Detroit, MI	James Balfour
Eli and Edythe Broad Art Museum, Michigan State University	East Lansing, MI	Zaha Hadid (UK)
Everson Museum of Art	Syracuse, NY	I.M. Pei & Associates
Figge Art Museum	Davenport, IA	David Chipperfield Architects (UK) with Herbert Lewis Kruse Blunck Architecture

Opened	Architect (expansion)
1897–1927	Prentice & Chan, Ohlhausen, 1978 addition; Arata Isozaki & Associates (Japan) and James Stewart Polshek & Partners, 1991 Iris and B. Gerald Cantor Auditorium; Polshek Partnership Architects, 2004 front entrance and public plaza addition
1919	Paul Boucherie, 1931 north and south wings; C. Robert Buchanan & Associates, 1967 addition; Buchanan, Ricciuti & Associates, 1986 west wing addition
2014	—
1970	Machado and Silvetti and Associates with Continuum Architects + Planners, 2011 expansion
1886	Daniel H. Burnham, 1907 Schmidlapp Wing; Garber and Woodward, 1910 Ropes Wing and 1930 Emery, Hanna & French Wings; Rendigs, Panzer and Martin, 1937 Alms Wing; Potter, Tyler, Martin and Roth, 1965 Adams-Emery Wing
1916	J. Byers Hays and Paul C. Ruth, 1958 addition; Marcel Breuer and Hamilton P. Smith, 1971 addition; Dalton, van Dijk, Johnson & Partners, 1984 addition; Rafael Viñoly Architects, 2009 East Wing
2011	—
1936	—
1931	Van Buren and Firestone, Architects, Inc., 1974 addition
2003	—
1972	—
1897	Charles Adams Platt, 1927 expansion
1941	Rafael Moneo (Spain), 2002 addition
1978	Gwathmey Siegel & Associates Architects with HMR Architects, Inc., 2010 expansion
2011	—
1984	Edward Larrabee Barnes Associates, 1985 decorative arts wing and 1991 Nancy and Jake L. Hamon Building
1930	Levin Porter Associates, 1997 expansion
2005	—
1971	Studio Daniel Libeskind with Davis Partnership Architects, 2006 Frederic C. Hamilton Building
2006	—
1948	I.M. Pei & Associates, 1968 addition; Richard Meier & Partners Architects, 1985 addition
1888	Cret, Zantzinger, Borie and Medary, 1927 addition; Harley, Ellington, Cowin and Stirton, with Gunnar Birkerts and Associates, 1966 south wings; Harley, Ellington, Cowin and Stirton, 1966 north wing; Michael Graves & Associates with SmithGroup, 2007 expansion
2012	—
1968	—
2005	—

Art Museums

Museum	Location	Architect (original)
Frances Lehman Loeb Art Center	Poughkeepsie, NY	Cesar Pelli & Associates
Fred Jones Jr. Museum of Art	Norman, OK	Howard and Smais
Frederick R. Weisman Art Museum	Minneapolis, MN	Frank O. Gehry and Associates, Inc.
Freer Gallery Art	Washington, DC	Charles Adams Platt
Frist Center for the Visual Arts	Nashville, TN	Tuck Hinton Architects (adapted the 1934 US Post Office by Marr and Holman Architects)
Frost Art Museum, Florida International University	Miami, FL	Hellmuth, Obata & Kassabaum
Frye Art Museum	Seattle, WA	Paul Albert Thiry
Grand Rapids Art Museum	Grand Rapids, MI	wHY Architecture with Design Plus
Harvard Art Museums	Cambridge, MA	Three separate museums: Arthur M. Sackler Museum, 1985 (James Stirling Michael Wilford and Associates (UK); Busch-Reisinger Museum, 1903; Fogg Art Museum, 1927 (Coolidge, Shepley, Bulfinch, and Abbott)
Herbert F. Johnson Museum of Art	Ithaca, NY	I.M. Pei & Partners
High Museum of Art	Atlanta, GA	Richard Meier & Partners Architects
Hirshhorn Museum and Sculpture Garden	Washington, DC	Skidmore, Owings & Merrill
Hood Museum of Art	Hanover, NH	Charles Moore and Centerbrook Architects and Planners
Hunter Museum of American Art	Chattanooga, TN	Mead and Garfield (architects of the 1905 mansion adapted to a museum in 1952)
Indiana University Art Museum	Bloomington, IN	I.M. Pei & Partners
Indianapolis Museum of Art	Indianapolis, IN	Richardson, Severns, Scheeler and Associates
Institute for Contemporary Art	Boston, MA	Diller Scofidio + Renfro
Iris & B. Gerald Cantor Center for Visual Arts	Stanford, CA	Percy & Hamilton Architects with Ernest J. Ransome
Isabella Stewart Gardner Museum	Boston, MA	Willard T. Sears
J. Paul Getty Museum	Los Angeles, CA	Richard Meier & Partners Architects
Joslyn Art Museum	Omaha, NE	John and Alan McDonald
Kemper Museum of Contemporary Art and Design	Kansas City, MO	Gunnar Birkerts and Associates
Kimbell Art Museum	Fort Worth, TX	Louis I. Kahn
Kreeger Museum	Washington, DC	Philip Johnson with Richard Foster
Lois & Richard Rosenthal Center for Contemporary Art	Cincinnati, OH	Zaha Hadid Architects (UK) with KZF Design

Opened	Architect (expansion)
1993	—
1971	Hugh Newell Jacobsen, 2005 Mary and Howard Lester Wing
1993	Gehry Partners, 2011 addition
1923	—
2001	—
2008	—
1952	Olson Sundberg Kundig Allen Architects, 1997 expansion
2007	—
2014	Renzo Piano Building Workshop (Italy), 2014 expansion to unify 3 museums under one roof
1973	Pei Cobb Freed & Partners, 2011 expansion
1983	Renzo Piano Building Workshop (Italy) with Lord, Aeck and Sargent, 2005 addition
1974	—
1985	—
1952	Derthick, Henley and Wilkerson Architects, 1975 addition; Randall Stout Architects with Derthick, Henley and Wilkerson Architects and Hefferlin + Kronenberg Architects, 2005 addition
1982	—
1970	Edward Larrabee Barnes Associates and John M.Y. Lee, 1990 Mary Fendrich Hulman Pavilion; Browning Day Mullins Dierdorf Architects, 2005 expansion
2006	—
1894	Polshek Partnership Architects, 1999 addition
1903	Renzo Piano Building Workshop (Italy), 2012 expansion
1997	—
1931	Foster + Partners (UK), 1994 Walter and Suzanne Scott Pavilion
1994	—
1972	Renzo Piano Building Workshop (Italy), 2013 expansion
1967	—
2003	—

Art Museums

Museum	Location	Architect (original)
Los Angeles County Museum of Art	Los Angeles, CA	William L. Pereira & Associates
Mead Art Museum	Amherst, MA	McKim, Mead and White
Memphis Brooks Museum of Art	Memphis, TN	James Gamble Rogers with Carl Gutherz
Menil Collection	Houston, TX	Renzo Piano Building Workshop (Italy) with Richard Fitzgerald & Partners
Metropolitan Museum of Art	New York, NY	Calvert Vaux and J. Wrey Mould
Milwaukee Art Museum	Milwaukee, WI	Eero Saarinen with Maynard Meyer
Minneapolis Institute of Arts	Minneapolis, MN	McKim, Mead and White
Modern Art Museum of Fort Worth	Fort Worth, TX	Tadao Ando (Japan)
Munson-Williams-Proctor Arts Institute	Utica, NY	Philip Johnson
Museum of Arts and Design	New York, NY	Allied Works Architecture (renovated the 1965 building by Edward Durrell Stone & Associates)
Museum of Contemporary Art Chicago	Chicago, IL	Josef Paul Kleihues (Germany)
Museum of Contemporary Art Cleveland	Cleveland, OH	Farshid Moussavi (UK) with Westlake Reed Leskosky
Museum of Contemporary Art Denver	Denver, CO	Adjaye Associates (UK)
Museum of Contemporary Art, Los Angeles	Los Angeles, CA	Arata Isozaki & Associates (Japan)
Museum of Contemporary Art San Diego	La Jolla, CA	Irving Gill (originally designed as a residence in 1916)
Museum of Fine Arts, Boston	Boston, MA	Guy Lowell
Museum of Fine Arts, Houston	Houston, TX	William Ward Watkin
Museum of Fine Arts, St. Petersburg	St. Petersburg, FL	John L. Volk

Opened	Architect (expansion)
1965	Hardy Holzman Pfeiffer Associates, 1986 Art of the Americas Building; Bruce Goff, 1988 Pavilion for Japanese Art; Albert C. Martin and Associates, 1998 LACAMA West building (originally the 1946 May Co. building); Renzo Piano Building Workshop (Italy), 2008 Broad Contemporary Art Museum
1949	—
1916	Walk Jones and Francis Mah, 1973 addition; Skidmore, Owings & Merrill with Askew, Nixon, Ferguson & Wolf, 1989 expansion
1987	—
1880	Theodore Weston, 1888 SW wing; Richard Morris Hunt and Richard Howland Hunt, 1902 Central Fifth Avenue facade; McKim, Mead and White, 1906 side wings along Fifth Avenue; Brown, Lawford & Forbes, 1965 Thomas J. Watson Library; Kevin Roche John Dinkeloo & Associates, 1975 Lehman Wing, 1979 Sackler Wing, 1980 American Wing, 1981 Michael C. Rockefeller Wing for Primitive Art, 1988 European Sculpture and Decorative Art Wing; Kevin Roche John Dinkeloo & Associates, 2012 American Wing renovation
1957	Kahler, Fitzhugh and Scott, 1975 addition; Santiago Calatrava (Spain) with Kahler Slater Architects, 2001 Quadracci Pavilion; HGA Architects and Engineers, 2015 expansion
1915	Kenzo Tange Associates (Japan), 1974 addition; Michael Graves & Associates with RSP Architects, 2006 Target Wing
2002	—
1960	Lund McGee Sharpe Architecture, 1995 Education Wing
2008	—
1996	—
2012	—
2007	—
1986	—
1941	Mosher & Drew, 1950 transition to museum; Mosher & Drew, 1959 Sherwood Auditorium; Venturi, Scott Brown and Associates, 1996 expansion and renovation
1909	Guy Lowell, 1915 Robert Dawson Evans Wing; John Singer Sargent, 1921 Rotunda and 1925 Colonnade; Guy Lowell, 1928 Decorative Arts Wing; Hugh Stubbins & Associates, 1968 Forsyth Wickes Galleries and 1970 George Robert White Wing; I.M. Pei & Partners, 1981 West Wing; Foster + Partners (UK) with Childs Bertman Tseckares, 2010 Art of the Americas Wing and Ruth and Carl J. Shapiro Family Courtyard
1924–26	Kenneth Franzheim, 1953 Robert Lee Blaffer Memorial Wing; Mies van der Rohe, 1958 Cullinan Hall and 1974 Brown Pavilion; Isamu Noguchi (Japan), 1986 Lillie and Hugh Roy Cullen Sculpture Garden; Rafael Moneo (Spain), 2000 Audrey Jones Beck Building
1965	Hellmuth, Obata & Kassabaum, 2008 Hazel Hough Wing

Art Museums

Museum	Location	Architect (original)
Museum of Modern Art	New York, NY	Philip L. Goodwin and Edward Durrell Stone & Associates
Nasher Museum of Art	Durham, NC	Rafael Viñoly Architects
Nasher Sculpture Center	Dallas, TX	Renzo Piano Building Workshop (Italy) with Peter Walker and Partners
National Gallery of Art, East Building	Washington, DC	I.M. Pei & Partners
National Gallery of Art, West Building	Washington, DC	John Russell Pope
National Portrait Gallery and American Art Museum	Washington, DC	Faulkner, Stenhouse, Fryer (adapted the 1836–67 Old Patent Office Building by Robert Mills and Thomas Ustick Walter)
Nelson Fine Arts Center	Tempe, AZ	Antoine Predock Architect
Nelson-Atkins Museum of Art	Kansas City, MO	Wight and Wight
Nevada Museum of Art	Reno, NV	will bruder + PARTNERS
New Museum of Contemporary Art	New York, NY	SANAA with Gensler
New Orleans Museum of Art	New Orleans, LA	Samuel Marx
North Carolina Museum of Art	Raleigh, NC	Edward Durell Stone
Oakland Museum of California	Oakland, CA	Kevin Roche John Dinkeloo & Associates
Ohr-O'Keefe Museum of Art	Biloxi, MS	Gehry Partners; Eley Guild Hardy Architects
Palm Springs Art Museum, Architecture & Design Center	Palm Springs, CA	Marmol Radziner (adapted from the 1961 Santa Fe Fersal Savings & Loan by E. Stewart Williams)
Parrish Art Museum	Southampton, NY	Grosvenor Atterbury
Pennsylvania Academy of the Fine Arts	Philadelphia, PA	Frank Furness and George W. Hewitt
Perez Art Museum	Miami, FL	Herzog & de Meuron (Switzerland)
Philadelphia Museum of Art	Philadelphia, PA	Horace Trumbauer with Zantzinger, Borie, and Medar
Phoenix Art Museum	Phoenix, AZ	Alden B. Dow
Portland Art Museum	Portland, OR	Pietro Belluschi
Portland Museum of Art	Portland, ME	John Calvin Stevens
Princeton University Art Museum	Princeton, NJ	Ralph Adams Cram
Pulitzer Foundation for the Arts	St. Louis, MO	Tadao Ando (Japan)
Queens Museum	New York, NY	Rafael Vinoly reconfigured original building (Aymar Embury II designed the building for the 1939 World's Fair; Daniel Chait renovated building for 1964 World's Fair)
Renwick Gallery	Washington, DC	James Renwick Jr.

Opened	Architect (expansion)
1939	Philip Johnson, 1964 east wing; Cesar Pelli & Associates, 1984 tower; Taniguchi Associates (Japan) with Kohn Pedersen Fox and Cooper, Robertson & Partners, 2004 expansion and 2006 Lewis B. and Dorothy Cullman Education Building
2005	—
2003	—
1978	—
1941	—
1968	Foster + Partners (UK) with SmithGroup, 2007 Robert and Arlene Kogod Courtyard
1989	—
1933	Steven Holl Architects with BNIM Architects, 2007 Bloch Building
2003	—
2007	—
1911	August Perez with Arthur Feitel, 1971 Wisner Education Wing, City Wing, and Stern Auditorium; Eskew Filson Architects with Billes/Manning Architects, 1993 expansion
1984	Thomas Phifer and Partners with Pierce Brinkley Cease + Lee, 2010 expansion
1969	Mark Cavagnero, 2012 expansion
2010	—
2014	—
1897	Grosvenor Atterbury, 1902 and 1913 wings; Herzog & de Meuron (Switzerland), 2012 expansion
1876	—
2013	—
1928	Gluckman Mayner Architects, 2008 renovation of the Perelman Building (originally designed by Zantzinger, Borie, and Medary in 1927)
1959	Alden B. Dow, 1965 east wing; Tod Williams Billie Tsien Architects, 1996 and 2006 expansions
1932	Pietro Belluschi, 1939 Hirsch Wing; Pietro Belluschi, with Wolff, Zimmer, Gunsul, Frasca, and Ritter, 1970 Hoffman Wing; Ann Beha Architects, 2000 expansion; Ann Beha Architects with SERA Architects, 2005 expansion
1911	I.M. Pei & Partners, 1983 Charles Shipman Payson Building
1922	Steinman and Cain, 1966 expansion; Mitchell	Giurgola Architects, 1989 Mitchell Wolfson Jr. Wing
2001	—
1972	Grimshaw Architects, 2013 expansion
1859	John Carl Warnecke & Associates and Hugh Newell Jacobsen, 1971 restoration

Art Museums

Museum	Location	Architect (original)
Rodin Museum	Philadelphia, PA	Paul Philippe Cret and Jacques Gréber
Saint Louis Art Museum	St. Louis, MO	Cass Gilbert
Salvador Dali Museum	St. Petersburg, FL	HOK
San Diego Museum of Art	San Diego, CA	William Templeton Johnson with Robert W. Snyder
San Francisco Museum of Modern Art	San Francisco, CA	Mario Botta (Italy)
Santa Barbara Museum of Art	Santa Barbara, CA	David Adler (adapted the 1914 Old Post Office designed by Francis Wilson)
Seattle Art Museum	Seattle, WA	Venturi, Scott Brown and Associates
Shaw Center for the Arts	Baton Rouge, LA	Schwartz/Silver Architects with Eskew+Dumez+ Ripple and Jerry M. Campbell Associates
Sheldon Memorial Art Gallery	Lincoln, NE	Philip Johnson
Solomon R. Guggenheim Museum	New York, NY	Frank Lloyd Wright
Speed Art Museum	Louisville, KY	Arthur Loomis
Sterling and Francine Clark Art Institute	Wiliamstown, MA	Daniel Perry
Tacoma Art Museum	Tacoma, WA	Antoine Predock Architect with Olson Sundberg Kundig Allen Architects
Tampa Museum of Art	Tampa, FL	Natoma Architects
Taubman Museum of Art	Roanoke, VA	Randall Stout Architects with Rodriguez Ripley Maddux Motley Architects
Terra Museum of American Art	Chicago, IL	Booth Hansen Associates
Toledo Museum of Art	Toledo, OH	Green & Wicks with Harry W. Wachter
UCLA Hammer Museum of Art	Los Angeles, CA	Edward Larrabee Barnes Associates
University of Michigan Museum of Art	Ann Arbor, MI	Donaldson and Meier Architects
Vincent Price Art Museum	Los Angeles, CA	Arquitectonica
Virginia Museum of Fine Arts	Richmond, VA	Peebles and Ferguson Architects
Wadsworth Atheneum Museum of Art	Hartford, CT	Ithiel Town and Alexander Jackson Davis
Walker Art Center	Minneapolis, MN	Edward Larrabee Barnes Associates
Wexner Center for the Arts	Columbus, OH	Eisenman Architects with Richard Trott & Partners

Opened	Architect (expansion)
1929	—
1903	David Chipperfield Architects with HOK, 2013 East Building
2011	—
1926	Robert Mosher & Roy Drew, Architects, 1966 west wing; Mosher, Drew, Watson & Associates with William Ferguson, 1974 east wing
1995	—
1941	Chester Carjola, 1942 Katherine Dexter McCormick Wing; Arendt/Mosher/Grants Architects, 1961 Preston Morton Wing and 1962 Sterling Morton Wing; Paul Gray, 1985 Alice Keck Park Wing; Edwards & Pitman, 1998 Peck Wing
1991	Allied Works Architecture with NBBJ, 2007 expansion
2005	—
1963	—
1959	Gwathmey Siegel & Associates Architects, 1992 addition
1927	Nevin and Morgan, 1954 Preston Pope Satterwhite Wing; Brenner, Danforth, and Rockwell, 1973 north wing; Robert Geddes, 1983 south wing
1955	Pietro Belluschi and The Architects Collaborative, 1973 addition; Tadao Ando Architect & Associates (Japan) and Gensler, 2008 Stone Hill Center; Tadao Ando Architect & Associates (Japan), 2014 new Visitor Center; Sellforf Architects, 2014 renovation
2003	Olson Kundig Architects, 2014 expansion
2010	—
2008	—
1987	—
1912	Edward B. Green and Sons, 1926 wing and 1933 expansion; Frank O. Gehry and Associates, Inc., 1992 Center for the Visual Arts addition; SANAA (Japan), 2006 Glass Pavilion
1990	—
1910	Allied Works Architecture with IDS, 2009 Maxine and Stuart Frankel and Frankel Family Wing
2011	—
1936	Merrill C. Lee, Architects, 1954 addition; Baskervill & Son Architects, 1970 South Wing; Hardwicke Associates, Inc., 1976 North Wing; Hardy Holzman Pfeiffer Associates, 1985 West Wing; Rick Mather Architect (UK) with SMBW, 2010 addition
1844	Benjamin Wistar Morris, 1910 Colt Memorial and 1915 Morgan Memorial; Morris & O'Connor, 1934 Avery Memorial; Huntington, Darbee & Dollard, Architects, 1969 Goodwin Wing
1971	Herzog & de Meuron (Switzerland) with Hammel, Green and Abrahamson, 2005 expansion
1989	—

Art Museums

Museum	Location	Architect (original)
Whitney Museum of American Art	New York, NY	Renzo Piano Building Workshop (Italy) with Cooper Robertson
Yale Center for British Art	New Haven, CT	Louis I. Kahn
Yale University Art Gallery	New Haven, CT	Louis I. Kahn

Source: DesignIntelligence

Opened	Architect (expansion)
2015	—
1977	—
1953	Ennead Architects, 2012 renovation of Swartwout Hall and Street Hall

Convention Centers

In the past decade public spending on convention centers has doubled to $2.4 billion annually, and since 1990 convention space in the US has increased by more than 50 percent. The following is *DesignIntelligence*'s list of the largest US convention centers with their requisite architectural statistics.

Convention Center	Location	Opened	Exhibit Halls (sq. ft.)
America's Center	St. Louis, MO	1977	502,000
AmericasMart Atlanta	Atlanta, GA	1961	800,000
Anaheim Convention Center	Anaheim, CA	1967	815,000
Atlantic City Convention Center	Atlantic City, NJ	1997	518,300
Austin Convention Center	Austin, TX	1992	246,097
Baltimore Convention Center	Baltimore, MD	1979	300,000
Boston Convention and Exhibition Center	Boston, MA	2004	516,000
Charlotte Convention Center	Charlotte, NC	1995	280,000
Cobo Conference/Exhibition Center	Detroit, MI	1960	700,000
Colorado Convention Center	Denver, CO	1990	584,000
Dallas Convention Center	Dallas, TX	1973	726,726
David L. Lawrence Convention Center	Pittsburgh, PA	2003	313,400
Donald E. Stephens Convention Center	Rosemont, IL	1974	840,000
Fort Worth Convention Center	Fort Worth, TX	1968	253,226
George R. Brown Convention Center	Houston, TX	1987	893,590

Architect (original)	Architect (expansion)
Hellmuth, Obata & Kassabaum	Hellmuth, Obata & Kassabaum, 1993 and 1995 expansions
Edwards and Portman, Architects (Merchandise Mart)	Edwards and Portman, Architects, 1968 Merchandise Mart addition; John Portman & Associates, Architects, 1979 Apparel Mart, 1986 Merchandise Mart addition, 1989 Apparel Mart addition, 1992 Gift Mart; John Portman & Associates, 2009 Building 2 WestWing
Adrian Wilson & Associates	HNTB Architecture, 1974, 1982, 1990, and 1993 expansions; HOK Sport + Venue + Event, 1999–2001 expansion
Wallace Roberts & Todd	—
PageSoutherlandPage	Austin Collaborative Venture (PageSoutherlandPage; Cotera Kolar Negrete & Reed Architects; Limbacher & Godfrey Architects), 2002 expansion
NBBJ with Cochran, Stephenson & Donkervoet expansion	LMN Architects with Cochran, Stephenson & Donkervoet, 1996
HNTB Architecture/Rafael Viñoly Architects, joint venture	—
Thompson, Ventulett, Stainback & Associates with The FWA Group	—
Giffels & Rossetti	Sims-Varner & Associates, 1989 expansion
Fentress Bradburn Architects	Fentress Bradburn Architects, 2004 expansion
Harrell + Hamilton Architects (adapted and expanded the 1957 Dallas Memorial Auditorium by George L. Dahl Architects and Engineers Inc.)	Omniplan, 1984 expansion; JPJ Architects, 1994 expansion; Skidmore, Owings & Merrill and HKS, Inc., 2002 expansion
Rafael Viñoly Architects	—
Anthony M. Rossi Limited	Anthony M. Rossi Limited, subsequent expansions
Parker Croston	Carter & Burgess, Inc. and HOK Sport + Venue + Event, 2003 addition
Goleman & Rolfe Associates, Inc.; John S. Chase; Molina & Associates; Haywood Jordan McCowan, Inc.; Moseley Architects with Bernard Johnson and 3D/International	Golemon & Bolullo Architects, 2003 expansion

Convention Centers

Convention Center	Location	Opened	Exhibit Halls (sq. ft.)
Georgia World Congress Center	Atlanta, GA	1976	1.4 M
Greater Columbus Convention Center	Columbus, OH	1993	426,000
Hawaii Convention Center	Honolulu, HI	1996	204,249
Henry B. Gonzalez Convention Center	San Antonio, TX	1968	440,000
Indianapolis Convention Center & RCA Dome	Indianapolis, IN	1972	567,000
Jacob K. Javits Convention Center	New York, NY	1986	924,000
Kansas City Convention Center	Kansas City, MO	1976	388,800
Las Vegas Convention Center	Las Vegas, NV	1959	2 M
Long Beach Convention & Entertainment Center	Long Beach, CA	1978	224,000
Los Angeles Convention Center	Los Angeles, CA	1972	720,000
Mandalay Bay Convention Center	Las Vegas, NV	2003	934,731
McCormick Place	Chicago, IL	1971	2.6 M
Miami Beach Convention Center	Miami Beach, FL	1958	503,000

Architect (original)	Architect (expansion)
Thompson, Ventulett, Stainback & Associates	Thompson, Ventulett, Stainback & Associates, 1985 and 1992 expansions; Thompson, Ventulett, Stainback & Associates with Heery International, 2003 expansion
Eisenman Architects with Richard Trott & Partners	Eisenman Architects, Karlsberger, and Thompson, Ventulett, Stainback & Associates, 2001 expansion
LMN Architects with Wimberly Allison Tong & Goo	—
Noonan and Krocker; Phelps and Simmons and Associates	Cerna Raba & Partners, 1986 expansion; Thompson, Ventulett, Stainback & Associates with Kell Muñoz Architects and Haywood Jordon McCowan, Inc., 2001 expansion
Lennox, James and Loebl (Lennox, Matthews, Simmons and Ford; James Associates; Loebl Schlossman Bennett & Dart)	Blackburn Architects and Browning Day Mullins Dierdorf Architects with Hellmuth, Obata & Kassabaum, 1993 and 2001 expansions; RATIO Architects with BSA LifeStructures, Blackburn Architects, and Domain Architecture Inc., 2011 expansion
I.M. Pei & Partners	FXFOWLE Epstein, 2015 expansion
C.F. Murphy Associates with Seligson Associates, Hormer and Blessing, and Howard Needles Tammen & Bergendoff	Convention Center Associates, Architects; BNIM Architects; HNTB Architecture, 1994 expansion
Adrian Wilson & Associates with Harry Whitney Consulting Architect	Jack Miller & Associates, 1967 South Hall; Adrian Wilson & Associates, 1971 C3 expansion; Jack Miller & Associates, 1975 C4 expansion; JMA, 1980 C5 expansion and 1990 expansion; Domingo Cambeiro Corp. Architects, 1998 North Hall and 2002 South Hall
Killingsworth, Brady, Smith and Associates	Thompson, Ventulett, Stainback & Associates, 1994 expansion
Charles Luckman & Associates	Pei Cobb Freed & Partners with Gruen Associates, 1993 expansion; Gruen Associates, 1997 Kentia Hall addition
Klai Juba Architects	—
C.F. Murphy Associates	Skidmore, Ownings & Merrill, 1986 North Hall; Thompson, Ventulett, Stainback & Associates with Architects Enterprise, 1996 South Hall; Thompson, Ventulett, Stainback & Associates and Mc4West, 2007 West Hall
B. Robert Swartburg	Gilbert M. Fein, 1968 Hall D; Edward Durrell Stone & Associates, Gilbert M. Fein, and Watson, Deutschmann, Kruse & Lyon, 1974 addition; Thompson, Ventulett, Stainback & Associates with Borrelli, Frankel, Biltstein, 1989 and 1991 expansions

Convention Centers

Convention Center	Location	Opened	Exhibit Halls (sq. ft.)
Minneapolis Convention Center	Minneapolis, MN	1989–91	475,000
Moscone Center	San Francisco, CA	1981	741,308
New Orleans Ernest N. Morial Convention Center	New Orleans, LA	1985	1.1 M
Orange County Convention Center	Orlando, FL	1983	2.1 M
Oregon Convention Center	Portland, OR	1990	315,000
Pennsylvania Convention Center	Philadelphia, PA	1993	679,000
Phoenix Convention Center	Phoenix, AZ	1985	502,500
Reliant Center	Houston, TX	2004	706,213
Reno-Sparks Convention Center	Reno, NV	1965	381,000
Salt Palace Convention Center	Salt Lake City, UT	1996	515,000
San Diego Convention Center	San Diego, CA	1989	615,701
Tampa Convention Center	Tampa, FL	1990	200,000
Washington Convention Center	Washington, DC	2003	703,000
Washington State Convention and Trade Center	Seattle, WA	1988	205,700

Source: DesignIntelligence

Architect (original)	Architect (expansion)
Leonard Parker Associates; Setter Leach & Lindstrom; LMN Architects	Convention Center Design Group (Leonard Parker Associates; Setter Leach & Lindstrom; LMN Architects), 2001 expansion
Hellmuth, Obata & Kassabaum	Gensler/DMJM Associate Architects, joint venture, 1992 North Hall; Gensler/Michael Willis Architects/Kwan Henmi, joint venture, 2003 West Hall
Perez & Associates and Perkins & James	Perez & Associates and Billes/Manning Architects, 1991 expansion; Convention Center III Architects (Cimini, Meric, Duplantier Architects/Planners, Billes/Manning Architects, and Hewitt Washington & Associates), 1999 expansion
Helman Hurley Charvat Peacock/Architects, Inc.	Hellmuth, Obata & Kassabaum and Vickey/Ovresat Assumb Associates, Inc., 1989-90 expansion; Hunton Brady Pryor Maso Architects and Thompson, Ventulett, Stainback & Associates, 1996 expansion; Helman Hurley Charvat Peacock/Architects, Thompson, Ventulett, Stainback & Associates, Inc. and Hunton Brady Pryor Maso Architects, 2003 expansion
Zimmer Gunsul Frasca Partnership	Zimmer Gunsul Frasca Architects, 2003 expansion
Thompson, Ventulett & Stainback Associates with VITETTA and Kelly/Maiello Architects and Planners (including the adaption of the 1893 Reading Terminal Headhouse by Wilson Brothers and F.H. Kimball)	tvsdesign with Vitetta Group and Kelly/Maiello Architects and and Planners, 2011 expansion
GSAS Architects and Planners, Inc. with Howard Needles Tammen & Bergendoff	LEO A DALY/HOK Sport + Venue + Event with van Dijk Westlake Reed Leskosky, 2006 expansion; HOK Sport + Venue + Event and SmithGroup, 2008 North Building
Hermes Reed Architects	—
Richard Neutra with Lockard, Casazza & Parsons	Parsons Design Group, 1981 North Hall; Sheehan, Van Woert Architects, 1991 East Hall; LMN Architects, 2002 expansion
Thompson, Ventulett, Stainback & Associates	Leonard Parker Associates with MHTB Architects, 2000 with GSBS Architects expansion; Edwards & Daniels Architects, Inc., 2006 expansion
Arthur Erickson Architect with Deems Lewis McKinley	HNTB Architecture with Tucker Sadler Architects, 2002 expansion
Hellmuth, Obata & Kassabaum	—
TVS–D&P–Mariani PLLC (Thompson, Ventulett, Stainback & Associates; Devrouax & Purnell Architects; and Mariani Architects Engineers)	—
TRA Architects	LMN Architects, 2001 expansion

Sports Stadiums

From classic ballparks to cutting-edge arenas and stadiums, the following charts provide statistical and architectural highlights for all major-league baseball, basketball, football, and hockey venues in the United States. All cost and architectural information refers to the stadiums as they were originally built and does not include additions, renovations, or expansions.

Baseball

Team	League	Stadium	Location	Opened
Arizona Diamondbacks	National	Chase Field	Phoenix, AZ	1998
Atlanta Braves	National	Turner Field	Atlanta, GA	1997
Baltimore Orioles	American	Oriole Park at Camden Yards	Baltimore, MD	1992
Boston Red Sox	American	Fenway Park	Boston, MA	1912
Chicago Cubs	National	Wrigley Field	Chicago, IL	1914
Chicago White Sox	American	U.S. Cellular Field	Chicago, IL	1991
Cincinnati Reds	National	Great American Ball Park	Cincinnati, OH	2003
Cleveland Indians	American	Progressive Field	Cleveland, OH	1994
Colorado Rockies	National	Coors Field	Denver, CO	1995
Detroit Tigers	American	Comerica Park	Detroit, MI	2000
Houston Astros	National	Minute Maid Park	Houston, TX	2000
Kansas City Royals	American	Kauffman Stadium	Kansas City, MO	1973
Los Angeles Angels of Anaheim	American	Angel Stadium of Anaheim	Anaheim, CA	1966
Los Angeles Dodgers	National	Dodger Stadium	Los Angeles, CA	1962
Miami Marlins	National	Marlins Park	Miami, FL	2012
Milwaukee Brewers	National	Miller Park	Milwaukee, WI	2001
Minnesota Twins	American	Target Field	Minneapolis, MN	2010
New York Mets	National	Citi Field	Flushing, NY	2009
New York Yankees	American	Yankee Stadium	Bronx, NY	2009
Oakland A's	American	O.co Coliseum	Oakland, CA	1966
Philadelphia Phillies	National	Citizens Bank Park	Philadelphia, PA	2004
Pittsburgh Pirates	National	PNC Park	Pittsburgh, PA	2001
San Diego Padres	National	Petco Park	San Diego, CA	2004

Architect	Cost (original)	Capacity (current)	Roof Type	Naming Rights (amt. & expiration)
Ellerbe Becket with Bill Johnson	$354 M	49,033	Convertible	$33.1 M (30 yrs.)
Heery International; Williams-Russell & Johnson, Inc.; Ellerbe Becket	$250 M	49,831	Open-Air	Undisclosed
HOK Sports Facilities Group with RTKL Associates Inc.	$210 M	48,876	Open-Air	—
Osborn Engineering Company	$365,000	33,871	Open-Air	—
Zachary Taylor Davis	$250,000	38,765	Open-Air	—
HOK Sports Facilities Group	$150 M	44,321	Open-Air	$68 M (20 yrs.)
HOK Sport + Venue + Event with GBBN Architects	$290 M	42,053	Open-Air	$75 M (30 yrs.)
HOK Sports Facilities Group	$173 M	43,345	Open-Air	$54 M (15 yrs.)
HOK Sports Facilities Group	$215 M	50,445	Open-Air	$15 M (indefinite)
HOK Sports Facilities Group; SHG Inc.	$300 M	40,637	Open-Air	$66 M (30 yrs.)
HOK Sports Facilities Group	$248.1 M	42,000	Retractable	$170 M (28 yrs.)
HNTB Architecture	$50.45 M	40,625	Open-Air	—
Robert A.M. Stern Architects	$25 M	45,050	Open-Air	—
Emil Praeger	$24.47 M	56,000	Open-Air	—
Populous	$634 M	36,742	Retractable	—
HKS, Inc. with NBBJ and Eppstein Uhen Architects	$399.4 M	42,500	Retractable	$41 M (20 yrs.)
Populous	$545 M	39,504	Open-Air	Undisclosed
Populous	$660 M	41,800	Open-Air	$400 M (20 yrs.)
Populous	$1.5 B	52,325	Open-Air	—
Skidmore, Owings & Merrill	$25.5 M	35,067	Open-Air	$1.2 M (6 yrs.)
EwingCole with HOK Sport + Venue + Event	$346 M	43,000	Open-Air	$57.5 M (25 yrs.)
HOK Sport + Venue + Event; L.D. Astorino Companies	$262 M	38,000	Open-Air	$30 M (20 yrs.)
Antoine Predock Architect with HOK Sport + Venue + Event	$453 M	42,524	Open-Air	$60 M (22 yrs.)

Sports Stadiums

Baseball

Team	League	Stadium	Location	Opened
San Francisco Giants	National	AT&T Park	San Francisco, CA	2000
Seattle Mariners	American	Safeco Field	Seattle, WA	1999
St. Louis Cardinals	National	Busch Stadium	St. Louis, MO	2006
Tampa Bay Rays	American	Tropicana Field	St. Petersburg, FL	1990
Texas Rangers	American	Rangers Ballpark in Arlington	Arlington, TX	1994
Toronto Blue Jays	American	Rogers Centre	Toronto, ON, Canada	1989
Washington Nationals	National	Nationals Park	Washington, DC	2008

Basketball

Team	Conference	Stadium	Location	Opened
Atlanta Hawks	Eastern	Philips Arena	Atlanta, GA	1999
Boston Celtics	Eastern	TD Garden	Boston, MA	1995
Brooklyn Nets	Eastern	Barclays Center	Brooklyn, NY	2012
Charlotte Hornets	Eastern	Time Warner Cable Arena	Charlotte, NC	2005
Chicago Bulls	Eastern	United Center	Chicago, IL	1994
Cleveland Cavaliers	Eastern	Quicken Loans Arena	Cleveland, OH	1994
Dallas Mavericks	Western	American Airlines Center	Dallas, TX	2001
Denver Nuggets	Western	Pepsi Center	Denver, CO	1999
Detroit Pistons	Eastern	Palace of Auburn Hills	Auburn Hills, MI	1988
Golden State Warriors	Western	Oracle Arena	Oakland, CA	1966
Houston Rockets	Western	Toyota Center	Houston, TX	2003
Indiana Pacers	Eastern	Bankers Life Fieldhouse	Indianapolis, IN	1999
Los Angeles Clippers	Western	Staples Center	Los Angeles, CA	1999
Los Angeles Lakers	Western	Staples Center	Los Angeles, CA	1999
Memphis Grizzlies	Western	FedEx Forum	Memphis, TN	2004
Miami Heat	Eastern	American Airlines Arena	Miami, FL	1999

Architect	Cost (original)	Capacity (current)	Roof Type	Naming Rights (amt. & expiration)
HOK Sports Facilities Group	$345 M	41,815	Open-Air	$50 M (24 yrs.)
NBBJ	$517.6 M	46,621	Retractable	$40 M (20 yrs.)
HOK Sport + Venue + Event	$344 M	46,816	Open-Air	Undisclosed
HOK Sports Facilities Group; Lescher & Mahoney Sports; Criswell, Blizzard & Blouin Architects	$138 M	45,360	Dome	$30 M (30 yrs.)
David M. Schwarz Architects; HKS, Inc.	$190 M	49,115	Open-Air	—
Rod Robbie and Michael Allen	C$500 M	50,516	Retractable	C$20 M (10 yrs.)
HOK Sport + Venue + Event with Devrouax & Purnell	$611 M	41,888	Open-Air	—

Architect	Cost (original)	Capacity (current)	Naming Rights (amt. & expiration)
HOK Sports Facilities Group; Arquitectonica	$213.5 M	20,300	$180 M (20 yrs.)
Ellerbe Becket	$160 M	18,624	Undisclosed
Ellerbe Becket with SHoP Architects	$950 M	18,103	$200 M (20 yrs.)
Ellerbe Becket with Odell & Associates and The Freelon Group, Inc.	$265 M	19,077	Undisclosed
HOK Sports Facilities Group; Marmon Mok; W.E. Simpson Company	$175 M	20,917	$25 M (20 yrs.)
Ellerbe Becket	$152 M	20,562	Undisclosed
David Schwarz/Architectural Services, Inc. with HKS, Inc.	$420 M	19,200	$40 M (20 yrs.)
HOK Sports Facilities Group	$160 M	19,309	$68 M (20 yrs.)
Rossetti	$70 M	21,454	—
HNTB Architecture	n/a	19,200	$30 M (10 yrs.)
HOK Sports + Venue + Event	$175 M	18,300	Undisclosed
Ellerbe Becket	$183 M	18,165	$40 M (20 yrs.)
NBBJ	$330 M	20,000	$100 M (20 yrs.)
NBBJ	$330 M	20,000	$100 M (20 yrs.)
Ellerbe Becket with Looney Ricks Kiss	$250 M	18,165	$90 M (20 yrs.)
Arquitectonica	$175 M	19,600	$42 M (20 yrs.)

Sports Stadiums

Basketball

Team	Conference	Stadium	Location	Opened
Milwaukee Bucks	Eastern	BMO Harris Bradley Center	Milwaukee, WI	1988
Minnesota Timberwolves	Western	Target Center	Minneapolis, MN	1990
New Orleans Pelicans	Western	New Orleans Arena	New Orleans, LA	1999
New York Knicks	Eastern	Madison Square Garden	New York, NY	1968
Oklahoma City Thunder	Western	Chesapeake Energy Arena	Oklahoma City, OK	2002
Orlando Magic	Eastern	Amway Center	Orlando, FL	2010
Philadelphia 76ers	Eastern	Wells Fargo Center	Philadelphia, PA	1996
Phoenix Suns	Western	US Airways Center	Phoenix, AZ	1992
Portland Trail Blazers	Western	Moda Center	Portland, OR	1995
Sacramento Kings	Western	Sleep Train Arena	Sacramento, CA	1988
San Antonio Spurs	Western	AT&T Center	San Antonio, TX	2002
Toronto Raptors	Eastern	Air Canada Centre	Toronto, ON, Canada	1999
Utah Jazz	Western	EnergySolutions Arena	Salt Lake City, UT	1991
Washington Wizards	Eastern	Verizon Center	Washington, DC	1997

Football

Team	League	Stadium	Location	Opened
Arizona Cardinals	NFC	University of Phoenix Stadium	Glendale, AZ	2006
Atlanta Falcons	NFC	Georgia Dome	Atlanta, GA	1992
Baltimore Ravens	AFC	M&T Bank Stadium	Baltimore, MD	1998
Buffalo Bills	AFC	Ralph Wilson Stadium	Orchard Park, NY	1973
Carolina Panthers	NFC	Bank of America Stadium	Charlotte, NC	1996
Chicago Bears	NFC	Soldier Field	Chicago, IL	2003
Cincinnati Bengals	AFC	Paul Brown Stadium	Cincinnati, OH	2000
Cleveland Browns	AFC	First Energy Stadium	Cleveland, OH	1999
Dallas Cowboys	NFC	Cowboys Stadium	Arlington, TX	2009

Architect	Cost (original)	Capacity (current)	Naming Rights (amt. & expiration)
HOK Sports Facilities Group	$90 M	19,000	—
KMR Architects	$104 M	19,006	$18.75 M (15 yrs.)
Arthur Q. Davis, FAIA & Partners	$112 M	18,500	—
Charles Luckman	$116 M	19,763	—
The Benham Companies	$89 M	19,599	$8.1 M (15 yrs.)
Populous	$480 M	18,500	$195 M (30 yrs.)
Ellerbe Becket	$206 M	20,444	$40 M (29 yrs.)
Ellerbe Becket	$90 M	19,023	$26 M (30 yrs.)
Ellerbe Becket	$262 M	19,980	—
Rann Haight Architect	$40 M	17,317	Undisclosed (5 yrs.)
Ellerbe Becket with Lake/Flato Architects and Kell Muñoz Architects	$186 M	18,581	$85 M (20 yrs.)
HOK Sports Facilities Group; Brisbin Brook Beynon Architects (Canada)	C$265 M	19,800	C$40 M (20 yrs.)
FFKR Architects	$94 M	19,911	$20 M (10 yrs.)
Ellerbe Becket	$260 M	20,308	$44 M (15 years)

Architect	Cost (original)	Capacity (current)	Roof Type	Naming Rights (amt. & expiration)
Peter Eisenman with HOK Sport + Venue + Event	$370.6 M	65,000	Retractable	$154.5 M (20 yrs.)
Heery International	$214 M	71,149	Dome	—
HOK Sports Facilities Group	$220 M	71,008	Open-Air	$75 M (15 yrs.)
HNTB Architecture	$22 M	73,800	Open-Air	—
HOK Sports Facilities Group	$248 M	73,258	Open-Air	Undisclosed
Wood + Zapata, Inc. with Lohan Caprile Goettsch	$365 M	61,500	Open-Air	—
NBBJ	$400 M	65,535	Open-Air	—
HOK Sports Facilities Group	$283 M	73,200	Open-Air	—
HKS, Inc.	$1.1 B	80,000	Retractable	—

Sports Stadiums

Football

Team	Conference	Stadium	Location	Opened
Denver Broncos	AFC	Sports Authority Field at Mile High Stadium	Denver, CO	2001
Detroit Lions	NFC	Ford Field	Allen Park, MI	2002
Green Bay Packers	NFC	Lambeau Field	Green Bay, WI	1957
Houston Texans	AFC	Reliant Stadium	Houston, TX	2002
Indianapolis Colts	AFC	Lucas Oil Stadium	Indianapolis, IN	2008
Jacksonville Jaguars	AFC	EverBank Field	Jacksonville, FL	1995
Kansas City Chiefs	AFC	Arrowhead Stadium	Kansas City, MO	1972
Miami Dolphins	AFC	Sun Life Stadium	Miami, FL	1987
Minnesota Vikings	NFC	Vikings Stadium	Minneapolis, MN	1982
New England Patriots	AFC	Gillette Stadium	Foxboro, MA	2002
New Orleans Saints	NFC	Mercedes-Benz Superdome	New Orleans, LA	1975
New York Giants	NFC	Met Life Stadium	E. Rutherford, NJ	2010
New York Jets	AFC	Met Life Stadium	E. Rutherford, NJ	2010
Oakland Raiders	AFC	O.co Coliseum	Oakland, CA	1966
Philadelphia Eagles	NFC	Lincoln Financial Field	Philadelphia, PA	2003
Pittsburgh Steelers	AFC	Heinz Field	Pittsburgh, PA	2001
San Diego Chargers	AFC	Qualcomm Stadium	San Diego, CA	1967
San Francisco 49ers	NFC	Levi's Stadium	Santa Clara, CA	2014
Seattle Seahawks	NFC	Century Link Field	Seattle, WA	2002
St. Louis Rams	NFC	Edward Jones Dome	St. Louis, MO	1995
Tampa Bay Buccaneers	NFC	Raymond James Stadium	Tampa, FL	1998
Tennessee Titans	AFC	LP Field	Nashville, TN	1999
Washington Redskins	NFC	FedEx Field	Landover, MD	1997

Architect	Cost (original)	Capacity (current)	Roof Type	Naming Rights (amt. & expiration)
HNTB Architecture with Fentress Bradburn Architects and Bertram A. Burton and Associates	$400.8 M	76,125	Open-Air	$120 M (20 yrs.)
SmithGroup	$500 M	64,355	Dome	$40 M (40 yrs.)
John Somerville	$960,000	72,928	Open-Air	—
HOK Sport + Venue + Event	$325 M	69,500	Retractable	$300 M (30 yrs.)
HKS, Inc.	$625 M	63,000	Retractable	$122 M (20 yrs.)
HOK Sports Facilities Group	$138 M	73,000	Open-Air	$16.6 M (5 yrs.)
Kivett and Meyers	$43 M	79,409	Open-Air	—
HOK Sports Facilities Group	$125 M	74,916	Open-Air	$20 M (5 yrs.)
Skidmore, Owings & Merrill	$55 M	64,121	Dome	—
HOK Sport + Venue + Event	$325 M	68,000	Open-Air	Undisclosed
Curtis & Davis Architects	$134 M	69,065	Dome	Undisclosed $ (10 yrs.)
EwingCole; Skanska; 360 Architecture	$1.6 B	82,566	Open-Air	$425 M–$450 M (25 yrs.)
EwingCole; Skanska; 360 Architecture	$1.6 B	82,566	Open-Air	$425 M–$450 M (25 yrs.)
Skidmore, Owings & Merrill	$25.5 M	53,200	Open-Air	$1.2 M (6 yrs.)
NBBJ	$320 M	66,000	Open-Air	$139.6 M (20 yrs.)
HOK Sport + Venue + Event with WTW Architects	$281 M	64,440	Open-Air	$58 M (20 yrs.)
Frank L. Hope and Associates	$27 M	71,294	Open-Air	$18 M (20 yrs.)
HNTB Architecture	$1.2 B	68,500	Open-Air	$220.3 M (20 yrs.); future option $75 M (5 yrs.)
Ellerbe Becket with LMN Architects	$360 M	67,000	Partial Roof	—
HOK Sports Facilities Group	$280 M	66,000	Dome	$31.8 M (12 yrs.)
HOK Sports Facilities Group	$168.5 M	66,000	Open-Air	$32.5 M (13 yrs.)
HOK Sports Facilities Group	$290 M	67,000	Open-Air	$30 M (10 yrs.)
HOK Sports Facilities Group	$250.5 M	80,116	Open-Air	$205 M (27 yrs.)

Sports Stadiums

Hockey

Team	Conference	Stadium	Location	Opened
Anaheim Ducks	Western	Honda Center	Anaheim, CA	1993
Arizona Coyotes	Western	Gila River Arena	Glendale, AZ	2003
Boston Bruins	Eastern	TD Garden	Boston, MA	1995
Buffalo Sabres	Eastern	First Niagara Center	Buffalo, NY	1996
Calgary Flames	Western	Scotiabank Saddledome	Calgary, AB, Canada	1983
Carolina Hurricanes	Eastern	PNC Arena	Raleigh, NC	1999
Chicago Blackhawks	Western	United Center	Chicago, IL	1994
Colorado Avalanche	Western	Pepsi Center	Denver, CO	1999
Columbus Blue Jackets	Western	Nationwide Arena	Columbus, OH	2000
Dallas Stars	Western	American Airlines Center	Dallas, TX	2001
Detroit Red Wings	Western	Joe Louis Arena	Detroit, MI	1979
Edmonton Oilers	Western	Rexall Place	Edmonton, AB, Canada	1974
Florida Panthers	Eastern	BB & T Center	Sunrise, FL	1998
Los Angeles Kings	Western	Staples Center	Los Angeles, CA	1999
Minnesota Wild	Western	Xcel Energy Center	St. Paul, MN	2000
Montreal Canadiens	Eastern	Bell Centre	Montreal, QC, Canada	1996
Nashville Predators	Western	Bridgestone Arena	Nashville, TN	1996
New Jersey Devils	Eastern	Prudential Center	Newark, NJ	2007
New York Islanders	Eastern	Nassau Veterans Memorial Coliseum	Uniondale, NY	1972
New York Rangers	Eastern	Madison Square Garden	New York, NY	1968
Ottawa Senators	Eastern	Canadian Tire Center	Kanata, ON, Canada	1996
Philadelphia Flyers	Eastern	Wells Fargo Center	Philadelphia, PA	1996
Pittsburgh Penguins	Eastern	Consol Energy Center	Pittsburgh, PA	2010
San Jose Sharks	Western	SAP Center at San Jose	San Jose, CA	1993
St. Louis Blues	Western	Scottrade Center	St. Louis, MO	1994
Tampa Bay Lightning	Eastern	Tampa Bay Times Forum	Tampa, FL	1996
Toronto Maple Leafs	Eastern	Air Canada Centre	Toronto, ON, Canada	1999
Vancouver Canucks	Western	Rogers Arena	Vancouver, BC, Canada	1995
Washington Capitals	Eastern	Verizon Center	Washington, DC	1997
Winnipeg Jets	Eastern	MTS Centre	Winnipeg, MB, Canada	2004

Source: DesignIntelligence

Architect	Cost (original)	Capacity (current)	Naming Rights (amt. & expiration)
HOK Sports Facilities Group	$120 M	17,174	$60 M (15 yrs.)
HOK Sport + Venue + Event	$220 M	17,653	Undisclosed $ (9 yrs.)
Ellerbe Becket	$160 M	17,565	Undisclosed
Ellerbe Becket	$127.5 M	18,595	Undisclosed (15 yrs.)
Graham Edmunds Architecture (Canada); Graham McCourt Architects (Canada)	C$176 M	20,140	C$20 M (20 yrs.)
Odell	$158 M	19,289	$80 M (20 yrs.)
HOK Sports Facilities Group; Marmon Mok; W.E. Simpson Co.	$175 M	20,500	$25 M (20 yrs.)
HOK Sports Facilities Group	$160 M	18,129	$68 M (20 yrs.)
Heinlein Schrock Stearns; NBBJ	$150 M	18,500	$135 M (indefinite)
David M. Schwarz Architects with HKS, Inc.	$420 M	18,000	$40 M (20 yrs.)
Smith, Hinchmen and Grylls Associates	$57 M	18,785	—
Phillips, Barrett, Hillier, Jones & Partners with Wynn, Forbes, Lord, Feldberg & Schmidt	C$22.5 M	16,900	Undisclosed
Ellerbe Becket	$212 M	20,737	$27 M (10 yrs.)
NBBJ	$330 M	18,500	$116 M (no expiration)
HOK Sports Facilities Group	$130 M	18,064	$75 M (25 yrs.)
Consortium of Quebec Architects (Canada)	C$280 M	21,273	$100 M (20 yrs.)
HOK Sports Facilities Group	$144 M	20,000	Undisclosed
HOK Sport + Venue + Event with Morris Adjmi Architects	$375 M	17,615	$105.3 M (20 yrs.)
Welton Becket	$31 M	16,297	—
Charles Luckman	$116 M	18,200	—
Rossetti	C$200 M	19,153	C$20 M (15 yrs.)
Ellerbe Becket	$206 M	18,168	$40 M (29 yrs.)
Populous	$321 M	18,087	Undisclosed
Sink Combs Dethlefs	$162.5 M	17,483	$55.8 M (18 yrs.)
Ellerbe Becket	$170 M	19,260	Undisclosed
Ellerbe Becket	$139 M	19,500	$25 M (to 2018)
HOK Sports Facilities Group; Brisbin Brook Beynon Architects (Canada)	C$265 M	18,800	C$40 M (20 yrs.)
Brisbin Brook Beynon Architects (Canada)	C$160 M	18,422	Undisclosed (15 yrs.)
Ellerbe Becket	$260 M	19,700	Undisclosed (10 yrs.)
Sink Combs Dethlefs; Number Ten Architectural Group (Canada)	C$133.5 M	15,004	—

AWARDS, STATISTICS & RESOURCES

Top awards to firms and individuals are included in this chapter. Numerous vital statistics for professional reference are also contained herein.

(Note: Bolded text indicates additions to the existing list.)

AIA Gold Medal

The Gold Medal is the **American Institute of Architects' highest award**. Eligibility is open to architects and non-architects, living or dead, whose contribution to the field of architecture has made a lasting impact. The AIA's board of directors grants at least one gold medal each year, occasionally granting none.

www.aia.org

1907	Sir Aston Webb (UK)
1909	Charles F. McKim
1911	George B. Post
1914	Jean Louis Pascal (France)
1922	Victor Laloux (France)
1923	Henry Bacon
1925	Sir Edwin Lutyens (UK)
1925	Bertram Grosvenor Goodhue
1927	Howard Van Doren Shaw
1929	Milton B. Medary
1933	Ragnar Östberg (Sweden)
1938	Paul Philippe Cret (France/US)
1944	Louis Sullivan
1947	Eliel Saarinen (Finland/US)
1948	Charles D. Maginnis
1949	Frank Lloyd Wright
1950	Sir Patrick Abercrombie (UK)
1951	Bernard Maybeck
1952	Auguste Perret (France)
1953	William Adams Delano
1955	Willem Marinus Dudok (Netherlands)
1956	Clarence S. Stein
1957	Ralph Thomas Walker
1957	Louis Skidmore
1958	John Wellborn Root II
1959	Walter Gropius (Germany/US)
1960	Ludwig Mies van der Rohe (Germany/US)
1961	Le Corbusier (Charles Édouard Jeanneret) (Switzerland/France)
1962	Eero Saarinen*
1963	Alvar Aalto (Finland)
1964	Pier Luigi Nervi (Italy)
1966	Kenzo Tange (Japan)
1967	Wallace K. Harrison
1968	Marcel Breuer
1969	William Wurster
1970	R. Buckminster Fuller

1971	Louis I. Kahn
1972	Pietro Belluschi
1977	Richard Neutra* (Germany/US)
1978	Philip Johnson
1979	I.M. Pei
1981	José Luis Sert (Spain)
1982	Romaldo Giurgola
1983	Nathaniel Owings
1985	William Wayne Caudill*
1986	Arthur C. Erickson (Canada)
1989	Joseph Esherick
1990	E. Fay Jones
1991	Charles Moore
1992	Benjamin Thompson
1993	Thomas Jefferson*
1993	Kevin Roche
1994	Sir Norman Foster (UK)
1995	Cesar Pelli
1997	Richard Meier
1999	Frank Gehry
2000	Ricardo Legorreta (Mexico)
2001	Michael Graves
2002	Tadao Ando (Japan)
2004	Samuel Mockbee*
2005	Santiago Calatrava (Spain)
2006	Antoine Predock
2007	Edward Larrabee Barnes*
2008	Renzo Piano (Italy)
2009	Glenn Murcutt (Australia)
2010	Peter Bohlin
2011	Fumihiko Maki (Japan)
2012	Steven Holl
2013	Thom Mayne
2014	Julia Morgan
2015	**Moshe Safdie**

* Honored posthumously

Source: American Institute of Architects

AIA Honor Awards

The American Institute of Architects' Honor Awards celebrate **outstanding design in three areas: architecture, interior architecture, and regional and urban design**. Juries for each category, comprised of designers and executives for the respective disciplines, select the winners.

www.aia.org

2015 Architecture Winners

28th Street Apartments
Los Angeles, CA
Koning Eizenberg Architecture

Brockman Hall for Physics
   Rice University
Houston, TX
KierenTimberlake

California Memorial Stadium &
   Simpson Training Center
University of California, Berkeley
Berkeley, CA
HNTB Architecture

Cambridge Public Library
Cambridge, MA
William Rawn Associates

Danish Maritime Museum
Elsinore, Denmark
BIG | Bjarke Ingels Group

John Jay College of Criminal Justice
   City University of New York
New York, NY
Skidmore, Owings & Merrill

Krishna P. Singh Center for Nanotechnology
   University of Pennsylvania
Philadelphia, PA
Weiss/Manfredi Architects

LeFrak Center at Lakeside Prospect Park
New York, NY
Tod Williams Billie Tsien Architects

Sant Lespwa, Center of Hope
Hinchi, Haiti
Rothschild Doyno Collaborative

United States Courthouse
Salt Lake City, UT
Thomas Phifer and Partners;
   Naylor Wentworth Lund Architects

Wild Turkey Bourbon Visitor Center
Lawrenceburg, KY
De Leon & Primmer Architecture Workshop

2015 Interior Architecture Winners

Arent Fox
Washington, DC
STUDIOS Architecture

The Barbarian Group
New York, NY
Clive Wilkinson Architects;
    Design Republic Partners Architects

Beats By Dre Headquarters
Culver City, CA
Bestor Architecture

Crystal Bridges Museum of American Art,
    Museum Store
Bentonville, AR
Marlon Blackwell Architects

Illinois State Capitol West Wing Restoration
Springfield, IL
Vinci Hamp Architects

Louisiana State Sports Hall of Fame
    and Regional History Museum
Natchitoches, LA
Trahan Architects

National September 11 Memorial Museum
New York, NY
Davis Brody Bond

Newport Beach Civic Center and Park
Newport Beach, CA
Bohlin Cywinski Jackson

2015 Regional & Urban Design Winners

Beijing Tianqiao (Bridge of Heaven) Performing
    Arts District Master Plan
Beijing, China
Skidmore, Owings & Merrill

The BIG U
New York, NY
BIG | Bjarke Ingels Group

Government Center Garage Redevelopment
Boston, MA
CBT Architects

Target Field Station
Minneapolis, MN
Perkins Eastman

Source: American Institute of Architects

Architecture Firm Award

The American Institute of Architects grants its Architecture Firm Award, **the highest honor the AIA can bestow on a firm, annually to an architecture firm for consistently producing distinguished architecture**. Eligible firms must claim collaboration within the practice as a hallmark of their methodology and must have been producing work as an entity for at least 10 years.

www.aia.org

1962	Skidmore, Owings & Merrill
1963	*No award granted*
1964	The Architects Collaborative
1965	Wurster, Bernardi & Emmons
1966	*No award granted*
1967	Hugh Stubbins & Associates
1968	I.M. Pei & Partners
1969	Jones & Emmons
1970	Ernest J. Kump Associates
1971	Albert Kahn Associates
1972	Caudill Rowlett Scott
1973	Shepley Bulfinch Richardson and Abbott
1974	Kevin Roche John Dinkeloo & Associates
1975	Davis, Brody & Associates
1976	Mitchell/Giurgola Architects
1977	Sert Jackson and Associates
1978	Harry Weese & Associates
1979	Geddes Brecher Qualls Cunningham
1980	Edward Larrabee Barnes Associates
1981	Hardy Holzman Pfeiffer Associates
1982	Gwathmey Siegel & Associates, Architects
1983	Holabird & Root
1984	Kallmann, McKinnell & Wood Architects
1985	Venturi, Rauch and Scott Brown
1986	Esherick Homsey Dodge and Davis
1987	Benjamin Thompson & Associates
1988	Hartman-Cox Architects
1989	Cesar Pelli & Associates

1990	Kohn Pedersen Fox Associates
1991	Zimmer Gunsul Frasca Partnership
1992	James Stewart Polshek & Partners
1993	Cambridge Seven Associates
1994	Bohlin Cywinski Jackson
1995	Beyer Blinder Belle
1996	Skidmore, Owings & Merrill
1997	R.M. Kliment & Frances Halsband Architects
1998	Centerbrook Architects and Planners
1999	Perkins+Will
2000	Gensler
2001	Herbert Lewis Kruse Blunck Architecture
2002	Thompson, Ventulett, Stainback & Associates
2003	Miller|Hull Partnership
2004	Lake/Flato Architects
2005	Murphy/Jahn Architects
2006	Moore Ruble Yudell Architects & Planners
2007	Leers Weinzapfel Associates
2008	KieranTimberlake Associates
2009	Olson Sundberg Kundig Allen Architects
2010	Pugh + Scarpa
2011	BNIM Architects
2012	VJAA
2013	Tod Williams Billie Tsien Architects
2014	Eskew+Dumez+Ripple
2015	**Ehrlich Architects**

Source: American Institute of Architects

Arnold W. Brunner Memorial Prize

The American Academy of Arts and Letters annually awards the Arnold W. Brunner Memorial Prize **to architects of any nationality who have contributed to architecture as an art**. The award consists of a $5,000 prize. The prize is named in honor of the notable New York architect and city planner, Arnold William Brunner, who died in 1925.

www.artsandletters.org

1955	Gordon Bunshaft	1986	John Hejduk
	Minoru Yamasaki*	1987	James Ingo Freed
1956	John Yeon	1988	Arata Isozaki (Japan)
1957	John Carl Warnecke	1989	Richard Rogers (UK)
1958	Paul Rudolph	1990	Steven Holl
1959	Edward Larrabee Barnes	1991	Tadao Ando (Japan)
1960	Louis I. Kahn	1992	Sir Norman Foster (UK)
1961	I.M. Pei	1993	Rafael Moneo (Spain)
1962	Ulrich Franzen	1994	Renzo Piano (Italy)
1963	Edward C. Bassett	1995	Daniel Urban Kiley
1964	Harry Weese	1996	Tod Williams and Billie Tsien
1965	Kevin Roche	1997	Henri Ciriani (France)
1966	Romaldo Giurgola	1998	Alvaro Siza (Portugal)
1967	No award granted	1999	Fumihiko Maki (Japan)
1968	John M. Johansen	2000	Toyo Ito (Japan)
1969	N. Michael McKinnell	2001	Henry Smith-Miller and
1970	Charles Gwathmey and		Laurie Hawkinson
	Richard Henderson	2002	Kazuyo Sejima + Ryue Nishizawa
1971	John H. Andrews (Australia)		(Japan)
1972	Richard Meier	2003	Elizabeth Diller and Ricardo Scofidio
1973	Robert Venturi	2004	Hans Hollein (Austria)
1974	Hugh Hardy with Norman Pfeiffer	2005	Shigeru Ban (Japan)
	and Malcolm Holzman	2006	Jean Nouvel (France)
1975	Lewis Davis and Samuel Brody	2007	Eric Owen Moss
1976	James Stirling (UK)	2008	Peter Zumthor (Switzerland)
1977	Henry N. Cobb	2009	Juhani Pallasmaa (Finland)
1978	Cesar Pelli	2010	Michael Van Valkenburgh
1979	Charles Moore	2011	Mack Scogin
1980	Michael Graves		Merrill Elam
1981	Gunnar Birkerts	2012	Kathryn Gustafson
1982	Helmut Jahn	2013	Alberto Campo Baeza (Spain)
1983	Frank Gehry	2014	Massimo Scolari (Italy)
1984	Peter Eisenman	**2015**	**Sheila O'Donnell and John Tuomey**
1985	William Pedersen and Arthur May		

* Honorable Mention

Source: American Academy of Arts and Letters

ASLA Firm Award

The American Society of Landscape Architects presents its annual ASLA Firm Award to a **landscape architecture firm that has produced a body of distinguished work for at least 10 years**. Nominees are reviewed for their influence on the profession, their collaborative environment, the consistent quality of their work, and their recognition among fellow practitioners, teachers, allied professionals, and the general public.

www.asla.org

2003	Jones & Jones Architects and Landscape Architects	2010	EDSA
2004	Wallace Roberts & Todd	2011	JJR
2005	SWA Group	2012	PWP Landscape Architecture
2006	OLIN	2013	Reed Hilderbrand
2007	Sasaki Associates, Inc.	2014	Oehme van Sweden & Associates
2008	Design Workshop	**2015**	**The Office of James Burnett**
2009	EDAW	AECOM		

Source: American Society of Landscape Architects

ASLA Medals

The American Society of Landscape Architects awards its highest honor, the ASLA Medal, to individuals who have made a **significant contribution to the field of landscape architecture** in such areas as landscape design, planning, writing, and public service. The ASLA Design Medal recognizes landscape architects who have produced a body of exceptional design work at a sustained level for at least 10 years.

www.asla.org

ASLA Medal

1971	Hideo Sasaki	1994	Edward D. Stone Jr.
1972	Conrad L. Wirth	1995	Ervin H. Zube
1973	John C. Simonds	1996	John Lyle
1974	Campbell E. Miller	1997	Julius Fabos
1975	Garrett Eckbo	1998	Carol R. Johnson
1976	Thomas Church	1999	Stuart C. Dawson
1977	Hubert B. Owens	2000	Carl D. Johnson
1978	Lawrence Halprin	2001	Robert E. Marvin
1979	Norman T. Newton	2002	Morgan (Bill) Evans
1980	William G. Swain	2003	Richard Haag
1981	Sir Geoffrey Jellicoe (UK)	2004	Peter Walker
1982	Charles W. Eliot II	2005	Jane Silverstein Ries
1983	Theodore Osmundson	2006	Cameron R.J. Man
1984	Ian McHarg	2007	William B. Callaway
1985	Roberto Burle Marx (Brazil)	2008	Joseph A. Porter
1986	William J. Johnson	2009	Joseph E. Brown
1987	Philip H. Lewis Jr.	2010	Edward L. Daugherty
1988	Dame Sylvia Crowe (UK)	2011	Laurie D. Olin
1989	Robert N. Royston	2012	Cornelia Hahn Oberlander
1990	Raymond L. Freeman	2013	Warren T. Byrd, Jr.
1991	Meade Palmer	2014	Richard Bell
1992	Robert S. (Doc) Reich	**2015**	**M. Paul Friedberg**
1993	Arthur E. Bye Jr.		

ASLA Design Medal

2003	Lawrence Halprin	2010	James van Sweden
2004	M. Paul Friedberg	2011	Michael Van Valkenburgh
2005	Laurie D. Olin	2012	Peter Walker
2006	Steve Martino	2013	Stuart O. Dawson
2007	Richard Haag	2014	Andrea Cochran
2008	Kathryn Gustafson	**2015**	**Thomas Balsley**
2009	Richard W. Shaw		

Source: American Society of Landscape Architects

ASLA Professional Awards

With the annual Professional Awards program, the American Society of Landscape Architects honors the **best in landscape architecture from around the globe**. Recipients receive coverage in *Landscape Architecture* magazine; winners in the residential category are also featured in *Garden Design* magazine. The Landmark Award recognizes a distinguished landscape architecture project completed 15 to 50 years ago that retains its original design integrity and contributes significantly to the public realm.

www.asla.org

2015 Award of Excellence Winners

Analysis & Planning
Penn's Landing Redevelopment
  and Feasibility Study
Philadelphia, PA
Hargreaves Associates

Communications
Landscape Performance Series:
  Demonstrating the Environmental,
  Social, and Economic Value of
  Sustainable Landscapes
Landscape Architecture Foundation

General Design
At the Hudson's Edge: Beacon's Long Dock
  as a Resilient Riverfront Park
Beacon, NY
Reed Hilderbrand

Landmark Award
The Art Institute of Chicago South Garden
Chicago, IL
Cultural Landscape Foundation

Residential Design Category
Cedar Creek
Trinidad, TX
Hocker Design Group

2015 Honor Award Winners

Analysis & Planning
Cornwall Park 100 Year Master Plan:
  Projecting a Resilient Future
Auckland, New Zealand
Nelson Byrd Woltz Landscape Architects

Fayetteville 2030: Food City Scenario
Fayetteville, AR
University of Arkansas Community
  Design Center

James Island
Gulf Islands, BC, Canada
Design Workshop

Communications
Composite Landscapes: Photomontage and
  Landscape Architecture
Charles Waldheim and Andrea Hansen

Ecological Restoration Journal: A New
  Platform for Dialogue Between Landscape
  Architects and Ecologists
Rutgers University

General Design

Perez Art Museum Miami: Resiliency
  by Design
Miami, FL
ArquitectonicaGEO

Art and Infrastructure: Community, Culture,
  and a Collection in the Berkshires
Williamstown, MA
Reed Hilderbrand

Phil Hardberger Park
San Antonio, TX
Stephen Stimson Associates
  Landscape Architects

The Lawn on D
Boston, MA
Sasaki Associates, Inc.

Residential Design

300 Ivy
San Francisco, CA
Fletcher Studio

Sweetwater Spectrum Residential Community
  for Adults with Autism Spectrum Disorders
Sonoma, CA
Roche + Roche Landscape Architecture

Mill Creek Ranch
Vanderpool, TX
Ten Eyck Landscape Architects

Brooklyn Oasis
Brooklyn, NY
Michael Van Valkenburgh Associates, Inc.

Source: American Society of Landscape Architects

Best in Green Awards

The National Association of Home Builders presents the annual Green Building Awards to recognize **leaders who have advanced green-home building**. With this program, the NAHB hopes to encourage builders to incorporate green practices into their developments, designs, and construction methodologies and to speed the public's acceptance of sustainable, environmentally friendly building. A jury of industry professionals selects the winners, who are celebrated at the annual NAHB National Green Building Conference.

www.nahb.org

2015 Winners

Development of the Year
Grow Community
Bainbridge Island, WA
PHC Construction

50+ Home or Community
Skylar
Playa Vista, CA
KTGY Group

Multifamily Project
Stack House Apartments
Seattle, WA
Vulcan Residential

Remodeling Project
Sustainable Urban Villa
Cambridge, MA
Wolf Architects

Single-Family Custom Home
Katie's Ridge
Asheville, NC
Red Tree Builders

Single-Family Production Home
ArtiZEN Plan
Denver, CO
New Town Builders

Source: National Association of Home Builders

Best Tall Building Awards

The Best Tall Building Awards recognize projects that have made **extraordinary contributions to the advancement of tall buildings and the urban environment, including sustainability**. The projects must also exhibit processes or innovations that have enhanced the design profession and enriched the cities and lives of their inhabitants. The program is sponsored by the Council on Tall Buildings and Urban Habitats.

www.ctbuh.org

2015 Winners

Americas
One World Trade Center
New York, NY
Skidmore, Owings & Merrell

Asia & Australasia
CapitaGreen
Singapore
Takenaka Corp. (Japan);
    Toyo Ito & Associates (Japan);
    RSP Architects

Europe
Bosco Verticale
Milan, IT
Stefano Boeri Architetti (Italy)

Middle East & Africa
Burj Mohammed Bin Rashid Tower
Abu Dhabi, UAE
Foster + Partners (UK)

Source: Council on Tall Buildings and Urban Habitats

Exhibition of School Architecture Awards

The Exhibition of School Architecture Awards, sponsored by the American Association of School Administrators, American Institute of Architects, and Council of Educational Facility Planners International, **showcase how well-designed schools facilitate student achievement**. The Shirley Cooper Award recognizes the project that best meets the educational needs of students. The Walter Taylor Award honors the project that best addresses a difficult design challenge.

www.aia.org

2015 Winners

Shirley Cooper Award
Penn State University Hort Woods Child
    Care Center/Lab School
State College, PA
studioMLA Architects

Walter Taylor Award
Tesla STEM High School
Redmond, WA
Integrus Architecture

Source: American Institute of Architects

Holcim Awards for Sustainable Construction

The Holcim Awards for Sustainable Construction encourage **future-oriented, tangible sustainable design initiatives in the building and construction industry**. The competition was created by the Swiss-based Holcim Foundation for Sustainable Construction and is conducted in partnership with some of the world's leading technical universities. Prize money totaling $2 million per three-year competition cycle encourages and inspires achievements that go beyond convention to explore new ways and means.

www.holcimfoundation.org

2015 North American Recipients

Gold
Poreform Porous Concrete, Water Absorptive
    Surface & Subterranean Basin
New York, NY
Water Pore Partnership

Silver
Big U Project, New York City Coastal
    Flooding Protection Plan
New York, NY
Bjarke Ingels Group; Starr Whitehouse
    Landscape Architects and Planners

Bronze
Hy-Fi, Zero Carbon Emissions Compostable
    Structure
New York, NY
The Living

Source: Holcim Foundation for Sustainable Construction

Housing Awards

The AIA's Housing Awards recognize the **importance of good housing as a necessity of life, a sanctuary for the human spirit, and a valuable national resource**. Licensed AIA-member architects are eligible to enter US-built projects.

www.aia.org

2015 Winners

One/Two Family Custom Housing
Bridge House
Kent, CT
Joeb Moore & Partners

Marlboro Music: Five Cottages
Marlboro, VT
HGA Architects and Engineers

Old Briar
Halls, TN
Applied Research

Studhorse
Winthrop, WA
Olson Kundig Architects

Multifamily Housing

North Parker
San Diego, CA
Jonathan Segal

Bayview Hill Gardens
San Francisco, CA
David Baker Architects

Broadway Affordable Housing
Santa Monica, CA
Kevin Daly Architects

Specialized Housing

160 Massachusetts Avenue Tower
    Berklee College of Music
Boston, MA
William Rawn Associates

John C. Anderson Apartments
Philadelphia, PA
WRT

La Casa Permanent Supportive Housing
Washington, DC
Studio 27 Architecture | Leo A. Daly

Source: American Institute of Architects

Interior Design Competition

The Interior Design Competition is presented jointly each year by the International Interior Design Association and *Interior Design* magazine. The program was established in 1973 to recognize **outstanding interior design projects and to foster new ideas and techniques**. Winning projects appear in the magazine, and the best-of-competition winner receives a $5,000 cash prize.

www.iida.org

2015 Winners

Windhover Contemplative Center
Stanford, CA
Aidlin Darling Design

Mark Lash Flagship
Toronto, ON, Canada
Burdifilek

Vancouver Grill
Nanjing, China
CL3 Architects Limited

Chilewich Store
New York, NY
de-spec, inc.

Newton Tudor Residence
Newton, MA
Hacin + Associates

Fort McMurray International Airport
Fort McMurray, Alberta, CA
office of mcfarlane biggar
    architects + designers inc.

Source: International Interior Design Association

International Design Excellence Awards

The annual International Design Excellence Awards (IDEA), produced by the Industrial Designers Society of America (IDSA) and sponsored by *Fast Company*, **honor outstanding industrial design projects worldwide**. A jury of business and design executives select winners from categories ranging from commercial and industrial products to interactive product experiences and service design. Gold, silver, and bronze awards are granted.

www.idsa.org

2015 Gold Winners

Automotive & Transportation
BLACKLINE Bicycle
MINIMAL; Method Bicycle

Commercial & Industrial Products
Black Onyx
ROE Visual Co., Ltd.

Blackmagic Cintel Film Scanner
Blackmagic Industrial Design Team

Communication Tools
Blackmagic URSA
Blackmagic Industrial Design Team

Logitech ConferenceCam Connect
MINIMAL and Logitech Design

Computer Equipment
Cardboard
Google

Seven Hard Drive
HUGE Design and Seagate Branded
    Innovation

Design Strategy
Coloplast Design DNA
Coloplast and Native

Innova Schools
InterGroup/Innova Schools and IDEO

Digital Design
NAVER Service History Wall
NAVER Corp; VINYL I

Post-it® Plus App
3M Design

Entertainment
NX mini
Samsung Electronics Company

Environments
National September 11 Memorial Museum
Thinc Design; Local Projects; Hadley
    Exhibits; Layman Design; Design and
    Production; Electrosonic; PPI Consulting;
    Fisher Marantz Stone Layman Design;
    Renfro Design Group; Jaffe Holden; Art
    Preservation Services; Zubatkin Owner
    Representation; Davis Brody Bond;
    Snøhetta; Lend Lease; National September 11
    Memorial Museum

Home & Bath
Living Square Washbasin with SaphirKeramik
platinumdesign for LAUFEN

Water Heater
Midea

Kitchens
Craft Beer Glasses
Spiegelau for Kristallglasfabrik Spiegelau
GmbH

GE Micro Kitchen
General Electric

Medical & Scientific Products
Brivo XR118
GE Healthcare (China)

da Vinci Xi Surgical System
Intuitive Surgical New Product Development
Team; Bould Design

LUMI Medical Advanced Concept
GE Healthcare

Outdoor & Garden
MultipliCITY
fuseproject; Landscape Forms Industrial
Design Group

Packaging & Graphics
Patagonia Baselayer Packaging
Capsule; Avery Dennison; and Lotus for
Patagonia

Social Impact Design
Design Kit
IDEO

Sports, Leisure & Recreation
CLUG Bike Rack
Hurdler Studios, Inc. ; CLUG Brands Inc.

Flip Reel by Squiddies
tillerdesign for Squiddies Pty. Ltd.

Source: Industrial Designers Society of America

Library Buildings Awards

The American Institute of Architects and American Library Association present the biennial Library Buildings Awards to encourage **excellence in the design and planning of libraries**. Architects licensed in the United States are eligible to enter any public or private library project from around the world, whether a renovation, addition, conversion, interior project, or new construction. The jury consists of three architects and three librarians with extensive library building experience.

www.ala.org

2015 Winners

Cedar Rapids Public Library
Cedar Rapids, IA
OPN Architects

Claire T. Carney Library Addition & Renovation
    University of Massachusetts
Dartmouth, MA
designLAB architects

Hillary Rodham Clinton Children's Library
    and Learning Center
Little Rock, AR
Polk Stanley Wilcox Architects

Mission Branch Library
San Antonio, TX
Muñoz and Company

Slover Library
Norfolk, VA
Newman Architects

Vancouver Community Library
Vancouver, BC, WA
The Miller Hull Partnership

Source: American Library Association

National Healthcare Design Awards

The National Healthcare Design Awards showcase the **best of healthcare building design and health design-oriented research**. The program is sponsored by the American Institute of Architects and the Academy of Architecture for Health. Winning projects exhibit conceptual strength and solve aesthetic, civic, urban, and social concerns in addition to the requisite functional and sustainability concerns of a healthcare facility.

www.aia.org/aah

2015 Winners

Built, Less Than $25 Million

New York Hospital of Queens Primary
　Care Satellite Clinic
Astoria, NY
Michielli + Wyetzner Architects

Vitenas Cosmetic Surgery and
　Mirror Mirror Beauty Boutique
Houston, TX
Perkins+Will; Harrell Architects

Providence Sacred Heart Medical Center
　Pediatric Emergency Department
Spokane, WA
Mahlum

Cleveland Clinic, Brunswick Family Health
　Center Emergency Department
Brunswick, OH
Westlake Reed Leskosky

Built, More Than $25 Million

Bridgepoint Active Healthcare
Toronto, ON, Canada
Stantec Architecture; KPMB; HDR
　Architecture; Diamond Schmitt Architects

Unbuilt

Fifth XiangYa Hospital
ChangSha, China
Payette

U.S. Department of Veterans Affairs, Robley
　Rex VA Replacement Medical Center
Louisville, KY
URS with SmithGroup

Innovations in Planning and Design Research, Built and Unbuilt

Studio Dental
San Francisco Bay Area, CA
Montalba Architects

Source: American Institute of Architects

National Planning Excellence Awards

Through its National Planning Awards program, the American Planning Association recognizes the role cutting-edge planning achievements and outstanding individual contributions play in creating **communities of lasting value**. Excellence Awards are granted to outstanding initiatives by planning agencies, planning teams or firms, community groups, and local authorities.

www.planning.org

2015 Winners

Daniel Burnham Award for a Comprehensive Plan
Vibrant NEO 2040: Northeast Ohio
    Sustainable Communities Consortium
Northeast Ohio

HUD Secretary's Opportunity and Empowerment Award
Mueller Redevelopment
Austin, TX

Best Practice
First Last Mile Strategic Plan &
    Planning Guidelines
Los Angeles, CA

Implementation
Green City, Clean Waters: Philadelphia's 21st
    Century Green Stormwater
     Infrastructure Program
Philadelphia, PA

Public Outreach
Making Planning Public: Newark
    Zoning Workshop
Newark, NJ

Communications Initiative
Boston Complete Streets Design Guidelines
Boston, MA

Transportation Planning
moveDC
Washington, DC

Environmental Planning
Greater New Orleans Urban Water Plan
New Orleans, LA

Economic Planning & Development
Phase 1 Glenwood Refinement Plan
Springfield, OR

Urban Design
The BIG U
New York, NY

Pierre L'Enfant International Planning Excellence Award
Tecnologico de Monterrey Urban
    Regeneration Plan
Monterrey, Mexico

Advancing Diversity & Social Change (in Honor of Paul Davidoff)
State Rep. Harold Mitchell, Jr. and the
    ReGenesis Project
Spartanburg, SC

Planning Firm
Perkins+Will
San Francisco, CA

Emerging Planning & Design Firm
Raimi + Associates
Berkeley, Los Angeles, and Riverside, CA

Planning Agency
Maryland Department of Planning
Baltimore, MD

Source: American Planning Association

National Preservation Dreihaus Awards

The National Trust for Historic Preservation annually recognizes citizens, organizations, and public and private entities for their dedication to and **support of historic preservation**. A jury of preservation professionals selects the winners of the National Preservation Dreihaus Awards using such criteria as the projects' positive effect on the community, pioneering nature, quality, and degree of difficulty. Special interest is also placed on projects that use historic preservation as a method of revitalization.

www.preservationnation.org

2015 Winners

JW Marriott Houston Downtown
Houston, TX

Dental Associates Iron Block Building
Milwaukee, WI

Baltimore Design School
Baltimore, MD

Ames Shovel Works Apartments
North Easton, MA

Source: National Trust for Historic Preservation

Praemium Imperiale

The Praemium Imperiale is awarded by the Japan Art Association, Japan's premier cultural institution, for **lifetime achievement in the fields of painting, sculpture, music, architecture, and theater/film**. The following individuals received this honor for architecture, which includes a commemorative medal and a 15,000,000 yen ($130,000) honorarium.

www.praemiumimperiale.org

1989	I.M. Pei	2003	Rem Koolhaas (Netherlands)
1990	James Stirling (UK)	2004	Oscar Niemeyer (Brazil)
1991	Gae Aulenti (Italy)	2005	Taniguchi Yoshio (Japan)
1992	Frank Gehry	2006	Frei Otto (Germany)
1993	Kenzo Tange (Japan)	2007	Jacques Herzog and Pierre de
1994	Charles Correa (India)		Meuron (Switzerland)
1995	Renzo Piano (Italy)	2008	Peter Zumthor (Switzerland)
1996	Tadao Ando (Japan)	2009	Zaha Hadid (UK)
1997	Richard Meier	2010	Toyo Ito (Japan)
1998	Alvaro Siza (Portugal)	2011	Ricardo Legorreta (Mexico)
1999	Fumihiko Maki (Japan)	2012	Henning Larsen (Denmark)
2000	Sir Richard Rogers (UK)	2013	David Chipperfield (UK)
2001	Jean Nouvel (France)	2014	Steven Holl
2002	Sir Norman Foster (UK)	**2015**	**Dominique Perrault**

Source: Japan Art Association

Pritzker Architecture Prize

In 1979, Jay and Cindy Pritzker established the Pritzker Architecture Prize to inspire **greater creativity in the profession** and to heighten public awareness about architecture. Today, it is revered as one of the field's highest honors. The prize, which includes a $100,000 grant, is awarded each year to a living architect whose body of work represents a long-standing, significant contribution to the built environment.

www.pritzkerprize.com

1979	Philip Johnson	1999	Sir Norman Foster (UK)
1980	Luis Barragán (Mexico)	2000	Rem Koolhaas (Netherlands)
1981	James Stirling (UK)	2001	Jacques Herzog and Pierre de
1982	Kevin Roche		Meuron (Switzerland)
1983	I.M. Pei	2002	Glenn Murcutt (Australia)
1984	Richard Meier	2003	Jørn Utzon (Denmark)
1985	Hans Hollein (Austria)	2004	Zaha Hadid (UK)
1986	Gottfried Boehm (Germany)	2005	Thom Mayne
1987	Kenzo Tange (Japan)	2006	Paulo Mendes da Rocha (Brazil)
1988	Gordon Bunshaft	2007	Sir Richard Rogers (UK)
	Oscar Niemeyer (Brazil)	2008	Jean Nouvel (France)
1989	Frank Gehry	2009	Peter Zumthor (Switzerland)
1990	Aldo Rossi (Italy)	2010	Kazuyo Sejima (Japan)
1991	Robert Venturi		Ryue Nishizawa (Japan)
1992	Alvaro Siza (Portugal)	2011	Eduardo Souto de Moura
1993	Fumihiko Maki (Japan)		(Portugal)
1994	Christian de Portzamparc (France)	2012	Wang Shu (China)
1995	Tadao Ando (Japan)	2013	Toyo Ito (Japan)
1996	Rafael Moneo (Spain)	2014	Shigeru Ban (Japan)
1997	Sverre Fehn (Norway)	**2015**	**Frei Otto (Germany)**
1998	Renzo Piano (Italy)		

Source: The Pritzker Architecture Prize

Religious Art & Architecture Design Awards

The annual Religious Art & Architecture Design Awards, co-sponsored by *Faith & Form* magazine and the Interfaith Forum on Religion, Art and Architecture (a professional interest area of the American Institute of Architects), reward the **highest achievements in architecture, liturgical design, and art for religious spaces**. Architects, liturgical consultants, interior designers, artists, and craftpersons worldwide are eligible to enter. Winning projects are featured in *Faith & Form*.

www.faithandform.com

2013 Honor Awards

New Facilities
Saint George Church and Parish Center
Pamplona, Navarra, Spain
Tabuenca & Leache, Arquitectos (Spain)

Renovation
Church of St. Brigid – St. Emeric
New York, NY
Acheson Doyle Partners Architects

Saint Nicholas Eastern Orthodox Church
Springdale, AR
Marlon Blackwell Architect

Restoration
Restoration and Adaptation of
   16th-Century Chapel
Guadalajara, Spain
Adam Bresnick Architects (Spain)

2013 Merit Awards

New Facilities
Colombiere Jesuit Community
   Residence and Chapel
Baltimore, MD
Bohlin Cywinski Jackson

Sayama Lakeside Cemetery Community Hall
Saitama, Japan
Hiroshi Nakamura & NAP Co. (Japan)

Children's Chapel and Education Center
   Korean Church of Boston
Brookline, MA
Brian Healy Architects

Shrine in an Air Pocket in the City
Ryuto-Ohashi, Chuo, Niigata, Japan
Kikuma Watanabe (Japan)

Renovation
St. Paul's Episcopal Church Renovation
Seattle, WA
atelierjones, llc

Restoration
Mission Nuestra Señora de la Purísima
   Concepción de Acuña
San Antonio, TX
Ford, Powell & Carson, Architects & Planners

La Lomita Chapel
Mission, TX
Muñoz & Company

Westwood Lutheran Church
   Sanctuary Restoration
St. Louis Park, MN
Kodet Architectural Group

Liturgical/Interior Design
Chapel of St. Monica
Des Moines, IA
Integrated Studio

Cathedral of Saint Paul Organ Case
Saint Paul, MN
Duncan G. Stroik Architect

Liturgical Furnishings
Pyx Tabernacle
Brooklyn, NY
Salvatore V. LaRosa

Visual Arts
"Meronymy / Sukkah 2012"
    Temple Adas Israel
Sag Harbor, NY
Erling Hope

Sacred Landscape
Terrace and Gardens Restoration
    Baha'i House of Worship
Wilmette, IL
One World Architecture

Unbuilt Work
Meditation House
Jebaa, Lebanon
MZ Architects

Source: Faith & Form

RIBA Royal Gold Medal

The Royal Institute of British Architects' Royal Gold Medal was inaugurated by Queen Victoria in 1848. It is conferred annually on a **distinguished architect, person, or firm "whose work has promoted, either directly or indirectly, the advancement of architecture."**

www.riba.org

1848	Charles Robert Cockerell (UK)
1849	Luigi Canina (Italy)
1850	Sir Charles Barry (UK)
1851	Thomas L. Donaldson (UK)
1852	Leo von Klenze (Germany)
1853	Sir Robert Smirke (UK)
1854	Philip Hardwick (UK)
1855	Jacques Ignace Hittorff (France)
1856	Sir William Tite (UK)
1857	Owen Jones (UK)
1858	Friedrich August Stuler (Germany)
1859	Sir George Gilbert Scott (UK)
1860	Sydney Smirke (UK)
1861	Jean-Baptiste Cicéron Lesueur (France)
1862	Robert Willis (UK)
1863	Anthony Salvin (UK)
1864	Eugène Emmanuel Violett-le-Duc (France)
1865	Sir James Pennethorne (UK)
1866	Sir Matthew Digby Wyatt (UK)
1867	Charles Texier (France)
1868	Sir Henry Layard (UK)
1869	C.R. Lepsius (Germany)
1870	Benjamin Ferrey (UK)
1871	James Fergusson (UK)
1872	Baron von Schmidt (Austria)
1873	Thomas Henry Wyatt (UK)
1874	George Edmund Street (UK)
1875	Edmund Sharpe (UK)
1876	Joseph Louis Duc (France)
1877	Charles Barry Jr. (UK)
1878	Alfred Waterhouse (UK)
1879	Marquis de Vogue (France)
1880	John L. Pearson (UK)
1881	George Godwin (UK)
1882	Baron von Ferstel (Austria)
1883	Francis C. Penrose (UK)
1884	William Butterfield (UK)
1885	H. Schliemann (Germany)
1886	Charles Garnier (France)
1887	Ewan Christian (UK)
1888	Baron von Hansen (Austria)
1889	Sir Charles T. Newton (UK)
1890	John Gibson (UK)
1891	Sir Arthur Blomfield (UK)
1892	Cesar Daly (France)
1893	Richard Morris Hunt
1894	Lord Frederic Leighton (UK)
1895	James Brooks (UK)
1896	Sir Ernest George (UK)
1897	Petrus Josephus Hubertus Cuypers (Netherlands)
1898	George Aitchison (UK)
1899	George Frederick Bodley (UK)
1900	Rodolfo Amadeo Lanciani (Italy)
1901	*No award granted due to the death of Queen Victoria*
1902	Thomas Edward Collcutt (UK)
1903	Charles F. McKim
1904	Auguste Choisy (France)
1905	Sir Aston Webb (UK)
1906	Sir Lawrence Alma-Tadema (UK)
1907	John Belcher (UK)
1908	Honore Daumet (France)
1909	Sir Arthur John Evans (UK)
1910	Sir Thomas Graham Jackson (UK)
1911	Wilhelm Dorpfeld (Germany)
1912	Basil Champneys (UK)
1913	Sir Reginald Blomfield (UK)
1914	Jean Louis Pascal (France)
1915	Frank Darling (Canada)
1916	Sir Robert Rowand Anderson (UK)
1917	Henri Paul Nenot (France)
1918	Ernest Newton (UK)
1919	Leonard Stokes (UK)
1920	Charles Louis Girault (France)
1921	Sir Edwin Lutyens (UK)
1922	Thomas Hastings
1923	Sir John James Burnet (UK)
1924	*No award granted*
1925	Sir Giles Gilbert Scott (UK)

1926	Ragnar Östberg (Sweden)	1972	Louis I. Kahn
1927	Sir Herbert Baker (UK)	1973	Sir Leslie Martin (UK)
1928	Sir Guy Dawber (UK)	1974	Powell & Moya (UK)
1929	Victor Laloux (France)	1975	Michael Scott (Ireland)
1930	Sir Percy Scott Worthington (UK)	1976	Sir John Summerson (UK)
1931	Sir Edwin Cooper (UK)	1977	Sir Denys Lasdun (UK)
1932	Hendrik Petrus Berlage (Netherlands)	1978	Jørn Utzon (Denmark)
1933	Sir Charles Reed Peers (UK)	1979	The Office of Charles and Ray Eames
1934	Henry Vaughan Lanchester (UK)	1980	James Stirling (UK)
1935	Willem Marinus Dudok (Netherlands)	1981	Sir Philip Dowson (UK)
1936	Charles Henry Holden (UK)	1982	Berthold Lubetkin (Georgia)
1937	Sir Raymond Unwin (UK)	1983	Sir Norman Foster (UK)
1938	Ivar Tengbom (Sweden)	1984	Charles Correa (India)
1939	Sir Percy Thomas (UK)	1985	Sir Richard Rogers (UK)
1940	Charles Francis Annesley Voysey (UK)	1986	Arata Isozaki (Japan)
1941	Frank Lloyd Wright	1987	Ralph Erskine (Sweden)
1942	William Curtis Green (UK)	1988	Richard Meier
1943	Sir Charles Herbert Reilly (UK)	1989	Renzo Piano (Italy)
1944	Sir Edward Maufe (UK)	1990	Aldo van Eyck (Netherlands)
1945	Victor Vesnin (USSR)	1991	Sir Colin Stansfield Smith (UK)
1946	Sir Patrick Abercrombie (UK)	1992	Peter Rice (UK)
1947	Sir Albert Edward Richardson (UK)	1993	Giancarlo de Carlo (Italy)
1948	Auguste Perret (France)	1994	Sir Michael and Lady Patricia
1949	Sir Howard Robertson (UK)		Hopkins (UK)
1950	Eleil Saarinen (Finland/US)	1995	Colin Rowe (UK/US)
1951	Emanuel Vincent Harris (UK)	1996	Harry Seidler (Australia)
1952	George Grey Wornum (UK)	1997	Tadao Ando (Japan)
1953	Le Corbusier (Charles-Édouard	1998	Oscar Niemeyer (Brazil)
	Jeanneret) (Switzerland/France)	1999	Barcelona, Spain
1954	Sir Arthur Stephenson (Australia)	2000	Frank Gehry
1955	John Murray Easton (UK)	2001	Jean Nouvel (France)
1956	Walter Gropius (Germany/US)	2002	Archigram (UK)
1957	Alvar Aalto (Finland)	2003	Rafael Moneo (Spain)
1958	Robert Schofield Morris (Canada)	2004	Rem Koolhaas (Netherlands)
1959	Ludwig Mies van der Rohe	2005	Frei Otto (Germany)
	(Germany/US)	2006	Toyo Ito (Japan)
1960	Pier Luigi Nervi (Italy)	2007	Jacques Herzog and Pierre
1961	Lewis Mumford		de Meuron (Switzerland)
1962	Sven Gottfrid Markelius (Sweden)	2008	Edward Cullinan (UK)
1963	Lord William Graham Holford (UK)	2009	Álvaro Siza (Portugal)
1964	E. Maxwell Fry (UK)	2010	I.M. Pei
1965	Kenzo Tange (Japan)	2011	David Chipperfield
1966	Ove Arup (UK)	2012	Herman Hertzberger (Netherlands)
1967	Sir Nikolaus Pevsner (UK)	2013	Peter Zumthor (Switzerland)
1968	R. Buckminster Fuller	2014	Joseph Rykwert
1969	Jack Antonio Coia (UK)	**2015**	**Sheila O'Donnell &**
1970	Sir Robert Matthew (UK)		**John Tuomey (Ireland)**
1971	Hubert de Cronin Hastings (UK)		

Source: Royal Institute of British Architects

SCUP/AIA-CAE Excellence in Planning, Landscape Architecture, and Architecture Awards

The Society for College and University Planning and the American Institute of Architects' Committee on Architecture for Education jointly present the annual Excellence in Planning, Landscape Architecture, and Architecture Awards to **outstanding projects developed for higher education institutions**. The jury considerations include the quality of the physical environment as well as the comprehensiveness of the planning process. The award is presented to all members of the project team.

www.scup.org

2015 Honor Awards

Planning for a District or Campus Component
Academic Core Replacement Buildings, Ohlone Community College District
Fremont and Newark, CA
Cannon Design; Anderson Brule Architects

Planning for an Existing Campus
South Mall Campus Master Plan, Smithsonian Institution
Washington, DC
BIG – Bjarke Ingels Group; Surfacedesign

Landscape Architecture – Open Space Planning and Design
West Village Implementation Plan, University of California Davis
Davis, CA
West Village Community Partnership; SWA Group; Studio E Architects

Landscape Architecture – General Design
Life Science Laboratories, University of Massachusetts Amherst
Amherst, MA
Towers Golde; Wilson Architects

Architecture for Building Additions or Adaptive Reuse
Baldwin Auditorium Renovation, Duke University
Durham, NC
Pfeiffer Partners Architects

Architecture for a New Building
Ashtonbee Campus, Centennial College
Scarborough, ON, Canada
MacLennan Jaunkains Miller Architects

Physical Sciences & Engineering Center, Foothill College
Los Altos Hills, CA
Ratcliff

2015 Merit Awards

Planning for a District or Campus Component

Medical District Master Plan: University
  of Texas at Austin
Austin, TX
Page Southerland Page; Sasaki Associates

Planning for an Existing Campus

Stormwater Management & Landscape Master
  Plan: Rowan University
Glassboro, NJ
Biohabitats, Inc; Ayers Saint Gross

Landscape Architecture – General Design

Global Plaza: Rochester Institute
  of Technology
Rochester, NY
SWA Group; ARC

Architecture for Building Additions or Adaptive Reuse

Academic Center, Cornell University
  Law School
Ithaca, NY
Ann Beha Architects

Kline Fitness and Squash Center,
  Dickinson College
St. Carlisle, PA
Andropogon Associates

Mariposa Hall, Los Angeles Trade
  Technical College
Los Angeles, CA
Harley Ellis Devereaux

Wood Center Expansion, University of Alaska
  Fairbanks
Fairbanks, AK
Perkins+Will; Ghemm Company;
  Design Alaska

Sawyer Library/Stetson Hall, Williams College
Williamstown, MA
Bohlin Cywinski Jackson

Architecture for Rehabilitation, Restoration, or Preservatione

Historic Old Administration Building;
  Fresno City College
Fresno, CA
ELS Architecture; Urban Design

Architecture for a New Building

Collaborative Life Science Building and
  Scourtes Tower; A partnership between
  Oregon Health Sciences University, Portland
  State University, and Oregon State
  University
Portland and Corvallis, OR
CO Architects; SERA Architects

Berklee Tower, Berklee College of Music
Boston, MA
William Rawn Associates

Nicholas School of the Environment,
  Duke University
Durham, NC
Payette; Stewart; Simpson Gumpertz & Heger

Milken Institute School of Public Health,
  George Washington University
Washington, DC
Payette; Ayers Saint Gross

Biosciences Research Building, National
  University of Ireland, Galway
Galway, Ireland
Payette; Reddy Architecture + Urbanism

Source: Society for College and University Planning

Star Award

The International Interior Design Association's Star Award celebrates **individuals and organizations that have made extraordinary contributions to the interior design profession**. As the Star Award is merit-based, it is not necessarily granted each year. Although non-members are eligible, the IIDA board of directors (the selection body) only accepts nominations from IIDA fellows, chapter presidents, and directors.

www.iida.org

1985	Lester Dundes	2001	Andrée Putman (France)
1986	William Sullivan	2002	Karim Rashid
1987	Orlando Diaz-Azcuy	2003	Ray Anderson
1988	Paul Brayton	2004	Kevin Kampschroer
1989	Florence Knoll Bassett	2005	Target Corporation
1990	Beverly Russell	2006	*Fast Company*
1991	Stanley Abercrombie	2007	Karen Stephenson
1992	M. Arthur Gensler Jr.	2008	Gordon Segal
1993	Sivon C. Reznikoff	2009	Hilda Longinotti
1994	Michael Kroelinger	2010	Majora Carter
1995	Douglas R. Parker	2011	The Center for Health Design
1997	Michael Wirtz	2012	Four Seasons Hotel Corporation
1998	Charles and Ray Eames	2013	Cooper-Hewitt, National Design Museum
1999	Michael Brill		
2000	Eva L. Maddox	2014	Yabu Pushelberg
		2015	**Yves Béhar**

Source: International Interior Designers Association

Top Green Projects

The American Institute of Architects' Committee on the Environment annually selects the Top Green Projects to highlight **viable architectural design solutions that protect and enhance the environment**. Winning projects address significant environmental challenges, such as energy and water conservation, use of recycled materials, and improved indoor air quality. Responsible use of building materials, daylighting, efficient heating and cooling, and sensitivity to local environmental issues are some of the jury's considerations.

www.aiatopten.org

2015 Winners

Bullitt Center
Seattle, WA
Miller Hull Partnership

CANMET Materials Technology Laboratory
Hamilton, ON, Canada
Diamond Schmitt

Collaborative Life Sciences Building for OHSU,
    PSU, and OSU
Portland, OR
SERA Architects; CO Architects

226-232 Highland Street Townhouses
Boston, MA
Interface Studio Architects;
    Urbanica Design

Hughes Warehouse Adaptive Reuse
San Antonio, TX
Overland Partners

Military Medical Hospital
San Antonio, TX
RTKL

New Orleans Bioinnovation Center
New Orleans, LA
Eskew+Dumez+Ripple

Sweetwater Spectrum Community
Sonoma, CA
LEDDY MAYTUM STACY Architects

Tassafaronga Village
Oakland, CA
David Baker Architects

University Center – The New School
New York, NY
Skidmore, Owings & Merrill

Source: American Institute of Architects

Twenty-five Year Award

The American Institute of Architects' Twenty-five Year Award celebrates **buildings that excel under the test of time**. Eligible projects must have been completed within the past 25 to 35 years by a licensed US architect, though the buildings may be located worldwide. Winning designs are still operating under the tenets of the original program, demonstrating continued viability in function and form, and contributing meaningfully to American life and architecture.

www.aia.org

1969	Rockefeller Center
	New York, NY, 1931–40
	Reinhard & Hofmeister with
	    Corbett, Harrison & MacMurray
	    and Hood & Fouilhoux

1971	Crow Island School Winnetka, IL, 1939 Perkins, Wheeler & Will and Eliel and Eero Saarinen

1972	Baldwin Hills Village
	Los Angeles, CA, 1941
	Reginald D. Johnson with Wilson,
	    Merrill & Alexander and
	    Clarence S. Stein

1973	Taliesin West Paradise Valley, AZ, 1938 Frank Lloyd Wright
1974	S.C. Johnson & Son Administration Building Racine, WI, 1939 Frank Lloyd Wright
1975	Philip Johnson Residence (The Glass House) New Canaan, CT, 1949 Philip Johnson
1976	860-880 North Lakeshore Drive Apartments Chicago, IL, 1948–51 Ludwig Mies van der Rohe
1977	Christ Lutheran Church Minneapolis, MN, 1948–51 Saarinen, Saarinen & Associates with Hills, Gilbertson & Hays
1978	Eames House Pacific Palisades, CA, 1949 Charles and Ray Eames

1979	Yale University Art Gallery New Haven, CT, 1954 Louis I. Kahn with Douglas W. Orr
1980	Lever House New York, NY, 1952 Skidmore, Owings & Merrill
1981	Farnsworth House Plano, IL, 1950 Ludwig Mies van der Rohe
1982	Equitable Savings and Loan Association Building Portland, OR, 1948 Pietro Belluschi
1983	Price Tower Bartlesville, OK, 1956 Frank Lloyd Wright
1984	Seagram Building New York, NY, 1957 Ludwig Mies van der Rohe

1985	General Motors Technical Center
	Warren, MI, 1951
	Saarinen, Saarinen & Associates
	    with Smith, Hinchman and
	    Grylls Associates

1986	Solomon R. Guggenheim Museum New York, NY, 1959 Frank Lloyd Wright
1987	Bavinger House Norman, OK, 1953 Bruce Goff
1988	Dulles International Airport Terminal Building Chantilly, VA, 1962 Eero Saarinen & Associates

1989	Vanna Venturi House Chestnut Hill, PA, 1964 Robert Venturi	2003	Design Research Headquarters Building Cambridge, MA, 1969 BTA Architects Inc.
1990	Gateway Arch St. Louis, MO, 1965 Eero Saarinen & Associates	2004	East Building, National Gallery of Art Washington, DC, 1978 I.M. Pei & Partners
1991	Sea Ranch Condominium I The Sea Ranch, CA, 1965 Moore Lyndon Turnbull Whitaker	2005	Yale Center for British Art New Haven, CT, 1977 Louis I. Kahn
1992	Salk Institute for Biological Studies La Jolla, CA, 1966 Louis I. Kahn	2006	Thorncrown Chapel Eureka Springs, AR, 1980 E. Fay Jones
1993	Deere & Company Administrative Center Moline, IL, 1963 Eero Saarinen & Associates	2007	Vietnam Veterans Memorial Washington, DC, 1982 Maya Lin
1994	Haystack Mountain School of Crafts Deer Isle, ME, 1962 Edward Larrabee Barnes Associates	2008	Atheneum New Harmony, IN, 1979 Richard Meier & Partners Architects
1995	Ford Foundation Headquarters New York, NY, 1968 Kevin Roche John Dinkeloo & Associates	2009	Faneuil Hall Marketplace Boston, MA various renovations Benjamin Thompson & Associates
1996	Air Force Academy Cadet Chapel Colorado Springs, CO, 1962 Skidmore, Owings & Merrill	2010	Hajj Terminal, King Abdul Aziz International Airport Jeddah, Saudi Arabia, 1981 Skidmore, Owings & Merrill
1997	Phillips Exeter Academy Library Exeter, NH, 1972 Louis I. Kahn	2011	John Hancock Tower Boston, MA I.M. Pei & Partners
1998	Kimbell Art Museum Fort Worth, TX, 1972 Louis I. Kahn	2012	Gehry Residence Santa Monica, CA, 1978 Gehry Partners
1999	John Hancock Center Chicago, IL, 1969 Skidmore, Owings & Merrill	2013	Menil Collection Houston, TX, 1987 Renzo Piano Building Workshop
2000	Smith House Darien, CT, 1967 Richard Meier & Partners Architects	2014	Washington Metropolitan Area Transit – METRO Washington, D.C. Harry Weese & Associates
2001	Weyerhaeuser Headquarters Tacoma, WA, 1971 Skidmore, Owings & Merrill	**2015**	**Broadgate Exchange House** **London, UK** **Skidmore, Owings & Merrill**
2002	Fundació Joan Miró Barcelona, Spain, 1975 Sert Jackson and Associates		

Source: American Institute of Architects

UIA Gold Medal

Every three years at its World Congress, the International Union of Architects awards its Gold Medal to a **living architect who has made outstanding achievements in the field of architecture**. This honor recognizes the recipient's lifetime of distinguished practice, contribution to the enrichment of mankind, and the promotion of the art of architecture.

www.uia-architectes.org

1984	Hassan Fathy (Egypt)	2002	Renzo Piano (Italy)
1987	Reima Pietila (Finland)	2005	Tadao Ando (Japan)
1990	Charles Correa (India)	2008	Teodoro González de León (Mexico)
1993	Fumihiko Maki (Japan)		
1996	Rafael Moneo (Spain)	2011	Alvaro Siza (Portugal)
1999	Ricardo Legorreta (Mexico)	2014	Ieoh Ming Pei

Source: International Union of Architects

America's Best Architecture & Design Schools

America's Best Architecture & Design Schools is conducted annually by *DesignIntelligence* on behalf of the Design Futures Council. The research ranks undergraduate and graduate programs from the perspective of leading practitioners. This 16th annual survey was conducted in mid-2015.

Selected professional practice leaders, with direct experience hiring and supervising the performance of recent architecture and design graduates, were invited to participate in the research. Survey participants, who are drawn from the Greenway Group database of leading firms throughout the United States, verified that they are currently responsible for hiring or supervising design professionals in each of the design fields for which they responded: architecture, industrial design, interior design, and landscape architecture. Surveys from non-qualifying individuals were excluded from the results.

Architecture Undergraduate Schools

1	Cornell University	18	University of Notre Dame
2	California Polytechnic State University, San Luis Obispo	19	California State Polytechnic University, Pomona
3	Virginia Polytechnic Institute and State University	20	Iowa State University
4	Syracuse University	21	Boston Architectural College
5	Rice University	22	University of Arizona
6	Rhode Island School of Design	23	North Carolina State University
7	University of Texas, Austin	24	Woodbury University
8	Auburn University	25	Mississippi State University
9	Carnegie Mellon University	26	University of Arkansas
10	University of Southern California	27	University of Tennessee, Knoxville
11	Pratt Institute	28	University of Miami
12	Southern California Institute of Architecture	29	University of North Carolina, Charlotte
13	Illinois Institute of Technology	30	Oklahoma State University
14	Cooper Union	31	New Jersey Institute of Technology
15	Rensselaer Polytechnic Institute	32	Louisiana State University
16	University of Oregon	33	California College of the Arts
17	Pennsylvania State University	34	New York Institute of Technology
		35	NewSchool of Architecture & Design

Architecture Graduate Schools

1	Harvard University	19	Clemson University
2	Cornell University	20	University of Southern California
3	Yale University	21	Kansas State University
4	Columbia University	22	Tulane University
5	Massachusetts Institute of Technology	23	Southern California Institute of Architecture
6	University of California, Berkeley	24	Georgia Institute of Technology
7	University of Michigan	25	Ohio State University
8	Rice University	25	Savannah College of Art and Design
9	Virginia Polytechnic Institute and State University	27	Pratt Institute
10	Washington University, St. Louis	27	University of Oregon
11	Syracuse University	29	California State Polytechnic University, Pomona
12	Princeton University	30	Texas A&M University
13	University of Virginia	31	Arizona State University
14	University of Texas, Austin	32	Illinois Institute of Technology
15	University of Pennsylvania	33	University of Illinois, Urbana-Champaign
16	Rhode Island School of Design	34	University of Washington
17	University of Cincinnati	35	Rensselaer Polytechnic Institute
18	University of California, Los Angeles		

America's Best Architecture & Design Schools

Interiors Undergraduate Schools

1	Savannah College of Art and Design	6	Kansas State University
2	Rhode Island School of Design	7	Cornell University
3	Pratt Institute	8	Parsons The New School for Design
4	University of Cincinnati	9	Auburn University
5	New York School of Interior Design	10	Drexel University

Interiors Graduate Schools

1	Savannah College of Art and Design	6	Parsons School of Design
2	Pratt Institute	7	Cornell University
3	Rhode Island School of Design	8	Boston Architectural College
4	Kansas State University	9	Florida State University
5	New York School of Interior Design	10	Drexel University

Landscape Architecture Undergraduate Programs

1	Louisiana State University	12	California State Polytechnic University, Pomona
2	Pennsylvania State University		
3	Cornell University	13	Virginia Polytechnic Institute & State University
4	University of Georgia		
5	Texas A&M University	14	University of Illinois at Urbana-Champaign
6	California Polytechnic State University, San Luis Obispo		
7	Purdue University	15	University of Oregon
8	Ball State University	16	University of Washington
9	Iowa State University	17	University of California at Davis
10	Ohio State University	18	Clemson University
11	Michigan State University	19	University of Wisconsin - Madison
		20	Arizona State University

Landscape Architecture Graduate Programs

1	Harvard University	13	California State Polytechnic University, Pomona
2	University of Pennsylvania		
3	Louisiana State University	14	University of Texas at Austin
4	Cornell University	15	University of Illinois at Urbana-Champaign
5	University of Virginia		
6	Kansas State University	16	University of Washington
7	Pennsylvania State University	17	Auburn University
8	University of California at Berkeley	18	Virginia Polytechnic Institute & State University
9	Texas A&M University		
10	University of Georgia	19	Ohio State University
11	Rhode Island School of Design	20	University of Oregon
12	Ball State University		

Fellows of the Design Futures Council

Senior fellowship in the Design Futures Council is granted annually to an outstanding individual(s) who has provided noteworthy leadership to the advancement of design, design solutions, and/or the design professions. Senior fellows of the DFC are recognized for significant contributions toward the understanding of changing trends, new research, and applied knowledge that improve the built environment and the human condition. Any person worldwide may nominate candidates. Final selection of the senior fellows is made by the Senior Fellows Selection Committee.

Ava Abramowitz, Professor, George Washington University Law School

Harold Adams, Chairman Emeritus, RTKL, Former Chairman, National Building Museum

David M. Adamson, Professor, University College London & Cambridge University

David Adjaye, Principal, Adjaye Associates

Natalia Allen, Fashion Designer, Natalia Allen LLC

Ray Anderson*, Founder & Chairman, Interface, Inc.

Rodrigo Arboleda, Chairman & CEO, One Laptop Per Child Association and MIT Fellow

James F. Barker, Architect & President, Clemson University

Peter Beck, Managing Partner & CEO, The Beck Group

Janine M. Benyus, Biomimicry & Sustainability Expert, Author

Robert J. Berkebile, Founding Principal, BNIM Architects

Phil Bernstein, Technology & Professional Practice Authority, Yale University

Peter Bohlin, Founder, Bohlin Cywinski Jackson

Friedl Bohm, Owner, White Oaks Partners, Former Chairman of NBBJ

Penny Bonda, Interior Designer, Author

John Seely Brown, Co-Chairman, Deloitte Center for Edge Innovation

Barbara White Bryson, Vice President, University of Arizona

Amanda Burden, Chair and Director, New York City Planning Commission

Carrie Byles, Managing Director & Partner, Skidmore, Owings & Merrill

Santiago Calatrava, Pioneering Forms & Spaces, Santiago Calatrava Architects

Rosalyn Cama, Author & Designer, Cama Inc., Evidence-Based Design Authority

Robert Campbell, Architect, Author, and Architecture Critic, The Boston Globe, Pulitzer Prize

John Cary, Public Interest Design Advocate & Author, The Power of Pro Bono

Wing T. Chao, Former Vice Chairman, Walt Disney World

David Childs, Partner Emeritus, Skidmore, Owings & Merrill

William Chilton, Architect, Educator, and Founding Principal, Pickard Chilton

Clayton Christensen, Harvard Business School, Author, The Innovator's Dilemma

Steve Chu, Nobel Laureate & Former Secretary of Energy, U.S. Dept. of Energy

Daniel P. Coffey, Founder & President, Daniel P. Coffey & Associates, Ltd.

Cindy Coleman, Strategic Planner, Gensler, Professor, Art Institute of Chicago

Carol Coletta, President, Coletta & Company

Maurice Cox, Planning Director, City of Detroit

James P. Cramer, Co-Founder of Design Futures Council; Chairman & Founder, Greenway Group, President, Greenway Communications

Michael Crichton*, Design Advocate, Author, Film Director

Sylvester Damianos, Architect, Sculptor, Damianosgroup, Former President, The American Institute of Architects

Fellows of the Design Futures Council

Nigel Dancey, Senior Partner, Foster + Partners

Clark Davis, Principal Consultant, Cameron MacAllister Group

Jack Davis, Dean and Reynolds Metal Professor of Architecture Virginia Polytechnic Institute

Joann Davis Brayman, Vice President, Armstrong World Industries

Betsy del Monte, Southern Methodist University

Lauren Della Bella, President, SHP Leading Design

Abel Joseph "Jack" Diamond, Principal, Diamond Schmitt Architects

Paul Doherty, Founder, The Digit Group, Inc.

Frank Duffy, Co-Founder of DEGW, Author

Trudy Dujardin, Founder, Dujardin Design

Williston (Bill) Dye, Architect, Disney Imagineering

Phil Enquist, Partner, Skidmore, Owings & Merrill

Del Eulberg, Booz Allen Hamilton; USAF (ret.)

Richard Farson, President, Western Behavioral Sciences Institute, Author of The Power of Design

Rick Fedrizzi, President & CEO, U.S. Green Building Council

Edward Feiner, Principal, Perkins + Will, Former Chief Architect, General Service Administration

Curtis Fentress, Founding Principal, Fentress Architects

Scott Findley, Design Partner, 10 Design

Martin Fischer, Director, Center for Integrated Facility Engineering, Stanford University

Tom Fisher, Design Educator, Author & Dean, College of Design, University of Minnesota

Steve Fiskum, Partner, Hammel, Green & Abrahamson

Richard Florida, Urban Advocate and Author

Jim Follett, Architect & Organizational Growth Pioneer, Gensler

Lord Norman Foster, Founder & Chairman, Foster + Partners

Harrison Fraker, Professor, University of California, Berkeley

Neil Frankel, Partner, Frankel + Coleman

Roger Frechette, Managing Principal, Interface Engineering

Cindy Frewen-Wuellner, Architect, Professor at University of Houston Graduate Program in Strategic Foresight, and Urban Futurist

Ed Friedrichs, Architect, Interior Designer, Author, Friedrichs Group

R. Buckminster (Bucky) Fuller*, Engineer, Inventor, Innovator

Thomas Galloway*, Georgia Institute of Technology

Jeanne Gang, Principal, Studio Gang Architects, MacArthur Fellow

Lisa Gansky, Author and Digital Entrepreneur, The Mesh: Why the Future of Business is Sharing

Jan Gehl, Principal, Gehl Architects

Frank Gehry, Architect, Gehry Partners

Arthur Gensler, Founder & Chairman, Gensler

David Gensler, Co-CEO, Gensler

Milton Glaser, Graphic Designer, Founder, Milton Glaser, Inc., Author

Roger Godwin, Architect, Interior Designer, Developer, DAG Architects

Paul Goldberger, Author & Architecture Critic, The New Yorker, Pulitzer Prize

Al Gore, Author & Former Vice President of the United States of America, Nobel Laureate

David Gottfried, Managing Partner, Regenerative Ventures, Founder, U.S. Green Building Council

Michael Graves*, Architect, Product Designer & Educator, Michael Graves & Associates

Robert Greenstreet, Urban Designer & Dean, University of Wisconsin - Milwaukee

Robert C. Grupe, Grupe Gypsum Consulting

Zaha Hadid, Zaha Hadid Architects

Gerry Hammond*, Architect & Educational Design Pioneer, SHP Leading Design

Jeremy Harris, former Mayor of Honolulu, Design Planning Advocate

Phil Harrison, President & CEO, Perkins + Will

Scott Harrison, President & Founder, charity: water

Craig W. Hartman, Design Partner, Skidmore, Owings & Merrill

Edwin B. (Ted) Hathaway, President & CEO, Oldcastle BuildingEnvelope

Paul Hawken, Founder, Natural Capital Institute

H. Ralph Hawkins, Chairman & CEO, HKS, Inc.

Barbara Heller, CEO, Design + Construction Strategies

Bill Hellmuth, President, HOK

Jerry Hobbs, Information Architect & New Media Pioneer, AC Neilson

Carl Hodges, Founder & Chairman, The Seawater Foundation

Steven Holl, Principal, Steven Holl Architects

Nicholas Holt, Director of Digital Design Innovation, Skidmore, Owings & Merrill

Diane Hoskins, Co-CEO, Gensler

Bjarke Ingels, Principal of BIG

Robert Ivy, Executive Vice President & CEO, The American Institute of Architects

Dr. Richard Jackson, Chair of Environmental Health Sciences at UCLA, Author

Jane Jacobs*, Urban Theorist, Author, Educator & Community Activist

Valerie Jacobs, Vice President, Group Director of Trends, LPK

Scott Jenkins, General Manager of the New Atlanta Stadium, Board Chair of Green Sports Alliance

Mary Margaret Jones, President & Senior Principal, Hargreaves Associates

Chris Jordan, Award-Winning Photographer

Louis I. Kahn*, Architect & Educator, University of Pennsylvania

Blair Kamin, Architecture Critic, The Chicago Tribune, Pulitzer Prize

Don Kasian, President & CEO, Architecture Interior Design & Planning

Bruce Katz, Vice President, Brookings Institution, and Founding Director, Brookings Metropolitan Policy Program

James P. Keane, President, Steelcase Group, Steelcase, Vecta, PolyVision

Larry Keeley, Co-Founder and President of Doblin, Inc.

Tom Kelley, Founder and General Manager, IDEO

Stephen Kieran, Founding Partner, KieranTimberlake

Eugene Kohn, Founding Partner & Chairman, Kohn Pedersen Fox Associates

Norman Koonce, Architect & Former CEO, The American Institute of Architects

Vijay Kumar, Illinois Institute of Technology, Author of 101 Design Methods

Ray Kurzweil, Inventor, Futurist, and Author, The Singularity is Near

Theodore C. Landsmark, Boston Redevelopment Authority

Gary Lawrence, Vice President & Chief Sustainability Officer, AECOM

Mary Ann Lazarus, Founder of Sustainable Design Initiative, HOK

Laura Lee, Professor, Carnegie Mellon University, Thinker in Residence, South Australia

Debra Lehman-Smith, Partner, Lehman Smith McLeish

Maya Lin, Artist & Designer, Maya Lin Studio

Vivian Loftness, Professor, Carnegie Mellon University

Amory Lovins, Author, Chief Scientist & Founder, Rocky Mountain Institute

Lucinda Ludwig*, Design Forum Advocate, Engineer, Design Integration & Value Innovator, Leo A. Daly

Chris Luebkeman, Author & Director for Global Foresight & Innovation, Arup

John Maeda, Design Partner, Kleiner Perkins Partners

Marvin Malecha, Dean, College of Design & Professor of Architecture, North Carolina State University & Former President, The American Institute of Architects

Janet Martin, President, Communication Arts, Inc. / Stantec

Fellows of the Design Futures Council

Bruce Mau, Author & Chief Creative Officer, Bruce Mau Design Inc.

Thom Mayne, Founder & Design Director, Morphosis

Ed Mazria, Environmental Advocate & Founder, Architecture 2030

William McDonough, Architect & Author, William McDonough + Partners

Alisdair McGregor, Engineer & Global Sustainability Leader, Arup

Steve McKay, Senior Principal, DLR Group

Jason McLennan, CEO, International Living Future Institute

Richard Meier, Managing Partner, Richard Meier & Partners Architects

Sandra Mendler, Author, Sustainability Leader & Principal, Mithun

Raymond F. Messer, Engineer, Chairman & CEO, Walter P. Moore

George Miller, Partner, Pei Cobb Freed & Partners

Gordon Mills, Architect, Former President, National Council of Architectural Registration Boards

Glen Morrison, President and CEO, Tarkett North America

Glenn Murcutt, Professor & Architect

John Ochsendorf, Massachusetts Institute of Technology, and MacArthur "Genius Award" Fellow

Liz Ogbu, Public Interest Design Expert and Design Director, Public Architecture

Lynn Osmond, President/CEO, Chicago Architecture Foundation

Ruy Ohtake, Architect

Neri Oxman, Professor of Media Arts and Sciences, MIT Media Lab

Doug Parker, Architect & Managing Principal, Greenway Group

Thompson Penney, Chairman/President/ CEO of LS3P

Alexander (Sandy) Pentland, Educator & Researcher, MIT Media Lab

John Peterson, Founder & President of Public Architecture; Curator of the Loeb Fellowship at Harvard

Renzo Piano, Renzo Piano Building Workshop

Joseph Pine II, Branding Strategist & Author, Strategic Horizons LLP

Dan Pink, Author

William Bradley (Brad) Pitt, Actor & Environmental Advocate

Jane Poynter, Chair & President, Paragon Space Development Corp.

Antoine Predock, Architect & Partner, Antoine Predock Architect PC

Raymond Ritchey, Executive Vice President, Boston Properties

Dan Rockhill, Executive Director, Studio 804 and J.L. Constant Distinguished Professor, University of Kansas School of Architecture

Richard Rogers, Architect, Pritzker Prize Laureate, RIBA Gold Medal Recipient

Tim Rowe, Founder/CEO, CIC

Witold Rybczynski, Author & Myerson Professor, Wharton School of Business, University of Pennsylvania, Author

Moshe Safdie, Architect & Global Peace Advocate, Moshe Safdie and Associates

Jonathan Salk, Psychiatrist, Private Practice

Jonas Salk*, Co-founder of the Design Futures Council, Founder of The Salk Institute, Presidential Medal of Freedom Recipient

Ken Sanders, Principal and Managing Director, Gensler

Adele Santos, Dean, School of Architecture & Planning, Massachusetts Institute of Technology

Edwin Schlossberg, Founder and Principal Designer, ESI Design

Michael Schrage, Innovation Expert, Author, and Research Fellow, Sloan School Center for Digital Business, Massachusetts Institute of Technology

Kenneth Schwartz, Dean of the Tulane School of Architecture

Peter Schwartz, Futurist, Author of The Long View, Co-founder, Global Business Network

Kate Schwennsen, Chair, School of Architecture, Clemson University, Former President, The American Institute of Architects

Terrence J. Sejnowski, Brain Scientist, The Salk Institute

Stephen J. Senkowski, CEO, Camino Modular Systems

William Sharples, Founding Principal, SHoP Architects

Scott Simpson, Co-Author of How Firms Succeed, Chair, DFC Senior Fellows

Cameron Sinclair, Global Humanitarian Design Leader & Co-Founder, Architecture for Humanity

Adrian Smith, Principal, Adrian Smith + Gordon Gill Architecture

Alex Steffen, Co-Founder, Worldchanging

Karen Stephenson, Professor, Rotterdam School of Management, Erasmus University & Founder, NetForm International

Robert A.M. Stern, Dean, Yale University School of Architecture

Cecil Steward, Architect, University of Nebraska-Lincoln & Joslyn Institute

RK Stewart, Architect, Former President, The American Institute of Architects

Sarah Susanka, Author & Architect, Susanka Studios

David Suzuki, Scientist, Environmentalist & Co-founder, David Suzuki Foundation

Hon. Richard N. Swett, Former U.S. Representative, Former U.S. Ambassador to Denmark, Climate Prosperity Solutions

Susan Szenasy, Chief Editor, Metropolis Magazine

Jack Tanis, Strategic Planning & Workplace Design Thought Leader

Marilyn Taylor, Dean, School of Design, University of Pennsylvania

April Thornton, Integrated Design Services Leader

James Timberlake, Founding Partner, KieranTimberlake

Lene Tranberg, Head Architect & Co-Founder, Lundgaard & Tranberg

Alan Traugott, Principal, CJL Engineering

Robert Tucker, Author & President, The Innovation Resource

Kent Turner, Architect, President, Cannon Design

Richard Varda, Vice President of Design, Target Corporation

John Carl Warnecke*, Architect & Contextual Design, Author

Alice Waters, Founder, Chez Panisse Foundation

Alan Webber, Author, Rules of Thumb; Founding Editor, Fast Company; Former Managing Editor, Harvard Business Review

Jon Westling, Professor & Former President, Boston University

Gary Wheeler, Architect & Workspace Design Leader, WheelerKänik

Mark Wight, Chairman and CEO of Wight & Co.

Doug Wignall, President, HDR Architecture

Allison Williams, Principal, Perkins + Will

Arol Wolford, President, VIMtrek/SmartBIM

Jane Wright, Architect, Partner, Hanbury Evans Wright Vlattas

Richard Saul Wurman, Author, Information Architect & Founder, Access Guide & TED

Jocelyn Wyatt, Co-Lead & Executive Director of IDEA

Scott Wyatt, Managing Partner, NBBJ, Chair of Nature Conservancy Board

Nicholas You, Planner & Director, UNESCO Executive Director

* Deceased

† Resident fellow and foresight advisor

Source: Design Futures Council

New Parkland Hospital, Dallas, TX | HDR and Corgan

© 2015 David Sundberg/Esto

Maryland Department of Health + Mental Hygiene, Public Health Lab, Baltimore, MD | HDR

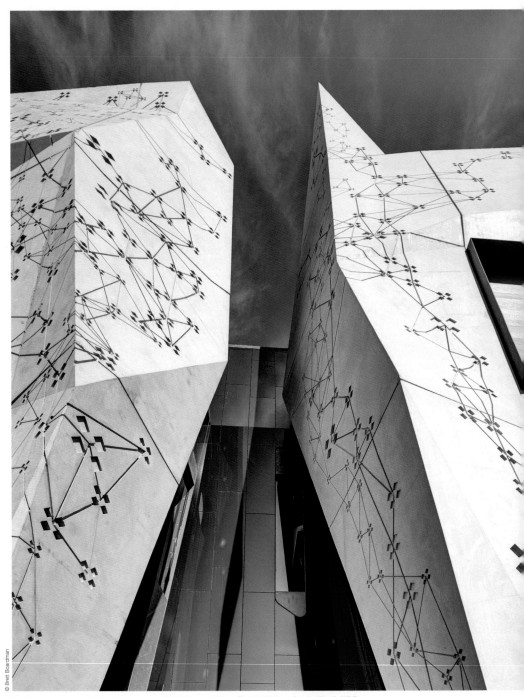

© Brett Boardman

Wollongong Central Shopping Center, Wollongong, New South Wales, Australia | HDR

Eaton Center, Beachwood, OH | Pickard Chilton

David Sundberg/Esto

Latino Baseball Town, La Romana, Dominican Republic | DLR Group

Pueblo County Courthouse, Pueblo, CO | DLR Group

Dilworth Park, Philadelphia
photo © James Ewing

© James Ewing

Dilworth Park, Philadelphia, PA | Kieran Timerlake

Bess Adler/Thornton Tomasetti

ARTIC/Anaheim Regional Transportation Intermodal Center, Anaheim, CA | HOK with Thornton Tomasetti (Structural Engineers)

Colorado Convention Center, Denver, CO | Fentress Architects

Green Square Museum and Offices, Raleigh, NC | Fentress Architects

James Ewing

Fulton Center, New York, NY | Arup

Martin Army Community Hospital, Fort Benning, GA | AECOM

Turner Construction Company

National Center for Civil and Human Rights, Atlanta, GA | Walter P. Moore

Gabe Guilliams, BuroHappold Engineering

Grace Farms, New Canaan, CT | BuroHappold

Gabe Guilliams, BuroHappold Engineering

Grace Farms, New Canaan, CT | BuroHappold

Firm Anniversaries

The following currently practicing US architecture firms were founded in 1916, 1966, and 1991 respectively.

Founded 1916 (Firms Celebrating their 100th Anniversaries)
Odle McGuire Shook, Indianapolis, IN

Founded 1966 (50th Anniversaries)
Carl Abbott Architect, Sarasota, FL
American Structurepoint, Indianapolis, IN
Banwell Architects, Lebanon, NH
BAR Architects, San Francisco, CA
Baughan & Baukhages Architects, Luray, VA
Beilharz Architects, Defiance, OH
Collins & Associates, Panama City, FL
Cope Linder Architects, Philadelphia, PA
DLR Group, Omaha, NE
Giattina Aycock Architecture Studio,
    Birmingham, AL
GMK Associates, Columbia, SC
Hinckley, Shepherd, Norden Architects,
    Warrenton, VA
KSK Architects Planners Historians,
    Philadelphia, PA
LHB, Duluth, MN
Nagle Hartray Architecture, Chicago, IL
RDG, Des Moines, IA
Stull and Lee, Boston, MA
Wilmot Sanz Architecture + Planning,
    Gaithersburg, MD
Wolf Architecture, Charlotte, NC

Founded 1991 (25th Anniversaries)
AJC Architects, Salt Lake City, UT
Alfandre Architecture, New Paltz, NY
JEA Architects, Eden Prairie, MN
Jon Anderson Architecture, Albuquerque, NM
Samuel Anderson Architects, New York, NY

Arcon Architects, Seabrook, TX
AK Architecture (Armstrong Kaulbach Architects),
    Philadelphia, PA
Atelier V, Los Angeles, CA
Bacon Group Inc. Architecture,
    Clearwater, FL
LNB Architecture & Interiors, St. Louis, MO
Thomas Baio Architect, Millburn, NJ
Alan Bell Architect, Inc., Carrollton, GA
Bernardo Wills Architects, Spokane, WA
Berrie Architecture & Design, Plantation, FL
Bickel Group Architecture,
    Newport Beach, CA
John Francis Borelli Architect, New York, NY
Bundy finkel Architects, Costa Mesa, CA
Harvey Cohn Architecture, New York, NY
CSArch (Colllins & Scovill Architects),
    Albany, NY
CORE, Washington, DC
Cornerstone Architects, Richmond, VA
CTA Design Builders, Seattle, WA
Culpen & Woods Architects, Stamford, CT
De Biasse & Seminara Architecture
    Planning Interiors, Martinsville, NJ
Design Alliance, Waukee, IA
DMR Architects, Hasbrouck Heights, NJ
DZN Partners, Encinitas, CA
E4 Architects, Los Angeles, CA
EOA Architects, Nashville, TN
Edward Farr Architects, Eden Prairie, MN
Earles Architects and Associates,
    Chicago, IL
Robert Flubacker Architects,
    Rolling Meadows, IL
FMK Architects, Charlotte, NC

Freyer Collaborative Architects, New York, NY
Gabellini Sheppard Associates, New York, NY
Garcia Teague Architecture + Interiors,
    San Jose, CA
GKKWorks, Irvine, CA
Goff-D'Antonio Associates, Charleston, SC
GTG Consultants, Chicago, IL
Habitat Architecture, Bloomington, MN
Sandberg Kessler Architecture, Jameston, NY
Harrison Woodfield Architects,
    Santa Rosa, CA
Johnson Architecture, Fresno, CA
JVC Architects, Las Vegas, NV
Kennan-Meyer Architecture, Seattle, WA
Lehman Smith McLeish, Washington, DC
Daniel Macdonald AIA Architects, Inc.,
    Novato, CA
Main Street Architecture, Berryville, VA
McGillin Architecture, Bala Cynwyd, PA
McKee and Associates, Montgomery, AL
Meeks, Coates + Eaton Architects,
    San Francisco, CA
Mikiten Architecture, Berkeley, CA
Pfau Long Architecture, San Francisco, CA
Pimsler Hoss Architects, Atlanta, GA
Platt Hichborn Architects, Exeter, NH
Ray + Hollington Architects (RHA),
    Houston, TX
RCG Architecture, San Mateo, CA
Candace Rosaen Renfro Architects,
    Brooklyn, NY
Ross Architecture, Chicago, IL
Saavedra Gehlhauser Architects,
    Rockford, IL
Saffran-Kilpatrick, Atlanta, GA
Michael Shilale Architects, New York, NY
Silver/Petrucelli + Associates, Hamden, CT
SMBW, Richmond, VA

Sonnenfeld & Trocchia Architects,
    Holmdel, NJ
Tracy A. Stone Architect, Los Angeles, CA
Studio B, Aspen, CO
Tennant/Wallace Architects, Manchester, NH
Thielsen Architects, Kirkland, WA
Constantine D. Vasilios & Associates,
    Chicago, IL
Clive Wilkinson Architects, Los Angeles, CA
Williams Architects, Madison, CT
Zagrodnik + Architects, San Diego, CA

Source: DesignIntelligence

Firm Statistics: Architecture

	Number of Establishments[1]	Annual Payroll ($1,000s)	Paid Employees[2]
Alabama	195	73,798	1,093
Alaska	43	26,574	320
Arizona	438	150,928	2,294
Arkansas	133	68,188	1,158
California	3,008	1,772,487	21,366
Colorado	711	224,233	3,229
Connecticut	278	150,227	1,887
Delaware	31	7,222	132
District of Columbia	163	286,599	3,254
Florida	1,469	433,498	6,659
Georgia	525	306,747	3,966
Hawaii	162	79,520	1,084
Idaho	111	32,992	594
Illinois	999	508,705	6,855
Indiana	235	112,905	1,806
Iowa	114	58,898	869
Kansas	139	86,875	1,289
Kentucky	142	47,528	774
Louisiana	272	116,850	1,748
Maine	115	35,923	621
Maryland	377	201,247	2,650
Massachusetts	700	481,216	5,981
Michigan	391	198,837	2,882
Minnesota	366	220,937	3,092
Mississippi	99	38,361	601
Missouri	360	249,261	3,473
Montana	133	38,867	699
Nebraska	95	82,189	1,119
Nevada	141	75,356	975
New Hampshire	67	21,456	309
New Jersey	626	226,062	3,312
New Mexico	139	45,285	827
New York	2,221	1,321,075	17,254

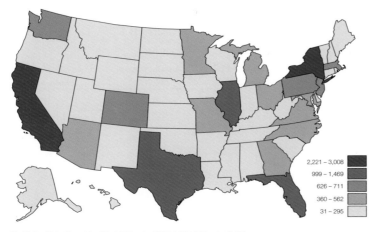

The District of Columbia contains 163 establishments. US Total of Establishments: 21,004.

	Number of Establishments[1]	Annual Payroll ($1,000s)	Paid Employees[2]
North Carolina	562	223,959	3,312
North Dakota	49	19,687	313
Ohio	547	307,868	4,576
Oklahoma	180	89,496	1,452
Oregon	295	158,540	2,363
Pennsylvania	669	378,933	5,419
Rhode Island	69	16,325	279
South Carolina	237	77,485	1,220
South Dakota	39	10,679	189
Tennessee	244	168,046	2,332
Texas	1,352	876,837	11,003
Utah	214	77,429	1,399
Vermont	85	21,141	386
Virginia	480	289,641	3,911
Washington	660	355,099	5,043
West Virginia	37	18,679	297
Wisconsin	237	134,218	2,040
Wyoming	50	13,109	197
US Total	21,004	11,018,017	149,903

[1] All numbers are 2013.
[2] Paid employees for the pay period including March 12.

Source: US Census Bureau

Firm Statistics: Industrial Design

	Number of Establishments[1]	Annual Payroll ($1,000s)	Paid Employees[2]
Alabama	5	876	13
Alaska	n/a	n/a	n/a
Arizona	25	8,049	155
Arkansas	6	1,023	n/a
California	286	239,300	2,522
Colorado	30	n/a	n/a
Connecticut	23	10,424	n/a
Delaware	2	n/a	n/a
District of Columbia	n/a	n/a	n/a
Florida	104	15,275	288
Georgia	29	21,116	234
Hawaii	3	n/a	n/a
Idaho	4	151	7
Illinois	91	27,404	409
Indiana	21	4,315	76
Iowa	9	n/a	n/a
Kansas	9	1,554	n/a
Kentucky	2	n/a	n/a
Louisiana	9	225	10
Maine	4	245	3
Maryland	13	5,851	n/a
Massachusetts	48	25,942	290
Michigan	85	n/a	n/a
Minnesota	28	8,828	120
Mississippi	5	n/a	n/a
Missouri	16	30,639	363
Montana	6	n/a	n/a
Nebraska	2	n/a	n/a
Nevada	10	733	n/a
New Hampshire	4	n/a	n/a
New Jersey	31	8,478	184
New Mexico	2	n/a	n/a
New York	165	80,497	987

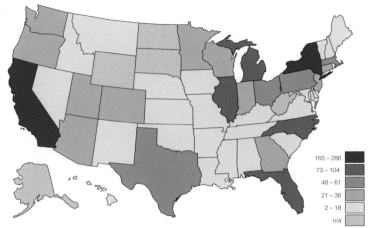

Information on the District of Columbia establishments was not available. US Total of Establishments: 1,509.

	Number of Establishments[1]	Annual Payroll ($1,000s)	Paid Employees[2]
North Carolina	73	22,429	n/a
North Dakota	n/a	n/a	n/a
Ohio	61	31,540	465
Oklahoma	3	n/a	n/a
Oregon	34	12,999	n/a
Pennsylvania	56	18,473	310
Rhode Island	17	11,784	142
South Carolina	7	n/a	n/a
South Dakota	n/a	n/a	n/a
Tennessee	8	n/a	n/a
Texas	61	31,765	418
Utah	27	4,848	106
Vermont	8	581	11
Virginia	18	4,916	n/a
Washington	36	40,170	493
West Virginia	n/a	n/a	n/a
Wisconsin	23	4,700	101
Wyoming	n/a	n/a	n/a
US Total	**1,509**	**675,130**	**7,707**

[1] All numbers are 2013.
[2] Paid employees for the pay period including March 12.
 n/a: not available

Source: US Census Bureau

Firm Statistics: Interior Design

	Number of Establishments[1]	Annual Payroll ($1,000s)	Paid Employees[2]
Alabama	102	10,886	275
Alaska	15	1,894	42
Arizona	236	27,535	608
Arkansas	55	3,364	126
California	1,633	345,215	5,983
Colorado	378	48,433	1,058
Connecticut	137	14,973	n/a
Delaware	31	4,189	n/a
District of Columbia	60	25,925	337
Florida	1,450	147,383	3,630
Georgia	431	56,389	1,157
Hawaii	33	4,356	98
Idaho	34	2,069	60
Illinois	544	81,723	1,682
Indiana	146	13,988	425
Iowa	54	4,524	n/a
Kansas	79	4,915	n/a
Kentucky	87	8,830	225
Louisiana	98	8,587	272
Maine	25	1,422	n/a
Maryland	208	37,850	739
Massachusetts	274	56,689	875
Michigan	227	20,651	599
Minnesota	203	21,745	515
Mississippi	32	4,330	130
Missouri	137	16,829	443
Montana	34	1,621	60
Nebraska	66	7,150	196
Nevada	79	15,884	367
New Hampshire	26	1,556	47
New Jersey	341	38,954	843
New Mexico	43	2,246	67
New York	1,251	299,927	4,278

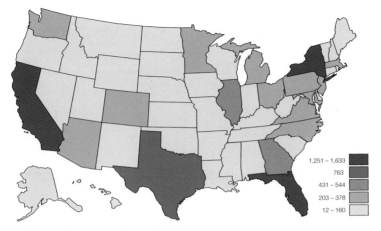

1,251 – 1,633
763
431 – 544
203 – 378
12 – 160

The District of Columbia contains 60 establishments. US Total of Establishments: 11,537.

	Number of Establishments[1]	Annual Payroll ($1,000s)	Paid Employees[2]
North Carolina	338	25,670	769
North Dakota	12	837	34
Ohio	225	50,025	950
Oklahoma	96	8,254	253
Oregon	127	14,412	364
Pennsylvania	280	62,146	1,120
Rhode Island	46	8,641	166
South Carolina	160	17,140	471
South Dakota	15	2,630	n/a
Tennessee	121	18,826	383
Texas	763	135,379	2,679
Utah	98	8,722	250
Vermont	17	1,621	43
Virginia	323	39,862	951
Washington	248	27,951	687
West Virginia	17	1,585	46
Wisconsin	84	8,613	253
Wyoming	18	2,679	47
US Total	**11,537**	**1,777,025**	**34,603**

[1] All numbers are 2013.
[2] Paid employees for the pay period including March 12.

Source: US Census Bureau

Firm Statistics: Landscape Architecture

	Number of Establishments[1]	Annual Payroll ($1,000s)	Paid Employees[2]
Alabama	32	4,991	138
Alaska	7	804	n/a
Arizona	112	19,332	419
Arkansas	14	1,960	47
California	828	289,915	4,820
Colorado	230	46,871	741
Connecticut	74	16,106	218
Delaware	9	2,476	58
District of Columbia	25	14,309	199
Florida	481	92,784	1,879
Georgia	136	18,772	477
Hawaii	30	11,598	145
Idaho	29	4,604	93
Illinois	289	51,714	778
Indiana	62	5,919	150
Iowa	20	1,943	53
Kansas	20	2,702	82
Kentucky	39	5,409	163
Louisiana	56	14,531	342
Maine	26	4,339	76
Maryland	107	30,945	564
Massachusetts	178	84,788	1,080
Michigan	121	20,417	333
Minnesota	85	10,871	179
Mississippi	22	2,302	74
Missouri	49	9,457	211
Montana	17	2,190	28
Nebraska	16	1,769	34
Nevada	26	4,488	90
New Hampshire	21	3,594	n/a
New Jersey	178	35,453	660
New Mexico	25	4,898	113
New York	358	98,555	1,533

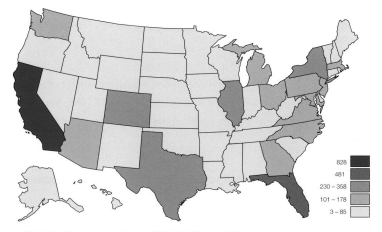

The District of Columbia contains 25 establishments. US Total of Establishments: 5,174.

	Number of Establishments[1]	Annual Payroll ($1,000s)	Paid Employees[2]
North Carolina	170	41,376	830
North Dakota	3	n/a	n/a
Ohio	101	17,741	348
Oklahoma	54	8,419	185
Oregon	85	16,323	349
Pennsylvania	175	51,499	937
Rhode Island	19	2,408	48
South Carolina	72	9,755	253
South Dakota	11	2,208	49
Tennessee	82	13,239	326
Texas	313	107,975	1,987
Utah	56	6,327	157
Vermont	29	3,358	58
Virginia	106	40,271	753
Washington	103	21,726	386
West Virginia	5	922	15
Wisconsin	62	10,590	214
Wyoming	6	1,834	n/a
US Total	**5,174**	**1,276,777**	**22,672**

[1] All numbers are 2013.
[2] Paid employees for the pay period including March 12.

Source: US Census Bureau

Number of Licensed Architects

Licensed architects in each state are divided into two categories: resident and recipro-cal, or non-resident, registrants. Based on current population levels, the chart below also calculates the per capita number of resident architects in each state. The following infor-mation is from the National Council of Architectural Registration Boards' 2014 survey.

State	Resident Architects	Reciprocal Registrations	Total	Population	Per capita # of Resident Arch. (per 100,000)
Alabama	900	1,841	2,741	4,849,377	19
Alaska	244	323	567	736,732	33
Arizona	2,217	2,703	5,780	6,731,484	33
Arkansas	495	850	1,345	2,966,369	17
California	16,618	3,977	20,595	38,802,500	43
Colorado	3,256	3,448	6,487	5,355,866	61
Connecticut	1,440	2,751	4,191	3,596,677	40
Delaware	111	1,479	1,590	935,614	12
D.C.	607	2,608	3,215	658,893	92
Florida	5,104	4,787	9,891	19,893,297	26
Georgia	2,404	2,952	5,356	10,097,343	24
Hawaii	1,003	1,260	2,263	1,419,561	71
Idaho	502	1,164	1,666	1,634,464	31
Illinois	5,306	3,740	9,046	12,880,580	41
Indiana	1,017	2,274	3,291	6,596,855	15
Iowa	565	1,409	1,974	3,107,126	18
Kansas	955	1,692	2,647	2,904,021	33
Kentucky	734	1,789	2,523	4,413,457	17
Louisiana	1,220	2,037	3,257	4,649,676	26
Maine	416	1,087	1,503	1,330,089	31
Maryland	2,616	3,832	5,848	5,976,407	44
Massachusetts	3,735	2,975	6,710	6,745,408	55
Michigan	2,548	3,135	5,683	9,909,877	26
Minnesota	1,820	1,389	3,209	5,457,173	33
Mississippi	356	1,408	1,764	2,994,079	12
Missouri	2,058	3,067	5,125	6,063,589	34
Montana	426	946	1,372	1,023,579	42

State	Resident Architects	Reciprocal Registrations	Total	Population	Per capita # of Resident Arch. (per 100,000)
Nebraska	539	1,245	1,784	1,881,503	29
Nevada	708	2,213	2,921	2,839,099	25
New Hampshire	313	1,509	1,822	1,326,813	24
New Jersey	3,402	4,662	8,064	8,938,175	38
New Mexico	680	1,420	2,100	2,085,572	33
New York	9,872	6,937	16,809	19,746,227	50
North Carolina	2,292	2,933	5,225	9,943,964	23
North Dakota	160	994	1,154	739,482	22
Ohio	3,234	3,080	6,314	11,594,163	28
Oklahoma	791	1,437	2,228	3,878,051	20
Oregon	1,690	1,331	3,021	3,970,239	43
Pennsylvania	3,653	4,212	7,865	12,787,209	29
Rhode Island	271	1,149	1,420	1,055,173	26
South Carolina	1,074	2,785	3,859	4,832,482	22
South Dakota	111	720	831	853,175	13
Tennessee	1,534	2,256	3,790	6,549,352	23
Texas	8,494	4,426	12,920	26,956,958	32
Utah	818	1,561	2,379	2,942,902	28
Vermont	321	821	1,142	626,562	51
Virginia	2,827	4,258	7,085	8,326,289	34
Washington	3,909	2,354	6,263	7,061,530	55
West Virginia	96	997	1,093	1,850,326	5
Wisconsin	1,456	2,794	4,250	5,757,564	25
Wyoming	126	1,055	1,181	584,153	22
Totals	**107,044**	**118,072**	**225,159**	**318,857,056**	**34**

Source: National Council of Architectural Registration Boards and DesignIntelligence

Oldest Architecture Firms

The following North American architecture firms were founded prior to 1917 (their specific founding dates indicated below) and are still operational today.

1853	Luckett & Farley, Louisville, KY SmithGroup JJR, Detroit, MI
1868	Jensen and Halstead, Chicago, IL King & King Architects, Syracyse, NY
1870	Harriman, Auburn, ME

1871	Scholtz Gowey Gere Marolf
	    Architects & Interior Designers
	    (SGGM), Davenport, IA

1874	Shepley Bulfinch Richardson and Abbott, Boston, MA
1876	Keffer/Overton Architects, Des Moines, IA
1878	The Austin Company, Kansas City, MO Ballinger, Philadelphia, PA
1880	Beatty, Harvey, Coco Architects, New York, NY Holabird & Root, Chicago, IL
1880	Zeidler Partnership Architects, Toronto, Canada
1884	SMRT, Portland, ME
1885	Cromwell Architects Engineers, Little Rock, AR HLW International, New York, NY
1887	Bradley & Bradley, Rockford, IL

1889	CSHQA, Boise, ID
	MacLachlan, Corneliu & Filoni,
	    Pittsburgh, PA
	WASA Studio,
	    New York, NY

1891	Mathes Brierre Architects,
	    New Orleans, LA
	SSP Architectural Group,
	    Somerville, NJ

1892	FreemanWhite, Raleigh, NC
1894	Colgan Perry Lawler Aurell Architects, Nyack, NY Freese and Nichols, Fort Worth, TX

1895	Brooks Borg Skiles Architecture
	    Engineering, Des Moines, IA
	Kahn (Albert Kahn Associates),
	    Detroit, MI

1896	Hummel Architects, Boise, ID
1897	Baskervill, Richmond, VA Ittner Architects, St. Louis, MO

1898	Beardsley Architects + Engineers,
	    Auburn, NY
	Berners-Schober Associates
	    (BSA, Inc.), Green Bay, WI
	Burns & McDonnell,
	    Kansas City, MO
	Eckles Architecture, New Castle, PA
	FEH Associates Inc., Des Moines, IA
	Foss Architecture & Interiors
	    Fargo, ND & Moorhead, MN
	Page, Austin, TX

1901	SHP Leading Design, Cincinnati, OH Wiley & Wilson, Lynchburg, VA
1902	WBRC Architects, Engineers, Bangor, ME

1906	AC Martin Partners, Los Angeles, CA
	CJMW, Winston Salem, NC
	Ratcliff, Emeryville, CA
	Zimmerman Architectural Studios,
	Milwaukee, WI

1907   Eppstein Uhen Architects,
       Milwaukee, WI
     Fletcher Thompson, Shelton, CT
     H2L2, Philadelphia, PA
     RCG Architects
       (Richter Cornbrooks Gribble),
       Baltimore, MD

1908   Harley Ellis Devereaux,
       Southfield, MI
     Kahler Slater Architects,
       Milwaukee, WI
     Somdal Associates,
       Shreveport, LA

1909   Howell Rusk Dodson Architects,
       Atlanta, GA
     Lionakis, Sacramento, CA
     Moeckel Carbonell Associates,
       Wilmington, DE
     TRO JB, Boston, MA

1910   HFR Design, Nashville, TN

1911   IKM Incorporated, Pittsburgh, PA

1912   Graham, Anderson, Probst, & White,
       Chicago, IL

1913   Potter Lawson, Madison, WI

1914   HNTB, Kansas City, MO

1915   Leo A Daly, Omaha, NE

1916   Odle McGuire Shook
       Indianapolis, IN

Source: DesignIntelligence

Tallest Buildings in the World

The following list ranks the world's 100 tallest buildings as determined by the Council on Tall Buildings and Urban Habitat. Buildings that have reached their full height but are still under construction are deemed eligible and are indicated with a UC in the year category along with the anticipated completion date, if known.

	Building	Yr.	Location	Height (ft./m.)	(# stories)	Architect
1	Burj Khalifa	2010	Dubai, UAE	2,717/828	163	Skidmore, Owings & Merrill
2	Shanghai Tower	UC15	Shanghai, China	2,073/632	128	Gensler; Architectural Design & Research Institute of Tongli University Co. (China)
3	Makkah Royal Clock Tower Hotel	2012	Mecca, Saudia Arabia	1,972/601	120	Dar Al-Handasah Architects (Lebanon)
4	One World Trade Center	2014	New York, NY	1,776/541	104	Skidmore, Owings & Merrill
5	CTF Finance Centre	UC16	Guangzhou, China	1,739/530	94	Kohn Pedersen Fox Associates; Dennis Lau & Ng Chun Man Architects & Engineers
6	Taipei 101	2004	Taipei, Taiwan	1,667/508	101	C.Y. Lee & Partners (Taiwan)
7	Shanghai World Financial Center	2008	Shanghai, China	1,614/492	101	Kohn Pedersen Fox Associates; East China Architectural Design & Research Institute Co. Ltd. (China)
8	International Commerce Centre	2010	Hong Kong, China	1,588/484	108	Wong & Ouyang Ltd. (Hong Kong); Kohn Pedersen Fox Associates
9	Petronas Tower 1	1998	Kuala Lumpur, Malaysia	1,483/452	88	Cesar Pelli & Associates
10	Petronas Tower 2	1998	Kuala Lumpur, Malaysia	1,483/452	88	Cesar Pelli & Associates
11	Zifeng Tower	2010	Nanjing, China	1,476/450	66	Skidmore, Owings & Merrill
12	Willis Tower	1974	Chicago, IL	1,451/442	108	Skidmore, Owings & Merrill
13	KK100 Development	2011	Shenzhen, China	1,449/442	100	TFP Farrells (UK)
14	Guangzhou International Finance Center	2010	Guangzhou, China	1,439/439	108	Wilkerson Eyre Architects (UK)
15	Trump International Hotel & Tower	2009	Chicago, IL	1,398/423	98	Skidmore, Owings & Merrill
16	Jin Mao Building	1999	Shanghai, China	1,380/421	88	Skidmore, Owings & Merrill
17	Princess Tower	2012	Dubai, UAE	1,356/413	101	Adnan Saffarini (UAE)
18	Al Hamra Firdous Tower	2011	Kuwait City, Kuwait	1,354/413	80	Skidmore, Owings & Merrill; Al Jazera Consultants (Kuwait); Callison

	Building	Yr.	Location	Height (ft./m.)	(# stories)	Architect
19	Two International Finance Centre	2003	Hong Kong, China	1,352/412	88	Cesar Pelli & Associates
20	23 Marina	2012	Dubai, UAE	1,289/393	90	Hafeez Contractor (India)
21	CITIC Plaza	1996	Guangzhou, China	1,280/390	80	Dennis Lau & Ng Chun Man Architects & Engineers (China)
22	Capital Market Authority Tower	UC15	Riyadh, Saudi Arabia	1,263/385	79	HOK; Omrania & Associates (UAE)
23	Shun Hing Square	1996	Shenzhen, China	1,260/384	69	K.Y. Cheung Design Associates (China)
24	Eton Place Dalian Tower 1	UC15	Dalian, China	1,257/383	80	NBBJ; China Northeast Architectural Design & Research Institute (China)
25	Burg Mohammed Bin Rashid	2014	Abu Dhabi, UAE	1,251/381	88	Foster + Partners (UK)
26	Empire State Building	1931	New York, NY	1,250/381	102	Shreve, Lamb & Harmon
27	Elite Residence	2012	Dubai, UAE	1,248/380	87	Adnan Saffarini (UAE)
28	Central Plaza	1992	Hong Kong, China	1,227/374	78	Ng Chun Man & Associates (China)
29	Bank of China Tower	1989	Hong Kong, China	1,205/367	72	Pei Cobb Freed & Partners
30	Bank of America Tower	2009	New York, NY	1,200/366	55	Cook+Fox Architects; Adamson Associates Architects
31	Almas Tower	2008	Dubai, UAE	1,181/360	68	WS Atkins & Partners (UK)
32	J.W. Marriott Marquis Hotel Dubai Tower 1	2012	Dubai, UAE	1,166/355	82	Archgroup Consultants (UAE)
33	J.W. Marriott Marquis Hotel Dubai Tower 2	2013	Dubai, UAE	1,166/355	82	Archgroup Consultants (UAE)
34	Emirates Tower One	2000	Dubai, UAE	1,163/355	54	Norr Group Consultants (Canada)
35	OKO Residential Tower	2015	Moscow, Russia	1,160/354	90	Skidmore, Owings & Merrill
36	The Torch	2011	Dubai, UAE	1,155/352	79	Khatib & Alami (UAE)
37	The Pinnacle	2012	Guangzhou, China	1,149/351	60	Make Architects (China)
38	T & C Tower	1997	Kaohsiung, Taiwan	1,140/348	85	C.Y. Lee & Partners (Taiwan); Hellmuth, Obata & Kassabaum
39	Aon Centre	1973	Chicago, IL	1,136/346	83	Edward Durrell Stone & Associates

Tallest Buildings in the World

	Building	Yr.	Location	Height (ft./m.)	(# stories)	Architect
40	The Center	1998	Hong Kong, China	1,135/346	73	Dennis Lau & Ng Chun Man Architects & Engineers (China)
41	John Hancock Center	1969	Chicago, IL	1,128/344	100	Skidmore, Owings & Merrill
42	ADNOC Headquarters	2015	Abu Dhabi, UAE	1,122/342	76	HOK
43	Ahmed Abdul Rahim Al Attar Tower	UC15	Dubai, UAE	1,122/342	76	Eng. Adnan Saffarini (UAE)
44	Mercury City Tower	2013	Moscow, Russia	1,112/339	75	Frank Williams & Associates; M. M. Posokhin (Russia)
45	Wuxi International Finance Square	2014	Wuxi, China	1,112/339	68	Aedas
46	Chongqing World Financial Center	2015	Chongqing, China	1,112/339	73	C. Y. Lee & Partners (Taiwan)
47	Tianjin World Financial Center	2011	Tianjin, China	1,105/337	76	Skidmore, Owings & Merrill
48	Shimao International Plaza	2006	Shanghai, China	1,094/333	60	Ingenhoven Architekten (Germany); East China Architectural Design & Research Institute Co. Ltd. (China)
49	Rose Rayhaan by Rotana	2007	Dubai, UAE	1,093/333	72	Khatib & Alami (Lebanon)
50	Minsheng Bank Building	2008	Wuhan, China	1,086/331	68	Wuhan Architectural Design Institute (China)
51	China World Tower	2009	Beijing, China	1,083/330	74	Skidmore, Owings & Merrill
52	Keangnam Hanoi Landmark Tower	2012	Hanoi, Vietnam	1,078/329	72	Heerim Architects & Planners (South Korea); Samoo Architects & Engineers (South Korea); HOK
53	Longxi International Hotel	2011	Jiangyin, China	1,076/328	74	A+E Design Co. (China)
54	Al Yaqoub Tower	2012	Dubai, UAE	1,076/328	69	Adnan Saffarini (UAE)
55	Wuxi Suning Plaza 1	2014	Wuxi, China	1,076/328	67	RTKL
56	The Index	2010	Dubai, UAE	1,070/326	80	Foster + Partners (UK); Woods Bagot (UAE); Khatib & Alami (UAE)
57	The Landmark	2013	Dubai, UAE	1,063/324	72	Cesar Pelli & Associates
58	Deji Plaza	2013	Nanjing, China	1,063/324	62	Deji Group (China) (developer); no architect listed
59	Yantai Shimao No. 1 The Harbour	UC15	Yantai, China	1,060/323	59	Wong Tung & Partners (China)
60	Q1 Tower	2005	Gold Coast, Australia	1,058/323	78	The Buchan Group (Australia)

Building	Yr.	Location	Height (ft./m.)	(# stories)	Architect
61 Wenzhou Trade Center	2010	Wenzhou, China	1,056,322	68	RTKL Associates Inc.; Shanghai Institute of Architectural Design & Research Co. (China)
62 Burj Al Arab Hotel	1999	Dubai, UAE	1,053/321	60	WS Atkins & Partners (UK)
63 Nina Tower	2007	Hong Kong, China	1,051/320	80	Arthur CS Kwok Architects & Associates (China); Casa Design International (China); Dennis Lau & Ng Chun Man Architects & Engineers (China)
64 Chrysler Building	1930	New York, NY	1,046/319	77	William Van Alen
65 New York Times Tower	2007	New York, NY	1,046/319	52	Renzo Piano Building Workshop (Italy); FXFOWLE Architects
66 HHHR Tower	2010	Dubai, UAE	1,042/318	72	Al Hashemi (UAE)
67 Nanjing International Youth Cultural Centre Tower 1	2015	Nanjing, China	1,032/315	68	Zaha Hadid Architects
68 Bank of America Plaza	1992	Atlanta, GA	1,023/312	55	Kevin Roche John Dinkeloo & Associates
69 Moi Center Tower A	2014	Shenyang, China	1,020/311	75	Shenzhen Tongi Architects (China)
70 U.S. Bank Tower	1990	Los Angeles, CA	1,018/310	73	Pei Cobb Freed & Partners
71 Ocean Heights	2010	Dubai, UAE	1,017/310	83	Aedas (UAE) with ECG Engineering Consultants Group (Egypt)
72 Menara Telekom	2000	Kuala Lumpur, Malaysia	1,017/310	55	Hijjas Kasturi Associates (Malaysia)
73 Fortune Center	2015	Guangzhou, China	1,015/310	73	Architectural Design and Research Institute of South China University of Technology (China)
74 Pearl River Tower	2013	Guangzhou, China	1,015/310	71	Skidmore, Owings & Merrill with Guangzhou Design Institute
75 Emirates Tower Two	2000	Dubai, UAE	1,014/309	56	Norr Group Consultants (Canada)
76 Stainaya Vershina	2015	Moscow, Russia	1,013/309	72	Swanke Hayden Connell Architects
77 Burg Rafal	2014	Riyadh, Saudi Arabia	1,010/308	68	P & T Architects and Engineers (China)
78 Franklin Center North Tower	1989	Chicago, IL	1,007/307	60	Skidmore, Owings & Merrill
79 Cayan Tower	2013	Dubai, UAE	1,005/306	76	Skidmore, Owings & Merrill
80 One57	2014	New York, NY	1,004/306	79	Atelier Christian de Portzamparc (France)

Tallest Buildings in the World

	Building	Yr.	Location	Height (ft./m.)	(# stories)	Architect
81	East Pacific Center Tower A	2013	Shenzhen, China	1,004/306	85	Wong & Ouyang (Hong Kong)
82	The Shard	2013	London, UK	1,004/306	73	Renzo Piano Building Workshop (Italy)
83	JP Morgan Chase Tower	1982	Houston, TX	1,002/305	75	I.M. Pei & Partners
84	Etihad Towers T2	2011	Abu Dhabi, UAE	1,002/305	80	DBI Design (Australia)
85	Northeast Asia Trade Tower	2010	Incheon, South Korea	1,001/305	68	Kohn Pedersen Fox Associates
86	Baiyoke Tower II	1997	Bangkok, Thailand	997/304	85	Plan Architects Co. (Thailand)
87	Wuxi Maoye City - Marriott Hotel	2014	Wuxi, China	997/304	68	N/A
88	Two Prudential Plaza	1990	Chicago, IL	995/303	64	Loebl Schlossman Dart & Hackl
89	Diwang International Fortune Center	2015	Liuzhou, China	994/303	75	AECOM
90	Jiangxi Nanchang Greenland Central Plaza 1	2015	Nanchang, China	994/303	59	Skidmore, Owings & Merrill with ECADI
91	Jiangxi Nanchang Greenland Central Plaza 2	2015	Nanchang, China	994/303	59	Skidmore, Owings & Merrill with ECADI
92	Shenzhen Changcheng Center	2014	Shenyang, China	994/303	61	Beijing Institute of Architectural Design
93	Leatop Plaza	2012	Guangzhou, China	993/303	64	Murphy/Jahn
94	Wells Fargo Plaza	1983	Houston, TX	992/302	71	Skidmore, Owings & Merrill
95	Kingdom Centre	2002	Riyadh, Saudi Arabia	991/302	41	Ellerbe Becket; Omrania & Associates (Saudi Arabia)
96	The Address	2008	Dubai, UAE	991/302	63	WS Atkins & Partners (UK)
97	Capital City Moscow Tower	2010	Moscow, Russia	990/302	76	NBBJ
98	Greenland Puli Center	2015	Jinan, China	988/301	61	Greenland Group Development
99	Doosan Haeundae We've the Zenith Tower A	2011	Busan, South Korea	984/300	80	DeStefano + Partners
100	Torre Costanera	2014	Santiago, Chile	984/300	64	Cesar Pelli & Associates

Source: ©Council on Tall Buildings and Urban Habitat

World's Best Skylines

This list ranks the impressiveness of the world's skylines by calculating the density and height of each city's skyscrapers. All buildings taller than 295 feet (90 meters)—excluding spires—contribute points to its home city's score equal to the number of feet it exceeds this benchmark height.

	City	Country	Points	# Bldgs over 295 ft/90 m
1	Hong Kong	China	92,628	3,266
2	New York (inc. Jersey City, Fort Lee, Guttenburg)	USA	39,772	938
3	Shanghai	China	26,530	855
4	Dubai	UAE	25,712	400
5	Tokyo (inc. Kawaguchi, Kawasaki, Ichikawa)	Japan	25,546	753
6	Shenzhen	China	21,194	442
7	Guangzhou	China	19,030	456
8	Bangkok	Thailand	17,867	581
9	Chicago	USA	17,830	375
10	Chongqing	China	15,717	398
11	Manila (inc. Makati, Mandaluyong, Ortigas, Quezon City, Pasig, Taguig, Muntinlupa)	Philippines	13,753	345
12	Singapore	Singapore	13,415	460
13	Seoul	South Korea	12,578	362
14	Kuala Lumpur (inc. Petaling Jaya, Subang Jaya)	Malaysia	12,192	325
15	Jakarta	Indonesia	11,755	280
16	Toronto (inc. Mississauga)	Canada	10,901	345
17	Panama City	Panama	9,731	229
18	Chengdu	China	8,964	201
19	Shenyang	China	8,607	153
20	Tianjin	China	8,395	135
21	Moscow	Russia	7,901	222
22	Nanjing	China	7,340	128
23	Busan	South Korea	7,168	125
24	Beijing	China	7,108	293
25	Osaka (inc. Sakai, Amagasaka)	Japan	6,960	183

Source: Egbert Gramsbergen and Paul Kazmierczak

AIGA, the professional association for design

One of the oldest and largest membership associations for professionals engaged in visual communication and graphic design, AIGA, the professional association for design was founded in 1914 as the American Institute of Graphic Arts. Its more than 25,000 members include professional designers, educators, and students in traditional communication design fields, such as type and book design, as well as such newer disciplines as interaction design, experience design, and motion graphics. In addition, AIGA supports the interests of those involved in design in other disciplines, professions, and businesses who are committed to advancing the understanding of the value of design. AIGA serves as a hub of information and activity within the design community through conferences, competitions, exhibitions, publications, educational activities, and its website.

the professional association for design

Address
233 Broadway, 17th Floor
New York, NY 10279
(212) 807-1990
www.aiga.org

Mission
AIGA's mission is to advance designing as a professional craft, strategic tool, and vital cultural force.

American Architectural Foundation

The American Architectural Foundation is a national nonprofit 501(c)(3) organization that educates individuals and communities about the power of architecture to transform lives and improve the places where we live, learn, work, and play. The AAF's programs include the Mayors' Institute on City Design and Great Schools by Design—highly regarded initiatives that help improve the built environment through the collaboration of thought leaders, designers, and local communities. Through its outreach programs, grants, exhibitions, and educational resources, the AAF helps people become thoughtful and engaged stewards of the world around them. The AAF is headquartered in The Octagon, an 1801 Federal-style home designed by William Thornton.

American Architectural Foundation

Address
740 15th Street NW, Suite 224
Washington, DC 20005
(202) 787-1001
www.archfoundation.org

Mission
The American Architectural Foundation's mission is to educate the public on the power of architecture to improve lives and transform communities. The AAF is a national resource that helps provide information and best practices to communities and leaders, promotes collaboration, and encourages design excellence.

American Institute of Architects

Representing the professional interests of America's architects since 1857, the American Institute of Architects provides education, government advocacy, community redevelopment, and public outreach activities with and for its 83,500 members. With more than 300 local and state AIA organizations, the institute closely monitors legislative and regulatory actions at all levels of government. It provides professional development opportunities, industry-standard contract documents, information services, and a comprehensive awards program.

Address

1735 New York Avenue NW
Washington, DC 20006
(800) AIA-3837
www.aia.org

Mission

The American Institute of Architects is the voice of the architecture profession dedicated to serving its members, advancing their value, and improving the quality of the built environment.

American Planning Association

The American Planning Association promotes good planning practices to build better communities while protecting the environment so residents have choices in housing, transportation, and employment. The group's 40,000 members include engaged citizens, planning professionals, and elected and appointed officials. The APA strives to engage all citizens in the planning process so it is open, transparent, and reflects the needs and desires of all community members. The association has offices in Washington, DC, and Chicago. It operates local chapters across the country as well as interest-specific divisions, and provides extensive research, publications, and training opportunities. The APA's professional institute, the American Institute of Certified Planners, certifies planners and promotes high ethical standards of professional practice.

Address

205 North Michigan Avenue	1030 15th Street NW
Suite 1200	Suite 750 West
Chicago, IL 60601	Washington, DC 20005
(312) 431-9100	(202) 872-0611
www.planning.org	www.planning.org

Mission

The American Planning Association is a nonprofit public interest and research organization committed to urban, suburban, regional, and rural planning. The APA and its professional institute, the American Institute of Certified Planners, advance the art and science of planning to meet the needs of people and society.

American Society of Interior Designers

The American Society of Interior Designers was formed in 1975 with the consolidation of the American Institute of Designers and the National Society of Interior Designers. It serves more than 24,000 members with continuing education and government affairs departments, conferences, publications, online services, and more. Members include residential and commercial designers and 5,000 interior design students. ASID operates 48 local chapters throughout the United States.

Address

AMERICAN
SOCIETY OF
INTERIOR
DESIGNERS

718 7th St NW, 4th Floor
Washington, DC 20001
(202) 546-3480
www.asid.org

Mission
The mission of the American Society of Interior Designers is to advance the interior design profession through knowledge generation and sharing, advocacy of interior designers' right to practice, professional and public education, and expansion of interior design markets.

American Society of Landscape Architects

Representing the landscape architecture profession in the United States since 1899, the American Society of Landscape Architects currently serves more than 15,000 members through 49 chapters across the country. The ASLA's goal is to advance knowledge, education, and skill in the art and science of landscape architecture. The benefits of membership include a national annual meeting, *Landscape Architecture* magazine, continuing education credits, seminars and workshops, professional interest groups, government advocacy, and award programs. In addition, the US Department of Education has certified the Landscape Architectural Accreditation Board of the ASLA as the accrediting agency for landscape architecture programs at US colleges and universities.

AMERICAN
SOCIETY OF
LANDSCAPE
ARCHITECTS

Address
636 Eye Street NW
Washington, DC 20001
(202) 898-2444
www.asla.org

Mission
The mission of the American Society of Landscape Architects is to lead, to educate, and to participate in the careful stewardship, wise planning, and artful design of our cultural and natural environments.

Construction History Society of America

Founded in 2007 as an independent branch of the British-based Construction History Society, the CHSA provides a forum for everyone interested in the history of the American construction industry in all its aspects. The society attracts members from all sectors of the industry. It publishes newsletters and a well-regarded journal called *Construction History*. Biennial national meetings are held and local interest groups are forming.

Address
PO Box 93461
Atlanta, GA 30377
www.constructionhistorysociety.org

Mission
The Construction History Society of America's mission is to encourage the study and research of the history of the American construction industry.

Design Futures Council

The Design Futures Council is a global think tank of design and building industry leaders who collaborate through a series of regular meetings, summits, and *DesignIntelligence*, the bi-monthly journal. The group shares information among its fellows and members on best practices and new trends in order to help member organizations anticipate change and increase competitive fitness. Recent summit topics have included sustainability and innovation. Members include leading architecture and design firms, preferred manufacturers, service providers, and forward-thinking AEC companies taking an active interest in their future.

Address
25 Technology Parkway South, Suite 101
Peachtree Corners, GA 30092
(678) 879-0929
www.di.net

Mission
The Design Futures Council is a think tank with the mission to explore trends, changes, and new opportunities in design, architecture, engineering, and building technology for the purpose of fostering innovation and improving the performance of member organizations.

Industrial Designers Society of America

Founded in 1965, the Industrial Designers Society of America is a professional association of industrial designers, educators, and students dedicated to the promotion of the profession. By fostering innovation and high standards of design, the IDSA communicates the value of design to the public and mentors young designers in their professional career development. The organization serves its constituency through the professional journal *Innovation*, award programs, an annual conference, research sponsorship, networking opportunities, and the promotion of the practice at all levels of government.

Address

555 Grove Street, Suite 200
Herndon, VA 20170
(703) 707-6000
www.idsa.org

Mission

The mission of the Industrial Designers Society of America is to lead the profession by expanding our horizons, connectivity and influence, and our service to members; inspire design quality and responsibility through professional development and education; and elevate the business of design and improve our industry's value.

International Interior Design Association

The International Interior Design Association provides a variety of services and benefits to its more than 13,000 members through 10 specialty forums, and more than 31 chapters around the world. This professional networking and educational association promotes the interior design practice to the public and serves its members as a clearinghouse for industry information. The IIDA was founded in 1994 as the result of a merger of the Institute of Business Designers, the International Society of Interior Designers, and the Council of Federal Interior Designers. The goal of the merger was to create an international association with a united mission that would represent interior designers worldwide.

Address

222 Merchandise Mart Plaza, Suite 567
Chicago, IL 60654
(312) 467-1950
www.iida.org

Mission

The International Interior Design Association is committed to enhancing the quality of life through excellence in interior design and advancing interior design through knowledge. The IIDA advocates for interior design excellence, provides superior industry information, nurtures a global interior design community, maintains educational standards, and responds to trends in business and design.

National Trust for Historic Preservation

The National Trust for Historic Preservation is a private nonprofit membership organization dedicated to saving historic places and revitalizing America's communities. Since NTHP's founding in 1949, it has worked to preserve historic buildings and neighborhoods through leadership, educational programs, publications (such as its award-winning *Preservation* magazine), financial assistance, and government advocacy. The National Trust has a staff of 300 employees based at headquarters in Washington, D.C., in field offices nationwide, and at historic sites in 15 states.

Address

National Trust *for*
Historic Preservation

Watergate Office Building
2600 Virginia Ave, Suite 1100
Washington, DC 20037
(202) 588-6000
www.preservationnation.org

Mission

The National Trust for Historic Preservation is a privately funded, nonprofit organization that provides leadership, education, advocacy, and resources to save America's diverse historic places and revitalize our communities.

Society for Environmental Graphic Design

The Society for Environmental Graphic Design is a nonprofit organization formed in 1973 to promote public awareness of and professional development in environmental graphic design. This interdisciplinary field encompasses the talents of many design professionals, including graphic designers, architects, landscape architects, product designers, planners, interior designers, and exhibition designers who create graphic elements to help identify, direct, inform, interpret, and visually enhance our surroundings through such means as wayfinding or maps. Resources available to SEGD members (totaling 1,500) include a quarterly color magazine, a bi-monthly newsletter, an annual conference, a design award program, technical bulletins, job bank listings, and many other formal and informal materials.

Address

1900 L St NW, Suite 710
Washington, DC 20036
(202) 638-5555
www.segd.org

Mission

The Society for Environmental Graphic Design is an international nonprofit educational organization providing resources for design specialists in the field of environmental graphic design; architecture; and landscape, interior, and industrial design.

Society for Marketing Professional Services

Established in 1973, the Society for Marketing Professional Services is a network of over 6,000 marketing and business development professionals representing architectural, engineering, planning, interior design, construction, and specialty consulting firms throughout the United States and Canada in 59 chapters. The society's benefits include a certification program (Certified Professional Services Marketer), an annual marketing and management conference (www.buildbusiness.org), an annual marketing communications competition, educational programs, resources, and publications highlighting the latest trends and best practices in professional services marketing in the AEC industry. SMPS is supported by 57 chapters in the United States.

Address

123 North Pitt Street, Suite 400
Alexandria, VA 22314
(800) 292-7677
www.smps.org

Mission

The mission of the Society for Marketing Professional Services is to advocate for, educate, and connect leaders in the building industry.

Society of Architectural Historians

Since its founding in 1940, the Society of Architectural Historians has sought to promote the history of architecture. The membership of the SAH ranges from professionals, such as architects, planners, preservationists, and academics, to those simply interested in architecture. The society produces a quarterly journal and monthly newsletter and organizes study tours and an annual conference. There are also a number of associated, although independent, local chapters. The SAH's national headquarters is located in Chicago's architecturally significant Charnley-Persky House, designed in 1891 by the firm of Dankmar Adler and Louis Sullivan. Guided tours of the house are offered.

Address

1365 North Astor Street
Chicago, IL 60610
(312) 573-1365
www.sah.org

Mission

The mission of the Society of Architectural Historians is to advance knowledge and understanding of the history of architecture, design, landscape, and urbanism worldwide.

Urban Land Institute

Formed in 1936 as a research arm of the National Association of Real Estate Boards (now the National Association of Realtors), the Urban Land Institute is an independent organization for those engaged in the entrepreneurial and collaborative process of real estate development and land-use policymaking. The ULI has more than 32,000 members worldwide. ULI members include the people that plan, develop, and redevelop neighborhoods, business districts, and communities across the United States and around the world, working in private enterprise and public service. The institute's activities include research, forums and task forces, awards, education, and publishing.

Address

1025 Thomas Jefferson Street NW
Suite 500 West
Washington, DC 20007
(202) 624-7000
www.uli.org

Mission

The mission of the Urban Land Institute is to provide responsible leadership in the use of land to enhance the total environment.

US Green Building Council

The US Green Building Council was formed in 1993 to integrate, educate, and provide leadership for building industry leaders, environmental groups, designers, retailers, and building owners as they strive to develop and market products and services that are environmentally progressive and responsible. The council includes nearly 12,800 member organizations, 193,000 LEED professionals, and 76 regional chapters with a common interest in green building practices, technologies, policies, and standards. Its most visible program, the LEED™ Green Building Rating System, is a voluntary consensus-based rating system that provides a national standard on what constitutes a green building. It also offers professional accreditation to certify individuals who have demonstrated the ability to serve on a LEED project team and provide detailed knowledge of LEED project certification requirements and processes.

Address

2101 L Street NW, Suite 500
Washington, DC 20037
(800) 795-1747
www.new.usgbc.org

Mission

The US Green Building Council's core purpose is to transform the way buildings and communities are designed, built, and operated, enabling an environmentally and socially responsible, healthy, and prosperous environment that improves the quality of life.

Architectural Outreach

Countless volunteer opportunities abound for architects, designers, and others interested in the built environment, ranging from disaster relief and recovery to community empowerment, restoration, and historic preservation. The following is a partial list of organizations, coalitions, and resources aimed at the coordination and operation of national and international volunteer programs that are focused on architecture, planning, design, and community development initiatives.

Adventures in Preservation (formerly Heritage Conservation Network)
1557 North Street
Boulder, CO 80304
(303) 444-0128
www.adventuresinpreservation.org

Adventures in Preservation has become a leader in offering volunteer vacations directed toward saving distinctive architecture that defines a region's history and culture. The fact that historic preservation is innately "green" provides yet another compelling reason for restoring historic buildings for integrated community use.

Builders Without Borders
119 Kingston Main Street
Hillsboro, NM 88042
(575) 895-5652
(510) 525-0525
www.builderswithoutborders.org

With volunteers, including architects, engineers, contractors, and others in the AEC field, Builders Without Borders specializes in affordable housing, both domestically and abroad, emphasizing sustainable structures built with locally available materials. Generally, BWB provides technical assistance to improve designs.

buildOn
P.O. Box 16741
Stamford, CT 06905
(203) 961-5041
www.buildon.org

buildOn enhances education and empowers youth in the United States to make a positive difference in their communities while helping people of developing countries increase their self-reliance through education and the development of educational resources.

Caribbean Volunteer Expeditions
PO Box 388
Corning, NY 14830
(607) 962-7846
www.cvexp.org

Caribbean Volunteer Expeditions is a non-profit agency dedicated to the preservation and documentation of the historical heritage of the Caribbean. Members and volunteers measure and document historical plantations, windmills, and other structures to help local Caribbean agencies keep a record of their architectural heritage. Professional assistance is appreciated.

Habitat for Humanity International

121 Habitat Street
Americus, GA 31709
(800) 422-4828
www.habitat.org

Habitat for Humanity International seeks to eliminate poverty housing and homelessness from the world and to make decent shelter a matter of conscience and action. Through volunteer labor and donations of money and materials, Habitat builds and rehabilitates simple, decent houses with the help of the homeowner (partner) families.

National Park Service Volunteers-In-Parks Program

1849 C Street NW
Washington, DC 20240
(202) 208-3818
www.nps.gov

The Volunteers-In-Parks Program provides a vehicle through which the National Park Service can accept and utilize voluntary help and services from the public.

Open Architecture Network Architecture for Humanity

695 Minna Street
San Francisco, CA 94103
(415) 963-3511
www.openarchitecturenetwork.org

The Open Architecture Network is an online, open-source community dedicated to improving living conditions through innovative and sustainable design. Here designers of all persuasions can share their ideas, designs and plans; view and review designs posted by others; collaborate to address specific design challenges; manage design projects from concept to implementation; protect their intellectual property rights using the Creative Commons licensing system; and build a more sustainable future.

Peace Corps

1111 20th Street NW
Washington, DC 20526
(855) 855-1961
www.peacecorps.gov

Peace Corps Volunteers serve in countries across the globe: Africa, Asia, the Caribbean, Central and South America, Europe, and the Middle East. Collaborating with local community members, volunteers work in such areas as education, youth outreach and community development, the environment, and information technology.

Public Architecture 1% Solution

1211 Folsom Street, 4th Floor
San Francisco, CA 94103
(415) 861-8200
www.theonepercent.org
www.publicarchitecture.org

The 1% Solution program grew out of a realization that there are no formal mechanisms supporting or recognizing pro bono architectural work within the profession. The goal of the 1% Solution is to direct one percent of all architects' working hours to matters of public interest, pro bono.

Rebuilding Together

1899 L Street NW, Suite 1000
Washington, DC 20036
(800) 473-4229
www.rebuildingtogether.org

Rebuilding Together preserves and revitalizes houses and communities, assuring that low-income homeowners, from the elderly and disabled to families with children, live in warmth, safety, and independence. Its goal is to make a sustainable impact in partnership with the community.

Architectural Outreach

Red Feather Development Group
PO Box 907
Bozeman, MT 59771
(406) 585-7188
www.redfeather.org

Red Feather educates and empowers American Indian nations to create sustain- able solutions to the severe housing crisis within reserva- tion communities. Red Feather teaches afford- able, replicable, and sustainable approaches to home construction, working with volunteers alongside tribal members to build desperately needed homes.

Shelter For Life International
10201 Wayzata Boulevard, Suite 230
Minnetonka, MN 55305
(763) 253-4082
www.shelter.org

Shelter for Life International is a faith-based humanitarian organization that enables people affected by conflict and disaster to rebuild their communities and restore their lives through appropriate shelter and community development programs. Shelter for Life has occasional volun- teer opportunities in project management, con- struction, community development, engineering, architecture, and cross-cultural relations.

slowLab
c/o New York Foundation for the Arts
20 Jay Street, 7th Floor
Brooklyn, NY 11201
(212) 366-6900
www.slowlab.net

The goal of slowLab is to promote slowness as a positive catalyst of individual, socio- cultural, and environmental well-being. Current and future programs include public lectures, discussions and exhibitions, a dynamic online project observatory and communication portal, academic programs, and publishing projects.

Southface Energy Institute
241 Pine Street NE
Atlanta, GA 30308
(404) 872-3549
www.southface.org

Southface promotes sustainable homes, work- places, and communities through education, research, advocacy, and technical assistance.

World Shelters for Humanitarian Needs
550 South G Street, Suite 3
Arcata, CA 95521
(707) 822-6600
www.worldshelters.org

World Shelters designs, produces, and delivers temporary and permanent structures for both emergency response and long-term humanitar- ian needs.

Source: DesignIntelligence

Architecture Critics

Below is a listing of major publications that regularly feature architectural writing and criticism. Some publications have a staff architecture critic while others an art critic or critic-at-large who routinely covers architecture stories.

Arizona Republic
Michelle Dodds
Historic Preservation Officer
200 East Van Buren Street
Phoenix, AZ 85004
(602) 444-8000
www.azcentral.com

**Atlanta Journal-
    Constitution**
Chris Quinn
Features Assignment Editor
cquinn@ajc.com
223 Perimeter Center Parkway
Atlanta, GA 30346
(404) 526-2160
www.ajc.com

**Austin American-
    Statesman**
Jeanne Claire van Ryzin
Arts Critic
jvanryzin@statesman.com
P.O. Box 670
Austin, Texas 78767
(512) 445-3699
www.statesman.com
www.austin360.com

Baltimore Sun
Mary Carole McCauley
Visual Arts Editor
501 North Calvert Street
Baltimore, MD 21278
(410) 332-6704
www.baltimoresun.com

Boston Globe
Robert Campbell
Architecture Critic
Rebecca Ostriker
Arts Editor
ostriker@globe.com
135 Morrissey Boulevard
Boston, MA 02125
(617) 929-2800
www.boston.com

Boston Herald
Sandra Kent
Arts and Lifestyle Editor
Sandra.kent@bostonherald.com
One Herald Square
Boston, MA 02118
(617) 426-3000
www.bostonherald.com

**Charleston Post
    and Courier**
Robert Behre
rbehre@postandcourier.com
Architecture Critic
134 Columbus Street
Charleston, SC 29403
(843) 577-7111
www.postandcourier.com

Charlotte Observer
Allen Norwood
Home Columnist
homeinfo@embarqmail.com
600 South Tryon Street
Charlotte, NC 28202
(704) 358-5000
www.charlotteobserver.com

Chicago Sun-Times
Fran Spielman
fspielman@suntimes.com
350 North Orleans Street
Chicago, IL 60654
(312) 321-3000
www.suntimes.com

Chicago Tribune
Blair Kamin
Architecture Critic
bkamin@tribune.com
435 North Michigan Avenue
Chicago, IL 60611
(312) 222-3232
www.chicagotribune.com

Cleveland Plain Dealer
Steven Litt
Art & Architecture Critic
Plain Dealer Plaza
1801 Superior Avenue
Cleveland, OH 44114
(216) 999-5000
www.plaindealer.com

Dallas Morning News
Mark Lamster
Architecture Critic
mlamster@dallasnews.com
508 Young Street
Dallas, TX 75202
(214) 977-8222
www.dallasnews.com

Architecture Critics

Denver Post
Ray Ranaldi
Fine Arts Critic
rranaldi@denverpost.com
101 West Colfax Avenue
Denver, CO 80202
(303) 954-1540
www.denverpost.com

Detroit Free Press
John Gallagher
Business and Architecture
    Writer
jgallagher@freepress.com
615 West Lafayette
    Boulevard
Detroit, MI 48226
(313) 222-6459
www.freep.com

Financial Times
Edwin Heathcote
Architecture Writer
1 Southwark Bridge
London SE1 9HL, UK
44 (0) 20 7873 3000
www.ft.com

Los Angeles Times
Christopher Hawthorne
Architecture Critic
christopher.hawthorne@atimes.com
202 West First Street
Los Angeles, CA 90012
(213) 237-5000
www.latimes.com

Louisville Courier-Journal
Elizabeth Kramer
Arts Reporter
ekramer@courier-journal.com
P.O. Box 740031
Louisville, KY 40201
(502) 582-4215
www.courier-journal.com

Milwaukee Journal Sentinel
Mary Louise Schumacher
Art and Architecture Critic
mschumacher@journalsentinel.com
P.O. Box 371
Milwaukee, WI 53201
(414) 224-2000
www.jsonline.com

New York Times
Michael Kimmelman
Architecture Critic
229 West 43rd Street
New York, NY 10036
(212) 556-1234
www.nytimes.com

Newark Star-Ledger
Dan Bischoff
Art Critic
dbischoff@starledger.com
1 Star-Ledger Plaza
Newark, NJ 07102
(973) 392-4040
www.nj.com/starledger

Newport News Daily Press
Mark St. John Erickson
Arts/Museum/History
    Reporter
merickson@dailypress.com
7505 Warwick Boulevard
Newport News, VA 23607
(757) 247-4600
www.dailypress.com

Philadelphia Inquirer
Inga Saffron
Architecture Critic
isaffron@phillynews.com
P.O. Box 8263
Philadelphia, PA 19101
(215) 854-2000
www.philly.com

Pittsburgh Post-Gazette
Marylynne Pitz
mpitz@post-gazette.com
34 Boulevard of the Allies
Pittsburgh, PA 15222
(412) 263-1100
www.post-gazette.com

Providence Journal
Bill Van Siclen
Art Critic
bvansicl@projo.com
75 Fountain Street
Providence, RI 02902
(401) 277-7000
www.providencejournal.com

The Record
John Zeaman
Art Critic
features@northjersey.com
North Jersey Media Group
1 Garret Mountain Plaza
Woodland Park, NJ 07424
(201) 646-4000
www.northjersey.com

San Antonio Express-News
Steve Bennett
Arts and Architecture Writer
sbennett@express-news.net
301 Avenue E
San Antonio, TX 78205
(210) 250-3000
www.mysanantonio.com

San Diego Union-Tribune
Roger Showley
Arts Reporter
350 Camino de la Reina
San Diego, CA 92108
(619) 299-3131
www.utsandiego.com

San Francisco Chronicle
John King
Urban Design Critic
jking@sfchronicle.com
901 Mission Street
San Francisco, CA 94103
(415) 777-1111
www.sfgate.com

Seattle Times
Rebecca Teagarden
Reporter, Pacific NW
    Magazine
bteagarden@seattletimes.com
P.O. Box 70
Seattle, WA 98111
(206) 748-5808
seattletimes.com

Wall Street Journal
Alastair Gordon
Contributing Editor for
    Architecture and Design
Robert Whelan
Reporter
Robert.whelan@wsj.com
1211 Avenue of the
    Americas
New York, NY, 10036
(212) 416-2000
www.wsj.com

Washington Post
Philip Kennicott
Chief Art & Architecture Critic
1150 15th Street NW
Washington, DC 20071
(202) 334-6000
www.washingtonpost.com

Source: DesignIntelligence

Bookstores

The following is a list of US architecture and design bookstores, including rare and out-of-print dealers that specialize in design titles.

ARIZONA
Builder's Book Depot
1001 East Jefferson, Suite 5
Phoenix, AZ 85034
(800) 284-3434
www.buildersbookdepot.com

CALIFORNIA
Arcana: Books on the Arts
@ The Historic Helms Bakery
8675 Washington Boulevard
Culver City, CA 90232
(310) 458-1499
www.arcanabooks.com

Builder's Book
8001 Canoga Avenue
Canoga Park, CA 91304
(800) 273-7375
www.buildersbook.com

Builders Booksource
1817 Fourth Street
Berkeley, CA 94710
(800) 843-2028
www.buildersbooksource.com

Hennessey + Ingalls
214 Wilshire Boulevard
Santa Monica, CA 90401
(310) 458-9074
www.hennesseyingalls.com

J.B. Muns Fine Arts Books
1162 Shattuck Avenue
Berkeley, CA 94707
(510) 525-2420

MAK Center for Art and Architecture Bookstore
835 North Kings Road
West Hollywood, CA 90069
(323) 651-1510
www.makcenter.org

Moe's Books
2476 Telegraph Avenue
Berkeley, CA 94704
(510) 849-2087
www.moesbooks.com

Sullivan Goss
7 East Anapamu Street
Santa Barbara, CA 93101
(805) 730-1460
www.sullivangoss.com

William Stout Architectural Books
804 Montgomery Street
San Francisco, CA 94133
(415) 391-6757
www.stoutbooks.com

1605 Solano at Tacoma
Berkeley, CA 94707
(510) 356-4740
www.stoutbooks.com

COLORADO
Tattered Cover Bookstore
2526 East Colfax Avenue
Denver, CO 80206
(303) 322-7727
www.tatteredcover.com

1628 16th Street
Denver, CO 80202
(303) 436-1070
www.tatteredcover.com

7301 S. Santa Fe Drive
Littleton, CO 80120
(303) 436-1070
www.tatteredcover.com

1701 Wynkoop Street
Denver, CO 80202
(303) 436-1070
www.tatteredcover.com

DISTRICT OF COLUMBIA
AIA Bookstore
1735 New York Avenue NW
Washington, DC 20006
(202) 626-7475
www.aia.org/store

National Building Museum Shop
401 F Street NW
Washington, DC 20001
(202) 272-2448
www.nbm.org

ILLINOIS
Chicago Architecture Foundation Bookstore
224 South Michigan Avenue
Chicago, IL 60604
(312) 322-1132
www.architecture.org/shop

INDIANA
AIA Indiana Bookstore
1028 Shelby Street
Indianapolis, IN 46203
(317) 634-3871
www.aiaindiana.org

MARYLAND

Baltimore AIA Bookstore
11 1/2 West Chase Street
Baltimore, MD 21201
(410) 625-2585
www.aiabalt.com

MASSACHUSETTS

Ars Libri
500 Harrison Avenue
Boston, MA 02118
(617) 357-5212
www.arslibri.com

**Charles B. Wood III
Antiquarian Booksellers**
PO Box 382369
Cambridge, MA 02238
(617) 868-1711
www.cbwoodbooks.com

F. A. Bernett
144 Lincoln Street
Boston, MA 02111
(617) 350-7778
www.fabernett.com

MISSOURI

St. Louis AIA Bookstore
911 Washington Avenue
Suite 100
St. Louis, MO 63101
(314) 621-3484
www.aia-stlouis.org

NEW YORK

Argosy Bookstore
116 East 59th Street
New York, NY 10022
(212) 753-4455
www.argosybooks.com

**Cooper-Hewitt
Museum Bookstore**
2 East 91st Street
New York, NY 10128
(212) 849-8400
www.cooperhewittshop.org

Strand-Hacker Art Books
45 W 57th Street
New York, NY 10019
(212) 688-7600

Neue Galeria Bookstore
1048 Fifth Avenue
New York, NY 10028
(212) 994-9492
www.neuegalerie.org

**New York School of
Interior Design Bookstore**
170 East 70th Street
New York, NY 10021
(212) 472-1500
www.nysid.edu

Potterton Books
New York Design Center
Suite 431, 4th Floor
200 Lexington Ave.
New York, NY 10016
(212) 644-2292
www.pottertonbooksusa.com

Rizzoli Bookstore
1133 Broadway
New York, NY 10010
(212) 759-2424
www.rizzolibookstore.com

Royoung Bookseller
564 Ashford Avenue
Ardsley, NY 10502
(914) 693-6116
www.royoung.com

Strand Book Store
828 Broadway
New York, NY 10003
(212) 473-1452
www.strandbooks.com

Ursus Books
699 Madison Avenue
3rd Floor
New York, NY 10065
(212) 772-8787
www.ursusbooks.com

OREGON

Powell's City of Books
1005 West Burnside
Portland, OR 97209
(503) 228-4651
www.powells.com

Powell's Books Building 2
40 Northwest 10th Avenue
Portland, OR 97209
(503) 228-4651
www.powells.com

**Powell's Books
at Cedar Hills Crossing**
3415 Southwest Cedar
Hills Boulevard
Beaverton, OR 97005
(503) 228-4651
www.powells.com

**Powell's Books
on Hawthorne**
3723 Southeast Hawthorne
Boulevard
Portland, OR 97214
(503) 228-4651
www.powells.com

**Powell's Books for Home
and Garden**
3747 Hawthorne
Portland, OR 97214
(503) 228-4651
www.powells.com

Powell's Books at PDX
7000 NE Airport Way
Suite 2250
Portland, OR 97218
(503) 228-4651
www.powells.com

Bookstores

PENNSYLVANIA

AIA Bookstore & Design Center
1218 Arch Street
Philadelphia, PA 19107
(215) 569-3188
www.aiaphila.org

Joseph Fox Bookshop
1724 Sansom Street
Philadelphia, PA 19103
(215) 563-4184
www.foxbookshop.com

TEXAS

Brazos Bookstore
2421 Bissonnet Street
Houston, TX 77005
(713) 523-0701
www.brazosbookstore.com

WASHINGTON

Peter Miller Architecture and Design Books
2326 Second Avenue
Seattle, WA 98121
(206) 441-4114
www.petermiller.com

Source: DesignIntelligence

Journals & Magazines

The following is a list of major architecture and design journals and magazines from around the world, ranging from the mainstream to the cutting edge. Whether looking for periodicals that take a less-traditional approach or for exposure to the most recent projects and design news, this list is intended to provide an opportunity to explore new ideas and perspectives about design and expand your knowledge about the profession.

US Publications

Architect's Newspaper
21 Murray Street, Fifth Floor
New York, NY 10007
(212) 966-0630
www.archpaper.com
Published monthly.

Architectural Digest
1 World Trade Center, Floor 26
New York, NY 10007
(800) 365-8032
www.architecturaldigest.com
Published monthly by Condé Nast
Publications, Inc.

Architectural Record
Two Penn Plaza, Ninth Floor
New York, NY 10121-2298
(212) 904-2594
www.archrecord.construction.com
Published monthly by Dodge Data & Analytics.

Architect
One Thomas Circle NW, Suite 600
Washington, DC 20005
(202) 452-0800
www.architectmagazine.com
Published monthly by Hanley Wood, LLC.

ASID ICON
718 7th Street NW
Washington, DC 20001
(202) 546-3480
www.icon.asid.org
The magazine of the American Society of
Interior Designers, published quarterly.

Building Design+Construction
3030 W. Salt Creek Lane, Suite 201
Arlington Heights, IL 60005
(847) 391-1000
www.bdcnetwork.com
Published monthly by Scranton Gillette
Communications, LLC.

Contract
85 Broad Street
New York, NY 10004
(646) 654-5000
www.contractdesign.com
Published monthly by Nielsen Business
Publications, USA, Inc.

Communication Arts
110 Constitution Drive
Menlo Park, CA 94025
(650) 326-6040
www.commarts.com
Published six times per year.

Dwell
111 Sutter Street, Suite 600
San Francisco, CA 94104
(415) 373-5100
www.dwell.com
Published 10 times per year.

EcoHome
One Thomas Circle, NW
Suite 600
Washington, DC 20005
(202) 452-0800
www.ecobuildingpulse.com
Published four times a year by Hanley Wood.

Journals & Magazines

EcoStructure
One Thomas Circle, NW
Suite 600
Washington, DC 20005
(202) 452-0800
www.ecobuildingpulse.com
Published four times a year by Hanley Wood.

Engineering News Record
Two Penn Plaza, 9th Floor
New York, NY 10121
(212) 904-3507
www.enr.com
Published weekly by Dodge Data & Analytics.

Faith & Form
100 North Tryon Street, Suite 3500
Charlotte, NC 28202
www.faithandform.com
Quarterly journal of the Interfaith Forum on
Religion, Art and Architecture.

Fine Homebuilding
Taunton Press
63 South Main Street
Newtown, CT 06470
(203) 426-8171
www.finehomebuilding.com
Published eight times a year by Taunton Press.

Harvard Design Magazine
48 Quincy Street, Gund Hall
Cambridge, MA 02138
(617) 495-7814
www.harvarddesignmagazine.org
Published twice a year by the Harvard
University Graduate School of Design.

Interior Design
1271 Avenue of the Americas, Floor 17
New York, NY 10020
(917) 934-2882
www.interiordesign.net
Published 15 times a year by
Sandow Media LLC.

Interiors & Sources
615 Fifth Street SE
Cedar Rapids, IA 52401
(319) 364-6167
www.interiorsandsources.com
Published nine times a year by
Stamats Communications, Inc.

Journal of Architectural Education
Association of Collegiate Schools of
Architecture
1735 New York Avenue, NW
Washington, DC 20006
(202) 785-2324
www.jaeonline.org
Published biannually by Routledge
for the ACSA.

Journal of Interior Design
Interior Design Educators Council, Inc.
One Parkview Plaza, #800
Oakbrook Terrace, IL 60181
(630) 544-5057
www.idec.org
Published three times a year.

Journal of the American Planning Association
205 N. Michigan Avenue, Suite 1200
Chicago, IL 60601
(312) 431-9100
www.planning.org/japa
Published quarterly by the
American Planning Association.

**Journal of the Society of
Architectural Historians**
1365 North Astor Street
Chicago, IL 60610-2144
(312) 573-1365
www.sah.org
Published quarterly by the Society of
Architectural Historians.

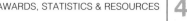

Landscape Architecture
636 Eye Street NW
Washington, DC 20001-3736
(202) 898-2444
www.landscapearchitecturemagazine.org
Published monthly by the American Society of
Landscape Architects.

Metropolis
61 West 23rd Street, 4th Floor
New York, NY 10010
(212) 627-9977
www.metropolismag.com
Published 11 times a year.

Old House Journal
4125 Lafayette Center Drive, Suite 100
Chantilly, VA 20151
(703) 222-9411
www.oldhousejournal.com
Published eight times annually by Home Buyer
Publications/Active Interest Media

Perspective
222 Merchandise Mart Plaza, Suite 567
Chicago, IL 60654
(888) 799-4432
www.iida.org
Published bi-annuallly by the
International Interior Design Association.

Places Journal
3536 California Street
San Francisco, CA 94118
(415) 497-6179
www.placesjournal.org

Preservation
2600 Virginia Avenue NW, Suite 1000
Washington, DC 20037
(800) 944-6847
www.preservationnation.org
Published bimonthly by the
National Trust for Historic Preservation.

International Publications

Abitare
Via Rizzoli 8
20132 Milano, Italy
+39 06 6500 0808
www.abitare.it
Monthly magazine in Italian and English
published by RCS Mediagroup S.p.A.

AD (Architectural Design)
25 John Street
London, WC1 N2BS, UK
+44 020 8326 3800
www.architectural-design-magazine.com
Published bi-monthly by John Wiley and Sons, Ltd.

AJ (Architects' Journal)
Telephone House
66-67 Paul Street
London, EC2A 4NQ, UK
+44 020 844 848 8858
www.architectsjournal.co.uk
Published by EMAP Construct.

l'Arca
31 ave Princesse Grace
MC 98000 Monaco
+377 92165154
www.arcadata.com
Six issues annually.

Architectural History: The Journal of the Society of Architectural Historians of Great Britain
SAHGB, Heritage House
PO Box 21
Baldock, Hertfordshire SG7 5SH
www.sahgb.org.uk
Published annually.

Architectural Review
69-77 Paul Street
London, EC2A 4NW, UK
+44 020 3033 2626
www.arplus.com
Published by EMAP Construct.

Journals & Magazines

Architecture Australia
Level 6, 163 Eastern Road
South Melbourne, Victoria
Australia 3205
+61 (03) 8699 1000
www.archmedia.com.au/aa/
Official magazine of the Australian Institute of
Architects published six times a year.

l'Architecture d'Aujourd'hui
10, Cité d'Angoulême
75010 Paris, France
+33 1 58051751
www.larchitecturedaujourdhui.fr
Published six times a year in
French and English.

Arkitektur
Birger Jarlsgatan 110
1 tr, SE 114 20 Stockholm, Sweden
+46 8 702 7850
www.arkitektur.se
Published eight times yearly by Arkitektur
Förlag AB with English summaries.

a+u magazine
Kasumigaseki Building 17F
3-2-5 Kasumigaseki, Chiyoda-ku
Tokyo, 100-6017, Japan
+81 36205 4380
www.japlusu.com
Published monthly in Japanese and English by
A+U Publishing Co., Ltd.

Blueprint
3rd Floor, Farringdon Place
Farringdon Road
London, EC1M 3HE, UK
www.blueprintmagazine.co.uk
+44 020 7936 6400
Published bi-monthly by Progressive
Media International Group.

Canadian Architect
80 Valleybrook Drive
Toronto, ON, M3B 2S9, Canada
(416) 510-6845
www.canadianarchitect.com
Published monthly by Business Information
Group, a division of Hollinger Canadian
Newspapers, LP.

Casabella
Via Mondadori 1
Segrate, 20090, Italy
+39 02 754 2 1
www.casabellaweb.eu
Published 11 times a year in Italian with an
English summary.

El Croquis
Av. de los Reyes Catolicos 9
E-28280 El Escorial
Madrid, Spain
+34 91 8969410
www.elcroquis.es
Published bimonthly in Spanish and English.

Domus
Via G. Mazzocchi 13
Rozzano
Milan, 20089, Italy
+39 0282472265
www.domusweb.it
Published 11 times a year in Italian and
English.

Hinge
24/F, Empire Land Commercial Centre
81 Lockhart Road
Wanchai
Hong Kong, China
+852 2520 2468
www.hinge.hk
Published monthly.

Japan Architect

Kasumigaseki Building 17F
3-2-5 Kasumigaseki, Chiyoda-ku
Tokyo, 100-6017, Japan
+81 3 6205 4380
www.japlusu.com
Published quarterly in Japanese and English.

Journal of Architecture

2 Park Square
Milton Park
Abingdon
Oxford, OX14 4RN, UK
+44 20 7017 5544
www.tandf.co.uk/journals/rjar/
Published six times a year by RIBA and
Routledge, an imprint of Taylor & Francis.

Journal of Sustainable Product Design

Centre for Sustainable Design
PO Box 990
3300 AZ Dordrecht
The Netherlands
+781 871 6600
www.cfsd.org.uk/journal
A quarterly journal published by Kluwer
Academic Publishers in partnership with the
Centre for Sustainable Design.

Journal of Urban Design

2 Park Square
Milton Park
Abingdon
Oxford, OX14 4RN, UK
+44 20 7017 5544
www.tandfonline.com
Published quarterly by Routledge, Taylor &
Francis Group.

Ottagono

Via Stalingrado, 97/2
40128 Bologna, Italy
+39 051 3540 111
www.ottagono.com
Published monthly in bilingual text (Italian and
English).

Volume

Archis Foundation
P.O. Box 14702
1001 LE Amsterdam, Netherlands
31 20 3203926
www.archis.org
Bilingual magazine published quarterly by
Stichting Archis in association with the
Netherlands Architecture Institute.

Wallpaper

Blue Fin Building
110 Southwark Street
London, SE1 0SU, UK
+44 20 3148 5000
www.wallpaper.com
Published 10 times a year.

Source: DesignIntelligence

Museums

There are many museums around the world devoted solely to architecture and design. In addition, many major museums maintain strong design collections and regularly host architecture and design-related exhibits. The following contains the contact information for these organizations.

US Museums

A+D Architecture and Design Museum
900 East 4th Street
Los Angeles, CA 90013
(213) 346-9734
www.aplusd.org

Art Institute of Chicago
111 South Michigan Avenue
Chicago, IL 60603
(312) 443-3600
www.artic.edu

Athenaeum of Philadelphia
219 South Sixth Street
Philadelphia, PA 19106
(215) 925-2688
www.philaathenaeum.org

Center for Architecture
536 LaGuardia Place
New York, NY 10012
(212) 683-0023
www.cfa.aiany.org

Chicago Architecture Foundation
224 South Michigan Avenue
Chicago, IL 60604
(312) 922-3432
www.architecture.org

**Cooper-Hewitt, National
Design Museum, Smithsonian Institution**
2 East 91st Street
New York, NY 10128
(212) 849-8400
www.cooperhewitt.org

Heinz Architectural Center
Carnegie Museum of Art
4400 Forbes Avenue
Pittsburgh, PA 15213
(412) 622-3131
www.cmoa.org

MAK Center for Art & Architecture L.A.
The Schindler House
835 North Kings Road
West Hollywood, CA 90069
(323) 651-1510
www.makcenter.org

Museum of Arts & Design
2 Columbus Circle #1
New York, NY 10019
(212) 299-7777
www.madmuseum.org

Museum of Contemporary Art, Los Angeles
MOCA Grand Avenue
250 South Grand Avenue
Los Angeles, CA 90012
(213) 626-6222
www.moca.org

Geffen Contemporary at MOCA
152 North Central Avenue
Los Angeles, CA 90012
(213) 633-5313
www.moca.org

MOCA Pacific Design Center
8678 Melrose Avenue
West Hollywood, CA 90069
(310) 289-5219
www.moca.org

Museum of Design
1315 Peachtree Street
Atlanta, GA 30309
(404) 979-6455
www.museumofdesign.org

Museum of Modern Art
11 West 53rd Street
New York, NY 10019
(212) 708-9400
www.moma.org

National Building Museum
401 F Street NW
Washington, DC 20001
(202) 272-2448
www.nbm.org

Price Tower Arts Center
510 Dewey Avenue
Bartlesville, OK 74003
(918) 336-4949
www.pricetower.org

San Francisco Museum of Craft + Design
2569 Third Street
San Francisco, CA 94107
(415) 773-0303
www.sfmcd.org

San Francisco Museum of Modern Art
151 Third Street
San Francisco, CA 94103
(415) 357-4000
www.sfmoma.org

Skyscraper Museum
39 Battery Place
New York, NY 10280
(212) 968-1961
www.skyscraper.org

Storefront for Art and Architecture
97 Kenmare Street
New York, NY 10012
(212) 431-5795
www.storefrontnews.org

Van Alen Institute
30 West 22 Street, 4th Floor
New York, NY 10010
(212) 924-7000
www.vanalen.org

Virginia Center for Architecture
The Branch House
2501 Monument Avenue
Richmond, VA 23220
(804) 644-3041
www.virginiaarchitecture.org

International Museums

Alvar Aalto Museum
(Alvar Aalto Museo)
Alvar Aallon katu 7
Jyväskylä, Finland
+358 14 266 7113
www.alvaraalto.fi

Architecture Center of Vienna
(Architekturzentrum Wien)
Museumsplatz 1
A-1070 Vienna, Austria
+43 522 3115
www.azw.at

Bauhaus Archive/Museum of Design
(Bauhaus-Archiv/Museum für Gestaltung)
Klingelhöferstraße 14
10785 Berlin, Germany
+49 30 254 00 20
www.bauhaus.de

Canadian Centre for Architecture
1920, rue Baile
Montreal, QC, Canada H3H 2S6
(514) 939-7026
www.cca.qc.ca

Museums

Danish Architecture Center
(Dansk Arkitektur Center)
Strandgade 27B
1401 Copenhagen K, Denmark
+45 32 57 19 30
www.dac.dk

Danish Design Center
(Dansk Design Center)
Frederiksholms Kanal 30
1220 Copenhagen K, Denmark
+45 33 69 33 69
www.ddc.dk

Design Museum, Finland
(Designmuseo)
Korkeavuorenkatu 23
00130 Helsinki, Finland
+35 809 622 0540
www.designmuseum.fi

Design Museum, London
Shad Thames
London SE1 2YD, UK
+44 20 7403 6933
www.designmuseum.org

**Design Museum at the
Cultural Center of Belém**
(Museu do Design,
Centro Cultural de Belém)
Praça do Império
1499-003 Lisbon, Portugal
+351 213 612 400
www.ccb.pt

German Centre for Architecture
(Deutsches Architektur Zentrum)
Direktorin Kristien Ring
Köpenicker Straße 48/49
10179 Berlin, Germany
+49 30 278799-29
www.daz.de

German Architecture Museum
(Deutsches Architektur Museum)
Schaumainkai 43
60596 Frankfurt am Main
Germany
+49 69-212 38844
www.dam-online.de

International Center for Urbanism
(Centre International pour la Ville,
l'Architecture et le Paysage)
Rue de l'Ermitage 55 Kluisstraat
Brussels 1050, Belgium
+32 (0)2 642 24 50
www.civa.be

**The Lighthouse: Scotland's Centre for
Architecture, Design & the City**
11 Mitchell Lane
Glasgow, G1 3NU, Scotland
United Kingdom
+44 141 276 5365
www.thelighthouse.co.uk

Museum of Architecture in Wroclaw
(Muzeum Architektury we Wroclawiu)
ul. Bernardynska 5
PL 50-156 Wroclaw, Poland
+48 (71) 344 82 79
www.ma.wroc.pl

Museum of Estonian Architecture
(Eesti Arhitektuurimuuseum)
Arts centre
Rotermann's Salt Storage
Ahtri 2, Tallinn 10151
tel. +372 625 7000
www.arhitektuurimuuseum.ee

Museum of Finnish Architecture
(Suomen Rakennustaiteen Museo)
Kasarmikatu 24, 00130
Helsinki, Finland
+358 9 8567 5100
www.mfa.fi

Netherlands Architecture Institute
(Het Nieuwe Instituut)
Museumpark 25
3000 AE Rotterdam, Netherlands
+3110-4401200
www.hetnieuweinstituut.nl

National Museum of Art,
Architecture and Design
(Nasjonalmuseet for Kunst,
Arkitektur og Design)
Kristian Augusts gate 23
Oslo, Norway
+47 21 98 20 00
www.nationalmuseum.no

Palladio Centre and Museum
(Centro Internazionale di Studi di Architettura
Andrea Palladio)
Palazzo Barbarano
Contra' Porti 11
I-36100 Vicenza, Italy
+39 (04) 44 32 30 14
www.palladiomuseum.org

RIBA Architecture Gallery
66 Portland Place
London W1B 1AD, UK
+44 20 7580 5533
www.architecture.com

Röhsska Museum of
Design and Applied Art
(Röhsska Museet för
Konsthantverk och Design)
Vasagatan 37-39
SE-400 15 Göteborg, Sweden
+46 31-36 83 150
www.rohsska.se

Schusev State
Museum of Architecture
Vozdvizhenka str., 5
119019 Moscow, Russia
+7 495 697 38 74
www.muar.ru

Swedish Centre for Architecture
and Design (ARKDES)
Skeppsholmen
SE-111 49 Stockholm, Sweden
+46 8 587 270 00
www.arkdes.se

Swiss Architecture Museum
(Schweizerisches Architekturmuseum)
Steinenberg 7
Postfach 911
CH-4051 Basel, Switzerland
+41 61 261 1413
www.sam-basel.org

Victoria and Albert Museum
Cromwell Road
London SW7 2RL, UK
+44 20 7942 2000
www.vam.ac.uk

Vitra Design Museum
Charles-Eames-Str. 2
D-79576 Weil am Rhein
Germany
+49 7621 702 32 00
www.design-museum.de

Zurich Museum of Design
(Museum für Gestaltung Schaudepot)
Toni-Areal, Pfingstweidstrasse 96
8005 Zürich, Switzerland
+41 43 446 67 67
www.museum-gestaltung.ch

Source: DesignIntelligence

About the Editors

James P. Cramer is founder and chairman of the Greenway Group, a management consulting firm specializing in strategy, leadership, and organizational health. He is the author of three best-selling books on professional practice leadership and the founding editor and publisher of the journal *DesignIntelligence*. Along with Jonas Salk, M.D., he founded the Design Futures Council in 1994 in La Jolla, CA, and in Washington, DC, at the Smithsonian Institute. Each year Cramer and his colleagues at Greenway Group conduct research on the future of the design professions. They currently have ongoing research in the fields of design education, executive compensation, business trends & shifts, and professional services value migration. His work has been featured in *Business Week*, the *Wall Street Journal, Architectural Record*, National Public Radio and elsewhere. Cramer is the former Executive Vice President and CEO of the American Institute of Architects and the former President of the American Architectural Foundation. He served as group publisher of *Architecture* magazine for eight years. He is an honorary member of the AIA, an honorary member of the International Interior Design Association (IIDA), and a Leadership Fellow of the Western Behavioral Sciences Institute (WBSI) in La Jolla. He is a Senior Fellow of the Design Futures Council, a Richard Upjohn Fellow of the American Institute of Architects, and past board director of the Society of Architectural Historians.

Jane Paradise Wolford, Ph.D., is an architectural historian and the editor of the *Almanac of Architecture & Design*. She is also a senior consultant with Greenway Communications and an editor for the Ostberg Library of Design Management. Wolford has a doctorate in architectural history, theory, and criticism from the Georgia Institute of Technology as well as a Master of Science degree in architectural history from there. Her doctoral thesis established the theoretical and practical framework for architectural contextualism in its definitions and aspects of construction that enable buildings to relate better to each other and encourage a more sustainable, cohesively built environment. She is a LEED accredited professional. She also studied at Westmont College in Santa Barbara, CA, where she earned her bachelor's degree in English, and the University of California Berkeley, where she received her teaching credential. She and her husband, Arol Wolford, founded Construction Market Data in 1981, a leading international construction information service. She served on the board of the American Architectural Foundation and the Octagon Museum for more than a decade. In our constantly changing environment she is passionate about the potential of architecture to transform our world—into a better place that nurtures our physical and spiritual health and supports our endeavors.

östberg

Library of Design Management

Every relationship of value requires constant care and commitment. At Östberg, we are relentless in our desire to create and bring forward only the best ideas in design, architecture, interiors, and design management. Using diverse mediums of communications, including books and the Internet, we are constantly searching for thoughtful ideas that are erudite, witty, and of lasting importance to the quality of life. Inspired by the architecture of Ragnar Östberg and the best of Scandinavian design and civility, the Östberg Library of Design Management seeks to restore the passion for creativity that makes better products, spaces, and communities. The essence of Östberg can be summed up in our quality charter to you: "Communicating concepts of leadership and design excellence."

DFC Research Partners

Armstrong

Oldcastle BuildingEnvelope®
Engineering your creativity™

■■**BASF**
We create chemistry

SCAD
The University for Creative Careers

CMD

shaw contract group®

Steelcase

Deltek Know more.
Do more.™

Tarkett
THE ULTIMATE FLOORING EXPERIENCE

DU PONT®

USG™

Greenway Group
Foresight for the Business of Design

KAWNEER
AN ALCOA COMPANY

VIMtrek™